Atlantic Canada Bed & Breakfasts

Second Edition

Formac Publishing Company Limited
Halifax, Nova Scotia

Formac Publishing acknowledges the support of the Nova Scotia Department of Education and Culture in the development of writing and publishing in Canada.

COVER: Detail from a painting by Joy Laking, Bass River, Nova Scotia

Canadian Cataloguing in Publication Data

Atlantic Canada bed & breakfasts

    2nd. ed.

ISBN 0-88780-346-6 (pbk.)

1. Bed and Breakfast accommodations — Atlantic Provinces — Guidebooks. 2. Atlantic Provinces — Guidebooks. I. Title: Atlantic Canada bed and breakfasts.

TX907.5.C22A85 1996	647.94715'03	C96-950094-7.

Formac Publishing Company Ltd., Publishers
5502 Atlantic Street
Halifax, Nova Scotia
B3H 1G4

Printed and bound in Canada

Distributed in the United States by
Seven Hills Book Distributors
49 Central Avenue, Cinncinnati, Ohio 45202

Distributed in the United Kingdom by
Springfield Books, Norman Rd., Denby Dale,
Huddersfield, W Yorkshire, England HD8 8TH

Contents

Introduction

Welcome to the first-ever complete guide to bed and breakfasts and small country inns in Atlantic Canada!

You'll be surprised by the friendly and hospitable attitude toward visitors you'll encounter everywhere in the four Atlantic provinces. In this part of the world, people take time to enjoy life and to get to know travellers and people 'from away'.

And one of the great appeals of bed and breakfast accommodation is that you meet and become acquainted with Maritimers and Newfoundlanders in their own homes. There's no better way to learn about the unique and diverse approaches to life you'll find in the communities of this region.

This guide has been compiled to give you a complete list of every bed and breakfast and small inn facility in Atlantic Canada. To prepare it, we obtained lists of all licensed accommodation from each of the four provinces. We then compiled detailed information on all of these properties, and put it together in this one handy book. The result is a unique resource for travellers — one single source, listing every B&B we could find in the region.

What is a B&B?

Of course B&Bs are only one of the many different kinds of accommodation you can choose. To compile the listings for this book we referred to the criteria used by the four provincial governments in preparing their tourist information material, and to other publications on B&Bs. For this guide, a B&B is:

- Accommodation in a home which guests share with their host
- With one or more guest bedrooms
- With a common living room for guests to use
- Where guests are offered breakfast

Often inns fit the above description of a B&B, but they have licensed dining rooms where dinner and often lunch is served, as well as breakfast. This year, we've expanded our range of listings to include small country inns which meet the other B&B criteria, and have identified them as such.

Tourist or guest homes are also similar to B&Bs, and although they don't always offer breakfast, they fall into the same catagory as B&Bs in provincial government material, so these accommodations have also been included in our listings.

Locations

While many B&Bs are located in the villages, towns and cities of the region, others are in smaller centres or in rural areas. As you'll see, for each listing we've provided the full address and often included directions about how to find the house. When an accommodation is not located in one of the larger communitites in the region, it is listed under the name of the nearest town or village. We've used the same method as is used in the provincial travel guides to decide locations for spots in rural areas or smaller centres.

Help us keep this guide up to date

As you'll see, we've tried to provide a complete description of each B&B and small inn — what it offers, and what features are available in the surrounding area to guests. There is also information about prices and terms. The information was compiled in March-April 1996.

Of course things are always changing. You should always reconfirm items that are important to you when you are booking your accommodation. On occasion you may find that some of the information in this guide may be out of date; please use the form at the back of the book to let us know. We'll be updating all our listings each time we go back to press, so that this volume is kept as up-to-date and as current as possible.

What the stars mean

For each property, we've provided information on their current rating according to the Canada Selection Accommodation Rating Program. Here's what the stars mean:

★	Basic, clean, comfortable
★★	Basic, clean, comfortable with some amenities
★★★	Better quality, more amentities and services
★★★★	High quality, extended facilities, amenities and services

More information

This guide is one of a growing series of guidebooks to the Atlantic Canada region which we have published. Our guides are independent — they're compiled by authors and editors based on their judgment about what visitors should know about and see. We don't seek or accept fees or anything else in exchange for listings or mentions in our books. That way, you can rely on our books as a source of trustworthy information.

On the back cover, you'll see several of the guides you can select for information on the unique heritage, culture, peoples and places of Atlantic Canada. They're available through bookstores everywhere.

Another great source of basic information on the four Atlantic provinces are the provincial departments of tourism. If you call their toll-free (in North America) phone numbers, you can obtain comprehensive basic information on tourist facilities in all provinces. Provincial literature is available free.

The numbers are:

New Brunswick	1-800-561-0123
Newfoundland	1-800-563-6353
Nova Scotia	1-800-565-0000
PEI	1-800-463-4734

We hope that you'll find this book helpful as you travel the Atlantic provinces!

The publishers

New Brunswick

Albert County
Coyote Ridge
Bed & Breakfast ★★½
RR 2, Albert, E0A 1A0
Tel & Fax (506) 882-2227
Rte. 915 • Waterfront property •
Three o/n units, shared B •
Centrally located TV • Pets
welcome • Non-smoking rooms
available
FEATURES: Laundry facilities •
Drive to beach • Off-street parking
*RATES: $40 (1), $55 (2) • Open
May-Nov. • Visa accepted*

Alma
Captain's Inn ★★★
John & Elsie O'Regan, Main Street,
Alma, E0A 1B0
(506) 887-2017
Fax (506) 887-2074
Rte. 114, Exit 430 • Waterfront
property • Ten o/n units, private B •
Private and centrally located TVs •
Telephone in rooms • Non-smoking
only
FEATURES: Coffee •
Air-conditioning • Housekeeping
unit available • Walk to beach •
Off-street parking
*RATES: $46-$49 (1), $54-$68 (2),
$7-$10 add'l person • Full
breakfast • Open year-round, winter
by reservation or chance • MC,
Visa accepted • Value Vacation
packages offered • TIANB Member*

Alma
Cleveland Place ★★½
Patricia J. West, North Main Street,
Alma, E0A 1B0
(506) 887-2213
Rte. 114 • Waterfront property •
Three o/n
units, shared
B&S •
Centrally
located TV •
Telephone in
rooms • Pets
permitted •
Non-smoking
only

FEATURES: Laundry facilities •
Walk to beach • Off-street parking
*RATES: $45-$65 (1), $56-$80 (2) •
Full home-baked breakfast • Open
year-round • MC, Visa accepted •
Lower rate for 2-night stay*

Alma
Florentine Manor ★★★½
Mary Tingley, RR 2, Albert, E0A 1A0
Tel & Fax (506) 882-2271
Rte. 915 • Nine o/n units, private B •
Centrally located TV • Non-smoking
only
FEATURES: Coffee • Drive to
beach • Off-street parking
*RATES: $45-$55 (1), $55-$70
(2), Honeymoon Suite $90, $10
add'l person • Full breakfast •
Open year-round • MC, Visa
accepted • Value Vacation packages
offered • NBHIA; TIANB Member*

Alma
Schools Out
Bed & Breakfast ★★
Ethel Duffy, Albert, RR 2, Albert
County, E0A 1A0
(506) 882-2630
Rte. 915 • Three o/n units, shared B
• Centrally located TV •
Non-smoking only
FEATURES: Coffee • Drive to
beach • Off-street parking
*RATES: $30 (1), $40-$45 (2) • Full
breakfast • Open May-Oct.*

Aroostook
La Ferme des
Erables # 2 ★★
RR 1, Aroostook, E0J 1B0
(506) 273-2510
Three o/n units, shared B •
Centrally located TV • Pets welcome
FEATURES: Laundry facilities •
Off-street parking • indoor
swimming pool
RATES: No rates available

Bathurst
Auberge Les Amis De
La Nature ★★★
Jocelyn Desgagné, 2183 chemin
Lincour, RR 1, Site 22, Boîte 23,
Robertville, E0B 2K0
Tel & Fax (506) 783-4797
Toll free 1-800-327-9999
Rte. 11 and 134, Exit 318 • Five o/n
units, private B • Non-smoking
rooms available
FEATURES: Laundry facilities •
Coffee • Licensed dining room •
Hot tub • Drive to beach •
Off-street parking
*RATES: $55-$65 (2) Full or
continental breakfast • Open
year-round • MC, Visa accepted •
AITNB Member*

Bathurst
The Harbour Inn
Bed & Breakfast ★★½
Barbara Richard, 262 Main Street,
Bathurst, E2A 2A8
(506) 546-4757
Rte. 134 • Waterfront property •
Three o/n units, shared B&S •
Centrally located TV
FEATURES: Drive 20 minutes to
beach • Off-street parking
*RATES: $30 (1), $35-$40 (2), $9
add'l person • Full breakfast •
Open year-round*

Bathurst
Ingle-Neuk Lodge Bed
& Breakfast ★★½
Ken & Jean Babin, 1330 Youghall
Drive, Bathurst, E2A 4Y3
(506) 546-5758
Off Rte. 134, Exit 310 off 11 •
Waterfront property • Three o/n
units, two shared B • Centrally
located TV • No smoking in rooms
FEATURES: Walk to beach •
Picnic tables • Bird-watching •
Off-street parking
*RATES: $35 (1), $40-$50(2), $9
add'l person • Full breakfast •
Open June to Oct. • Tourism
Chaleur Member*

Bathurst
Les Peupliers/
The Poplars ★★
Marianne Schwartz, RR 1, Site 11,
Box 16, Kent Lodge Road,
Beresford, E0B 1H0
(506) 546-5271
Waterfront property • Two o/n
units, private and shared B • Private
and centrally located TV •
Telephone in rooms • Pets welcome
• Non-smoking only

RATES: $45 (2), $60 (family) •
Open June to Sept.

Bertrand
Chez Claude et
Pauline ★★½
784 boulevarde des Acadiens,
Bertrand, E0B 1J0
(506) 727-2368
Rte. 11 • One o/n unit, private B •
TV in room • Telephone in room
FEATURES: Laundry facilities •
Housekeeping unit available • Drive
to beach • Off-street parking
*RATES: Two-bedroom suite $80 (2),
$10 add'l person* • *Full breakfast* •
Open year-round • *Visa accepted*

Bertrand
Hébergement
Clément ★★½
856 boulevarde des Acadiens, CP
161, Bertrand, E0B 1J0
(506) 727-2322
Rte. 11 • Three o/n units, shared B •
Centrally located TV •
Non-smoking rooms available
FEATURES: Drive to beach •
Off-street parking
RATES: $40 (2), $10 add'l person •
Full breakfast • *Open June to Sept.* •
Off-season by reservation only

Blackville
Oak Hill Bed &
Breakfast ★★½
Joan Coughlan, RR 1, Upper
Blackville, E0C 2C0
(506) 843-2805
Rte. 8 • Three o/n units, shared B •
Non-smoking rooms available
FEATURES: Coffee
RATES: $35 (1), $40-$45 (2) • *Full
breakfast* • *Open year-round*

Bouctouche
Au Bord de la Mer
Bed & Breakfast ★★
Rita Caissie, Box 1098, RR 1,
Sainte-Anne-de-Kent, E0A 2V0
(506) 743-5329
Off Rte. 11, on Rte. 505, on Rte.
475, Exit 42 • Two o/n units,
private and shared B • TV in rooms
FEATURES: Air-conditioning •
Housekeeping/efficiency unit
available • Off-street parking
RATES: $40 (1), $45 (2) • *Open
June-Sept.*

Bouctouche
Aux P'tits Oiseaux ★★½
Guylaine Castonguay & Maurice
Cullen, 124, chemin du Couvent,
Bouctouche, E0A 1G0
(506) 743-8196
Off Rte. 11 on 475, Exit 32 • Two
o/n units, shared B&S • Centrally
located TV • Children under 6 free
• Non-smoking only
FEATURES: Drive to beach, golf
and Le Pays de la Sagouine •
Halfway between Parlee Beach and
Kouchibouguac National Park
*RATES: $40 (1), $45 (2), $10 add'l
person* • *Full breakfast* • *Open
year-round*

Bouctouche
Bouctouche Bay Inn ★★½
George & Erika Klomfass, Box 445, Bouctouche, E0A 1G0
(506) 743-2726
Off Rte. 11, Rte. 134, Exits 27, 32A • Waterfront property • Twenty-seven o/n units, private and shared B • Private and centrally located TVs • Telephone in rooms
FEATURES: Restaurant/licensed dining room • Licensed lounge bar • Coffee • Air-conditioning • Walk or drive to beach • Off-street parking
RATES: $40-75, $10 add'l person • Open year-round • AE, ER, MC, Visa accepted • CRFA Member

Bouctouche
J and J
Bed & Breakfast ★★
Jackie Dominique, RR 3, Box 207, Bouctouche, E0A 1G0
(506) 743-9012
Rte. 134 • Two o/n units, shared B • Private and centrally located TVs • Non-smoking rooms available
FEATURES: Laundry facilities • Drive to beach • Off-street parking
RATES: $45 (2), $10 add'l person • Full breakfast • Open May-Oct.

Bouctouche
Le Vieux Presbytère de Bouctouche ★★★½
157, chemin de Couvent, Bouctouche, E0A 1G0
(506) 743-5568
Off Rte. 11, on Rte. 475, Exit 32 • Waterfront property • Twenty-two o/n units, private B • TV in rooms • Telephone in rooms • Non-smoking only
FEATURES: Restaurant/licensed dining room • Licensed lounge bar •

Coffee • Drive to beach • Off-street parking
RATES: $57-$70 (2), $110-125 (suite) • Full or continental breakfast • Open May-Oct. • Major credit cards accepted • Value Vacation packages offered • ATK; TIANB Member

Burnt Church
Prospect Hotel Ltd. ★½
Box 108 B, Burnt Church, E0C 1K0
(506) 776-3217
Off Rte. 11 • Waterfront property • Shared B • Centrally located TV
FEATURES: Laundry facilities • Meals on request • Walk to beach Housekeeping unit available • Off-street parking
RATES: $25 (1), $35 (2) • Open year-round

Cambridge-Narrows
Cambridge-Narrows Bed & Breakfast ★★½
Washademoak Lake, Cambridge-Narrows, E0E 1E0
(506) 488-2000
Fax (506) 488-2000
Off Rte. 2 and 695, Exit 343 • Three o/n units, private and shared B • Two TVs • No alcohol • Non-smoking only
FEATURES: Laundry facilities • Swimming pool • Housekeeping unit available • Walk to beach • Off-street parking
RATES: $25 (1), $35-40 (2), $5 add'l person • Full breakfast • Open year-round • Pantel; NBBBA Member

Campbellton
Aylesford Inn
Bed & Breakfast ★★½
Richard Ayles, 8 McMillan
Avenue, Campbellton, E3N 1E9
506) 759-7672
Off Rte. 11 and Rte. 134 • Six o/n
units, private and shared B • Private
and centrally located TVs •
Telephone in rooms
FEATURES: Licensed dining room
• Drive to beach • Off-street parking
*RATES: • $50 (1) $50-$60 (2),
$100 (Suite), $8 add'l person •
Full-breakfast • Open year-round •
AE, Dis, MC, Visa accepted
NBHIA; TIANB Member*

Campobello Island
Owen House ★★★
Welshpool, Campobello, E0G 3H0
(506) 752-2977
Waterfront property • Nine o/n units,
private and shared B • Centrally
located TV • Non-smoking only
FEATURES: Walk or drive to
beach • Off-street parking
*RATES: $56 (1), $85 (2), taxes not
incl. • Open May 27-Oct. 15 • Visa
accepted*

Campobello Island
The Welshpool
House ★★
Box 2, Welshpool, Campobello,
E0G 3H0
(506) 752-2040
Waterfront property • Three o/n
units, private and shared B •
Centrally located TV • Telephone in
rooms
FEATURES: Housekeeping/
efficiency units available • Walk or
drive to beach • Off-street parking
RATES: $165

Cap-Pelé
Ocean Retreat
Bed & Breakfast ★★
Oasis de la Mer, Cap-Pelé, E0A 1J0
(506) 577-6070
Exit 950 off Rte. 15 • Waterfront
property • Seven o/n units, private
and shared B • Private & centrally
located TVs • Non-smoking only
FEATURES: Laundry facilities •
Restaurant/licensed dining room •
Housekeeping/efficiency unit
available • Walk to beach •
Off-street parking
*RATES: $30 (1), $38-$57(2), $10
add'l person • Full breakfast •
Open year-round • MC, Visa
accepted • TIANB Member*

Cape Tormentine
Briggs Homestead ★★★½
Eric & Debbie Sloan, RR 1,
Bayfield, E0A 1E0
(506) 538-2313
Rte. 955, off 15 and 16 •
Waterfront property • Four o/n
units, private B • Centrally located
TV • Children under 12 yrs free •
Non-smoking only
FEATURES: Laundry facilities •
Coffee • Air-conditioning • Drive to
beach • Off-street parking
*RATES: $55 (1), $65-$70 (2), $10
add'l person • Full breakfast •
Open year-round • Visa accepted •
NBBBA Member*

Cape Tormentine
Hilltop
Bed & Breakfast ★★½
Garth & Joan Trenholm, Main
Street, Cape Tormentine, E0A 1H0
(506) 538-7747
Off Rte. 955 and 16, Exit 550 •
Waterfront property • Three o/n
units, shared B • Centrally located
TV • Non-smoking only
FEATURES: Coffee • Hot tub •
Walk or drive to beach • Off-street
parking
*RATES: $30 (1), $40-$50 (2), $10
add'l person • Full breakfast •
Open year-round*

Caraquet
Hotel Paulin ★★★
Gerard R. Paulin, 143, boulevarde
St. Pierre ouest, Caraquet, E1W 1B6
(506) 727-9981/3165
Rte. 11 • Waterfront property • Ten
o/n units, private and shared B •
Centrally located TV
FEATURES: Licensed dining room
• Walk to beach • Off-street parking
*RATES: $40-$60 (1), $45-$85 (2)
Open May-Oct. • MC, Visa accepted*

Caraquet
Auberge Le Goéland
(Seagull) ★★
44, boulevarde St. Pierre est,
Caraquet, E1W 1B6
(506) 727-2919
Rte. 145 • Four o/n units, shared B
• Centrally located TV •
Non-smoking rooms available
FEATURES: Drive to beach •
Off-street parking
*RATES: $35 (1), $35-$40 (2)
Continental breakfast • Open
May-Sept.*

Caraquet
Chez Rhéa
Bed & Breakfast ★★
236, boulevarde St. Pierre ouest,
Caraquet, E1W 1A4
(506) 727-4275
Rte. 11 • Two o/n units, shared B
• Centrally located TV •
Non-smoking only
FEATURES: Walk or drive to
beach • Off-street parking
*RATES: $34 (1), $44-$48 (2), $8
add'l person • Open year-round*

Caraquet
La Maison Touristique
Dugas ★★½
683, boulevarde St. Pierre ouest,
Caraquet, E1W 1A1
(506) 727-3195
Rte. 11 • Eighteen o/n units, shared
B • Centrally located TV •
Non-smoking rooms available
FEATURES: Housekeeping/
efficiency units available • Drive to
beach • Off-street parking
*RATES: $23-45 (1), $29-$55 (2),
$5 add'l person • Full breakfast
Open-year-round • (thirteen units
Nov.-Apr.) • MC, Visa accepted*

Caraquet
Le Pignon Rouge ★★½
Raymond & Thérèse Albert, 338,
boulevarde St. Pierre est, Caraquet,
E1W 1B4
(506) 727-5983
Rte. 145 • Waterfront property •
Three o/n units, shared B • Centrally
located TV • Non-smoking only
FEATURES: Walk or drive to
beach • Off-street parking
*RATES: $40-45 (1), $45-$55 (2),
$5-10 add'l person • Continental
breakfast • Open June 15-Sept. 30 •
Visa accepted • Off-season by*

reservation only • Value Vacation packages offered

Centreville
Reid's Farm Vacation, Bed & Breakfast ★★★
Shirley Reid, RR 1, Knoxford, Centreville, E0J 1H0
(506) 276-4787
Fax (506) 276-4292
Off Rte. 2, Rte. 560 • Three o/n units, shared B • Centrally located TV • No alcohol • Non-smoking only
FEATURES: Laundry facilities • Housekeeping unit available • Off-street parking
RATES: $30 (1), $40 (2) • Full breakfast • Open year-round • NBFVA Member

Chance Harbour
Mariner's Inn ★★★
Matthew & Valerie Mawhinney, RR 2, Mawhinney Cove Road, Box 645, Chance Harbour, Lepreau, E0G 2H0
(506) 659-2619
Toll free 1-800-463-6062
Off Rte. 1, Rte. 790, Exit 85 • Waterfront property • Nine o/n units, private B • Centrally located TV • Non-smoking only
FEATURES: Licensed dining room • Walk or drive to beach • Off-street parking
RATES: $65-$85 (1), $75-$95 (2), $10 add'l person • Contintental breakfast • Open June to Oct. • MC, Visa accepted • TIANB Member

Charlo
Aunt Maud's Place ★★★
Anne Coughlan, 996 Chaleur Street, PO Box 137, Charlo, E0B 1M0
(506) 684-2483
Rte. 134, Exit 375 • Three o/n units, shared B&S • Centrally located TV • Non-smoking only
FEATURES: Laundry facilities • Coffee • Drive to beach • Off-street parking
RATES: $45 (1), $50-$60 (2), $10 add'l person • Full breakfast • Open May to Oct. • Visa accepted • AAWBO; TIANB Member

Chipman
Speakman's Bed & Breakfast ★★
Anne Coughlan, 162 Bridge Street, Chipman, E0E 1C0
(506) 339-6387
Rte. 10 • Three o/n units, shared B • Centrally located TV • Non-smoking rooms available
FEATURES: Laundry facilities • Coffee • Meals on request • Outdoor swimming pool • Air-conditioning • Drive to beach • Off-street parking
RATES: $50 (2) • Full breakfast • Open year-round • Family rates available

Deer Island
Clam Cove Farm
Bed & Breakfast ★★★
Marie Dolan, Fairhaven, Deer
Island, E0G 1R0
(506) 747-2025
Rte. 772, Exit 40 or 43 • Waterfront
property • Two housekeeping units,
private B, telephone, TV • No
alcohol • Non-smoking only
FEATURES: Coffee • Swimming
pool • Air-conditioning • Off-street
parking
*RATES: $60 (2), $5 add'l person,
maximum 2 adults & 2 children •
Full breakfast • Open year-round •
Visa accepted • Weekly rates
available*

Deer Island
Gardner House Fine
Dining and Bed &
Breakfast ★★½
Audrey Stuart, Lambert's Cove,
Deer Island, E0G 2J0
(506) 747-2462/2109
Rte. 772, Exit 40 or 43 • Waterfront
property • Three o/n units, shared B
• Telephone in rooms •
Non-smoking rooms available
FEATURES: Licensed dining room
• Walk to beach • Off-street parking
*RATES: $35 (1), $45 (2), $10 add'l
person • Open May-Oct. • MC, Visa
accepted • Value Vacation packages
offered*

Deer Island
West Isles World
Bed & Breakfast ★★½
Audrey J. Cline, Lambert's Cove,
Deer Island, E0G 2E0
(506) 747-2946
Rte. 772, Exits 43, 40 • Waterfront
property • Two o/n units, private B

• Private & centrally located TVs •
Non-smoking only
FEATURES: Meals on request •
Complimentary coffee • Walk or
drive to beach • Off-street parking •
Dryer available
*RATES: $40 (1), $50 (2), $7 add'l
person • Full or continental
breakfast • Open May to Oct. •
Reservations required • 3-day
minimum stay • Value Vacation
packages offered*

Dorchester
Rocklyn Inn
Bed & Breakfast ★★½
Sylvia Yeoman, Dorchester, E0A 1M0
(506) 379-2205
Toll free 1-800-822-6633
Rte. 106 • National Historic Site,
home of E.B. Chandler, a Father of
Confederation, built 1831 • Three
o/n units, private and shared B •
Private & centrally located TVs •
Telephone in rooms • Pets welcome
• Non-smoking rooms available
FEATURES: Meals on request •
Library of books and records •
Piano • Large garden summer house
*RATES: $30 (1), $40 (2), $10 add'l
person • Full breakfast • Open
year-round • NBBBA Member*

Edmundston
Beaulieu Tourist
Home ★★
Patsy-Ann Lynch, 255, rue de
Pouvoir, Edmundston, E3V 2Y6
(506) 735-5781
Off Rte. 2, Exit 18 • Five o/n units,
shared B • Centrally located TV
FEATURES: Laundry facilities •
Coffee • Housekeeping/efficiency
units available • Off-street parking
*RATES: $20-30 (1), $22-$32 (2),
$3-$5 add'l person • Open season*

Edmundston
Ginik's
Bed & Breakfast ★★½
Ginette Bossé, 241 rue Principale, PO
Box 432, Saint-Jacques, E0L 1K0
(506) 739-6008
Rte. 2, Exit 8, 15 • Four o/n units
including two suites, private &
shared B • TV in rooms •
Non-smoking only
FEATURES: Laundry facilities •
Hot tub • Air-conditioning •
Off-street parking
*RATES: $45 (1), Suite $80, $10
add'l person • Full breakfast •
Open year-round • MC, Visa
accepted • Off-season by
reservation only*

Edmundston
La Maison du Lac ★½
CP 678, 5979 Route 120, Lac
Baker, Edmundston, E3V 3S1
(506) 992-6202
Fax (506) 739-9275
Six o/n units
RATES: No rates available

Edmundston
Le Fief ★★★
Sharon or Phil Bélanger, 87 Church
Street, Edmundston, E3V 1J6
(506) 735-0400
Rte. 2, Exit 18 • Six o/n units,
private & shared B • Private and
centrally located TVs • Telephone
in rooms • Non-smoking only
FEATURES: Licensed dining room
• Air-conditioning • Efficiency unit
available • Off-street parking
*RATES: $39.95-$59.95 (1),
$49.95-$79.95 (2), $10 add'l person
Full breakfast • Open year-round •
MC, Visa accepted • Off-season by
reservation only*

Florenceville
Wicklow House
Bed & Breakfast ★★★
Floyd & Irene Ritchie, RR 2,
Wicklow, E0J 1K0
(506) 278-3047
Rte. 2 • Three o/n units, private &
shared B • Private and centrally
located TVs • Telephone in rooms •
Non-smoking only
FEATURES: Laundry facilities •
Coffee • Air-conditioning •
Off-street parking
*RATES: $50-60 (2) • Full
breakfast • Open year-round*

Fredericton Area
Appelot
Bed & Breakfast ★★★
Elsie Myshrall, RR 4, Hwy 105,
#1272, Fredericton, E3B 4X5
(506) 444-8083
Rte. 105 • Waterfront property •
Three o/n units, private and shared
B • Centrally located TV •
Telephone in rooms • No alcohol •
Non-smoking only
FEATURES: Laundry facilities •
Coffee • Drive to beach • Off-street
parking
*RATES: $40 (1), $55-$60 (2), $15
add'l person Full breakfast • Open
season • Off-season by reservation
only • NBBBA Member*

Fredericton Area
Carriage House Inn ★★★
Joan & Nathan Gorham,
Innkeepers, 230 University Avenue,
Fredericton, E3B 4H7
(506) 452-9924
Fax (506) 458-0799
Toll free 1-800-267-6068
Off Rte. 2 and 102, Exit 295 • Ten
o/n units, private and shared B •
Private and centrally located TVs •
Telephone in rooms • Non-smoking
rooms available
FEATURES: Laundry facilities •
Coffee • Meals on request •
Air-conditioning • Drive to beach •
Off-street parking
*RATES: $55-$70 (1), $59-$75 (2),
$15 add'l person • Full breakfast •
Open year-round • MC, Visa
accepted • NBHIA; TIANB Member*

Fredericton Area
Chickadee Lodge
Bed & Breakfast ★★★
Vaughn & Bunny Schriver, Prince
William, E0H 1S0
(506) 363-2759 (Lodge May-Nov.) or
(506) 363-2288 (Residence Nov.-April)

Rte. 2, 5 km
from Kings
Landing •
Waterfront
property •
Five o/n
units, shared
B •
Centrally
located TV • Non-smoking rooms
available
FEATURES: Laundry facilities •
Coffee • Air-conditioning • Canoes
available • Off-street parking
*RATES: $40 (1), $45 (2), $10 add'l
person • Full breakfast • Open May
to Nov. • MC, Visa accepted •
NBBBA Member*

Fredericton Area
Cornish Corner Inn ★★½
Sheelah Wagener, Box 40, Main
Street, Stanley, E0H 1T0
(506) 367-2239
Off Rte. 8 • Seven o/n units,
private and shared B • Centrally
located TVs • Pets welcome •
Non-smoking rooms available
FEATURES: Laundry facilities •
Licensed dining room • Efficiency
units available • Off-street parking
*RATES: $30-$35 (1), $35-$45 (2),
$5 add'l person • Full breakfast •
Open year-round • AE, MC, Visa
accepted • NBHIA Member*

Fredericton Area
Country Lane ★★★
James & Sheila MacIsaac, Lakeville
Corner, RR 1, Ripples, E0E 1N0
(506) 385-2398/1999
Rte. 690, Exit 325 • Waterfront
property • Two o/n units, shared B •
Centrally located TV •
Non-smoking only
FEATURES: Drive to beach •
Off-street parking • Barbecue •
Pedal boat, canoe
*RATES: $40 (1), $50 (2), $5 add'l
person, taxes incl. • Full breakfast
Open year-round • MC, Visa
accepted • NBBBA Member*

Fredericton Area
Fowler House ★★★
Rita Fowler, RR 6, Silverwood,
Fredericton, E3B 4X7
(506) 459-7766
2 km from Fredericton, welcome
sign on Riverside • Waterfront
property • Two o/n units, private
and shared B • Centrally located TV
FEATURES: Laundry facilities •
Outdoor swimming pool • Off-street
parking

RATES: $62 (1), $65 (2) Full breakfast • Open May-Nov. • Visa accepted • NBBBA; TIANB Member

Fredericton Area
The Hawks Nest ★★★
Lorne & Kathleen Hawkins, 150 Rocky Road, Keswick Ridge, E0H 1N0
(506) 363-3645
Off Rte. 2 and 105, Exit 274 • Three o/n units, shared B • Centrally located TV • Non-smoking only
FEATURES: Laundry facilities • Drive to beach • Off-street parking
RATES: $40 (1), $55 (2) • Full breakfast • Open year-round

Gagetown
Broadview Bed & Breakfast ★★½
Mildred Eveleigh, Queenstown, Gagetown, E0G 1V0
(506) 488-2266
Rte. 102 • Three o/n units, shared B • Centrally located TV
FEATURES: Laundry facilities • Restaurant • Off-street parking
RATES: $35 (1), $45-$55 (2), $10 add'l person • Full breakfast • Open season • MC, Visa accepted

Gagetown
Loaves & Calico Country Inn ★★½
Marie Anne Godin, Box 175, Gagetown, E0G 1V0
(506) 488-3018
Off Rte. 102 • Four o/n units, shared B • Centrally located TV • Non-smoking only
FEATURES: Licensed dining room
RATES: $35 (1), $45-$50 (2), $10 add'l person • Open April-Dec. • Visa accepted • CRFA; TIANB Member

Gagetown
Hewlett House ~ 1785 ~ ★★★
Anne Fawcett, 4683 Queenstown, Gagetown, E0G 1V0
(506) 488-2673
Fax (506) 488-1011
Rte. 102 • Waterfront property • Three o/n units, shared B, one ½ B ensuite • Centrally located TV • Telephone in rooms • Non-smoking only
FEATURES: Laundry facilities • Informal garden • Dock • Canoeing, sailing, swimming, cross-country skiing, snowshoeing • Walk to beach • Off-street parking
RATES: $45-$52 (1), $60-$67 (2) Full breakfast • Open year-round • MC, Visa accepted • By reservation only • Painting, photography, birding packages • Value Vacation packages offered Superhost; TIANB; TMAC Member

Gagetown
Steamers Stop Inn ★★★
Vic & Pat Stewart, Box 155, Front Street, Gagetown, E0G 1V0
(506) 488-2903
Fax (506) 488-1116
Off Rte. 102 • Waterfront property • Seven o/n units, private B • Centrally located TV
FEATURES: Licensed dining room • On and off-street parking
RATES: $65 (2), $15 add'l person Open May-Oct. • MC, Visa accepted • Off-season by reservation only • NBHIA; TIANB Member

Grand Falls/Grand-Sault
Auberge Heritage Tourist Home ★★½
Roger & Ginette Desmeules, Box 2529, Grand Falls, E3Z 1E6
(506) 473-4806
Rte. 2 • Three o/n units, shared B • Centrally located TV • Non-smoking rooms available
FEATURES: Laundry facilities • Air-conditioning • Golf • Drive to beach • Off-street parking
RATES: $40 (1), $50 (2), $10 add'l person • Continental breakfast Open May-Sept. • Visa accepted • NBBBA Member

Grand Falls/Grand-Sault
Coté Bed & Breakfast ★★★
Norma Coté, 575 Broadway Street, PO Box 2526, Grand Falls, E3Z 1E6
(506) 473-1415
Rte. 2, Exits 75, 76 and 81 • Five o/n units, two private and one shared B • Centrally located TV • Telephone in rooms • Non-smoking only
FEATURES: Coffee • Air-conditioning • Drive to beach • Off-street parking
RATES: $35-$55 (1), $40-$55 (2), $10 add'l person • Full breakfast • Open year-round • MC and Visa accepted • NBBBA Member

Grand Falls/Grand-Sault
Farm House ★★★
Margaret & Eugene McCarthy, RR 1, Grand Falls, E0J 1M0
(506) 473-2867
Rte. 2 • Two o/n units, shared B • Centrally located TV • Non-smoking rooms available
FEATURES: Laundry facilities • Off-street parking

RATES: $30 (1), $40-45 (2), $10 add'l person • Open year-round • NBBBA Member

Grand Falls/Grand-Sault
Maple Tourist Home Bed & Breakfast ★★★½
Rachel Crawford, 142 Main Street, PO Box 1785, Grand Falls, E3Z 1E1
(506) 473-1763
Off Rte. 2, Exit 76 or 81 • Three o/n units, private and shared B • Private and centrally located TV • Telephone in rooms • No alcohol • Non-smoking only
FEATURES: Laundry facilities • Air-conditioning • Walk to beach • Off-street parking
RATES: $45-$50 (2), $15 add'l person • Full breakfast • Open year- round MC and Visa accepted • NBBBA Member

Grand Falls/Grand-Sault
Mont Assomption Bed & Breakfast ★★½
Mariette Gagnon/Vincent Ouellet, Rte. 2, Grand Falls, E0J 1M0
(506) 473-3562
Toll free 1-800-509-7223
Twelve o/n units, private and shared B
FEATURES: Laundry facilities
RATES: $40 (1), $48 (2), $8 add'l person • Continental breakfast • Open year-round • MC, Visa accepted

Grand Manan Island
Aristotles Lantern ★★½
Helen Charters, North Head, PO Box 208, Grand Manan, E0G 2M0
(506) 662-3788
Rte. 776 • Three o/n units, shared B • Centrally located TV • Non-smoking only • waterfront property

FEATURES: Coffee • Afternoon tea room and art gallery • Walk or drive to beach • Off-street parking *RATES: $50-$60 (2), $5 add'l person • Full gourmet breakfast • Open June to Sept. • Visa accepted*

Grand Manan Island
Baldwin's
Bed & Breakfast ★★★
Donald & Maureen Baldwin, Seal Cove, Grand Manan, E0G 3B0
(506) 662-8801
Rte. 776 • Waterfront property • Two o/n units, shared B • Centrally located TV • Telephone in rooms • Non-smoking rooms available
FEATURES: Laundry facilities • Walk to beach • Off-street parking *RATES: $37 (1), $59 (2), $11 add'l person, all taxes incl. • Full breakfast • Open May to Oct. • Grand Manan Tourist Assoc.*

Grand Manan Island
The Compass Rose ★★½
Nora & Ed Parker, North Head, Grand Manan, E0G 2M0
(506) 662-8570
Rte. 776 • Waterfront property • Eight o/n units, shared B • Non-smoking only
FEATURES: Laundry facilities • Restaurant/licensed dining room • Off-street parking *RATES: $49 (1), $59 (2), $10 add'l person • Full breakfast • Open May to Oct. • MC, Visa accepted • HIAC; NBHIA; TIANB Member*

Grand Manan Island
Crosstree Guest
Home ★★½
Hazel Zwicker, Seal Cove, Grand Manan, E0G 3B0

(506) 662-8263
Rte. 776 • Three o/n units, shared B • Centrally located TV • Telephone in rooms
FEATURES: Laundry facilities • Meals on request • Walk to beach • Off-street parking
RATES: $37 (1), $56 (2), $10 add'l person, taxes incl. • Full breakfast • Open year-round • Visa accepted

Grand Manan Island
The Fount Inn
Bed & Breakfast ★★½
Frances Bainbridge, Box 157, Seal Cove, Grand Manan, E0G 3B0
(506) 662-3725
Three o/n units, shared B • TV in rooms • No alcohol • Non-smoking only
FEATURES: Laundry facilities • Walk or drive to beach • Off-street parking
RATES: Value Vacation packages offered

Grand Manan Island
Manan Inn Island and
Spa ★★½
Susan Wilcox, North Head, Grand Manan, E0G 2M0
(506) 662-8624
Rte. 776 • Seven o/n units, shared B • Centrally located TV • Non-smoking only
FEATURES: Off-street parking
RATES: $59-$69 (2) • Open year-round • MC, Visa accepted

Grand Manan Island
Marathon Inn ★★½
Jim Leslie & Elizabeth Crompton,
North Head, Grand Manan, E0G 2M0
(506) 662-8144
Rte. 776 • Twenty-eight o/n units,
private and shared B • Private and
centrally located TV • Non-smoking
rooms available
FEATURES: Laundry facilities •
Restaurant/licensed dining room •
Licensed lounge bar • Outdoor
swimming pool • Tennis • Walk to
beach • Off-street parking
*RATES: $44-84 (1), $49-$89 (2), $6
add'l person • Open year-round •
MC, Visa accepted • TIANB Member
• Off-season by reservation only*

Grand Manan Island
McLaughlin's Wharf Inn ★★½
Mrs. Brenda McLaughlin, Seal
Cove, Grand Manan, E0G 3B0
(506) 662-8760
Rte. 776 • Waterfront property • Six
o/n units, shared B • Centrally
located TV • Non-smoking only
FEATURES: Restaurant/licensed
dining room • Walk to beach •
Off-street parking
*RATES: $59 (1), $69 (2), $10 add'l
person • Continental breakfast Open
June-Sept. • AE, MC, Visa accepted •
Off-season by reservation only*

Grand Manan Island
Rosalie's Guest Home ★★
Rosalie Harvey, Seal Cove, Grand
Manan, E0G 3B0
(506) 662-3344
Rte. 176 • Three o/n units, shared B
• Centrally located TV
FEATURES: Drive to beach •
Off-street parking

*RATES: $35 (1), $45 (2) • Open
May-Oct.*

Grand Manan Island
Shorecrest Lodge Country Inn ★★½
Andrew & Cynthia Normandeau,
North Head, Grand Manan,
E0G 2M0
(506) 662-3216
Rte. 776 • Waterfront property •
Ten o/n units, private B • Centrally
located TV • Non-smoking only
FEATURES: Restaurant/licensed
dining room • Walk or drive to
beach • Off-street parking
*RATES: $55-$65 (1), $65-$78 (2),
$8 add'l person • Continental
breakfast • Open May-Oct. • MC,
Visa accepted*

Grand Manan Island
Whale Cove Cottage Inn ★★½
Laura Buckley, North Head, Grand
Manan, E0G 2M0
(506) 662-3181/3241
Rte. 776, Whistle Rd. • Three o/n
units, private B
FEATURES: Licensed dining room
• Coffee • Drive to beach •
Off-street parking
*RATES: $50 (1), $65 (2) • Full or
continental breakfast • Open
May-Oct. • Visa accepted • Grand
Manan Tourism Assoc. Member*

Grande-Anse
Auberge de L'Anse ★★
Aurore Blanchard, 317 rue Acadie,
Grande-Anse, E0B 1R0
(506) 732-5204 or (506) 546-5667
Rte. 11 • Ten o/n units, private and
shared B • Private and centrally
located TVs • Pets welcome

FEATURES: Walk or drive to beach • Off-street parking
RATES: $35-$45 (2), $5 add'l person • Full breakfast • Open June to Aug.

Grande-Anse
L'Auberge aux Portes de l'Acadie ★★
Michelle Cormier, 108, rue Acadie, Grande-Anse, E0B 1R0
Tel/Fax (506) 732-5229
Rte. 11 • Two o/n units, private B • TV in rooms • Non-smoking rooms available
FEATURES: Drive to beach • Off-street parking
RATES: $48-$52 (2), $9 add'l person • Continental breakfast • Open May-Oct. • Visa accepted • Off-season by reservation only

Grande-Digue
Le Sous-Bois ★★½
Roger & Marilyn Tremblay, RR 1, Boîte 103, Grand-Digue, E0A 1S0
(506) 576-1183
Route 530, Cap de Cocagne, Exit 37 • Two o/n units, private and shared B • Centrally located TV • Telephone in rooms • Pets welcome • Non-smoking only
FEATURES: Laundry facilities • Walk or drive to beach • Off-street parking
RATES: $40 (1), $50 (2) • Continental breakfast • Open year-round • AE, MC, Visa accepted

Hampton
Bamara Inn ★★½
316 Main Street, Hampton, E0G 1Z0
(506) 832-9099
Off 1, on 121, Exit 143 or 145 • Three o/n units, private B • TV in rooms

FEATURES: Laundry facilities • Restaurant/licensed dining room • Walk to beach • Off-street parking
RATES: $50-75 (2) • Full breakfast • Open year-round • DC, ER, MC, Visa accepted • Value Vacation packages offered • AAWBO; C of C; TIANB Member

Hampton
Evelyn's Bed & Breakfast ★★★
David & Evelyn Cassidy, Ox-Bow Farm, Hwy 121, Bloomfield, Kings Co., E0G 1J0
(506) 832-4450
Rte. 121 off 1 • Waterfront property • Three o/n units, shared B, telephone in room • Private & centrally located TVs • Families welcome • Non-smoking rooms available
FEATURES: Laundry facilities • Meals on request • Coffee • Outdoor Swimming pool • Hot tub • Walk or drive to beach • Off-street parking
RATES: $37 (1), $55-$65 (2), $10 add'l person • Full country breakfast • Open year-round • Visa accepted • NBBBA Member

Hartland
Campbell's
Bed & Breakfast ★★★
Howard & Rosemary Campbell,
Hartland, E0J 1N0
(506) 375-4775
Off Rte. 2, 105 north 2 km, Exit
170 • Waterfront property • Three
o/n units, private and shared B •
Centrally located TV • Telephone in
rooms • Non-smoking only
FEATURES: Meals on request •
Coffee • Kitchen available •
Air-conditioning • Efficiency unit
available
*RATES: $30-$45 (1), $35-$45(2),
$5-$10 add'l person • Full
breakfast • Open year-round •
NBBBA; TIANB Member*

Hartland
Hatfield Heritage
House ★★★½
Box 210, Hartland, E0J 1N0
(506) 375-9092
Rte. 105 S, Exit 170 • Three o/n
units, shared B • Centrally located
TV • Non-smoking rooms available
FEATURES: Laundry facilities •
Restaurant/licensed dining room •
Coffee • On and off-street parking
*RATES: $45 (1), $50 (2), $5 add'l
person • Full breakfast • Open
year-round • DC, MC, Visa accepted*

Harvey
Myrna's Manor ★★½
Myrna Dery, RR 4, Harvey Station,
E0H 1H0
(506) 366-3127
Rte. 3, Exit 263 • Three o/n units,
private and shared B • Private and
centrally-located TVs • Pets
welcome • Non-smoking rooms
available

FEATURES: Laundry facilities •
Restaurant • Coffee • Drive to
beach • Off-street parking
*RATES: $35 (1), $45 (2), $8 add'l
person • Open year-round*

Hillsborough
Lakewood Estate
Bed & Breakfast ★★★
Lynne Liptay, 1 Lake Road, Box
118, Hillsborough, E0A 1X0
(506) 734-3108
Rte. 114, Lake Road • Two o/n
units, private B • Centrally located
TV • Non-smoking only
FEATURES: Laundry facilities •
Off-street parking
*RATES: $40-$50 (1), $45-$55 (2)
Full breakfast • Open year-round*

Hopewell Cape
Aiko's Villa
Bed & Breakfast ★★★
Aiko M. Hawkes, PO Box 45,
Hopewell Cape, E0A 1Y0
(506) 734-3160
Off Rte. 114 at Museum • Two o/n
units, private and shared B •
Centrally located TV • Telephone in
rooms • Non-smoking only
FEATURES: Laundry facilities •
Coffee • Drive to beach • Off-street
parking
*RATES: $32 (1), $40-$45 (2), $10
add'l person • Full breakfast •
Open season • Off-season by
reservation only • Value Vacation
packages offered • NBBBA Member*

Hopewell Cape
Broadleaf "Too" ★★½
Vernon & Joyce Hudson, Hopewell
Hill, E0A 1Z0
(506) 882-2803
Rte. 114, Exits 430, 488A or 540 •
Three o/n units, shared B •
Centrally-located TV
FEATURES: Laundry facilities •
Meals on request • Efficiency unit
available • Drive to beach •
Off-street parking
RATES: $40 (1), $45-$50 (2), $10
add'l person • Full breakfast •
Open year-round • NBBBA; NBFVA
Member

Hopewell Cape
Dutch Treat Farm ★★★
Glenn and Pat Treat, RR 1,
Hopewell Cape, Shepody, Albert
Co., E0A 1Y0
(506) 882-2569
Rte. 114, Exit 430, 540 and 488A •
Waterfront property • Three o/n
units, shared B • Centrally located
TV • Pets welcome • Non-smoking
rooms available
FEATURES: Drive to beach •
Off-street parking
RATES: $30-$35 (1), $40-$50 (2),
$10 add'l person • Full breakfast •
Open June to Sept. • NBBBA;
Albert Co. Tourist Assoc.

Hopewell Cape
Peck Colonial House Bed & Breakfast & Tea Room★★½
Elaine Holmstrom, Hopewell Hill,
E0A 1Z0
(506) 882-2114
Rte. 114, Exit 430, 540 and 488A •
Three o/n units, shared B •
Centrally located TV •
Non-smoking only

FEATURES:
Meals on
request •
Drive to
beach •
Off-street
parking
RATES:
$35-$40 (1), • $45-$55 (2), $10
add'l person, taxes incl. • All you
can eat breakfast • Open
year-round • Visa accepted
Off-season rates • NBBBA; TIANB
Member

Millville
Larsen Log Lodge Bed & Breakfast ★★★★
Marianne Larsen, 658B Hawkins
Corner, RR 1, Millville, E0H 1M0
(506) 463-2731
Rte. 585, Jct. 104 & 585 • Two o/n
units, private B&S • Television in
rooms • Telephone in rooms •
Non-smoking only
FEATURES: Laundry facilities •
Coffee • Meals on request • Hot tub
• Drive to beach • Off-street parking
RATES: $35-$55 (1), $45-$75 (2),
$7.50 add'l person • Full breakfast
Open year-round • MC, Visa
accepted • Value Vacation packages
offered • NBBBA Member

Minto
Bailey's Guest Home
& Motel ★½
Kevin Bailey, 2 Bridge Street,
Minto, E0E 1K0
(506) 327-4256
Off Rte. 10 • Eight o/n units,
private B • TV in rooms
FEATURES: Housekeeping/
efficiency units available •
Off-street parking
*RATES: $35-$45 (1), $40-$60 (2),
$10 add'l person • Open year-round
• Visa accepted*

Miramichi
Betts Homestead ★★★
Annie & John Betts, RR 1, Site 14,
Box 5, Millerton, E0C 1R0
(506) 622-2511
Fax (506) 622-5157
Rte. 108, off 8 at Millerton •
Overlooks river • Six o/n units,
shared B • Centrally located TV
FEATURES: Laundry facilities •
Meals on request • Lawn games •
Canoe available • Off-street parking
*RATES: $30-$50 (1), $45-$55 (2),
$5 add'l person • Full breakfast •
Open year-round • Visa accepted •
MRTA Member*

Mirimichi
Fourth Generation
Bed & Breakfast ★★½
John McLean/Marcel Quirion, RR
1, Strathadam, Newcastle,
Mirimichi, E1V 3M3
(506) 622-3221
Rte. 425, Exit 8 • Waterfront
property • Three o/n units, • shared
and private B • Private and centrally
located TVs • Telephone in rooms •
Non-smoking only
FEATURES: Laundry facilities •
Drive to beach • Off-street parking

*RATES: $40-$50 (1), $45-$55 (2)
Open year-round • Visa accepted*

Moncton Area
Aspen Poolside
Bed & Breakfast ★★★
Gary & Leona Geldart, Hiltz Road,
Berry Mills, RR 7, Moncton, E1C 8Z4
(506) 852-9303
Hiltz Rd. off Rte. 2 in Berry Mills •
Three o/n units, shared B, one
queen, private B • Centrally located
TV • Telephone in rooms •
Non-smoking only
FEATURES: Laundry facilities •
Outdoor swimming pool • Drive to
beach • Off-street parking
*RATES: $35 (1), $45-$55 (2), taxes
incl. • Full breakfast • Open
year-round*

Moncton Area
Au Mille Fleurs ★★★
Celyne or Richard LaFleur, 30
Courteney, Moncton, E1C 9L2
(506) 853-7263
One o/n unit, private B • TV in
room • Telephone in room • Pets
welcome • Non-smoking only
FEATURES: Meals on request •
Outdoor swimming pool • Drive to
beach • Off-street parking
*RATES: $50 (1), $55 (2), $10 add'l
person • Open year-round*

Moncton Area
Bonaccord House
Bed & Breakfast ★★★½
Patricia Townsend & Jeremy
Martin, 250 Bonaccord Street,
Moncton, E1C 5M6
(506) 388-1535
Fax (506) 853-7191
Five o/n units, private and shared B
• Centrally located TV • Telephone
in rooms • Non-smoking only

FEATURES: Coffee •
Air-conditioning • Drive to beach •
On and off-street parking
*RATES: $40-$45 (1), $50-$58 (2),
$10 add'l person • Full breakfast •
Open year-round • Visa accepted •
Family suite from $53 • C of C;
TIANB; NBBBA; AAWBO Member*

Moncton Area
Canadiana Inn ★★★
46 Archibald Street, Moncton,
E1C 5H9
(506) 382-1054
 Exit 8 off Rte. 15, Archibald St.
exit • Seventeen o/n units, private B
• TV in rooms • Non-smoking
rooms available
FEATURES: Coffee • Drive to
beach • Off-street parking
*RATES: $60-$75 (1), $65-$110 (2),
$10 add'l person • Open
March-Nov. • MC, Visa accepted •
TIANB Member*

Moncton Area
Downtown
Bed & Breakfast ★★★
Paul & Alice Boudreau, 101 Alma
Street, PO Box 113, Moncton,
E1C 4Y5
(506) 855-7108
Four o/n units, shared B • Centrally
located TV • Non-smoking rooms
available
FEATURES: Laundry facilities •
Coffee • Dining facilities • Drive to
beach • On-street parking
*RATES: $39-$45 (1), $49-$55 (2)
Full breakfast • Open year-round •
NBBBA Member*

Moncton Area
Kozy Kate's
Bed & Breakfast ★★½
Peter & Gisele Dickson, RR 3,
Moncton, E1C 8J7
(506) 386-0113
Rte. 114 • Waterfront property •
Two o/n units, shared B •
Centrally-located TV •
Non-smoking only
FEATURES: Laundry facilities •
Off-street parking
*RATES: $40 (1), $45 (2), $10 add'l
person • Full breakfast • Open
year-round • MC, Visa accepted •
NBBBA Member*

Moncton Area
Le Petunia ★★½
53 Hillside Drive, Moncton, E1A 3S2
(506) 853-9367
Three o/n units, shared B •
Centrally-located TV •
Non-smoking only
FEATURES: Drive to beach •
Close to university • Off-street
parking
*RATES: $35 (1), $40-$50 (2), $10
add'l person • Full breakfast •
Open year-round • NBBBA Member*

Moncton Area
McCarthy
Bed & Breakfast ★★★
Gerry McCarthy, 82 Peter Street,
Moncton, E1A 3W5
(506) 383-9152
Off 2, Exit 496A • Three o/n units,
private and shared B • Private and
centrally located TVs • Telephone
in rooms • Non-smoking only
FEATURES: Laundry facilities •
Guest fridge • Drive to beach •
Off-street parking
*RATES: $28 (1), $38-$43 (2), $8
add'l person • Full breakfast •
Open May to Aug. • Family suite 2
people $50 • CAA; TIANB; AAA
Member*

Moncton Area
Mountain View
Bed & Breakfast ★★½
Dave & Dawn Lutes, 2166
Mountain Road, Moncton, E1G 1B3
(506) 384-0290
Off Rte. 2, Exit 488A • One o/n unit
• No alcohol • Non-smoking only
FEATURES: Coffee • Drive to
beach • Off-street parking
*RATES: $33 (1), $43 (2), $10 add'l
person • Continental breakfast •
Open year-round*

Moncton Area
Park View
Bed & Breakfast ★★★
Carson & Gladys Langille, 254
Cameron Street, Moncton, E1C 5Z3
(506) 382-4504
Three o/n units, shared B • Private &
centrally located TVs • Telephone in
rooms • Non-smoking only
FEATURES: Laundry facilities •
Air-conditioning • Drive to beach •
On and off-street parking

*RATES: $40 (1), $50 (2), $10 add'l
person • Full breakfast • Open
year-round • NBBBA Member*

Moncton Area
Victoria
Bed & Breakfast ★★★★
Sharon LeBlanc, 71 Park Street,
Moncton, E1C 2B2
(506) 389-8296
Three o/n units, private B • Private
TV • Telephone in rooms •
Non-smoking only
FEATURES: Laundry facilities •
Air-conditioning • Drive to beach •
On and off-street parking
*RATES: $65 (1), $75 (2), $10 add'l
person • Full breakfast • Open
year-round • MC, Visa accepted •
TIANB, NBBBA Member*

Nackawick
Hilltop
Bed & Breakfast ★★
RR 3, Meductic, Nackawick, E0H 1P0
(506) 272-2012
Three o/n units
RATES: No rates available

New Denmark
Nyborg's Bed &
Breakfast ★★
Joan Nyborg, Box 109, Foley Brook
Road, New Denmark, E0J 1T0
(506) 553-6490
Rte. 108 • Three o/n units, shared B
• Centrally located TV • Pets
welcome • No alcohol •
Non-smoking rooms available
FEATURES: Coffee • Off-street
parking
*RATES: $35 (1), $45-$50 (2), $10
add'l person • Full breakfast •
Open year-round*

Nigadoo
La Fine Grobe Sur-Mer (By The Sea) ★★
C.P. 219, Nigadoo, E0B 2A0
(506) 783-3138
Off Rte. 11, 134, Exit 321 •
Waterfront property • Three o/n
units, private B • TV in rooms
FEATURES: Coffee • Licensed
dining room • Air-conditioning •
Off-street parking
RATES: $39-$80 (2) • *Open
May-Dec.* • *AE, CB, Dis, DC, MC,
Visa accepted AAA; CAA; TIANB
Member*

Perth-Andover
DeMerchants Bed & Breakfast and Tourist Home ★★★
Stephen & Shirley DeMerchant,
Trans Canada Highway,
Perth-Andover, E0J 1V0
(506) 273-6152
 Rte. 2 • Three o/n units, shared B •
Private and centrally located TVs •
Telephone in rooms
FEATURES: Laundry facilities •
Coffee • Off-street parking
*RATES: $35 (1), $40-$45 (2), $7
add'l person* • *Full breakfast* •
Open year-round • *NBBBA Member*

Petitcodiac
3 J's Bed & Breakfast ★★
Edith Corey, RR 2, Petitcodiac,
E0A 2H0
(506) 756-2958
Rte. 2 • Three o/n units, shared B •
Centrally located TV Telephone in
rooms • Pets welcome •
Non-smoking only
FEATURES: Laundry facilities •
Coffee • Off-street parking

*RATES: $25 (1), $40 (2), $8 add'l
person under 17* • *Full breakfast*
Open year-round • *NBBBA Member*

Petit-Rocher
Auberge d'Anjou ★★★
Lione Landry, 587 rue Principal,
PO Box 1076, Petit-Rocher,
E0B 2E0
(506) 783-0587
Fax (506) 783-5587
Rte. 134, Exit 326 • Fifteen o/n
units, private and shared B • Private
and centrally located TVs •
Telephone in rooms • Non-smoking
rooms available
FEATURES: Laundry facilities •
Licensed dining room • Efficiency
unit available • Walk to beach •
Off-street parking
*RATES: $40-$80 (1), $45-$85 (2),
$7 add'l person* • *Full breakfast* •
Open year-round • *AE, MC, Visa
accepted* • *AAPA Member*

Pocologan/Lepreau
By The Sea Bed & Breakfast ★★★
Carol Moore, Pocologan, E0G 2S0
(506) 755-2498
Rte. 1 • Three o/n units, shared B •
Centrally located TV • Pets
welcome • Non-smoking only
FEATURES: Laundry facilities •
Coffee • Walk to beach • Off-street
parking
*RATES: $25-$35 (1), $30-$40 (2),
$10 add'l person* • *Open season*

Pocologan/Lepreau
Pocologan House Bed & Breakfast ★★
Janice Gowan, General Delivery,
Pocologan, E0G 2S0
(506) 755-2915
Rte. 1 • Oceanfront property •
Three o/n units, shared B •
Centrally located TV • No alcohol •
Non-smoking rooms available
FEATURES: Coffee • Walk or
drive to beach • Off-street parking
RATES: *$40 • Full and continental
breakfast • Open June to Oct. • MC,
Visa accepted • NBBBA Member*

Port Elgin
A & A Jacobs Bed & Breakfast ★★
RR 2, Box 98, Melrose, E0A 2K0
(506) 538-9980
Off Hwy 16 • Shared B • Centrally
located TV • Telephone in rooms •
No alcohol • Non-smoking only
FEATURES: Drive to beach •
Off-street parking
RATES: *$35 (1), $45 (2), $10 add'l
person ($5 child) • Complimentary
breakfast • Open Apr.-Oct.*

Port Elgin
Little Shemoque Country Inn ★★★★
Klaus & Petra Sudbrack, Hwy 955,
Port Elgin, E0A 2K0
(506) 538-2320
Fax **(506) 538-7494**
Rte. 955 off Hwy 15 • Waterfront
property • Five o/n units, private B
• TV in rooms • Telephone in
rooms • Non-smoking only
FEATURES: Licensed dining room
• Laundry facilities • Walk to beach
Off-street parking
RATES: *$79 (1), $98 (2), $20 add'l
person • Full breakfast • Open*

*year-round • MC, Visa accepted •
Value Vacation packages offered •
HIAC; HINB Member*

Port Elgin
Roga Farm Bed & Breakfast #1 ★★½
Adriana Rommens, PO Box 75,
Port Elgin, E0A 2K0
(506) 538-7763
Trans Canada Hwy, Rte. 16 • Three
o/n units, private and shared Bs •
Private & centrally located TV •
Non-smoking only
FEATURES: Coffee • Drive to
beach • Off-street parking
RATES: *$35 (1), $40-$45 (2), $10
add'l person • Full breakfast •
Open year-round*

Port Elgin
Roga Farm Bed & Breakfast #2 ★★★
Rose Rommens, PO Box 75, Port
Elgin, E0A 2K0
(506) 538-2667
Off Rte. 15 on 16E • One o/n unit,
private B • TV in room
FEATURES: Coffee • Drive to
beach • Off-street parking
RATES: *$35 (1), $40-$45 (2), $10
add'l person • Full breakfast •
Open year-round*

Richibucto
L'Auberge O'Leary Inn ★★½
101 rue Main, Richibucto, E0A 2M0
(506) 523-7515
Rte. 134, Exit 57 • Waterfront
property • Seven o/n units, private
and shared B • Centrally located TV
• Non-smoking only
FEATURES: Drive to beach •
Off-street parking

RATES: $45 (1), $40-$50 (2), $10 add'l person • Continental breakfast • Open June to August

Richibucto
Mazerolle
Bed & Breakfast ★★
CP 706, 175 rue Main, Richibucto, E0A 2M0
(506) 523-6824
Three o/n units
RATES: No rates available

Riverside-Albert
Cailswick Babbling
Brook Bed &
Breakfast ★★★
Eunice Cail, Riverside-Albert, E0A 2R0
(506) 882-2079
Rte. 114 • Three o/n units, shared B • Centrally located TV • Non-smoking only
FEATURES: Laundry facilities • Drive to beach •

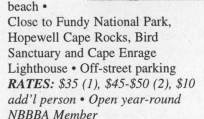

Close to Fundy National Park, Hopewell Cape Rocks, Bird Sanctuary and Cape Enrage Lighthouse • Off-street parking
RATES: $35 (1), $45-$50 (2), $10 add'l person • Open year-round
NBBBA Member

Sackville
Cosmic Tree ★★½
J. Robertson, 20 Church Street, Sackville, E0A 3C0
(506) 536-3504
Rte. 541, Exit 940 • Two o/n units, shared B • Centrally located TV • Pets welcome • Non-smoking only

FEATURES: Walk to beach • Close to hiking trails • Off-street parking
RATES: $40 (1), $50 (2)
Home-baked continental breakfast • Open May to Oct. • Visa accepted • NBBBA Member

Sackville
The Different
Drummer ★★★
R. Hanrahan, 82 W. Main St., PO Box 188, Sackville, E0A 3C0
(506) 536-1291
Rte. 2, Exit 541 • Eight o/n units, private B • Private & centrally located TVs • Non-smoking only
FEATURES: Coffee • Off-street parking
RATES: $45 (1), $49-$52 (2), $9 add'l person • Open year-round • MC, Visa accepted • TIANB; TTA Member

Sackville
Glenwater
Bed & Breakfast ★★½
Ralph & Emeline Oulton, Michael Oulton, Jolicure Road, RR 3, Sackville
Rte. 2, 15, 16, Exit to Jolicure Road • Two o/n units, shared B • Centrally located TV • Pets welcome
FEATURES: Outdoor swimming pool • Off-street parking
RATES: $45 (2), $5 add'l person • Full breakfast • Visa accepted

Sackville
The Harbourmaster's House ★★½
Sandra Cant, 30 Squire Street, Box
1482, Sackville, E0A 3C0
(506) 536-0452
Three o/n units, shared B • Pets
welcome • Non-smoking only
FEATURES: Laundry facilities •
Coffee • Drive to beach • Off-street
parking
*RATES: $35 (1), $45 (2)
Continental breakfast • Open
May-Oct. NBBBA • Member*

Sackville
Marshlands Inn ★★★
59 Bridge Street, Box 1440,
Sackville, E0A 3C0
(506) 536-0170
Fax (506) 536-0721
Rte. 106, Exit 541 • Twenty-one
o/n units, private and shared B •
Private and centrally located TVs •
Telephone in rooms • Non-smoking
rooms available
FEATURES: Restaurant/licensed
dining room • Drive to beach •
Off-street parking
*RATES: $50-$69 (1), $55-$95 (2),
$15 add'l person • Open
year-round • DC, AE, ER, MC and
VISA accepted • HIAC; NBHIA;
TIANB; TIANS Member*

Sackville
Rest in the Nest/ Repos au Nid ★★★
Bonnie & Murray Richardson, 6
Mount View Road, RR 2, Sackville,
E0A 3C0
(506) 364-8996
Three o/n units, private and shared
B • Centrally located TV • Pets
welcome • Non-smoking only

FEATURES: Laundry facilities •
Drive to beach • Off-street parking
*RATES: No rates available • Open
May-Sept.*

Sackville
Savoy Arms Bed & Breakfast ★★★½
Bill & Jean Young, 55 Bridge Street,
PO Box 785, Sackville, E0A 3C0
Tel & Fax (506) 536-0790
Rte. 106, Exit 541 • Three o/n units,
private B • Centrally located TV
and VCR • Non-smoking only
FEATURES: Hot and cold drinks •
3 sitting rooms • Fireplaces • Deck
• Drive to beach • Off-street parking
*RATES: $49.50 (1), $55 (2) • Full
buffet breakfast • Open year-round
NBBBA; TTA Member*

Sainte-Anne-de-Kent
Les Pins Maritimes ★★
Jeanne Brideau, Côte St. Anne,
Sainte-Anne-de-Kent, E0A 2V0
(506) 743-8450
Rte. 11, Exit 42 • Waterfront
property • Two o/n units, shared B •
Non-smoking only
FEATURES: Walk to beach •
Off-street parking
*RATES: $50-$60 (1-2) • Open July
to Sept.*

Saint John Area
The Blossoms Bed & Breakfast ★★★½
Bert & Berna Critchlow, RR 1,
Westfield, E0G 3J0
(506) 757-2962
Off Hwy 7, Exit 80 to Rte. 102 •
Waterfront property • Three o/n
units, private B • TV in rooms •
Telephone in rooms • Non-smoking
only

FEATURES: Meals on request •
Craft and gift store, herbal gardens
and workshop • Walk to beach •
Off-street parking
*RATES: $45-$50 (1), $55-$65 (2),
$15 add'l person • Full breakfast •
Open year-round • Visa accepted •
NBBBA Member*

Saint John Area
Dufferin Inn & San Martello Dining Room ★★★

Axel & Margret Begner, 357
Dufferin Row, Saint John, E2M 2J7
(506) 635-5968
Off Rte. 1 and 100, Exit 109 • Six
o/n units, private B • Centrally
located TV • Non-smoking rooms
available
FEATURES: Licensed dining room
• Licensed lounge bar • Coffee •
Off-street parking
*RATES: $45-$50 (1), $55-$75 (2),
$10-$15 add'l person • Full or
continental breakfast • Open
year-round • MC, Visa accepted*

Saint John Area
Earle of Leinster "Inn Style" Bed & Breakfast ★★★

Lauree & Stephen Savoie, 96
Leinster Street, Saint John, E2L 1J3
(506) 652-3275
Off Rte. 1 and 100, Exit 111 and
113 • Seven o/n units, private B,
suites available, private entrance •
TV in rooms • Telephone in rooms
• Pets welcome • Non-smoking
rooms available
FEATURES: Laundry facilities •
Coffee/tea • Microwave • Common
area with pool table, tourist
information, video library, VCR •
Drive to beach • On-street parking

*RATES: $32-$53.05 (1),
$37.89-$61.47 (2), $8.42 add'l
person • Full breakfast • Open
year-round • Visa accepted •
Discount for cash*

Saint John Area
Five Chimneys Bed & Breakfast ★★★½

Linda Gates, 238 Charlotte Street
West, Saint John, E2M 1Y3
(506) 635-1888
Fax (506) 635-8402
Off Rte. 1, Exit 109, 6 blocks to
Charlotte • Two o/n units, private
and shared B, telephone in room •
Private and centrally located TVs •
Non-smoking only
FEATURES: Coffee • Homemade
bread and jams • Walk to beach •
On and off-street parking
*RATES: $50-$60 (1), $50-$65 (2),
$10 add'l person • Full breakfast •
Meals on request • Open
year-round • MC, Visa accepted •
NBBBA Member*

Saint John Area
Fox Croft
Bed & Breakfast &
Women's Retreat ★★½
Marilynn Fox, 479 Gondola Point
Road, Rothesay, E2E 1E3
(506) 847-0818
Off Rte. 1 and 100, Exit 125B and
129 • Waterfront property • Three
o/n units, private B, telephone in
room • Private & centrally located
TVs • Pets welcome • Non-smoking
rooms available
FEATURES: Laundry facilities •
Meals on request • Coffee • Walk
and drive to beaches • Off-street
parking
*RATES: $40 (1), $40-$55 (2), $5
add'l person • Full breakfast •
Open year-round • MC, Visa
accepted • Off-season rates •
Women's retreat packages by
reservation only, $65 per day,
meals incl., min. 5 persons, 2 days •
NBBBA Member*

Saint John Area
Garden House
Bed & Breakfast ★★½
Diane Marks, 28 Garden Street,
Saint John, E2L 3K3
(506) 646-9093
Rte. 1, Exit 112 • Three o/n units,
private and shared B • Private and
centrally located TVs
FEATURES: Laundry facilities •
Meals on request • Coffee •
Off-street parking
*RATES: $35-$50 (1), $45-$65 (2),
$8 add'l person • Full breakfast •
Open year-round • Visa accepted •
NBBBA Member*

Saint John Area
Inn on the Cove ★★★½
Willa & Ross Mavis, 1371 Sand
Cove Road, PO Box 3113 Stn. B,
Saint John, E2M 4X7
(506) 672-7799
Fax (506) 635-5455
Hwy 1, Exit 107A • Waterfront
property • Five o/n units, private B
• Centrally located TV • Adults
only • Non-smoking only
FEATURES: Meals on request •
Off-street parking
*RATES: $60-$75 (twin doubles),
$90-$115 (Queen) • Full breakfast •
Open year-round • MC, Visa
accepted • SJBOT; HIONB; IBEX;
ACIA; OAOA; TIANB Member*

Saint John Area
La Belle Vie Restaurant
& Inn ★★½
325 Lancaster Avenue, Box 3550,
Station B, Saint John, E2M 4Y1
(506) 6735-1155
Off Rte. 1, 100, Exit 104, 107 or
109 • Six o/n units, private B •
Centrally located TV
FEATURES: Restaurant/licensed
dining room • Coffee
*RATES: $35-$100 (1), $45-$120
(2), $10 add'l person • Open
year-round • AE, DC, ER, MC, Visa
accepted • TIANB Member*

Saint John Area
Mahogany Manor ★★★
220 Germain Street, Saint John,
E2L 2G4
(506) 636-8000
Rte. 1. Exit 111 or 112 • Three o/n
units, private B • Centrally located
TV • Telephone in rooms •
Non-smoking only
FEATURES: Laundry facilities •
Drive to beach • Off-street parking

RATES: $55-$65 • Full breakfast • Open year-round • MC, Visa accepted • MRC Member

Saint John Area
Manawagonish
Bed & Breakfast ★★

Jean Poirier, 941 Manawagonish Road, Saint John, E2M 3X2
(506) 672-5843
Off Rte. 1 and 100, Exit 107B North • Two o/n units, private and shared B • Centrally located TV • Telephone in rooms • No alcohol • Non-smoking only
FEATURES: Air-conditioning • Drive to beach • Off-street parking
RATES: $40-$50 (1), $45-$55 (2) • Full breakfast • Open year-round • Visa accepted

Saint John Area
Mount Hope
Bed & Breakfast ★★½

Charlotte Lohnes, 690 Nerepis Road, RR 2, Westfield, E0G 3J0
Tel & Fax (506) 757-8608
Rte. 177 • Two o/n units, private B • Centrally located TV • Non-smoking only
FEATURES: Meals on request • Walk or drive to beach • Off-street parking
RATES: $50 (2), $10 add'l person, suite $129.50 • Full breakfast • Open year-round • Visa accepted

Saint John Area
O'Neill's
Bed & Breakfast ★★½

Fay & Gregg O'Neill, 982 Manawagonish Road, Saint John, E2M 3X1
(506) 672-0111, Cell. (506) 653-0949
Off Rte. 1, Exit 107B to Caterwood St., on to Manawagonish Rd and turn left, 2½ blocks • Three o/n units, shared B, ceiling fans • Centrally located TV • Non-smoking only
FEATURES: Laundry facilities • Coffee/tea, ice cubes • Help with luggage • Off-street parking
RATES: $45 (1), $49 (2), taxes incl. • Full or continental breakfast • Open year-round • MC, Visa accepted

Saint John Area
Phyl's Beverly Hills
Bed & Breakfast ★★★½

Phyllis Finkle, 8 Beverly Hills Drive, Box 315, Grand Bay, E0G 1W0
(506) 738-2337
Off Rte. 7, Exit 80 or 90 • View of water • Three o/n units, private B • Private and centrally located TVs • Telephone in rooms • Children under 6 yrs free, 6-12 yrs $7.50 • Non-smoking only
FEATURES: Laundry facilities • Hot tub • Drive to beach • Off-street parking
RATES: $50 (1), $65-$85 (2), $15 add'l person • Open year-round • NBBBA Member

Saint John Area
Riverside
Bed & Breakfast ★★★
Thomas & Connie Greene, Beulah
Road, Saint John, E0G 1K0
(506) 468-2820
Off Rte. 7 on 102, Exit 80 •
Waterfront property • Two o/n
units, private B, one suite on
separate floor • TV in rooms
Telephone in rooms • Non-smoking
only
FEATURES: Laundry facilities •
Coffee • Deck • Drive to beach •
Off-street parking
*RATES: $39 (1), $49 • (2), $14
add'l person • Full or continental
breakfast • Open June to Oct.*

Saint John Area
Shadow Lawn Inn ★★★★
3180 Rothesay Road, Box 41,
Rothesay, E2E 5A3
(506) 847-7539
Fax (506) 849-9238
Toll free 1-800-561-4166
Rte. 100, Exit 125 or 121 to I00 E •
Nine o/n units, private B • TV in
rooms • Telephone in rooms •
Non-smoking rooms available
FEATURES: Restaurant/Licensed
dining room • Licensed lounge bar •
Coffee Hot tub • Air conditioning •
Housekeeping/efficiency unit
available • Walk or drive to beach •
Off-street parking
*RATES: $79-$125, $15 add'l
person • Full or continental
breakfast • Open year-round • AE,
CB, DC, ER, MC, Visa accepted •
AAA; CAA; HIAC; HINB Member*

Saint John Area
Travis House
Bed & Breakfast ★★★½
Peter Godin, 280 Douglas Avenue,
Saint John, E2K 1E7
(506) 693-0475
Three o/n units, shared B • TV in
rooms • Telephone in rooms •
Non-smoking only
FEATURES: Laundry facilities •
Meals on request • Coffee
Air-conditioning • Drive to beach •
Off-street parking
*RATES: $45 (1), $55-$60 (2), $10
add'l person*

Saint-Louis-de-Kent
Le Gite de l'Oasis
Acadienne
Bed & Breakfast ★★
169 rue Principale, Site 17, Box 11,
Saint-Louis-de-Kent, E0A 2Z0
(506) 876-1199
Rte. 134, Exit 69 • Waterfront
property • Three o/n units, shared B
• Centrally located TV •
Non-smoking only
FEATURES: Laundry facilities •
Drive to beach • Off-street parking
*RATES: $30 (1), $40 (2), $5 add'l
person • Full breakfast • Open
April-October • Off-season by
reservation only*

Salisbury
Salisbury
Bed & Breakfast ★★
Dorothy Archibald, PO Box 551,
Salisbury, E0A 3E0
(506) 372-9754, Cell. (506) 863-4586
Rte. 112 • Three o/n units, shared B
• Centrally located TV • Telephone
in rooms
FEATURES: Air-conditioning •
Off-street parking

RATES: $25 (1), $35 (2) • Full breakfast • Open year-round • NBBBA Member

Shediac
Alcorn's Country Inn Bed & Breakfast ★★½
Barb J. Alcorn, Box 358, Shediac, E0A 3G0
(506) 532-8222
Rte. 134 • Two o/n units, shared B • Private and centrally located TVs • Telephone in rooms • Children under 10 free • Non-smoking only
FEATURES: Laundry facilities • Air-conditioning • Walk to beach • Off-street parking
RATES: $40 (1), $60-$70 (2), $10 add'l person • Full breakfast • Open year-round • Visa accepted • CAA; NBBBA Member

Shediac
Auberge Belcourt Inn ★★★½
Alcide & Thérèse Arsenault, 112 Main Street, Box 631, Shediac, E0A 3G0
(506) 532-6098
Rte. 133 • Seven o/n units, private and shared B • Centrally located TV
FEATURES: Drive to beach • Off-street parking
RATES: $79-$89, $10 add'l person • Full breakfast • Open April-Oct. • AE, DC, ER, MC, Visa accepted • HIAC; HBHIA; TIANB Member

Shediac
Auberge Seaside Haven Inn ★★★
75 Calder Street, Box 1921, Shediac, E0A 3G0
(506) 532-9025
Rte. 133, Exits 2A, 31B, 37, off Main at Centreville Mall Seven o/n

units, private B • TV in rooms • Non-smoking rooms available
FEATURES: Coffee • Efficiency unit available • Walk or drive to beach • On or off-street parking
RATES: $50-$70 (1), $50-$85 (2) • Open season • MC, Visa accepted

Shediac
Chez Françoise ★★½
Hélène & Jacques Johanny, 93 Main Street, CP 715, Shediac, E0A 3G0
(506) 532-4233
Rte. 133 • Nineteen o/n units, private and shared B • Centrally located TV
FEATURES: Licensed dining room • Drive to beach • Off-street parking
RATES: $50-$75, $10 add'l person • Complimentary breakfast • Open Apr.-Dec. • AE, DC, ER, MC, Visa accepted • HIAC; TIANB Member

Shediac
Morgan's Place/ Place Morgan ★★½
Monty V. & Georgette M. Morgan, 668 East Main Street, General Delivery, Shediac, E0A 3G0
(506) 532-8570
Rte. 133, Exits 31B, 37, 2A • Three o/n units, shared B • Private & centrally located TVs • Non-smoking rooms available
FEATURES: Laundry facilities • Coffee • Drive to beach • Off-street parking
RATES: $45-$50 (1), $50-$60 (2), $5-$10 add'l person • Full or continental breakfast • Open season • TIANB Member

Shippagan
Hébergement Dugay ★★½
160 rue des Saules, Shippagan,
E0B 2P0
(506) 336-9135
Two o/n units, private B • TV in
rooms • Telephone in rooms •
Non-smoking rooms available
FEATURES: Laundry facilities •
Housekeeping unit available • Drive
to beach • Off-street parking
RATES: No rates available

Shippagan
Maison Touristique Mallet ★★½
Alice Mallet, RR 2, CP 4, Site 20,
Haut Shippagan, E0B 2P0
(506) 336-4167
Rte. 113 • Waterfront property •
Eight o/n units, private or shared
B&S • Centrally located TV •
Non-smoking only
FEATURES: Indoor swimming
pool • Walk or drive to beach •
Off-street parking
*RATES: $30 (2) with shared B, $40
(2), $5 add'l person, with private B
• Open year-round • MC, Visa
accepted • ATPA; TIANB Member*

Shippagan
O Meunier Tudor ★★
Jeanne-Mance Noël, 279
boulevarde J. D. Gauthier, CP 863,
Shippagan, E0B 2P0
(506) 336-9490
Fax (506) 344-0363
Rte. 113, Exit 310 • Three o/n units,
shared B • Centrally located TV •
Non-smoking rooms available
FEATURES: Housekeeping unit
available • Drive to restaurant,
beach, aquarium, Miscou Island •
Off-street parking

*RATES: $40 (1), $45 (2), $20 add'l
person • Continental breakfast •
Open May to Sept.*

St. Andrews
A. Hiram Walker Heritage Inn ★★★½
Elizabeth Cooney, 109 Reed
Avenue, St. Andrews, E0G 2X0
(506) 529-4210
Fax (506) 529-4311
Toll free 1-800-470-4088
Off Rte. 1 on 127, Exit 14 and 29 •
Five o/n units, private B TV in
rooms • Telephone in rooms •
Non-smoking only
FEATURES: Laundry facilities •
Meals on request • Coffee • Walk to
beach • Off-street parking
*RATES: $95-$195 • Full breakfast
• Open year-round • MC, Visa
accepted • Value Vacation packages
offered • NBHIA; TIANB Member*

St. Andrews
Along the Shore Bed & Breakfast ★★★
RR 1, Bayside, St. Andrews,
E0G 2X0
Tel (506) 529-4323
Rte. 127, Exits 14 off Rte. 1 •
Waterfront property • Two o/n units,
private B • TV in rooms • Telephone
in rooms • Non-smoking only
FEATURES: Coffee • Hiking trails
• Walk to beach • Off-street parking
*RATES: $50-$65, $10 add'l person
• Full breakfast • Open May-Nov.
Value Vacation packages offered •
MC, Visa accepted*

St. Andrews
Chamcook Forest Lodge Bed & Breakfast ★★★

Don & Jenny Menton, RR 2, St. Andrews, E0G 2X0
(506) 529-4778
Off Rte. 1 on 127, Exit 14 and 29 • Waterfront property • Three o/n units, shared B • Centrally located TV • Families welcome • Non-smoking only
FEATURES: Spanish and Portuguese spoken • Laundry facilities • Coffee • Drive to beach • Off-street parking
RATES: $40-$50 (1), $50-$65 (2), $5-$10 add'l person • Full or continental breakfast • Open year-round • MC, Visa accepted Value Vacation packages offered • C of C; NBBBA Member

St. Andrews
Hanson House ★★½

Ann McIntosh, 62 Edward Street, St. Andrews, E0G 2X0
(506) 529-4947
Off Rte. 127, Exit 14 and 29 • Four o/n units, shared B • Centrally located TV • Pets welcome • Non-smoking only
FEATURES: Off-street parking
RATES: $45-$55 (1), $60-$70 (2), $8 add'l person • Full breakfast • Open May to Oct. • Nov.-May by reservation only

St. Andrews
Heritage Guest House ★½

Erma Trudeau, 100 Queen Street, PO Box 476, St. Andrews, E0G 2X0
(506) 529-3875
Off Rte. 1 on 127, Exits 14 and 29 • Three o/n units, private B • Private TV
FEATURES: Laundry facilities • Coffee • Housekeeping unit

available • Drive to beach • Off-street parking
RATES: $50 (1), $55-$60 (2), $5 add'l person • Continental breakfast • Open season • NBBBA Member

St. Andrews
It's the Cat's Meow ★★★½

Bonnie Nelson, 62 Water Street, St. Andrews, E0G 2X0
(506) 529-4717
Rte. 127 • Waterfront property • Two o/n units, private B • TV in rooms • Telephone in rooms • Non-smoking only
FEATURES: Laundry facilities • Drive to beach • Off-street parking
RATES: $85 (2), add'l person $15 Open May-Oct. • MC, Visa accepted NBBBA; TIANB Member • Off-season by reservation only

St. Andrews
Marcia's Garden Corner Bed & Breakfast ★★★½

Marcia Thomson, 364 Montague Street, St. Andrews, E0G 2X0
(506) 529-4453
Rte. 127, Exits 14 and 29 • Four o/n units, private B • Private and centrally located TVs • Telephone in rooms • Non-smoking rooms available
FEATURES: Laundry facilities • Coffee • Drive to beach • Off-street parking
RATES: $70 (1), $75 (2), $10 add'l person, taxes incl. • Full breakfast • Open season • Visa accepted • C of C Member

St. Andrews
The Mulberry Bed & Breakfast ★★½
96 Water Street, St. Andrews,
E0G 2X0
Tel & Fax (506) 529-4948
Rte. 127, Exits 14 and 29 •
Waterfront property • Three o/n
units, private and shared B •
Centrally located TV • Pets
welcome • Non-smoking only
FEATURES: Coffee • Walk or
drive to beach • Off-street parking
*RATES: $60-$75 (2) • Full or
continental breakfast • Open
year-round • MC, Visa accepted •
NBBBA Member*

St. Andrews
Pansy Patch Heritage B&B ★★★★
59 Carleton Street, St. Andrews,
E0G 2X0
(506) 529-3834
Fax (506) 529-9042
Rte. 1, Exits 14 and 29 to Rte. 127,
 adjacent to
Algonquin
Resort •
Waterfront
property •
Five o/n
units,
private B •
Centrally
located TV and VCR • Telephone
in rooms • Non-smoking only
FEATURES: On-site art gallery •
Laundry facilities • Coffee • Meals
on request • Restaurant • Valet
service • Tennis, racquetball courts,
bike rentals • Spa, outdoor
swimming pool, hot tub, sauna •
Walk to beach • Off-street parking
*RATES: $75-$115 (1), $85-$125
(2), $120-$160 (suite), $15 add'l
person • Full breakfast • Open May*

to Nov. • *MC, Visa accepted •
Off-season rates, multiple-night
discounts • Value Vacation
packages offered • NBBBA; TIANB;
C of C Member*

St. Andrews
Rossmount Inn ★★★
Webber & Alice Burns, RR 2, St.
Andrews, E0G 2X0
Tel (506) 529-3351
Fax (506) 529-1920
Rte. 127, Exits 14 and 29 •
Seventeen o/n units, private B •
Centrally located TV •
Non-smoking rooms available
FEATURES: Licensed dining room
• Licensed lounge bar • Outdoor
swimming pool • Drive to beach •
Off-street parking
*RATES: $65-$85 (1), $75-$95 (2),
$10 add'l person • Full breakfast •
Open year-round • MC, Visa
accepted • AAA; CAA; TIANB;
UCT Member*

St. Andrews
Salty Towers ★★
340 Water Street, St. Andrews,
E0G 2X0
Tel (506) 529-4585
Eleven o/n units, private and shared
B • Centrally located TV •
Non-smoking only
FEATURES: Walk to beach •
Off-street parking
*RATES: $31 (1), $59.94 (2), $5
add'l person • Open year-round •
Visa accepted*

St. Andrews
Tara Manor Inn ★★★★
N. & S. Ryall, 559 Mowatt Drive,
Box 30, St. Andrews, E0G 2X0
Tel (506) 529-3304

Rte. 127, Exits 14 and 29 •
Twenty-five o/n units, private B TV
in rooms • Telephone in rooms
FEATURES: Licensed dining room
• Tennis • Outdoor swimming pool
• Hot tub • Air-conditioning • Drive
to beach • Off-street parking
RATES: $96-$108, $138 suites,
$10 add'l person • Full breakfast •
Open season • AE, MC, Visa
accepted • Value Vacation packages
offered • AAA; CAA; DAA; TIANB
Member

St. Andrews
Treadwell Inn ★★★
129 Water Street, St. Andrews,
E0G 2X0
Tel (506) 529-1011
Fax (506) 529-4826
Rte. 127, Exits 14 and 29 •
Waterfront property • Six o/n units,
private B • Private and centrally
located TVs • Non-smoking only
FEATURES: Laundry facilities •
Coffee • Efficiency unit available •
Walk or drive to beach • On and
off-street parking
RATES: $75-$95 (2), $150 deluxe
suite, $10 add'l person • Full
breakfast • Open June -Sept. • MC,
Visa accepted • AAA; CAA; NBBBA
Member

St. George
Bonny River House
Bed & Breakfast ★★★
Eleanor & Harvey Dougherty, RR 3,
Bonny River, St. George, E0G 2Y0
(506) 755-2248
Rte. 770, Exits 40 and 43 •
Waterfront property • Three o/n
units, private B • Centrally located
TV • Non-smoking only
FEATURES: French spoken •
Drive to beach • Off-street parking

RATES: $45 (1), $55 (2), $10 add'l
person • Full breakfast • Open May
to Oct., other months by reservation
only • Visa accepted NBBBA; C of
C; TIANB Member

St. Martins
Bayview
Bed & Breakfast ★★
Main Street, St. Martins, E0G 2Z0
(506) 833-4723
Rte. 111, Exit 125 • Three o/n units,
shared B • Centrally located TV •
Non-smoking rooms available
FEATURES: Laundry facilities •
Meals on request • Kitchenette •
Efficiency unit available • Walk to
beach • Off-street parking
RATES: $48-$50 (2), $8 add'l
person • Open April to Oct. • AE,
MC, Visa accepted

St. Martins
Fundy Breeze
Lodge ★★★
Main Street, St. Martins, E0G 2Z0
(506) 833-4723
Off Rte. 111 • Waterfront property •
Three o/n units, shared B •
Centrally located TV •
Non-smoking rooms available
FEATURES: Laundry facilities •
Restaurant • Coffee • Golf • Walk
to beach • Off-street parking
RATES: $48-$50 (2), $8 add'l
person • Open April to Nov. • AE,
MC, Visa accepted

St. Martins
The Quaco Inn ★★★★½
Betty Ann & Bill Murray, Beach
Street, Box 15, St. Martins, E0G 2Z0
(506) 833-4772
Off 111 • Waterfront property •
Seven o/n units, private B •
Centrally located TV • Telephone in
rooms • Non-smoking only
FEATURES: Laundry facilities •
Licensed dining room • Coffee •
Hot tub • Air-conditioning • Walk
to beach • Off-street parking
*RATES: $60-$80 (1), $65-$85 (2),
$10 add'l person • Full or
continental breakfast • Open
year-round • MC, Visa accepted •
Value Vacation packages offered •
CRFA; NBHIA Member*

St. Martins
St. Martins Country Inn ★★★★½
Myrna & Al LeClair, St. Martins,
E0G 2Z0
(506) 833-4534
Toll free 1-800-565-5257
Off 111, Exit 125 • Waterfront
property • Twelve o/n units, private B
• Centrally located TV • Telephone in
rooms • Non-smoking only
FEATURES: Laundry facilities •
Restaurant/licensed dining room •
Licensed lounge bar • Coffee •
Air-conditioning • Off-street parking
*RATES: $65-$95, $10 add'l person
Full breakfast • Open year-round •
MC, Visa accepted • Value
Vacation packages offered • ACIA;
CAA; NBHIA Member*

St. Stephen
Bay's Edge Bed & Breakfast ★★★
Duncan & Florence McGeachy, RR
3, St. Stephen, E3L 2Y1

(506) 466-5401
Off Rte. 1 on Ledge Road •
Waterfront property • Two o/n units
Centrally located TV • Non-smoking
only
FEATURES: Outdoor swimming
pool • Walk to beach • Off-street
parking
*RATES: $50-$55 (1), $56-$58 (2),
$8 add'l person • Continental
breakfast • Open April to Nov. •
MC, Visa accepted • IODE;
NBBBA; KIWANIS; C of C Member*

St. Stephen
Blair House Bed & Breakfast ★★★
Betty Whittingham, 38 Prince
William Street, Box 112, St.
Stephen, E3L 2W5
(506) 466-2233
Fax (506) 466-5636
Off Rte. 1, 3rd house past the

church on
left • Three
o/n units,
private B,
ceiling fans
• Telephone
in rooms
Centrally
located TV •
Non-smoking only
FEATURES: Laundry facilities •
Coffee • Drive to beach • Off-street
parking
*RATES: $40-$46 (1), $48-$56 (2),
family suite $61, $10 add'l person
Full breakfast • Open year-round •
MC, Visa accepted • C of C; IODE;
NBBBA; TIANB Member*

St. Stephen
Elim Lodge Bed & Breakfast ★★★
Doran & Anne Hooper, 477
Milltown boulevarde, St. Stephen,
E3L 1K2
(506) 466-3521, Cell. (506) 466-8971
Off Rte. 1 • Three o/n units, private
B, ceiling fans, hair dryers,
individual thermostats, clock radios
• Centrally located TV • No alcohol
permitted • Non-smoking only
FEATURES: Laundry facilities •
Library, pool table • Self-guided
historical walking tours • Walk to
tennis, public pool and museum •
Drive to beach • Off-street parking
*RATES: $35 (1), $50-$60 (2), $10
add'l person • Full breakfast •
Open year-round • IIBBEX;
INNCROWD; NBBBA Member*

St. Stephen
The Tides Retreat ★★★
Polly Steele, Todd's Point
(Charlotte County), Box 71, St.
Stephen, E3L 2W9
(506) 466-3040
Fax (506) 466-2143
Rte. 3 • Waterfront property • Four
o/n units, private B • Centrally
located TV • Pets welcome •
Non-smoking only
FEATURES: Laundry facilities •
Licensed dining room • Hot tub •
Walk to beach • Off-street parking
*RATES: $65-$75 (1), $130-$150 (2),
all meals and gratuities incl. • Full
breakfast • Open year-round • Visa
accepted • Group rates available,
Value Vacation packages offered*

Sussex
Anderson's Holiday Farm Bed & Breakfast ★★
RR 2, Sussex, E0E 1P0

(506) 433-3786
Rte. 890, Exit 416 • Three o/n units,
shared B • Centrally located TV
FEATURES: Off-street parking
*RATES: $35-$45 (2) • Full
breakfast • Open year-round*

Sussex
Apohaqui Inn ★★★
Louise & Doug Cosman, 7 Foster
Avenue, PO Box 25, Apohaqui,
E0G 1A0
(506) 433-4149
Off Rte. 1 • Seven o/n units, four
with private ½ B, three with shared B
• Centrally located TV •
Non-smoking only
FEATURES: Laundry facilities •
Coffee • Meals on request
Air-conditioning • Off-street parking
*RATES: $35 (1), $45-$50 (2), $10
add'l person • Full breakfast •
Open year-round • MC, Visa
accepted • Family rate $60 •
NBBBA; TIANB Member*

Sussex
Dutch Valley Heritage Inn ★★★
Vickey S. Bell, RR 4, Waterford
Road, Sussex, E0E 1P0
(506) 433-1339
Fax (506) 433-4287
Off Rte. 1, off Rte. 2, Exits 416,
179, 413, 420 • Three o/n units,
private B • Centrally located TV •
Non-smoking only
FEATURES: Coffee • Meals on
request • Off-street parking
*RATES: $45 (1), $55 (2), $10 add'l
person • Continental breakfast •
Open year-round • Visa accepted •
NBBBA Member*

Sussex
Stark's Hillside Bed & Breakfast ★★★½
Peter & Elizabeth Stark, RR 4
Waterford, Sussex, E0E 1P0
(506) 433-3764
Off Rte. 1, 2 and 111, Exits 416,
420, 179, 3 km past Poley
Mountain • Three o/n units, private
B • Centrally located TV •
Non-smoking only
FEATURES: Meals on request •
Air-conditioning • Off-street parking
*RATES: $50 (1), $60 (2), $10 add'l
person • Full breakfast • Open
year-round • Visa accepted • Value
Vacation packages offered NBBBA;
TIANB Member*

Tracadie
Chez Prime Bed & Breakfast ★★
Jocelyne Losier, 8796 Rte. 11, •
Losier Settlement, E1X 3B9
(506) 395-6884
Rte. 11 and 160 • Four o/n units,
shared B
FEATURES: Drive to beach •
Off-street parking
*RATES: $30 (1), $40-$45 (2), $7
child • Full breakfast • Open season
ATPA Member*

Woodstock
Down Home Bed 'n' Breakfast ★★★
Traci Jones, 698 Main Street,
Woodstock, E0J 2B0
(506) 328-1819
Three o/n units, shared and private
B • TV in rooms • Pets welcome
FEATURES: Laundry facilities •
Air-conditioning • On and off-street
parking
RATES: No rates available

Woodstock
Edgewater Pines Bed & Breakfast ★★½
Bulls Creek, RR 1, Woodstock,
E0J 2B0
(506) 328-3285
Off Trans Canada Hwy, Rte. 103,
Exit 199 • One o/n unit, private B •
Centrally located TV • Telephone in
room • Non-smoking only
FEATURES: On-street parking
*RATES: $60 (1) • Full breakfast •
Open July-Aug.*

Woodstock
The Foot of the Hill/Au Pied de la Colline ★★★
Jean & Tom Bridgeo, 109
Sherwood Drive, Box 56,
Woodstock, E0J 2B0
(506) 328-3585
Exit 188 • Waterfront property •
Three o/n units • Private and
centrally located TVs • Telephone
in room • Non-smoking only
FEATURES: Laundry facilities •
Coffee • Air-conditioning •
Off-street parking
*RATES: $40-$55 (1), $50-$55 (2),
$20 add'l person • Full or
continental breakfast • Open
year-round*

Woodstock
Froehlich's Swiss Chalet Bed & Breakfast ★★½
Edgar & Elfi Froehlich, RR 2, PO
Box 1983, Woodstock, E0J 2B0
(506) 328-6751
Rte. 105 • Waterfront property •
Two o/n units, private B • Centrally
located TV
FEATURES: Laundry facilities •
Off-street parking

RATES: $40 (1), $45 (2), $10 add'l person • Full breakfast • Open May to Oct. • NBBBA Member

Woodstock
Pembroke Place
Inn ★★★
Elizabeth & Phillip Merrithew, RR 5, Newburg Road, Woodstock, E0J 2B0
(506) 328-3599
Fax (506) 325-2430
Toll free 1-800-282-1822
1.5 km off Rte. 105, Exits 191 and 199 • Three o/n units, private B • Centrally located TV • No alcohol • Non-smoking only
FEATURES: Spa treatments (by appointment), specialty travel agency, full office services, all on premises • Air-conditioning • Off-street parking
RATES: $55 (1-2), $15 add'l person • Full breakfast • Open year-round • Visa accepted • Value Vacation packages offered

Youngs Cove Road
Black Bear Lodge
Bed & Breakfast ★★
Gilbert Pelletier, Youngs Cove Road, Queen's County, E0E 1S0
(506) 488-2244
Rte. 2, Grand Lake Drive • Waterfront property • Three o/n units, shared B • Centrally located TV • Telephone in rooms • Pets welcome • Non-smoking rooms available
FEATURES: Laundry facilities • Walk to beach • Off-street parking
RATES: $35 (1), $40 (2), $6 add'l person • Continental breakfast Open year-round • Visa accepted

2

Newfoundland

Aquaforte
Hagan's Hospitality Home ★★★
Mrs. Rita Hagan, General Delivery, Aquaforte, A0A 1A0
(709) 363-2688/363-2213/432-2712
Aquaforte Rte. 10 • Three o/n units, shared B • Colour cable TV and telephone • Children under 10 yrs free
FEATURES: Laundry facilities • Dining room with home-cooked Newfoundland cuisine — fresh seafood • Playground, fishing nearby • Nine km from archaeological dig in historic Ferryland • Two hour drive from Argentia ferry
RATES: $35 (1), $45 (2), $10 add'l person • Full breakfast • Open year-round • Senior citizens' rates

Avondale
Country Lane ★★½
Masons Road, Avondale
(709) 229-4413
Rte. 60 • Bright and airy modern home • Three o/n units, shared B • Colour cable TV • Non-smoking rooms
FEATURES: Quiet and peaceful • Laundry facilites • Whale and iceberg-watching, fishing and hiking nearby
RATES: $35-$45 • Continental breakfast • Open May 15-Oct. 15

Badger
Woodlands Kettle Bed & Breakfast ★★★
19 Church Street, Box 70, Badger, A0H 1A0
(709) 539-2588 or
Fax (709) 539-2788
In Ontario (905) 549-4241,
Fax (905) 549-2488
Badger Rte. 1 Central Newfoundland • Old convent, built c.1900 • Four o/n units, private B • Wheelchair accessible • TV and telephone • Radio • Non-smoking only
FEATURES: Coffee Shop • Restaurant/dining room • Elegant entertainment area • Salmon fishing area • 30 km to Grand Falls, Windsor
RATES: $40 (1), $59 (2) • Full breakfast • Open May 1-Nov. 30 • Major credit cards accepted

Baie Verte
Dorset Bed and Breakfast ★★½
Box 606, Baie Verte, A0K 1B0
(709) 532-8031/4587
Fax (709) 532-4517
Baie Verte Rte. 410 • Three o/n units, private B • Colour cable TV • Radio
RATES: $39 (1), $45 (2), $10 add'l person, $5 child under 15 yrs • Complimentary breakfast • Open year-round

Bay Bulls
Gatherall's Hospitality Home (B&B)
Mike & Rosemary Gatherall,
Northside Road, Bay Bulls, A0A 1C0
(709) 334-2887
Fax (709) 334-2176
Toll free 1-800-41-WHALE
Bay Bulls Rte. 10, follow blue signs
for Gatherall's Boat Tours • Seaside
accommodations • Three o/n units •
Telephone • Non-smoking
FEATURES: Dining room •
Interpretive boat tours to Witless
Bay Seabird Ecological Reserve
(Puffins guaranteed) •
Whale-watching, hiking nearby
*RATES: $42 (1), $52 (2) $12 add'l
person • Continental breakfast •
Open May -Oct.*

Bay Roberts
Dawe's Country Manor ★★★
Box 802, Bay Roberts, A0A 1G0
(709) 786-6505
Rte. 70 • Two o/n units, private
B&S • Wheelchair accessible •
Colour cable TV • Non-smoking
rooms
FEATURES: Restaurant/dining
room • Coffee shop • Room service
• Banquet/meeting facilities
*RATES: $55-$65 • Continental
breakfast • Open June 1-Sept. 30 •
Major credit cards accepted*

Bell Island
Wabana Inn Inc. ★★½
Box 1278, The Front, Bell Island,
A0A 4H0
(709) 488-2944/2497
Off Rte. 40 via ferry from Portugal
Cove • 12 o/n units, private B&S •
Wheelchair accessible •
Non-smoking rooms

FEATURES: Restaurant/dining
room • Whale, iceberg and
bird-watching, fishing, golf and
hiking nearby
*RATES: $50-$60 • Open
year-round • Major credit cards
accepted*

Bonavista
Butler's By The Sea ★★½
Box 642, Bonavista, A0C 1B0
(709) 468-2445
Bonavista Rte. 230 • Two o/n units
• Colour cable TV • Pets allowed •
Non-smoking rooms
FEATURES: Laundry facilities •
Dining room • Barbecue • Picnic
area • Kitchenette available • Whale
and iceberg-watching nearby
*RATES: $45-$55 • Full breakfast •
Open year-round*

Bonavista
Silver Linings Bed & Breakfast ★★½
Chapel Hill Road, Bonavista,
A0C 1B0
Tel & Fax (709) 468-1278
Bonavista Rte. 230 • Registered
Gothic-style heritage home,
Victorian tones • Three o/n units •
Colour cable TV • Non-smoking
rooms
FEATURES: Antiques incl. Lionel
trains • Laundry facilities • Library
• Three fireplaces • Whale, iceberg
and bird-watching, National
Historic Site nearby
*RATES: $50-$60 • Full breakfast •
Open year-round • Visa accepted*

Bonavista
White's
Bed and Breakfast ★★½
21 Windlas Drive, Box 323,
Bonavista, A0C 1B0
(709) 468-7018
Bonavista Rte. 230 • Three o/n
units, one with 1/2 B, two with
shared B • Remote colour cable TV
and clock radio in room • Children
welcome • Non-smoking only
FEATURES: Laundry facilities •
Dining room • Evening snack •
Bicycle rentals • Whale-watching,
iceberg and sea bird viewing
*RATES: $40-$50 (2), $10 add'l
person, $5 under 12 yrs. •
Complimentary breakfast • Open
year-round*

Botwood
Bluejay
Bed & Breakfast ★★★
497 Main Street, Box 815,
Botwood, A0H 1E0
(709) 257-2143
Fax (709) 257-4863
Toll free 1-800-565-4782
Northern Arm Rte. 350-352 •
Comfortable, modern home in rural
location overlooking Bay of Exploits
• Three o/n units • Colour satellite
TV • Telephone • Non-smoking only
FEATURES: In historic, scenic area
• Evening snack • Hiking, ice fishing
• Whale, iceberg and bird-watching
nearby • Tours available
*RATES: $45-$55 (2) • Full
breakfast • Open year-round*

Boxey
Auntie's Inn
Hospitality Home
Box 10, Site 4A, Boxey, A0H 1M0
(709) 888-6581/5211

Boxey Rte. 363 • Four o/n units,
shared B
FEATURES: Meals on request
RATES: $39-$44 • Open year-round

Boyd's Cove
T & K
Bed and Breakfast ★★½
Box 51, Boyd's Cove, A0G 1G0
(709) 656-3551
Boyd's Cove Rte. 340, Located 55
km from Rte. 1 on Rte. 340 • Two
o/n units, shared B • Colour TV and
telephone • Cots available
FEATURES: Beothuk village
nearby • Approx. 33 km from
Twillingate and 25 km from Fogo
and Change Islands
*RATES: $30 (1), $35 (2), $10 add'l
person • Full breakfast • Open July
1-Aug. 31*

Branch
Whalen's Hospitality
Home ★★½
Box 46, Branch, St. Mary's Bay,
A0B 1E0
Tel & Fax (709) 338-2506
Branch Rte. 100 • Four o/n units,
shared B&S • Colour cable TV,
radio and telephone in rooms •
Non-smoking rooms
FEATURES: Best traditional
home-cooked meals • Whale, bird-
watching and fishing nearby •
Thirty minute drive from Cape St.
Mary's Ecological Reserve
*RATES: $42 (1), $48 (2), $10 add'l
person • Continental breakfast •
Open year-round • Major credit
cards accepted*

Brigus
Brittoner ★★½
12 Water Street, Box 163, Brigus,
Conception Bay, A0A 1K0
(709) 528-3412
Brigus off Rte. 70, near Hawthorne
Cottage and Olde Stone Barn •
Restored Victorian home, waterfront
property • Three o/n units, private
B&S • Pets permitted • Non-smoking
rooms
FEATURES: Laundry facilities •
Picnic area • Playground • Fishing
and hiking nearby
*RATES: $50-$55 (2), $55 (3) • Full
breakfast • Open year-round*

Brigus
Brookdale Manor ★★½
Frank & Shirley Roberts, Farm
Road, Box 121, Brigus, A0A 1K0
(709) 528-4544
Brigus Rte. 60, 20 km from Rte. 1
on Rte. 70 • Quiet country setting •
Four o/n units, private B&S •
Wheelchair accessible • Colour
cable TV and telephone •
Non-smoking only
FEATURES: Tea room •
Restaurant/dining room •
Banquet/meeting facilities • Patio
deck • Picnic tables •
Whale-watching nearby
*RATES: $45-$55 (2) • Continental
breakfast • Open year-round •
Major credit cards accepted • HNF
& LB Member*

Brigus
The Cabot Inn
Bed & Breakfast ★★
Box 89, Brigus, Conception Bay,
A0A 1K0
(709) 528-4959
Brigus centre, minutes away from
all historic sites • Colonial-style
interior • Six o/n units, private B •

Wheelchair accessible • Colour
cable TV and telephone in family
room • Non-smoking only
FEATURES: Room service •
Whale, iceberg and bird-watching,
fishing and hiking nearby
*RATES: $40 (1), $45 (2), $10
add'l person • Full breakfast •
Open June-Oct.*

Brigus
Riverhead Chalet
Bed & Breakfast ★★½
Box 71, Brigus, Conception Bay,
A0A 1K0
(709) 528-3295
Brigus Rte. 60 • Waterfront
property, mature grounds, antique
furnishings • Three o/n units, two
shared B • Colour cable TV and
telephone • Non-smoking only
FEATURES: Beautiful view •
Laundry facilities • Traditional
Newfoundland meals on request •
Banquet/meeting facilities • 42 ft.
tour boat • Whale, iceberg and
bird-watching, fishing and hiking
nearby
*RATES: $50-$60 • Full breakfast •
Open May-Oct.*

Brigus
Seaport Cottage ★★
Brigus, Conception Bay, A0A 1K0
(709) 528-4943
Brigus Rte. 60, 20 km from Rte. 1
on Roaches Line, Rte. 70 • Four o/n
units • Colour TV
FEATURES: Beautiful view •
Fireplace • Patio
*RATES: Rates starting from $30,
suites available • Continental
breakfast • Open April-Oct. •
Senior citizens' rates*

Brookfield
Yellow Teapot Inn ★★
Brookfield, Bonavista Bay, A0G 1B0
(709) 536-5858
Brookfield off Rte. 320 • Four o/n
units • Colour cable TV in sitting
room • Pets permitted, usually on
leash
FEATURES: Laundry facilities •
Restaurant • Craft shop, Provincial
Park nearby • Sitting room
*RATES: $35 (1), $40 (2), $5 add'l
person • Continental breakfast •
Open year-round*

Brooklyn
Old Caleb's Place
Vacation Home ★★
Brooklyn, Bonavista, Site 3 Box 11,
RR 1, Lethbridge, A0C 1V0
(709) 467-5436
Brooklyn off Rte. 234 • Farmhouse
style vacation in a seaside setting •
Three bedroom home, private B&S
• Colour TV and telephone
FEATURES: Private surroundings
on 8 acres • Laundry facilities •
Housekeeping services • Picnic area
• Whale and iceberg-watching,
golfing, hiking and National Park
nearby
*RATES: $85 per day, $7 add'l
person over 5 people • Open
year-round • Senior citizens' rates*

Buchans
Harris' Hospitality
Home
137 Gilcrest Road., Box 317,
Buchans, A0H 1G0
(709) 672-3348
Buchans Rte. 370 • Four o/n units,
shared B • Colour TV and
telephone • Radio • Pets permitted,
usually on leash • Non-smoking only

FEATURES: Sitting room •
Playground • Recreation facilities •
Fishing nearby
*RATES: $35 (1), $45 (2), $10 add'l
person • Complimentary breakfast •
Open year-round*

Burgeo
Burgeo Haven
Bed & Breakfast ★★½
Anne & Bill Parsons, 63 Reach
Road, Box 414, Burgeo, A0M 1A0
Tel & Fax (709) 886-2544

Burgeo Rte.
480 •
Waterfront
property •
Four o/n
units, one
private B•
Colour cable
TV •
Telephone • Non-smoking rooms
FEATURES: Laundry facilities •
Room service • Patio • Picnic area •
Sandy beaches, bird-watching and
hiking nearby • Ferry to
Ramea-Francois nearby
*RATES: $40 (1), $50 (2), $10 add'l
person • Full breakfast • Open
year-round • Visa accepted •
Romantic packages, family and
group rates, and Senior citizens'
discount • HNL Member*

Burin
Country Frills
Bed & Breakfast ★★
Winterland Road, Burin, A0E 1E0
(709) 891-2897
Rte. 221 • Country home, close to
nature • Two o/n units, large B with
whirlpool
FEATURES: Evening snack
*RATES: $48 • Complimentary
breakfast • Family rate available*

Burin
Evergreen House & Crafts ★★½
7 Winterland Road, Burin Bay Arm, A0E 1G0
(709) 891-4177
Fax (709) 279-2857
Burin, Rte. 221 • Two o/n units • Colour cable big screen TV and telephone • Non-smoking rooms
FEATURES: Country elegance surrounded by wood • Laundry facilities • Evening snack • Fireplaces • Whirlpool • Bird-watching, fishing, golf and hiking all nearby
RATES: Complimentary breakfast • Open year-round • Major credit cards accepted

Campbellton
P.J.'s Bed and Breakfast ★★
Pauline and Joan Fudge, Box 179, Campbellton, A0G 1L0
(709) 261-2786
Campbellton Rte. 340 • Two o/n units, shared B • Colour cable TV and telephone • Radio
FEATURES: Laundry facilities • Meals on request • Dining room • Two lounging areas
RATES: $35 (1), $5 add'l person • Complimentary breakfast • Open year-round

Cape Onion
Tickle Inn at Cape Onion ★★½
David and Barbara Adams, RR 1, Box 62, Cape Onion, A0K 4J0
Tel & Fax (709) 452-4321
Off-season (709) 739-5503
Cape Onion Rte. 437 • Century-old Newfoundland Heritage Home, beach front property in pastoral setting • Four o/n units, two shared B • Telephone • Non-smoking rooms
FEATURES: Home-cooked Newfoundland meals on request • Dining room • Parlour • Picnic area • Nine acres of meadows and hills for hiking • Whale, iceberg and bird-watching nearby • Close to L'Anse aux Meadows and St. Anthony
RATES: $45 (1), $50-$55 (2), $10 add'l person • Continental breakfast • Open June-Sept. • MC, Visa accepted • HNL; NFBBA; VTA Member

Carbonear
Keneally Manor Heritage Inn ★★½
8 Patrick Street, Carbonear, A1C 5X3
(709) 596-1221
Fax (709) 596-0744
Rte. 70 • Historic property with antique furnishings • Four o/n units, private B&S • Telephone
FEATURES: Southcott award winner • Meeting facilities • Picnic area • Gift shop • Whale, iceberg and bird-watching and fishing nearby
RATES: $45-$65 • Continental breakfast • Open year-round • MC, Visa accepted

Carmanville
Carmanville Olde Inn
Box 16, Carmanville, A0G 1N0
(709) 534-2544/2825
Carmanville Rte. 330 • Three o/n
units • Cable TV • Radio
FEATURES: Meals on request •
Evening snack • Salmon fishing
nearby • Patio deck, picnic table
available • Approx. 60 km from
town of Gander
*RATES: $35 (1), $40 (2), $5 add'l
person • Continental breakfast •
Open May-Sept.*

Carter's Cove
Highway
Bed & Breakfast
Barbara Burt, Main Road, Box 11,
Carters Cove, A0G 1P0
(709) 629-3484
Virgin Arm Rte. 345 • Two o/n
units, shared B • Colour TV and
telephone
FEATURES: Whale, iceberg and
bird-watching, fishing and hiking
nearby
*RATES: $35-$40 • Continental
breakfast • Open June-Sept.*

Cartyville
Hulan's Tourist
Home ★★½
Box 13, Cartyville, A0N 1G0
(709) 645-2376
Cartyville Rte. 404 • Two o/n units
• Colour TV • Children free •
Non-smoking only
FEATURES: Cottages available •
Park nearby • Port aux Basques
Ferry Terminal 110 km
*RATES: $35-$40, $5 add'l adult •
Complimentary breakfast • Open
May 1-Oct. 31 • Major credit cards
accepted*

Change Island
Seven Oakes Inn ★★★
Box 57, Change Island, A0G 1R0
Off-season: Box 123, Deer Lake,
A0K 2E0
(709) 621-3256
Off-season (709) 635-2247
Farewell off Rte. 335, 20 minute
car ferry to Change Islands • Eight
o/n units, private B&S • TV • No
pets, please
FEATURES: Laundry facilities •
Newfoundland meals • Dining room
• Parlour with fireplace •
Playground and picnic area •
Cottages available • Whale and
iceberg-watching and hiking nearby
*RATES: $49-$69 • Open May to
Oct. 31*

Channel-Port aux Basques
Caribou
Bed & Breakfast ★★½
30 Grand Bay Road, Box 53, Port
aux Basques, A0N 1K0
(709) 695-3408
Channel-Port aux Basques Rte. 1 •
Four o/n units, private B&S •
Colour cable TV and telephone •
Non-smoking only
FEATURES: 10,000 happy
travellers served • Coffee/tea •
Room service • Craft shop •
Bird-watching, fishing and hiking
nearby
*RATES: $43-$49 (2), $10 add'l
person • Continental breakfast
before ferry departure • Open May
1-Oct. 31 • Major credit cards
accepted*

Channel-Port aux Basques
Four Seasons Bed & Breakfast ★★½
82 High Street, Port aux Basques, A0M 1C0
(709) 695-3826
Channel-Port aux Basques Rte. 1 • Four o/n units, shared B&S • Colour cable TV and telephone • Rollaway cot • No pets, please • Non-smoking rooms
FEATURES: Complimentary fresh home-baked goods • Laundry facilities • Picnic area • One km to ferry terminal • Parking
RATES: $40-$45, $10 add'l person • Continental breakfast • Open year-round • Major credit cards accepted

Channel-Port aux Basques
Heritage Home ★★½
11 Caribou Road, Box 1187, Port aux Basques, A0M 1C0
(709) 695-3240
Channel-Port aux Basques Rte. 1 • Five o/n units, private B&S, family suite with 2 double beds • Colour cable TV and telephone • Cot available • No pets, please • Non-smoking only
FEATURES: Room service • Lounge • Walk to ferry terminal, shopping and other businesses • Bird-watching and hiking nearby
RATES: $37-$60, $10 add'l person (cot) • Continental breakfast • Open May-Oct. • MC, Visa accepted

Clarenville
Island View Hospitality Home ★★½
128 Memorial Drive, Box 1465, Clarenville, A0E 1J0
(709) 466-2062
Four o/n units • Colour cable TV and telephone in living room • Non-smoking only

FEATURES: Well-informed hosts display fishing, culture, antiques • Coffee/tea • Evening snack • Fitness facilities • Hiking and National Park nearby • Twenty-five minutes to Twin Rivers Golf Course
RATES: $39 (1), $65 (4) • Continental breakfast • Open year-round • Major credit cards accepted

Clarenville
Janes' Tourist Home ★★½
Ms. Sadie Thistle, Manageress, 261 Marine Drive, Box 431, Clarenville, A0E 1J0
(709) 466-1329
5 km from Rte. 1 • Attractively restored century old heritage home with original slate roof in quiet location • Three o/n units, private B • Colour cable TV and telephone • Radio • Non-smoking only • Offering all commercial amenities
FEATURES: Laundry facilities • Dining room • Golf and gourmet restaurant nearby
RATES: $35-$60 • Continental breakfast • Open June 1-Sept. 30

Clarenville
Patrick's Bed & Breakfast ★★
25 Balbo Drive, Shoal Harbour, A0E 1J0
(709) 466-1906
Clarenville Rte. 1 • Four o/n units • Cable colour TV • Clock radio
FEATURES: French spoken • Laundry facilities • Meals on request • Off-street parking
RATES: $30 (1), $35 (2) • Full breakfast • Open year-round • Weekly/monthly rates available

Sanctuary Country Inn ★★★

23 Balbo Drive, Box 1448,
Clarenville, A0E 1J0
(709) 466-3103
Two o/n units, private B • Colour
cable TV and telephone • Clock
radio • Non-smoking only
FEATURES: Laundry facilities •
Licensed • Coffee/tea • Living room
with fireplace, formal dining room
(breakfast only) • VCR/movie
rentals • Central air conditioning •
Overlooking the Shoal Harbour
Canada Goose Sanctuary, near
Trinity Pageant, Hibernia Project
tours • Outdoor dog kennel
*RATES: $59 (1), $69 (2), $15 add'l
person, no PST • Full breakfast •
Open year-round • Discovery Trail
Tourism Assoc; HNL Member*

Clarke's Beach
Country Manor B&B ★★

Box 28192, St. John's, A1B 4J8
(709) 786-9000
Rte. 70, Clarke's Beach • Three o/n
units, private and shared B
FEATURES: Tennis Court
*RATES: $45-$60 • Call for season
and more information*

Clarke's Beach
Kaldory Inn Bed and Breakfast ★★½

Cal & Doris Dory, Main Street,
Box 361, Clarke's Beach, A0A 1W0
(709) 786-0900
Clarke's Beach Rte. 70 • Waterfront
property snuggled beneath a
mountain • Four o/n units, private B
• Colour cable TV • Non-smoking
rooms

FEATURES:
Sitting
room,
library •
Housekeeping
services •
Large patio
with gas
barbecue • Kitchenette available •
Bird-watching, fishing and hiking
nearby • Country Emporium Craft
and Antique Shop
*RATES: $45-$65, $10 add'l person
• Full breakfast • Open May-Oct. •
Visa accepted*

Clarke's Beach
Otterbury Hollow ★★

Box 113, Paradise, A1L 1C4
(709) 782-1288
Clarke's Beach, Rte. 70 off Rte. 1
to North River Intersection, turn
right along Dock Road 2 km •
Private, scenic retreat offering
comfort and seclusion • Three o/n
units, private B&S • Colour cable
TV, VCRs and movies • Telephone
• Pets permitted • Non-smoking
rooms
FEATURES: Fireplaces • Barbecue
• Outdoor pool • Whale and bird-
watching and hiking nearby
*RATES: $120-$150, $700 per week
• Open year-round • Visa accepted*

Conception Bay South
Sleep Inn Bed & Breakfast ★★½

Ivimey Place, Box 4032, Manuels,
Conception Bay South, A1W 1G5
(709) 834-2905
Three o/n units, shared B • Cable
TV and telephone
FEATURES: Laundry facilities •
Playground • Outdoor swimming
pool (heated) • Scenic river walking
trails • Whale, iceberg and bird-

watching, fishing nearby, twenty minute drive from St. John's
RATES: $48-$58, $10 add'l person • Full breakfast • Open year-round

Conception Bay South
Villa Nova
Bed & Breakfast ★★
Long Pond, Conception Bay South, A1W 1J9
(709) 834-1659
Rte. 60 • Three o/n units, shared B • Colour cable TV • Non-smoking rooms
FEATURES: Laundry facilities • Scenic living room • Patio deck with barbecue • Iceberg-watching and hiking nearby • Ten minutes to marina/yacht club
RATES: $40-$50 • Open May-Oct.

Conception Harbour
Conception Tourist
Inn ★★½
Conception Harbour, Conception Bay, A0A 1Z0
(709) 229-3988
Rte. 60 • Country Inn with bed and breakfast atmosphere • Seven o/n units, private B&S • Colour cable TV
FEATURES: Laundry facilities • Restaurant/dining room • Picnic area • Whale, iceberg and bird-watching, fishing and hiking nearby
RATES: $44-$49 • Open year-round • Major credit cards accepted

Conche
Seashell Hospitality
Home ★½
Box 86, Conche, A0K 1Y0
(709) 622-4151
Conche Rte. 434 • Quiet setting, scenic view next to the sea • Three

o/n units, shared B • Colour cable TV and telephone • Non-smoking rooms
FEATURES: Laundry facilities • Whale and iceberg-watching, fishing and hiking nearby
RATES: $35-$40 • Continental breakfast • Open year-round

Corner Brook
Bell's
Bed & Breakfast ★★★
2 Fords Road, Corner Brook, A2H 1S6
(709) 634-5736
Corner Brook Rte. 1 • Located corner of St. Mark's Ave. and Fords Rd. • Four o/n units, private B • Colour cable TV in sitting room • Telephone • Radio
FEATURES: Laundry facilities • Ensuite fireplaces • Propane barbecue • Recreational facilities, fishing nearby • Close to Terra Transport Bus Terminal
RATES: $44-$64• Full breakfast • Open year-round • Major credit cards accepted

Corner Brook
Bide-A-Night
Hospitality Home ★★
11 Wellington Street, Corner Brook, A2H 5H3
(709) 634-7578
Corner Brook Rte. 1 • Centrally located • Two o/n units • Colour TV • Radio
FEATURES: Home baking • Picnic area • Fishing, golf, hiking and National Park nearby
RATES: $30 (1), $40 (2) • Full breakfast • Open year-round

Corner Brook
Humber Gallery Hospitality Home ★★½
26 Roberts Drive, Little Rapids,
Box 15, Corner Brook, A2H 6C3
(709) 634-2660
Little Rapids Rte. 1, 15 km east of
Corner Brook • Three o/n units •
Colour TV and telephone •
Non-smoking rooms
FEATURES: Laundry facilities •
Fireplace • Sundeck • Picnic area •
Fishing nearby • Close to Marble
Mountain, overnight stop to Gros
Morne Park
*RATES: $35-$40 (2), $6 add'l
person • Continental breakfast •
Open June 15-Sept. 15; Feb. 1-Mar.
31 • Visa accepted • 10% discount
for Senior citizens*

Corner Brook
Mary's Bed and Breakfast ★★
127 Little Port Road, Lark Harbour.
Mailing address: Box 231, Corner
Brook, A2H 6C9
(709) 681-2210
Off-season (709) 789-3642
Located at end of Captain Cook's
trail • Two o/n units • Non-smoking
FEATURES: Beautiful sunset •
Hiking trails • Close to restaurant •
Whale and iceberg-watching nearby
*RATES: $35 (1), $45 (2) •
Continental or full breakfast • Open
June 1-Sept. 4*

Cow Head
A & A Guest Home ★★
Box 147, Cow Head, A0K 2A0
(709) 243-2389
Cow Head Rte. 430 • Two o/n
units, shared B • Colour cable TV
in living room • Radio • Pets
permitted, usually on leash

FEATURES: Barbecue •
Housekeeping unit available •
Beach • Boat tours, nature walks
nearby • Close to Gros Morne
National Park
*RATES: $40 (1), $45 (2)• Full
breakfast • Open June-Labour Day*

Cow Head
J. & J. Hospitality Home ★★
Box 107, Cow Head, A0K 2A0
(709) 243-2521
Cow Head Rte. 430, within
boundaries of Gros Morne National
Park • Four o/n units, two private
B&S, two shared • Wheelchair
accessible • Colour cable TV and
telephone • Non-smoking only
FEATURES: Laundry facilities •
Barbecue • Outdoor swimming pool
• Hiking trails, bird-watching nearby
*RATES: $40 (1), $50 (2), $8 add'l
person, $4 children under 12 yrs
Four-choice breakfast with Nfld.
jams and homemade bread • Open
June 1-Oct. 31 • Major credit cards
accepted*

Creston South
Creston House Bed & Breakfast ★★½
Box 34, Creston South, Marystown,
A0E 1K0
(709) 279-3384
Creston South Rte. 210 • Three o/n
units, private B&S • Non-smoking
only
FEATURES: Local Newfoundland
jams • Golf and hiking nearby
*RATES: $35 (1), $45-$55 (2) • Full
breakfast • Open year-round •
Major credit cards accepted*

Daniel's Harbour
Seaview
Bed & Breakfast ★★
182 Main Street, Box 38, Daniel's Harbour, A0K 2C0
(709) 898-2581
Daniel's Harbour Rte. 430 • Three o/n units, shared B • Colour TV and telephone • Pets permitted, usually on leash • Non-smoking only
FEATURES: Laundry facilities • Picnic area, playground • Whale, iceberg and bird-watching, fishing, hiking and National Park nearby
RATES: $36 (1), $40 (2), $8 add'l person • Full breakfast • Open year-round

Doyles
Long Range
Bed & Breakfast ★★½
Box 823, RR 1, Doyles, A0N 1J0
(709) 955-2901
Upper Ferry, Rte. 406 • Beautiful scenery, quiet surroundings • Two o/n units, private B&S • Telephone • Non-smoking rooms
FEATURES: Traditional Newfoundland warmth and hospitality • Laundry facilities • Thirty minutes from ferry • Bird-watching, fishing and hiking nearby
RATES: Continental breakfast • Open June 1-Sept. 30

Eastport
Pinsent's
Bed & Breakfast and
Art Studio ★★½
17 Church Street, Box 85, Eastport, A0G 1Z0
(709) 677-3021
Eastport Rte. 310 • Two o/n units • Colour cable TV and Telephone • Radio • Non-smoking rooms

FEATURES: Art studio • Laundry facilities • Meals on request in off-season • Whale, iceberg and-bird watching, fishing, golfing and hiking nearby
RATES: $35 (1), $45 (2), $10 add'l person • Full breakfast • Open year-round

Eastport
Sharoz Inn ★★½
5 Burden's Road, Box 115, Eastport, A0G 1Z0
(709) 677-3539
Eastport Rte. 310 • Country inn with warm and personal atmosphere, delicious food and immaculate lodgings • Six o/n units, private B&S • Wheelchair accessible • Colour cable TV
FEATURES: Restaurant/dining room • Housekeeping services • Whale and iceberg-watching, golf, hiking and National Park nearby
RATES: $44-$75 • Continental breakfast • Open May-Nov. • Major credit cards accepted

Englee
Reeves Ocean View
Bed & Breakfast ★★½
Church Road, Box 217, Englee, A0K 2J0
(709) 866-2531
Englee Rte. 433 • Two o/n units, private B
FEATURES: View of icebergs and whales from balcony overlooking the ocean • Laundry facilities • Bird-watching, fishing and hiking nearby
RATES: $45 (1), $50 (2), $10 add'l person (cot) • Full breakfast • Open year-round • Visa accepted

English Harbour West
Olde Oven Inn ★★½
Box 40, English Harbour West,
Fortune Bay, A0H 1M0
(709) 888-3461/4402
Fax (709) 888-3441
English Harbour West Rte. 360 •
Traditional Newfoundland home
with view of harbour • Four o/n
units, shared B • Colour cable TV
and telephone • Pets permitted,
usually on leash
FEATURES: Laundry facilities •
Kitchenette available •
Bird-watching, fishing and hiking
nearby
RATES: $40 (1), $50 (2) •
Continental breakfast • Open
year-round • Major credit cards
accepted

Exploits Island
Devon House ★★½
Exploits Island, Notre Dame Bay
(709) 541-3230
Fax (709) 535-0805
Heritage home on remote resettled
island • Four o/n units, shared B •
Telephone • Pets permitted •
Non-smoking rooms
FEATURES: Laundry facilities •
Restaurant/dining room •
Housekeeping services • Outdoor hot
tub • Whale and iceberg-watching
RATES: $40-$70, Open May-Oct. •
Major credit cards accepted

Ferryland
The Ark of Avalon
Bed & Breakfast ★★½
General Delivery, Ferryland,
A0A 2H0
(709) 432-2861
Ferryland Rte. 10 • Four o/n units,
two shared B, newly built private
entrance • Spacious TV room and
satellite TV • Telephone • Radio

FEATURES: Laundry facilities •
Home-cooked meals • Dining room
• Patio deck with barbecue
RATES: No rates available • Full
breakfast • Open year-round

Ferryland
The Downs Inn
Box 15, Ferryland, A0A 2H0
(709) 432-2808
Ferryland Rte. 10 • Four o/n units,
shared B • Telephone •
Non-smoking rooms
FEATURES: Laundry facilities •
Tea room • Room service • Whale,
iceberg, and bird-watching and
fishing all nearby
RATES: $35-$45 • Full breakfast •
Open year-round

Flower's Cove
Labrador "Vue"
Bed & Breakfast
Box 145, Flower's Cove, A0K 2N0
(709) 456-2396/2526
Flower's Cove off Rte. 430 • Three
o/n units, two shared B • Cable TV
in living room
FEATURES: Access to kitchen •
Hunting, fishing nearby • Icebergs,
whales, seals (watch the running of
seals in the spring) • Centrally
located to Strait of Belle Isle ferry,
St. Anthony Airport, Sandy Cove
Airstrip, L'Anse aux Meadows
Viking site or Port au Choix Point
Rich Indian Burial Grounds (all
within one hour drive) • Three
hours from Gros Morne National
Park
RATES: $40 (1), $45 (2), $10 add'l
person • Open Apr.-Oct.

Fogo Island
Payne's Hospitality Home ★½
Box 201, Fogo, A0G 2B0
(709) 266-2359
Fogo Island off Rte. 335 via ferry from Farewell • Three o/n units, shared B • Colour cable TV and telephone • Non-smoking rooms
FEATURES: Playground and picnic area • Close to museum, craft shop, scenic areas • Whale, iceberg and bird-watching, fishing and hiking all nearby
RATES: $28-$56, meals included • Open year-round

Fogo Island
Alma's Bed and Breakfast ★★½
Alma Kinden, Box 90, Stag Harbour, Fogo Island, A0G 4B0
(709) 627-3302/3225
Fogo Island Rte. 333 • Three o/n units, two with double, one with two singles • Colour cable TV, telephone • Radio • Non-smoking only
FEATURES: Laundry facilities • Evening snack • Picnic area • Hiking trails • Snowmobiling, cross-country skiing • Bird and whale-watching, fishing, swimming, beaches, icebergs nearby • Craft shop/museums nearby • Boat tours available
RATES: $43.50 (1), $48.50 (2), $5.00 add'l person (cot) • Full hot breakfast • Open year-round

Forteau
Grenfell Louie A. Hall
3 Willow Avenue, Box 137, Forteau, A0K 2P0
(709) 931-2916
Forteau Rte. 510 • Formerly known as the International Grenfell Nursing Association, built 1946 • Five o/n units, two shared B • Colour cable TV/VCR in living room • Children stay free • Non-smoking rooms
FEATURES: Laundry facilities • Meals on request • Dining room, living room with fireplace • Close to playground • Whale, iceberg and bird-watching and fishing nearby
RATES: $32 (1), $40 (2), $7 add'l person • Open May-Jan. • Continental breakfast • Visa accepted

Fortune
Eldon House Country Inn ★★½
31 Eldon Street, Fortune, A0E 1P0
(709) 832-0442
Fortune Rte. 210 • Turn of the century home • Three o/n units, private B • Colour cable TV, telephone • Non-smoking rooms
FEATURES: Glassware collection • Laundry facilities • Room service • Picnic area • Fishing, golf and hiking nearby • Complimentary guest parking while visiting St. Pierre
RATES: $35 (1), $45 (2) • Full breakfast • Open May 1-Nov. 30

Gander
Cape Cod Inn B&B ★★★
66 Bennett Drive, Gander, A1V 1M9
Tel/Fax (709) 651-2269
Gander Rte. 1 • Four o/n units,
private B • Colour cable TV and
telephone • Non-smoking rooms
FEATURES: Maid service •
Fishing, golf nearby • Thirty minutes
to whale and iceberg-watching
RATES: *$45-$75 (1-2)* •
*Continental breakfast • Open
year-round • Major credit cards
accepted*

Gander
Country Inn ★★½
315 Gander Bay Road, Box 154,
Gander, A1V 1W6
(709) 256-4005
Rte. 330, 4 km from Rte. 1 • Nine
o/n units, private B&S • Wheelchair
accessible • Colour cable TV and
telephone • Rollaway cots • Pets
permitted, usually on leash
FEATURES: Coffee/tea • Room
service • Playground • Golf and
hiking nearby
RATES: *$42 (1), $48 (2)* •
*Continental breakfast • Open
year-round • MC, Visa accepted •
Winter rates $34 (1-2) • Seniors'
discount 10% • C of C; HN&L;
KTA Member*

Gander
Travellers Choice Inn Bed & Breakfast ★★½
303 Gander Bay Road, Box 183,
A1V 1W6
(709) 256-7846
Rte. 330 off Rte. 1, three minute
drive from Gander • Three o/n
units, shared B • Colour TV and
telephone • Children under 12 free
FEATURES: Laundry facilities •
Dining room • Complimentary

tea/coffee • Spacious sundeck •
Hand-crafted items on sale
RATES: *$40 (1), $45 (2), $10 add'l
person over 12 yrs • Full breakfast
• Open year-round*

Gaskiers
Tobin's Gaskiers Bay ★★½
Box 143, Gaskiers, A0B 3B0
(709) 525-2463/2849
Gaskiers Rte. 90 • Overlooks St.
Mary's Bay • Two o/n units •
Colour cable TV and telephone •
Non-smoking rooms
FEATURES: Laundry facilities •
Home-cooked meals on request •
Whale, iceberg and bird-watching,
hiking and caribou herd all nearby
RATES: *$40-$60 • Open year-round*

Gaultois
Gaultois Inn
Box 151, Gaultois, A0H 1N0
(709) 841-4141
Gaultois off Rte. 364 via ferry from
Hermitage-Sandyville • Six o/n
units, private B&S • Colour cable
TV and telephone • Pets permitted
FEATURES: Laundry facilities •
Specializing in fresh seafood •
Restaurant/dining room • Lounge •
Room service
RATES: *$50-$60 • Continental
breakfast • Open year-round*

Glovertown
30 Main Bed & Breakfast ★★
Box 58, Glovertown, A0G 2L0
(709) 533-2559
Fax (709) 533-2640
Glovertown Rte. 310 • Three o/n
units, shared B • Colour cable TV
and telephone • Non-smoking only

FEATURES: Modern, comfortable surroundings • Whale, iceberg and bird-watching, fishing, golf and hiking nearby • Close to Terra Nova National Park
RATES: $35-$65 • Continental breakfast • Open year-round

Glovertown
Ackerman's
Bed & Breakfast ★★½
Box 239, Glovertown, A0G 2L0
(709) 533-2811/2810
Glovertown Rte. 310, on the border of Terra Nova National Park • Four o/n units, private B • Pets permitted
FEATURES: Home away from home • Golf nearby
RATES: $40 (1), $50 (2), $5 add'l person • Continental breakfast • Open year-round

Grand Bank
Thorndyke
Bed & Breakfast ★★½
Box 39, Grand Bank, A0E 1W0
(709) 832-0820/279-3384
Grand Bank Rte. 210 • Sea captain's mansion (1917) overlooking Fortune Bay • Four o/n units, private B&S • Non-smoking only
FEATURES: Golf and hiking nearby
RATES: $35-$50 • Full breakfast • Open May-Sept. • Visa accepted

Grand Bruit
Dutch Inn ★½
Grand Bruit, A0M 1G0
(709) 492-2730/2665
Grand Bruit off Rte. 470 via coastal boat from Rose Blanche • Colour TV and telephone • Radio
FEATURES: Dining room • Lounge • Guide service available

RATES: $50, $10 add'l person • Open year-round

Grand Falls-Windsor
Carriage House Inn ★★★½
181 Grenfell Heights, Grand Falls-Windsor, A2A 2J2
Tel & Fax (709) 489-7185
Toll free 1-800-563-7133 reservations only
Grand Falls-Windsor Rte. 1 • Country decor, quiet setting on six acres • Four o/n units, private B&S • Colour cable TV and telephone • Non-smoking only
FEATURES: • Library • Spacious sun deck • Full equestrian facility, stable tours, Nfld. dog and pony • Golf nearby
RATES: $49-$79 • Full breakfast • Open year-round • Visa accepted • Seniors discount 10%

Grand Falls-Windsor
Poplar Inn
Bed & Breakfast ★★½
Wayne and Beth Thorne, 22 Poplar Road, Grand Falls-Windsor, A2A 1V5
(709) 489-2546, call after 5 p.m. Sept.-June
Grand Falls-Windsor Rte. 1, Exit 19, keep right • Three o/n units, private B&S • TV and clock radio in rooms • Telephone • Non-smoking only
FEATURES: Elegant, comfortable, quiet surroundings • Golf, playground nearby • Centre town location close to a variety of services, restaurant, shopping
RATES: $45-$65, $10 add'l person • Full (season) or continental (off-season) breakfast • Open year-round • MC, Visa accepted

Gunners Cove
Valhalla
Bed and Breakfast ★★
Box 10, Gunners Cove, L'Anse aux
Meadows, A0K 2X0
(709) 623-2018
Fax (709) 623-2144
Off-season (709) 896-5519
Off-season Fax (709) 896-0239
Gunners Cove Rte. 436 • Six o/n
units, private B • Wheelchair
accessible • Telephone • Radio •
Pets permitted • Non-smoking only
FEATURES: Annie Proulx stayed
here • Room service • Living room
• Kitchenette available
RATES: $40 (1), $55 (2) •
Continental breakfast • Open
June-Oct. • Visa accepted •
Off-season rates available

Happy Valley-Goose Bay
Bradley's
Bed and Breakfast
13 MacKenzie Drive, Happy
Valley-Goose Bay, PO Box 164,
Stn. C, LB A0K 1C0
(709) 896-8006
Fax (709) 896-9344
Happy Valley-Goose Bay Rte. 500
• Two o/n units • Colour cable TV
and telephone • Non-smoking rooms
FEATURES: Home made bread,
muffins, jams • Laundry facilities •
Lounge • Room service • Picnic
area • Electric/water/sewage hookup
• Walk to golf course, local bars,
restaurants and shops
RATES: $40-$55 • Continental
breakfast • Open year-round •
Major credit cards accepted

Happy Valley-Goose Bay
Davis Bed and Breakfast
14 Cabot Crescent, Box 811, Stn.
B, Happy Valley-Goose Bay, LB,
A0P 1E0
(709) 896-5077
Happy Valley-Goose Bay Rte. 520
• Four o/n units, private B •
Wheelchair accessible • Colour
cable TV in sitting room •
Telephone • Radio • Non-smoking
only
FEATURES: Laundry facilities •
Best homemade bread and jams •
Banks, restaurants, post office, car
rentals nearby
RATES: $40-$60 (2-3) •
Continental breakfast • Open
year-round • Visa accepted

Harbour Grace
Garrison House Inn
Box 736, Harbour Grace, A0A 2M0
(709) 596-3658
Rte. 70 • 1811 Heritage home
furnished with antiques • Three o/n
units, private B&S • Wheelchair
accessible • Telephone •
Non-smoking rooms
FEATURES: Laundry facilities •
Restaurant/dining room • Room
service • Garden • Whale and
iceberg-watching and hiking nearby
RATES:$45-$59 • Open year-round
• Major credit cards accepted

Harbour Grace
Rothesay ★★½
Box 78, Harbour Grace, A0A 2M0
(709) 596-2268
Rte. 70 • Victorian house in
heritage district, on the ocean •
Four o/n units, private B&S •
Colour cable TV and telephone •
Non-smoking rooms
FEATURES: Laundry facilities •
Room service • Whale, iceberg and

bird-watching and hiking nearby •
Sixty minutes from St. John's
*RATES: $45-$59 • Open
year-round • Major credit cards
accepted*

Harbour Main
Kennedy's Country Corner Bed and Breakfast ★★½

Box 74, Lakeside, Harbour Main,
A0A 2P0
(709) 229-6568
Lakeview Rte. 60 • Two o/n units,
private B • Colour cable TV and
telephone • Clock radio •
Non-smoking rooms available
FEATURES: Beautiful scenery
overlooking pond • Laundry
facilities • Room service • Propane
barbecue on veranda • Whale,
iceberg- watching, fishing and
hiking nearby
*RATES; $40 - $45 • Full breakfast
• Open year-round*

Harcourt
Hollingside Bed & Breakfast ★★

Harcourt, Trinity Bay, A0E 1J0
(709) 747-3663
Harcourt Rte. 232 • Clean, comfortable
accomodation • Three o/n units, shared
B • Non-smoking only
*RATES: $50-$60 • Continental
breakfast • Open year-round • Two
cats and one dog on site •
Reservations required*

Hawke's Bay
Baie View Bed and Breakfast ★★

Miranda Mouland, Box 54,
Hawke's Bay, A0K 3B0
(709) 248-5270

Fax (709) 248-5155
Hawke's Bay Rte. 430 • Three o/n
units, two shared Bs • Wheelchair
accessible • Colour cable TV •
Radio • Pets permitted, usually on
leash • Designated smoking area
FEATURES: Laundry facilities •
Meals on request • Evening snack •
Cocktail drinks permitted •
Barbecues • Playground
*RATES: $30 (1), $35 (2), $5 add'l
person • Open year-round • AE,
MC, Visa accepted •*

Hawke's Bay
Gloria's Bed and Breakfast ★★½

Box 26, Hawke's Bay, A0K 3B0
(709) 248-5131
Hawke's Bay Rte. 430 • Three o/n
units • Colour cable TV and
telephone • Non-smoking only
FEATURES: Clean, quiet, homey
atmosphere
• Laundry
facilities •
Picnic area •
Fishing,
hiking
nearby
*RATES:
$35 (1), $40
(2), $7 add'l person • Full
breakfast • Open May-Oct.*

Heart's Delight
Farm House Hospitality Home ★★½
Box 72, Heart's Delight, Trinity
Bay, A0B 2A0
(709) 588-2393
Heart's Delight Rte. 80 • Three o/n
units, one with private B • Colour
cable TV and telephone in family
room • Radio • Non-smoking only
FEATURES: Playground • Fishing,
beach, swimming nearby •
Provincial Park and Museum
nearby • Historic "Trans Atlantic
Cable Station" nearby • Craft shop
nearby
*RATES: $40-$50, $10 add'l
person, $5 per child • Continental
breakfast • Open May 15-Dec. 15*

Hillgrade
Sunset Bed and Breakfast ★★
General Delivery, Hillgrade,
A0G 2S0
(709) 628-5209
Off Rte. 340 • Quiet, peaceful area
• Three o/n units, private B • Cable
TV • Non-smoking rooms
FEATURES: Sunroom overlooking
bay, with telescope • Laundry
facilities • Homemade baked goods
• Kitchenette available • Whale,
iceberg-watching nearby
*RATES: $45-$50 • Continental
breakfast*

Holyrood
Beach Cottage Bed & Breakfast ★★½
Holyrood, Conception Bay,
A0A 2R0
(709) 229-4801
Holyrood Rte. 60 • Three o/n units,
private B • Colour TV in sitting
room • Non-smoking rooms

FEATURES: Ocean view •
Restaurant/dining room • Picnic area
• Outdoor swimming • Twenty-five
minutes from St. John's and Brigus •
Whale, iceberg-watching nearby
*RATES: $44-$49 (2) • Open June
15-Sept. 15*

Horwood
Bennings Bed & Breakfast ★★
General Delivery, Stoneville,
A0G 4C0
(709) 541-3091
Horwood off Rte. 331 • Two o/n
units, shared B •
FEATURES: Many rivers, ponds
for trouting • Ice fishing in winter
and skidooing • Salmon river 800
ft. away • Twenty minutes to Fogo
and Change Island Farewell Ferry
RATES: $40-$45 • Open year-round

Jackson's Arm
Peggy's Hospitality Home ★★
Box 39, Jackson's Arm, White Bay,
A0K 3H0
(709) 459-3333/3136
Jackson's Arm Rte. 420 • Four o/n
units, two shared B • Colour cable
TV and telephone • Rollaway cots
available • Pets permitted, usually
on leash • Non-smoking only
*RATES: $40 (1-2), $15 add'l
person • Complimentary breakfast •
Open year-round*

L'Anse-Amour
Davis
Bed & Breakfast ★★
Rita Davis, General Delivery,
L'Anse-Amour, LB, A0K 3L0
(709) 927-5690
L'Anse-Amour Rte. 510 • Three o/n
units, two full B • Colour cable TV
and telephone • Non-smoking only
FEATURES: Home away from
home • Laundry facilities •
Housekeeping services • Barbecue,
picnic table • Playground • Whale
and iceberg-watching nearby
RATES: $32 (1), $36 (2) •
Continental breakfast • Open
May-Oct. • MC accepted

L'Anse au Clair
Beachside Hospitality
Home
L'Anse au Clair, LB, A0K 3K0
(709) 931-2662/2053
L'Anse au Clair Rte. 510 • Three
o/n units, shared B • Telephone •
Pets permitted • Non-smoking rooms
FEATURES: "Labrador's
elemental appeal...owner's
knowledge of Labrador tradition
goes way back", *New York Times*,
July 17, 1995 • Laundry facilities •
Whale and iceberg-watching,
fishing and hiking nearby
RATES: $32-$38 • Continental
breakfast • Open year-round •
Major credit cards accepted

L'Anse-Au-Loup
Barney's
Bed & Breakfast
L'Anse-Au-Loup, LB
(709) 927-5634
L'Anse-Au-Loup Rte. 510 • Clean
comfortable accomodation • Three
o/n units, shared B • Telephone

FEATURES: Laundry facilities •
Home cooked seafood meals •
Home made bread/pies made from
bakeapples/partridge jam • Picnic
area • Indoor swimming • Whale,
iceberg and bird-watching and
fishing nearby
RATES: $30-$45 • Continental
breakfast • Open year-round

L'Anse aux Meadows
Marilyn's Hospitality
Home ★★
Box 5, Hay Cove, L'Anse aux
Meadows, A0K 2X0
(709) 623-2811
Hay Cove Rte. 436 • Three o/n
units, shared B • Colour cable TV
and telephone
FEATURES: L'Anse aux
Meadows Viking site and straits
view only 1 km away • Meals on
request • Whale, iceberg and
bird-watching, hiking nearby
RATES: $35 (1) $40 (2) • Full
breakfast • Open May -Nov. • Visa
accepted

LaScie
Rogers'
Bed & Breakfast ★★½
6 Rogers Lane, LaScie, A0K 3M0
(709) 675-2505
LaScie Rte. 414 • Four o/n units,
three with double and single bed,
one room wheelchair accessible, all
rooms private B&S
RATES: $35 (1), $40 (2) •
Complimentary breakfast • Open
year-round

Lewisporte
Northgate
Bed & Breakfast ★★½

June Leschied, 106 Main Street,
Lewisporte, A0G 3A0
(709) 535-2258
Country-style home • Four o/n
units, private B • Cable TV and
telephone • Non-smoking only •
Pets permittted, usually on leash
FEATURES: Sitting rooms with
fireplace • Picnic area • Whale,
iceberg-watching, fishing, hiking and
boat tours nearby • Near Labrador
ferry terminal • Laundry facilities •
Afternoon tea • Overnight island
cabin camping by arr.
*RATES: $40-$55 • Full breakfast •
Open year-round • NFBBA*

Little Bay Islands
Sheltered Harbour
Inn ★★

Box 22, Little Bay Islands,
A0E 2M0
(709) 626-5341/5476
Little Bay Islands off Rte. 392 via
ferry from Shoal Arm • Three o/n
units, shared B • Colour cable TV •
Radio • Rollaway cots •
Non-smoking rooms
FEATURES: Laundry facilities
nearby • Restaurant/dining room •
Evening snack • Sundeck •
Barbecue • Picnic area • Gazebo
*RATES: $35-$45 • Complimentary
breakfast • Open year-round • Visa
accepted • Senior citizens' discount
10%*

Makkovik
Chelsea's

Box 131, Makkovik, LB, A0P 1J0
(709) 923-2335
Coastal Labrador (Accessible by
coastal boat from St. Anthony or

Happy Valley-Goose Bay) • Five
o/n units • One wheelchair
accessible room
FEATURES: Free transportation to
and from airport • Laundry facilities
• Dining room • Small conference
room
*RATES: $67-$100.50 • Open
year-round*

Marystown
Cozy Corners ★★½

150 Ville Marie Drive, Marystown,
A0E 2M0
(709) 279-2620
Marystown Rte. 210 • Eight o/n
units, shared B&S • Colour cable
TV in guest lounge • Non-smoking
rooms
FEATURES: Newly renovated,
quiet, overlooking the ocean •
Coffee shop • Room service • Five
minute walk from all amenities •
Outdoor swimming pool, fishing,
golf and hiking nearby
*RATES: $35-$45 • Full breakfast •
Open year-round • MC accepted*

Marystown
Shirley's
Bed and Breakfast ★★

929 Ville Marie Drive, Marystown,
A0E 1L0
(709) 279-1440
Marystown Rte. 210 • Quiet
location overlooking Creston Inlet •
Three o/n units, shared B • Colour
cable TV and telephone • Radio •
Non-smoking only
FEATURES: Cosy, comfortable
rooms • Laundry facilities • Meals
on request • Housekeeping services
• Playground • Fishing and golf
nearby • Thirty minutes from St.
Pierre-Miquelon ferry

RATES: $30 (1), $40 (2), $10 add'l person • Full breakfast • Open year- round

Millertown
Hoffe's Tourist Home ★½
Box 41, Millertown, A0H 1V0
(709) 852-6411
Millertown Rte. 370 • Five o/n units • Colour cable TV and telephone • Radio • Pets permitted, usually on leash • Non-smoking only
FEATURES: Dining room
RATES: $18 (1), $22 (2) • Complimentary breakfast • Open year-round

Ming's Bight
M & M's Hospitality Home ★★½
Box 33, Ming's Bight, A0K 3S0
(709) 254-8221
Ming's Bight Rte. 418 • Three o/n units, private and shared bath • Non-smoking rooms
FEATURES: Laundry facilities • Patio deck • Whale and iceberg-watching and fishing
RATES: $38-$45 • Full breakfast • Open year-round

Nain
Atsanik Lodge
Box 10, Nain, LB, A0P 1L0
(709) 922-2910
Fax (709) 922-2101
Coastal Labrador (Accessible by coastal boat from St. Anthony or Happy Valley-Goose Bay) • Nine o/n units • Colour cable TV and telephone • Radio
FEATURES: Restaurant/dining room • Lounge • Room service • Housekeeping services • Banquet/meeting facilities • Airport shuttle/taxi service • Fishing nearby

RATES: $73-$90 • Open year-round • Major credit cards accepted • Special tour group rates available

Norris Point
Earle's
Bed & Breakfast ★★
Box 99, Norris Point, A0K 3V0
(709) 458-2345
Norris Point Rte. 430 • Two o/n units
FEATURES: Located in Gros Morne National Park
RATES: $30 (1), $35 (2), $5 add'l person • Complimentary breakfast • Open June 15-Sept. 15

Norris Point
Eileen's
Bed & Breakfast ★★
Eileen James, Box 159, Norris Point, A0K 3V0
(709) 458-2427
Norris Point Rte. 430 • Three o/n units, private and shared B • Colour cable TV and telephone • Cots available • Non-smoking only
FEATURES: Located in the centre of Gros Morne National Park with one of the best views • Fishing, golfing, and hiking nearby
RATES: $30 (1), $40 (2), $5 add'l person • Complimentary breakfast • Open year-round

Norris Point
Sugar Hill Inn ★★★
115-129 Rte. 431, Box 100, Norris
Point, A0K 3V0
Tel/Fax (709) 458-2147
Norris Point Rte. 430 •
"Civilization in the wilderness" •
Four o/n units, private B • Colour
cable TV and telephone • Pets
permitted • Non-smoking rooms
FEATURES: Gourmet cuisine, fine
wines • Laundry facilities •
Restaurant/dining room • Room
service • Hot tub • Sauna • National
Park nearby
*RATES: $76-$96 • Open Jan. 15-Oct.
15 • Major credit cards accepted*

Norris Point
Terry's
Bed and Breakfast ★½
Box 167, Norris Point, Bonne Bay,
A0K 3V0
(709) 458-2373
Norris Point Rte. 430 • Five o/n
units, shared B • Colour TV and
telephone • Pets permitted, usually
on leash • Non-smoking only
FEATURES: Stay at Terry's in Gros
Morne Park for spectacular view of
world-famous tableland • Laundry
facilities • Playground, picnic area •
Fishing and hiking nearby
*RATES: $40 (1), $45 (2) • Full
breakfast • Open June-Sept.*

North West River
Blake's
Bed & Breakfast
Box 81, North West River, A0P 1M0
(709) 497-8348
Rte. 520, North West River • Four
o/n units, shared B • Colour cable
TV • Radio
FEATURES: Large, old-fashioned
kitchen • Laundry facilities $5 extra •

Meals on request • Kitchen facilities
$5 extra
*RATES: $45 (2) • Self-serve
continental breakfast • Open
year-round*

Old Perlican
Captain's Inn ★★½
Box 48, Old Perlican, Trinity Bay,
A0A 3G0
(709) 587-2626
Fax (709) 587-2447
Rte. 70 • Four o/n units • Cable TV
FEATURES: Home cooking •
Dining room • Meeting facilities •
Group tours to Baccalieu Island
arranged
*RATES: $55, $5 add'l person •
Open year-round*

Petite Forte
Anchor's Down Inn ★★
181 Middle Cove, Torbay, A1K 1G1
(709) 428-4251
Petite Forte Rte. 210 • Peaceful and
serene, located in isolated fishing
community now linked by road to
Burin Peninsula • Three o/n units,
private B • Telephone •
Non-smoking rooms
FEATURES: Art workshops
arranged through MUN extension •
Laundry facilities • Meals on
request • Outdoor swimming • Bird-
watching, golf and hiking nearby •
*RATES: $40 (1), $50 (2) • Full
breakfast • Open May-Oct. • MC,
Visa accepted*

Petty Harbour
Orca Inn Hospitality
Home ★★½
Reg & Mildred Carter, Box 197,
Petty Harbour, A0A 3H0
(709) 747-9676

Petty Harbour Rte. 11 • Scenic fishing village • Four o/n units, two shared Bs • Colour cable TV and telephone • Radio • Non-smoking only
FEATURES: Room service • Whale and iceberg-watching nearby • Close to sea bird sanctuary • Fifteen minutes from downtown St. John's, Cape Spear
RATES: *$43 (1), $50 (2) • Full breakfast • Open year-round • MC, Visa accepted • NFBBA Member*

Placentia
Linehan's Hospitality Home ★★
RR 1, Box 186, Placentia, A0B 2Y0
(709) 227-5717
Placentia Rte. 100 • Country setting • Four o/n units • Colour cable TV • Pets permitted • Non-smoking rooms
FEATURES: Good food, relaxed at-home atmosphere • Picnic area • Nature walks • Trout and salmon fishing in ocean behind house
RATES: *$45-$50, $15 add'l person • Open year-round*

Placentia
Rosedale Manor ★★½
Riverside Drive, Box 329, Placentia, A0B 2Y0
(709) 227-3613
Placentia Rte. 100 • Heritage home • Four o/n units, private two piece B • Colour cable TV • Telephone • Non-smoking only
FEATURES: Picnic area • Bird-watching, hiking and National Historic Site nearby • Close to Argentia ferry
RATES: *$50-$70 • Complimentary continental breakfast • Open year-round • Visa accepted*

Placentia
Trudon Hospitality House ★★½
Freshwater, Placentia Bay, A0B 1W0
(709) 227-2774
Fax (709) 227-5555
Freshwater Rte. 100, 2 km from Nova Scotia ferry • Six o/n units, private B • Colour cable TV/VCR, telephone • Pets permitted
FEATURES: Laundry facilities • Lounge • Banquet/meeting facilities • Bird-watching nearby
RATES: *$50 • Continental breakfast • Open year-round*

Point Leamington
Skipper's View Bed & Breakfast ★★½
259A Main Street, Box 154, Point Leamington, A0H 1Z0
(709) 484-3415/3271
Point Leamington Rte. 350 • One o/n unit accommodates up to 4 persons, private B • Colour TV and telephone • Non-smoking only
FEATURES: Traditional Newfoundland music • Piano • Picnic area • Visit/photograph Newfoundland pony sanctuary • Whale, iceberg and bird-watching, fishing and hiking nearby • Close to playground
RATES: *$40 (1), $45 (2), $15 add'l person • Breakfast included • Open year-round*

Pool's Cove
By the Bay
Bed & Breakfast ★★
Pool's Cove, Fortune Bay, A0H 2B0
(709) 665-3176
Pool's Cove off Rte. 362 • Three
o/n units • Colour cable TV and
telephone • Pets permitted •
Non-smoking rooms
FEATURES: Laundry facilities •
Bird-watching, fishing and hiking
nearby
*RATES: $35, $5 add'l person, $10
rollaway cot • Full breakfast •
Open year-round • Major credit
cards accepted*

Port au Choix
Jean-Marie Guest
Home ★★½
Box 286, Port au Choix, A0K 4C0
(709) 861-3023
Port au Choix Rte. 430 • Your
home away from home • Three o/n
units, shared B • Colour cable TV •
Telephone • Radio • Non-smoking
rooms
FEATURES: Laundry facilities •
Kitchen facilities • Room service •
Patio, barbecue, picnic tables •
Bird-watching, hiking and National
Park nearby
*RATES: $40 (1), $50 (2), $10 add'l
person • Continental breakfast •
Open June 15-Sept. 15*

Port Blandford
Terra Nova Hospitality
Home and Cottages ★★½
General Delivery, Port Blandford,
A0C 2G0
(709) 543-2260
Fax (709) 543-2241
Port Blandford Rte. 233 • Six o/n
units, private B&S • Wheelchair
accessible • Non-smoking rooms

FEATURES:
Picturesque
scenery,
tasteful
decor,
friendly
atmosphere,
great food
and activities galore •
Banquet/meeting facilities •
Cottages available • Whale and
iceberg watching, golfing and
National Park nearby • Close to
Discovery Trail
*RATES: $45 (1), $55-$65 (2) •
Open year-round • Major credit
cards accepted • NFHA Member*

Port Rexton
Parkside Inn
Box 132, Port Rexton, A0C 2H0
(709) 464-2151
Port Rexton, Rte. 230 • Six o/n
units, private B&S • Colour cable
TV
FEATURES: Restaurant/Dining
room • Lounge • Close to historic
Trinity, central to major tourist
attractions • Whale, iceberg and
bird watching, fishing and hiking
nearby
*RATES: $45-$55 • Full breakfast •
Open year-round • Major credit
cards accepted*

Port Saunders
Biggin Hospitality
Home ★★
Main Street, Box 100, Port
Saunders, A0K 4H0
(709) 861-3523
Fax (709) 861-3620
Port Saunders off Rte. 430 • Four
o/n units • Cable TV • Radio
FEATURES: Dining room •
Evening snack

RATES: $35-$39, $7 add'l person • *Continental breakfast* • *Open May 15-Sept. 15*

Portland Creek
Entente Cordiale ★★
General Delivery, Portland Creek, A0K 4G0
(709) 898-2288
Off season (709) 634-7407
Portland Creek Rte. 430 • Secluded property with historic decor • Four o/n units, private B&S • Centrally located TV • Non-smoking rooms
FEATURES: Dining room • Outdoor swimming on sandy beach • Close to "Arches" scenic attraction • Fishing, hiking and National Park nearby
RATES: $50 • *Continental breakfast* • *Open July-Sept.* • *Major credit cards accepted*

Portugal Cove-St. Phillips
Beachy Cove Bed and Breakfast ★★
Box 159, Portugal Cove, A0A 3K0
(709) 895-2920
Two o/n units, shared B • Pets permitted
FEATURES: Beautiful view of Conception Bay• Whale and iceberg watching and hiking nearby • Ten minutes from St. John's Airport
RATES: $45 (1), $50 (2) • *Full breakfast* • *Open year-round* • *Visa accepted*

Portugal Cove-St. Phillips
Country Loft ★★½
Dogberry Hill Road, Box 441, RR 1, St. Phillips, A1L 1C1
(709) 895-2615
Rtes. 40, 41 • Two o/n units, shared B • Colour cable TV • Non-smoking only

FEATURES: Many festive occasions celebrated • Newfoundland library collection • Toothbrush, bathrobe, slippers available • Whale and iceberg watching nearby • Fifteen minutes to Airport and St. John's
RATES: $50-$55 • *Breakfast in bed* • *Open year-round*

Raleigh
Taylor's Bed and Breakfast ★★
Box 99, Raleigh, A0K 4J0
(709) 452-3521/2112/2136
Raleigh Rte. 437 • Four o/n units, shared B • Colour TV and telephone • Radio • Rollaway cots • Non-smoking only
FEATURES: Laundry facilities available • Home-cooked meals on request • Dining room • Lounge • Near L'Anse aux Meadows • Close to Burnt Island Cape with 200 species of flowers, 33 rare
RATES: $32 (1), $42 (2), $10 add'l person (cot) • *Full breakfast* • *Open June-Sept.* • *Visa accepted*

Rigolet
Sivulik Country Inn
Box 58, Rigolet, LB, A0P 1P0
(709) 947-3444
Coastal Labrador (Accessible by coastal boat from St. Anthony or Happy Valley-Goose Bay) • Seven o/n units • Cable TV
FEATURES: Restaurant/dining room • Room service • Banquet/meeting facilities • Whale-watching, fishing and hiking nearby
RATES: $85-$100 • *Open year-round* • *Visa accepted*

Roberts Arm
Lake Crescent Inn ★★½
Evelyn & Bruce Warr, Box 69,
Roberts Arm, A0J 1R0
(709) 652-3067
Fax (709) 652-3056
Beothuck Trail Roberts Arm, Rte.
380, located 26 km from Rte. 1 on
Rte. 380 • Four o/n units, shared B
• Colour cable TV and telephone •
Non-smoking only
FEATURES: Laundry facilities •
Room service • Whirlpool • Beach,
boating, hiking trails, snowmobiling
• Salmon fishing nearby • Located
half-way between Port aux Basques
and St. John's
*RATES: $32 (1), $37 (2), $10 add'l
person • Complimentary breakfast •
Open year-round • MC, Visa
accepted*

Rocky Harbour
Evergreen
Bed & Breakfast ★★
Donald & Annie Shears, Evergreen
Lane, Box 141, Rocky Harbour,
A0K 4N0
(709) 458-2692
Rocky Harbour Rte. 430 • Four o/n
units, two with shared B • Colour
cable TV • Telephone • Pets
permitted • Non-smoking rooms
FEATURES: Homemade bread and
a variety of Newfoundland jams •
Whale, iceberg and bird-watching,
fishing, hiking and National Park
nearby • Close to swimming pool,
mini golf and go-carts
*RATES: $35 (1), $39 (2), $5 add'l
person (cot) • Full breakfast • Open
May 1-Sept. 30 • MC, Visa accepted*

Rocky Harbour
Major's Hospitality
Home ★½
General Delivery, Rocky Harbour,
A0K 4N0
(709) 458-2537
Rocky Harbour Rte. 430 • Four o/n
units, shared B • Colour cable TV •
Telephone • Radio • Pets permitted,
usually on leash
FEATURES: Living room •
Laundry service • Picnic tables,
patio, barbecue • Swimming pool •
Close to Funland Resort
*RATES: $25 (1), $45 (2) •
Complimentary breakfast • Open
year-round*

Rocky Harbour
Ocean Acre Inn
Bed and Breakfast ★★
Main Street North, Rocky Harbour,
A0K 4N0
(709) 458-2272
Off-season (902) 865-5397
Rocky Harbour Rte. 430 • Ocean
front accomodation located in the
heart of Gros Morne National Park
• Four o/n units, shared B • Colour
cable TV in living room •
Telephone • Clock radio •
Non-smoking only
FEATURES: Newfoundland library
• Bird-watching and hiking nearby
*RATES: $35 (1), $40-$50 (2), $10
add'l person • Full breakfast •
Open July 1-Sept. 6 • MC, Visa
accepted*

Rocky Harbour
Wildflowers
Bed and Breakfast ★★
Main St. North, Rocky Harbour,
A0K 4N0
Tel & Fax (709) 458-2625
Rocky Harbour Rte. 430 • Three
o/n units, shared B
FEATURES: Laundromat •
Restaurant • Craft shop • Near
Lobster Cove Lighthouse
*RATES: No rates available •
Continental breakfast • Open
year-round*

Roddickton
Betty's
Bed & Breakfast ★½
Box 194, Roddickton, A0K 4P0
(709) 457-2371
Roddickton Rte. 433 • Three o/n
units, shared B • Colour cable TV
and telephone • Pets permitted •
Non-smoking rooms
FEATURES: Clean and affordable
• Laundry facilities • Electric/water/
sewage hookup/dumping station •
View the cloud hills and watch the
whales in the bay • Whale and
iceberg-watching and fishing nearby
*RATES: $35-$42 • Continental
breakfast • Open year-round*

Southport
By The Pond
Bed and Breakfast ★★
RR 2, Box 502, Southport, A0E 2A0
(709) 548-2248
Tel/Fax (709) 548-2580
Southport Rte. 204 • Two o/n units,
shared B • Colour cable TV and
telephone • Non-smoking only
FEATURES: Fishing on location •
Meet locals • Laundry facilities •
Whale, iceberg and bird-watching

nearby • One hour and ten minutes
from Terra Nova
*RATES: $35 (1), $45 (2) • Full
breakfast • Open May-Oct. • Visa
accepted • Combine accomodation
with boat tours for a discount*

Spaniards Bay
Bay Ridge Cottage
Main Highway, Box 401, Bay
Roberts, Spaniards Bay, A0A 1G0
Tel & Fax (709) 786-3006
Spaniards Bay Rte. 70 • Four o/n
units, shared B • Colour cable TV
(Closed captioned) • Telephone on
each floor • Radio • Rollaway cots
• Children under 5 yrs free •
Non-smoking only
FEATURES: Meals on request •
Barbecue pits • Art/craft shops
*RATES: $37 (1), $47 (2), $10
add'l person • Full breakfast •
Open year-round*

Springdale
Hull's Riverview
Bed & Breakfast ★★½
Box 729, Springdale, A0J 1T0
(709) 673-4518/3835
Fax (709) 673-3177
Springdale Rte. 390, 2 km off Rte. 1
• Quiet, overlooking salmon river •
Two o/n units • Colour cable TV and
telephone • Pets permitted, usually on
leash • Non-smoking only
FEATURES: Homemade bread
and jams • Picnic area • Whale,
iceberg and bird-watching, fishing
and hiking nearby
*RATES: $35-$45 (2) • Open
year-round • Major credit cards
accepted*

St. Anthony
Dogberry Cottage Bed & Breakfast ★½
Jeanette Hostetter, 15A Tuckers Lane, Box 702, St. Anthony, A0K 4J0
(709) 454-3539
St. Anthony Rte. 430 • Two o/n units, shared B • Colour cable TV in living room • Telephone in hall • Non-smoking only
FEATURES: Peaceful and quiet • Dining room for breakfast • Whale and iceberg-watching and hiking nearby
RATES: $32-$38 • Continental breakfast • Open mid-June to Sept. 30

St. Anthony
Howell's Tourist Home ★★
1 Spruce Lane, Box 214, St. Anthony, A0K 4S0
(709) 454-3402/454-8494
St. Anthony Rte. 430 • Four o/n units • Centrally located TV • Telephone • Radio
FEATURES: Laundry facilities • Coffee/tea • Sitting room with Newfoundland literature and magazines
RATES: $31-$39 • Open year-round • Visa accepted

St. Anthony
Trailsend Hospitality Home ★★
1 Cormack Street, Box 392, St. Anthony, A0K 4S0
(709) 454-2024/8477
St. Anthony Rte. 430 • Four o/n units, two shared B • Colour cable TV and telephone • Wheelchair accessible • Non-smoking rooms
FEATURES: Our home is your home • Laundry facilities • Whale and iceberg-watching and National Park nearby
RATES: $35 (1), $55 (2), $6 add'l person • Full breakfast • Open year-round • Visa accepted

St. Barbe
Toope's Hospitality Home Ltd. ★★
St. Barbe, A0K 1M0
(709) 877-2413/2340
St. Barbe Rte. 430, adjacent to Labrador-St. Barbe ferry terminal • Three o/n units, shared B • Colour cable TV and telephone • Radio
FEATURES: Traditional Newfoundland meals on request • Whale, iceberg and bird-watching nearby
RATES: $30 (1), $35 (2), $5 add'l person • Complimentary breakfast • Open year-round

St. Bride's
Atlantica Inn ★★
St. Bride's, A0B 2Z0
(709) 337-2860
St. Bride's Rte. 100 • Five o/n units • Colour cable TV and telephone • Rollaway cots • Children under 13 yrs free
FEATURES: Coffee Shop • Close to Cape St. Mary's Bird Sanctuary • One hour from Argentia ferry terminal
RATES: $35-$40, $500 add'l person • Open year-round • Visa accepted

St. John's
A Bonne Esperance House ★★½
20 Gower Street, St. John's, A1C 1N1
(709) 726-3835
Fax (709) 739-0496
Downtown St. John's • Spacious Victorian house • Four o/n units,

private ensuite B, clock radio in each room, fireplaces in bedrooms • Colour cable TV and telephone • Pets permitted • Non-smoking only
FEATURES: Period furnishings • Five minute walk to downtown and Provincial Archives, minutes from Signal Hill • Off-street parking
RATES: from $45 • Full breakfast • Open year-round • MC, Visa accepted

St. John's
A Gower Street House ★★★
Leonard Clarke, 180 Gower Street, St. John's, A1C 1P9
(709) 754-0047
Fax (709) 754-5721
Toll Free 1-800-563-3959
Four o/n units, private B, queen and twin beds, telephone, remote TV • Designated smoking area
FEATURES: Heritage building, Newfoundland art displayed throughout • Laundry facilities • Light snacks on request • Room service • Housekeeping services • Five minute walk to harbour, major hotels, museum, cathedrals, tours, archives • Off-street parking
RATES: $45-$55 • Continental breakfast • Open year-round • Major credit cards and cheques accepted • Cancellation notice required • Off-season (Nov.-Apr.) $35 • Extended rates available

St. John's
Balmoral Inn ★★★
Maria Petrov, 38 Queen's Road, St. John's, A1C 2A5
Tel & Fax (709) 754-5721
St. John's • Three o/n units, fireplace, king and queen beds and ensuite B • Colour TV in rooms • Telephone • Non-smoking rooms

FEATURES: Antique furnishings • Laundry facilities • Sitting room • Historical artwork • Afternoon tea • Air-conditioning • Five minute walk to harbour, major hotels, museum, cathedrals, courts, archives, galleries, live theatre and most restaurants • Off-street parking
RATES: From $65 • Continental breakfast • Open year-round • Major credit cards and cheques • Off-season (Nov.-Apr.) from $55 • Extended rates available

St. John's
Bird Island Guest Home ★★½
150 Old Topsail Road, St. John's, A1E 2B1
(709) 753-4850, 722-1675
Fax (709) 753-3140
Two o/n units, shared B • Colour cable TV and telephone
FEATURES: Meet our Newfoundland dog, Cabot • Laundromat • Restaurant/dining room • Daily trips for bird-watching and whale-watching available with shuttle service
RATES: $50 (1), $60 (2) • Continental breakfast • Open year-round • HNL Member

St. John's
Compton House ★★★
26 Waterford Bridge Road, St. John's, A1E 1C6
(709) 739-5789
Elegant Victorian mansion • Four  o/n units, three with whirlpool and fireplace, private B&S • Colour cable TV • Radio • Telephone in rooms • No pets, please • Non-smoking rooms
FEATURES: Period furnishings • Housekeeping services • Whale and iceberg-watching, golfing and hiking all nearby
RATES: $59-$119 (1), $69-$159 (2), $15 add'l person • Full breakfast • Open year-round • AE, ER, MC, Visa accepted • • HNL; NFBBA Member

St. John's
English Ryall House ★★½
6 Wood Street, St. John's, A1C 3K9
(709) 726-3835
Fax (709) 739-0496
Turn of the century house • Four o/n units, private B&S, clock radio in each room • Colour cable TV • Pets permitted • Non-smoking rooms
FEATURES: Victorian house • Laundry facilities • National Park nearby
RATES: $50-$90 • Full breakfast • Open year-round • MC, Visa accepted

St. John's
Fairmede Century Farm Bed & Breakfast ★★½
179 Brookfield Road, Box 7095, St. John's, A1E 3Y3
(709) 364-3980
St. John's • Four o/n units, two B • Colour cable TV and telephone • Radio • Non-smoking only
FEATURES: Dining room • Playground • Picnic area • Winter weekend packages include sleigh rides and cross-country skiing
RATES: $40 (1), $55-$60 (2), $5 add'l person • Open year-round • Weekend packages available

St. John's
Fireside Bed and Breakfast ★★½
28 Wicklow Street, St. John's, A1B 3H2
(709) 726-0237
Two o/n units • Colour cable TV and telephone • Non-smoking rooms
FEATURES: Laundry facilities • Whale and iceberg-watching, golfing and hiking nearby
RATES: $35 (1), $40 (2) • Full breakfast • Open year-round

St. John's
Fort William Bed & Breakfast ★★½
5 Gower Street, St. John's, A1C 1M9
(709) 726-3161
Fax (709) 576-0849
St. John's • Three o/n units, one suite, private B, telephones in each room • Colour cable TV • Non-smoking only
FEATURES: Heritage home • Antique furnishings • Sitting room with fireplace • Near major hotels and downtown area

RATES: $50-$80 • Full breakfast •
Open year-round

St. John's
Kincora ★★★
36 Kings Bridge Road, St. John's,
A1C 3K6
(709) 576-7415
Downtown • Victorian heritage
home • Four o/n units, private B&S,
fireplaces, antiques • Colour cable
TV and telephone • Non-smoking
rooms
FEATURES: Dining room • Living
room • Banquet/meeting facilities •
Golf nearby
RATES: $50-$75, $15 add'l person
• Continental breakfast • Open
year-round • Cats on premises •
Major credit cards accepted

St. John's
Monroe House
Bed & Breakfast ★★★
8a Forest Road, St. John's, A1C 2B9
(709) 754-0610
E-mail: monhouse@newcomm.net
HTTP://www.monhouse.nf.ca
Former Prime Minister's home •
Three o/n units, private B&S •
Colour cable TV and telephone •
Clock radio •
FEATURES: Laundry facilities •
Evening wine • Separate guest
living room
RATES: $59, $15 add'l person •
Full breakfast • Cats on premises •
Major credit cards accepted

St. John's
Oh What A View ★★½
184 Signal Hill Road, St. John's,
A1A 1B3
(709) 576-7063
View of old St. John's and the
harbour • Four o/n units, private

and shared B&S • No pets, please •
Non-smoking only
FEATURES: Plain old
Newfoundland hospitality • Whale,
iceberg and bird-watching, fishing,
golf and hiking nearby
RATES: $45-$65 • Continental
breakfast • Open May 15-Oct. 15 •
Major credit cards accepted

St. John's
Prescott Inn ★★½
19 Military Road, St. John's,
A1C 2C3
(709) 753-7733
Fax (709) 579-7774
Downtown heritage houses •
Fourteen o/n units, private and
shared B • Colour cable TV and
telephone • Non-smoking rooms
FEATURES: Antiques,
Newfoundland books and arts and
crafts • Fireplaces • Balconies •
Housekeeping services • Banquet/
meeting facilities • Effiency units
available • Whale, iceberg and
bird-watching and hiking nearby
RATES: $40-$95 • Gourmet
breakfast • Open year-round •
Major credit cards accepted

St. John's
Rose au Rue ★★½
215 Hamilton Avenue, St. John's,
A1E 1J6
(709) 579-3201
Charming old St. John's house •
Two o/n units, shared B • Colour
cable TV and telephone •
Non-smoking only
FEATURES: Antique furnishings •
Restaurant/dining room • Lounge •
Close to downtown
RATES: $50-$60 • Continental
breakfast

St. John's
The Roses
Bed and Breakfast ★★½
9 Military Road, St. John's, A1C 2C3
(709) 726-3336
Four o/n units, private B • TV in
rooms • Non-smoking rooms
FEATURES: Housetop kitchen
with panoramic view of St. John's •
Whale, iceberg and bird-watching,
hiking and National Historic Site
nearby
*RATES: $53-$69 • Full breakfast •
Open year-round • AE, MC and
Visa accepted*

St. John's
Waterford Manor
Victorian Style
Bed and Breakfast ★★★
185 Waterford Bridge Road, St.
John's, A1E 1C7
(709) 754-4139
Fax (709) 754-4155
St. John's • Five o/n units, private
B&S • Colour cable TV and
telephone • Smoking area
FEATURES: Elegant living room
with fireplace • Room service •
Complimentary wine • Banquet/
meeting facilities • Suites, Jacuzzi
available • Winner of 1994 Southcott
Award • Five minutes to downtown
and Bowring Park • Whale, iceberg
and bird-watching nearby
*RATES: $75-$150 • Full breakfast
• Open year-round • MC, Visa
accepted • HIAC Member*

St. John's
Winterholme Heritage
Inn ★★★
79 Rennies Mill Road, St. John's,
A1C 3R1
(709) 739-7979
Fax (709) 753-9411

National historic property centrally
located in heritage district • Six o/n
units, private B&S • Colour cable
TV and telephone
FEATURES: Laundry facilities •
Fireplaces • Housekeeping services
• Golf, hiking and National Park
nearby
*RATES: $69-$169 • Continental
breakfast • Open year-round •
Major credit cards accepted*

Steady Brook
Edgewater Inn ★★½
14 Forest Drive, Box 202, RR 1,
Steady Brook, A2H 2N2
(709) 634-3474
Steady Brook Rte. 1 • Three o/n
units, shared B • Telephone •
Non-smoking rooms
FEATURES: Dining room •
Fishing nearby • Boat tours arranged
*RATES: $30 (1), $40 (2) • Full
breakfast • Open year-round • •
NFBBA • HNL Member*

Steady Brook
Huxter's
Bed and Breakfast ★★½
Ken & Cheryl Huxter, 2 Forest
Drive, Box 170, Steady Brook,
A2H 2N2
(709) 634-4999
Steady Brook Rte. 1 • River front
property • Three o/n units, shared B
• Colour cable TV and telephone •
Non-smoking only
FEATURES: Salmon outfitting •
Patio deck • On Humber River, near
Marble Mountain skiing and Corner
Brook • Golf, hiking, swimming
and National Park nearby
*RATES: $29 (1), $39 (2), $10 add'l
person • Deluxe continental
breakfast • Open year-round • Visa
accepted • HNL; NFBBA Member*

Steady Brook
View Marble
Bed and Breakfast ★★
Clarence & Betty Jackson, 21
Forest Drive, Box 201, RR 1,
Steady Brook, A2H 2N2
(709) 634-6616
Fax (709) 632-2145
Steady Brook Rte. 1 • Two o/n
units, shared B • Colour cable TV
and telephone • Radio •
Non-smoking rooms
FEATURES: View of Steady
Brook Falls and Marble Mountain •
Meals on request • Swimming pool
• Playground • Minutes from base
of Marble Mountain and a view of
Steady Brook Falls • Bird-watching,
fishing, golf, hiking and National
Park nearby
*RATES: $30 (1), $40 (2) • Full
breakfast • Open year-round*

Steady Brook
Wilton's
Bed & Breakfast ★★
Marble Drive, Box 160, Steady
Brook, A2H 2N2
Tel/Fax (709) 634-5796
Exit 8 at Steady Brook • Three o/n
units, shared
B • Colour
cable TV and
telephone •
Non-smoking
only
FEATURES:
Playground
and picnic
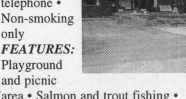
area • Salmon and trout fishing •
Hiking and National Park nearby •
Two minutes from Marble
Mountain Ski Resort, five minutes
from Corner Brook
*RATES: $35 (1), $40 (2), $10 add'l
person • Full breakfast • Open
year-round*

Stephenville
"Harmon House"
Billard's Bed &
Breakfast ★★½
George & Myra Billard, 144 New
Mexico Drive, Box 656,
Stephenville, A2N 3B5
Tel & Fax (709) 643-4673
Best of Newfoundland award B&B
1995 (Newfoundland *Herald*) •
Four o/n units • Colour cable TV in
rooms • Non-smoking only
FEATURES: Newfoundlandia and
local knowledge a specialty •
Laundry
facilities •
Room
service •
Coffee/tea •
Fishing, golf
and National
Park nearby

RATES:
*$40-$50 (2) • Continental breakfast
• Open year-round • MC, Visa
accepted • Off-season rates $35 (1),
$45 (2)*

Summerford
Joan's Seabreeze
Bed & Breakfast ★★½
Summerford, A0G 4E0
(709) 629-3657/7400
Fax (709) 629-3691
Summerford Rte. 344 • Spectacular
view of the ocean • Two o/n units,
shared B • Wheelchair accessible •
Colour cable TV • Non-smoking
rooms
FEATURES: Laundry facilities •
Homemade bread, jam and muffins
• Housekeeping services •
Kitchenette available • Whale and
iceberg- watching nearby
*RATES: $40-$45 • Continental
breakfast • Open year-round*

Sunnyside
Brookside Hospitality Home ★★

Box 104, Sunnyside, A0B 3J0
(709) 472-4515
Sunnyside, 2 km off Rte. 1 • Two o/n units, shared B • Wheelchair accessible • Colour cable TV and telephone • Radio • Pets permitted • Non-smoking only
FEATURES: Laundry facilities • Evening snack • Hiking nearby • Close to Hibernia project
RATES: $35 (1), $42-$45 (2) • Continental breakfast • Open year-round

Torbay
See the Sea Bed & Breakfast ★★½

102 Marine Drive, Torbay, A1K 1A7
(709) 437-1915
Torbay Rte. 20 • Two o/n units, shared B • Colour cable TV • Restricted smoking
FEATURES: Host singer/songwriter Mickey Michael entertains you with romantic songs of the 30s and 40s • Ici on parle français • View of ocean and whales • Minutes from St. John's and airport
RATES: $45 (1), $50 (2) • Full breakfast • Open year-round

Tors Cove
The Chalet ★★

T58 Tors Cove Pond
Mailing address: c/o 45 Gower Street, St. John's, A1C 1N3
(709) 754-7703
Tors Cove Rte. 10 • Private fully equipped all-pine chalet with beach on scenic lake • Two o/n units, private B&S • Pets permitted

FEATURES: Sun deck • Rock gardens • Picnic area • Outdoor swimming • Whale. iceberg and bird-watching, fishing and hiking all nearby
RATES: $60-$90 • Open year-round

Traytown
Janes' Tourist Home ★★★

Mill Cove, Traytown, A0G 4K0
(709) 533-2221
Traytown Rte. 310, borders on Terra Nova National Park • Four o/n units, private and shared B • Non-smoking only
FEATURES: Health conscious people will appreciate ocean and mountain view, clean fresh air and drinking water • Laundry facilities • Whale, iceberg and bird-watching, fishing, golf and hiking nearby
RATES: $35-$60 • Continental breakfast • Open June 1-Sept. 30

Trepassey
Northwest Bed and Breakfast ★★½

Harold and Marie Pennell, Box 5, Site 14, Trepassey, A0A 4B0
(709) 438-2888
Trepassey Rte. 10 • Four o/n units (double) with private entrance, shared B • Colour cable TV • Telephone • Pets permitted
FEATURES: Friendly atmosphere • Laundry facilities • Meals on request • Comfortable beds • Picnic area • Playground • Outdoor swimming • Can arrange lighthouse tour, seabird sanctuary tour, and whale and bird boat tour
RATES: $40, $10 add'l person (cot) • Continental breakfast • Open year-round • Visa accepted • Packages available

Trinity
Beach
Bed & Breakfast ★★½
Box 17, Trinity, Trinity Bay,
A0C 2S0
(709) 464-3695
Trinity Rte. 239 • Three o/n units,
private B&S • Colour cable TV •
Non-smoking only
FEATURES: Laundry facilities •
Dining room • Room service •
Whale, iceberg and bird-watching
nearby
*RATES: $45-$62 • Full breakfast •
Open May 15-Oct. 15*

Trinity
Campbell House
Bed & Breakfast ★★★
Tineke Gow & family, Trinity,
Trinity Bay, A0C 2S0
Mailing address: 24 Circular Road,
St. John's, A1C 2Z1
Tel/Fax (709) 464-3377
Off-season Tel/Fax (709) 753-8945
Trans Canada Hwy to Clarenville,
Exit Rte. 230, 70 km toward
Bonavista on Discovery Trail, Rte.
239 to Trinity Bay • Restored
property
(circa 1840)
by the sea •
Four o/n
units, private
B • Colour
cable TV
and VCR •
Telephone •

Clock radio • Children 7 yrs and
older welcome • No pets, please •
Non-smoking only
FEATURES: Recipient of the
Southcott Award by the
Newfoundland Historic Trust for
excellence in restoration • Antique
furnishings • Guest refrigerator •
Parlour with fireplace •

Housekeeping services • Fax on
permises • Hiking trails • View of
icebergs, whales • Restaurants
nearby
*RATES: $60-$75 (1), $75-$85 (2),
$10 add'l person • Full breakfast •
Open May-Oct. • Major credit
cards accepted • HNL; NFBBA
Member*

Trinity
Eriksen Premises
General Delivery, Trinity, Trinity
Bay, A0C 2S0
(709) 464-3698
Fax (709) 464-2104
Trinity Rte. 239 • Victorian
building with fantastic view in
historic Trinity • Four o/n units,
private B&S • Non-smoking rooms
FEATURES: Restaurant/Dining
room • Whale, iceberg and
bird-watching, fishing and hiking
nearby
*RATES: $70-$90 • Full breakfast •
Open May-Oct.*

Trinity
Village Inn ★★½
Box 10, Trinity, Trinity Bay,
A0C 2S0
(709) 464-3269
Trinity Rte. 239 • Historic Inn c.
1910 • Eight o/n units, private B&S
• Non-smoking rooms
FEATURES: Resident
world-renowned whale scientist •
Restaurant/dining room • Coffee
shop • Lounge • Whale, iceberg and
bird watching, fishing and hiking
nearby
*RATES: $51-$61, $10 add'l person
• Open year-round • Major credit
cards accepted*

Trinity East
Peace Cove Inn ★★½
Art & Louise Andrews, Box 48,
Paradise, A1L 1C4
(709) 781-2255/464-3738/464-2133
Trinity East off Rte. 230 at Port
Rexton • Original turn of the
century sea captain's home • Five
o/n units, private and shared B
FEATURES: Located in scenic
fishing village in Trinity harbour •
Meals on request • Restaurant •
View whales, icebergs, seabirds and
bald eagles aboard 46 ft. sailing
yacht • Hike country and coastal
trails, explore abandoned villages •
Historical presentations • Art
gallery and gift shop
*RATES: $44-$55 (1-2), $10 add'l
person • Open May-Oct. •
Continental breakfast • Visa
accepted • HNL; NFBBA Member*

Triton
Bridger's
Bed & Breakfast ★★½
Sylvia & Eugene Bridger, 4 Mount
Tan Heights, Box 69, Triton, A0J 1V0
(709) 263-7324
Off TransCanada Hwy at South
Brook, Halls Bay, 41 km. on Rte
380 • Two o/n units, one queen bed,
one with two single beds, one
shared B • TV and telephone
FEATURES: Laundry facilities •
Home-cooked meals on request •
Evening snack • Coffee/tea • Patio
and back yard • Home-made jams
and jellies available
*RATES: $30 (1), $35 (2) •
Complimentary breakfast*

Trout River
Crocker's
Bed & Breakfast ★½
Box 10, Trout River, A0K 5P0
(709) 451-5220/3141
Trout River Rte. 431, within Gros
Morne National Park • Ocean view
• Three o/n units, shared B • Colour
cable TV and telephone
FEATURES: Friendly, relaxing
atmosphere • Laundry facilities •
Playground and picnic area • Whale
and iceberg-watching, fishing and
hiking nearby
*RATES: $30 (1-2) • Continental
breakfast • Open May 15-Sept. 15*

Trouty
Riverside Lodge ★★
Box 9, Site 3, Trouty, Trinity Bay
(709) 464-3780
Trouty Rte. 239 • Ten o/n units •
Wheelchair accessible •
Non-smoking rooms
FEATURES: Warm hospitality •
Home cooking • Restaurant/Dining
room • Picnic area • Housekeeping
unit available • Close to historic
Trinity • Whale, iceberg and
bird-watching, fishing and hiking
nearby
*RATES: $39-$52, $5 add'l person •
Open Apr.-Oct.*

Twillingate
Beach Rock
Bed & Breakfast ★★
RR 1, Little Harbour, Box 350,
Twillingate, A0G 4M0
(709) 884-2292
Twillingate Rte. 340 • Two o/n
units, shared B • Colour cable TV
and telephone • Non-smoking rooms
FEATURES: Laundry facilities •
Coffee shop • Electrical/water

hook-ups • Whale and
iceberg-watching and hiking nearby
*RATES: $35 (1), $40 (2) • Open
year-round • Continental breakfast
• HNL Member*

Twillingate
Harbour Lights Inn ★★½
189 Main Street, Twillingate, A0G 4M0
(709) 884-2703
Fax (709) 884-2701
Twillingate Rte. 340 • Eighteenth-
century house • Five o/n units •
Wheelchair accessible • Colour
cable TV and telephone • Pets
permitted • Non-smoking rooms
FEATURES: Laundry facilities •
Meals on request • Dining room •
Coffee shop • Kitchen available
*RATES: $55-$85 • Open
year-round • Major credit cards
accepted*

Twillingate
Hillside
Bed & Breakfast ★★½
5 Young's Lane, Box 4,
Twillingate, A0G 4M0
(709) 884-5761
Twillingate Rte. 340 • House built
in 1874 • Four o/n units, shared B,
radio in each room • Colour cable
TV and telephone • Room service •
Non-smoking only
FEATURES: View of icebergs •
Laundry facilities • Lounge • Trails
to hilltop lookout • Home-made
bread and jams our specialty •
Whale-watching nearby
*RATES: $35 (1), $40-$45 (2), $10
add'l person • Continental
breakfast • Open June 1- Sept. 30 •
HNL; NFBBA Member*

Twillingate
Toulinguet Inn
Bed and Breakfast ★★★
Cecile Mast & Hazel Young, 56
Main Street, Box 610, Twillingate,
A0G 4M0
(709) 884-2080
Fax (709) 884-2936
Off-season (709) 884-2028
Twillingate Rte. 340 • Three o/n
units, private B • Colour cable TV •
Radio • Rollaway cots available •
Pets permitted, usually on leash •
Non-smoking only
FEATURES: Ocean view •
Laundry facilities • Tea room •
Dining room • Living room and
sitting room • Balcony
*RATES: $40 (1), $45 (2), $10
add'l person • Continental
breakfast • Open June-Sept. • Visa
accepted • HNL; NFBBA Member*

Winterhouse
Lainey Hospitality
Home ★½
Box 334, Black Duck Brook, A0N
1R0
(709) 642-5556
Winterhouse off Rte. 463 • Four
o/n units • Colour TV • Radio
FEATURES: Dining room •
Lounge • Horse riding
RATES: $30-$50 • Open May-Sept.

Witless Bay
Armstrong's Bed & Breakfast ★★
Box 39, Witless Bay
(709) 334-2201
Rte. 10 • Two o/n units • Colour cable TV and telephone
FEATURES: Laundry facilities • Whale, iceberg and bird-watching and fishing nearby • Close to Witless Bay Ecological Reserve and boat tours
RATES: *$40-$45 • Continental breakfast • Open year-round*

Witless Bay
Aunt Clara's Bed & Breakfast ★★½
Gallows Cove Road, Witless Bay, A0A 4K0
(709) 334-2228
Witless Bay Rte. 10 • Three o/n units, shared B&S • Colour cable TV and telephone• Non-smoking only
FEATURES: Specialize in catering to seniors 55 and over • Laundry facilities • Room service • Whale and iceberg-watching and hiking nearby
RATES: *$40-$50 • Continental breakfast • Open May-Sept.*

Witless Bay
Elaine's Seaside Bed & Breakfast ★★
Box 125, Witless Bay, Lower Loop Place
(709) 334-2722
Witless Bay Rte. 10 • Spectacular ocean view • Three o/n units • Colour cable TV • Pets permitted • Non-smoking rooms
FEATURES: Laundry facilities • Room service • Kitchenette available • Close to caribou herd

and archaeological dig • Whale, iceberg and bird-watching nearby
RATES: *$40-$52, $10 add'l person • Continental breakfast • Open June 1-Sept. 30*

Witless Bay
Jean's Bed and Breakfast By the Sea ★★
Witless Bay, A0A 4K0
(709) 334-2075
Witless Bay Rte. 10 • Two o/n units, shared B • Colour cable TV
FEATURES: Ocean view and scenic seashore walks • Sunroom • Gazebo • Whale, iceberg and bird-watching, hiking, fishing and National Park nearby • Close to laundry facilities, restaurant, ocean tours and craft shops • Thirty minutes from St. John's
RATES: *$40 (1), $47 (2) • Full breakfast • Open mid-June-mid-Sept.*

Woody Island
Island Rendezvous ★★
Woody Island, Placentia Bay
Mailing address: 14 Westminister Drive, Mt. Pearl, A1N 4N1
(709) 747-7253
Fax (709) 364-3701
Toll free 1-800-504-1066
Woody Island off Rte. 210 via tour boat from Garden Cove • A unique two-day adventure on a deserted island • Sixteen o/n units •
FEATURES: Dining room • Home-cooked meals • Boat tour
RATES: *$89 (1) for complete package • Open Apr.-Nov. • Major credit cards accepted*

Woody Point
Victorian Manor
Hospitality Home ★★½
Stan & Jenny Parsons, Gros Morne
National Park, Box 165, Woody
Point, A0K 1P0
Tel/Fax (709) 453-2485
Victorian home • Seven o/n units,
private and shared B • Colour cable
TV and telephone • Clock radio •
No pets, please • Non-smoking only
FEATURES: Laundry facilities •
Dining room • Housekeeping
services •
Barbecue •
Efficiency
units
available •
Cross-country
skiing, sea
kayaking •
Whale and

iceberg-watching and hiking nearby
• Close to playground, restaurant
and swimming
RATES: $50 (1), $50-$70 (2) •
Continental breakfast • Open year-
round • Major credit cards
accepted • HNL; VTA Member

3

Nova Scotia

Advocate Harbour
Reid's Century Farm Bed & Breakfast
Donna Reid, 1391 West Advocate
Road, (West Advocate) RR 3,
Parrsboro, B0M 1S0
(902) 392-2592
Rte. 209 • Working beef farm •
Three o/n units, private B&S • TV
in family room, also in two rooms •
No pets, please
FEATURES: Barbecue • Cottage
available • Near West Advocate
entrance to Cape Chignecto Park
*RATES: $30 (1), $40 (2), $10 add'l
person (STC), check out by 11 a.m.
• Full breakfast 7-9 • Open
June 1-Sept. 30 • Off-season by
arrangement • Family rates
available • NSFC Member*

Afton
Chestnut Corner Bed & Breakfast ★★★
Gordon & Joan Randall, RR 1,
Afton Station, B0H 1A0
(902) 386-2403
Hwy 104, 20 km (12.5 mi) east of
Antigonish, Exit 36A, 3 km (2
mi) • Three o/n units, one B&S
shared • TV/VCR in living room
Non-smoking only
*FEATURES:*Barbecue • Hiking trail
*RATES: $30-$35 (1), $35-$40 (2),
$5-$10 add'l person • Full
breakfast 7-9:30 • Open
May 15-Oct. 15 • Visa accepted •
IGNS; NSRS Member*

Albert Bridge
Sunlit Valley Farm B&B
Hazel Ferguson, 821 Brickyard
Road, RR 2 Albert Bridge, Marion
Bridge, B0A 1P0
(902) 562-7663
Fax (902) 562-2222
From Port Hawkesbury, Rte. 4 or
Hwy 105 to Sydney area, then Rte.
22 toward Louisbourg, cross Mira
River, left on Brickyard Rd. • Four
o/n units, two shared B&S • TV in
lounge • Cot available • Children
welcome • No pets, please
Non-smoking only
*RATES: $35 (1), $45 (2), $16 add'l
person • Full breakfast 7:30-9:30 •
Open May 1-Oct. 31 • MC, Visa
accepted • Off-season by
reservation • NSRS Member*

Alma
Pine Hedge Bed & Breakfast
Theresa & John Patton, RR 1,
Westville, B0K 2A0
(902) 396-5726
Hwy 104, Exit at Granton, turn at
Irving garage, or Hwy 106, Exit
2 (from Pictou Rotary) • Three o/n
units, shared B&S • TV in rooms •
Telephone in rooms • Cot available •
No pets, please • Non-smoking only
FEATURES: Laundry facilities •
Screened patio, barbecue •
Air-conditioning • Close to beaches,
golf course, family amusement park

RATES: $35 (1), $40 (2), $10 add'l person • Full home-baked breakfast 7:30-10:00 • Open May 15-Oct. 15 Off-season by reservation • Visa accepted • Brian Moore & Euravec; NSRS Member

Alma
Stoneycombe Lodge ★★★
Keith & Edith Selwyn-Smith, RR 3, Westville, B0K 2A0
Tel & Fax (902) 396-3954
Toll free 1-800-461-5999
North off Hwy 104 on Alma Rd. at Alma • Three o/n units, private B • Colour cable TV and radio in lounge • No pets, please • Non-smoking only
FEATURES: Stereo in lounge • Evening refreshments • Heated swimming pool • Housekeeping unit available, three-day minimum stay
RATES: $30-$45 (1), $45-$55 (2), $10 add'l person (STC) • Full or continental breakfast 7:30-9 • Open year-round MC, Visa accepted • Off-season rates Oct. 1-June 1 by reservation only • NSRS Member

Amherst
Bonnvie
Bed & Breakfast ★★★
Barb Clarke, 54 Albion Street, Amherst, B4H 2V8
Tel & Fax (902) 667-7430
Hwy 104, Exit 4, approx. 2.5 km (1.5 mi) towards Amherst, on the corner of Albion and Queen Street • Restored Victorian home • Three o/n units, shared B&S • Colour cable TV in games room • No pets, please • Smoking area
FEATURES: Laundry facilities • Screened deck • Fax machine and photocopier available

RATES: $35-$40 (1), $50-$55 (2), $10 add'l person • Full breakfast 8-9 • Open year-round • MC accepted • Off-season rates available

Amherst
Breeze In
Bed & Breakfast
Gerald & Lu Freeman, Box 153, Amherst, B4H 3Z2
(902) 667-5518
Fax (902) 667-4998
Hwy 104, Exit 3 right toward Amherst on Rte. 6 East, first driveway on the left, long lane, white fence • Renovated former  farmhouse, c.1890 • Two o/n units, one housekeeping suite, skylit and ensuite B&S • Cot available • Non-smoking only
FEATURES: Housekeeping unit is fully equipped
RATES: $40 (1), $50 (2), Housekeeping suite two-night minimum $120, $10 add'l person • Choice of breakfast • Weekly $360 • Open June 1-Oct. 1 • Special rates for longer stays • CNTA, NSRS Member

Amherst
Brown's Guest Home
Deane & Nancy Allen, 158 Victoria Street East, Amherst, B4H 1Y5
(902) 667-9769
Three o/n units, two shared B • TV in lounge • No pets, please
RATES: $28-$30 (1), $30-$38 (2) (STC) • Open May 1-Oct. 31 • MC, Visa accepted

Amherst
MacKay's Guest Home B&B
Carol & Edward MacKay, 149 East
Victoria Street, Amherst, B4H 1Y2
(902) 667-9935
Three o/n units, one full B&S •
Non-smoking only
FEATURES: Music room
containing large collection of
Broadway musicals • Theatre
packages arranged
RATES: $35 (1), $40-$45 (2) •
Continental breakfast 7-9 • Open
year-round

Amherst
Seven Gables Bed & Breakfast ★★★
Lorne & Hazel McMullin, Tidnish
Crossroads, RR 2, Amherst, B4H 3X9
(902) 661-2377
From Amherst 26 km (16 mi), Rte.
366 on Northumberland Strait •

Tastefully
restored
Victorian-style
home with
period
furnishings •
Four
period-furnish
ed guest
rooms, private B&S • No pets,
please • Non-smoking only
FEATURES: Furnished with
antiques • Meals on request •
Afternoon/ evening refreshments •
Natural pine floors • One whirlpool
• Spacious lawns and gardens
RATES: $48-$55 (1-2), $60 queen,
$8 add'l person • Full breakfast 7-9
• Open May 15-Oct. 15 • MC, Visa
accepted • Off-season by
reservation • Brian Moore; CNTA;
NSFC; NSRS Member

Amherst
Treen Mansion Bed & Breakfast ★★½
Marilyn Boss, 113 Spring Street,
Amherst, B4H 1T2
(902) 667-2146
Hwy 104, Exit 3 (Victoria Street)
right to Regeut St., left on Spring •
Three o/n units, one private B&S,
one shared B, Colour cable TV in
living room • No smoking in
bedrooms, please
FEATURES: Laundry facilities
RATES: $25 (1), $45-$48 (2)
(STC) • Continental breakfast 7-9 •
Open year-round • NSRS Member

Amherst
Victoria Garden Bed & Breakfast (c. 1903) ★★★½
Carl & Beatrice Brander, 196 Victoria
Street East, Amherst, B4H 1Y9
(902) 667-2278
Hwy 104, Exit 1A at Information
Centre to Laplanche St. to Victoria
St. East • Three o/n units, one with
queen bed, one private B&S, one
shared B&S • Colour cable TV in
living room • Cot available • Small
pets with permission • Smoking
outdoors
FEATURES: Evening tea and
sweets • Pleased to cater to special
diets (with prior notice) • Various
tours arranged
RATES: $40 (1), $50-$60 (2), $10
add'l person (STC) • Full breakfast
7:30-9:30 • Open May 1-Sept. 30 •

MC, Visa
accepted •
Off-season
by
arrangements
• NSRS
Member

Annapolis Royal
Bread and Roses Country Inn

Richard & Monica Cobb, 82 Victoria Street, Box 177, Annapolis Royal, B0S 1A0
(902) 532-5727
Toll free 1-800-906-5727
Registered Provincial Heritage Property (c. 1882) • Nine o/n units, private B • Not suitable for children under 12 yrs • No pets, please • Non-smoking only
FEATURES: Antique furnishings, Nova Scotia folk art, contemporary Canadian and Inuit art • Complimentary evening tea and breakfast
RATES: $60 (1), $70 (2), $85 (3 or suite), $15 add'l person • Open Mar. 1-Oct. 30 • Small dog on premises MC, Visa accepted • 10% discount for 3-night stay • NSRS; UCI Member

Annapolis Royal
English Oaks B&B

Fran & Gordon Atwell, Box 233, Annapolis Royal, B0S 1A0
(902) 532-2066
Off Rte. 201, east end of Annapolis Royal at Alden Hubley Dr. • Spacious parklike setting with panoramic view • Three o/n units, two suites with private B&S, one queen ensuite full B&S with balcony, clock-radio in rooms • Colour cable TV in lounge • Children under 3 yrs free, under 12 yrs $10
FEATURES: Screened veranda, picnic table, barbecue • Trout pond
RATES: $45-$50, $15 add'l person, under 12 yrs $10 • Full breakfast 7-9 • Open April 1-Oct. 31 • NSRS Member

Annapolis Royal
Garrison House Inn

Patrick Redgrave, 350 St. George Street, Box 108, Annapolis Royal, B0S 1A0
(902) 532-5750
Fax (902) 532-5501
Registered Historic Property (1854) • Seven o/n units, five private B, one shared B, one suite
FEATURES: Licensed dining room
RATES: $45-$65 (1), $48-$78 (2-3), $10 add'l person • Breakfast 8-9:30 • Open May-Nov. • AE, MC, Visa accepted • CAA; NSRS Member

Annapolis Royal
Grange Cottage Bed & Breakfast

Ray & Maude Marshall, 102 Ritchie Street, Box 536, Annapolis Royal, B0S 1A0
(902) 532-7993
St. George Street onto Grange St., left to Ritchie St. Three o/n units, shared B • Colour cable TV and VCR in lounge
FEATURES: Whirlpool • Sunporch
RATES: $32-$38 (1), $44 (2) • Breakfast 7-9 • Open year-round • MC, Visa accepted • NSRS Member

Annapolis Royal
JoyQua Lodging B&B
Giselle Beauchamp, 3602 Hwy 1,
RR 2, Annapolis Royal, B0S 1A0
Tel & Fax (902) 532-2209
Four km (2.5 mi) west of town •
Between two brooks overlooking
Annapolis Basin • Three o/n units,
shared B • TV in living room •
Clock radio • Cot available
FEATURES: Artwork for sale •
French spoken barbecue • Picnic area
*RATES: $35 (1), $45 (2), add'l
person $5 • Continental breakfast
7:30-9 • Open May 20-Oct. 20 •
Dog on permises • NSRS member*

Annapolis Royal
Hillsdale House
Leslie Langille, 519 St. George
Street, Box 148, Annapolis Royal,
B0S 1A0
(902) 532-2345
Fax (902) 532-7850
Registered Heritage Property (1849) •
Ten o/n units, private B • Colour
cable TV in lounge • Non-smoking
only
FEATURES: Patio • Bird sanctuary
• Historic Gardens next door • Walk
to Fort Anne, museums, art
galleries, restaurants • Close to
Upper Clements Theme Park, Tidal
Hydro Electric Plant, The Habitation
*RATES: $60-$90, $10 add'l person
• Full country breakfast 8-10 •
Open May 1-Oct. 15 • MC, Visa
accepted*

Annapolis Royal
King George Inn
Donna & Michael Susnick, Faye
McStravick, 548 Upper St. George
Street, Box 34, Annapolis Royal,
B0S 1A0
(902) 532-5286
Off-season (902) 425-5626

Registered Heritage Property
(c. 1868) • Four o/n units, two
shared B&S, two-room suite,
private 1/2 bath • Cable TV in
parlour • Pay telephone • Crib
available • Non-smoking only
FEATURES: Victorian sea
captain's home with antique
furnishings • French spoken •
Evening tea/coffee • Library •
Fireplaces • Classic movies in
parlour • Piano • Board games •
Lawn games • Bicycles
*RATES: $43 (1), $48 (2), $55 (3),
$88 (suite), $7 add'l person • Full
country breakfast 7-9 • Open June
1-Sept. 30 • NSRS Member*

Annapolis Royal
Poplars
Bed & Breakfast
Syd & Iris Williams, 124 Victoria
Street, Box 277, Annapolis Royal,
B0S 1A0
(902) 532-7936
  Rte. 1, one block east of traffic
light • Nine o/n units, six with
private B, two with powder room,
one shared B, three units at ground
level • Colour cable TV in lounge •
Baby bed and cot available •
Wheelchair accessible • No pets,
please • Non-smoking only
FEATURES: Fireplace in lounge
*RATES: $33-$45 (1-2), $53-$55
(private B), $8 add'l person (STC) •
Continental breakfast 7:30-8:45 •
Open year-round, three rooms
Oct. 15-May 15 • Visa accepted
NSRS Member*

Annapolis Royal
Queen Anne Inn
Leslie J. Langille, 494 Upper St.
George Street, Annapolis Royal,
B0S 1A0
(902) 532-7850

Registered Heritage Property (c. 1865) • Ten o/n units, private B • Colour cable TV in sitting room • Non-smoking only
RATES: $50-$90 (2) • Full breakfast • Open year-round • MC, Visa accepted

Annapolis Royal
Turret
Bed & Breakfast
Barb & George Dunlop, 372 St. George Street, Annapolis Royal, B0S 1A0
(902) 532-5770
Registered Historic Property • Three o/n units, 1 1/2 shared Bs • TV in lounge
RATES: $35 (1), $45 (2-3), $10 add'l person • Full breakfast 7:30-9:30 • Open year-round

Antigonish
Bekkers
Bed & Breakfast ★★★
John & Sisca Bekkers, RR 2, Antigonish, B2G 2K9
(902) 863-3194/1713
Hwy 104, Exit 32 to Rte. 245, 3 km (1.5 mi) to Clydesdale Rd., turn left 1.5 km (1 mi) on the left • Three o/n units, one queen, two B&S •

Colour cable TV in living room • No pets, please • Non-smoking only
RATES: $40-$50 (2) • Full breakfast 7-9 • Open June 1-Oct. 31

Antigonish
Green Haven
Bed & Breakfast
Al & Martha Balawyder, 27 Greening Drive, Antigonish, B2G 1R1
(902) 863-2884/5059
From Hwy 104, Exit 31, first left • Three o/n units, one queen with private B, one double and one twin with shared B • TV, radio and telephone in lounge • No pets, please • Non-smoking only
FEATURES: Bilingual • Stereo and piano in lounge
RATES: $38.85-$55.50 (2), taxes incl. • Full breakfast 7-9 • Open year-round

Antigonish
MacIsaac's
Bed & Breakfast ★★★
Hugh & Bev MacIsaac, 18 Hillcrest Street, Antigonish, B2G 1Z3
(902) 863-2947
Hwy 104, Exit 32 at traffic lights onto West St., bear right to St. Ninian St., take second street past St. Ninian's Cathedral, turn right at Hillcrest St., second house on right • Quiet residential area • Three o/n units, 1 1/2 B&S • Remote colour cable TV in room • Clock radio in rooms • Cot available
FEATURES: Downtown one block • Picnic table Off-street parking
RATES: $35 (1), $45-$50 (2) • Full breakfast 7:30-9 • Open May 1-Oct. 15 • MC, Visa accepted • NSRS Member

Antigonish
Old Manse Inn (c. 1872)
Leonard & Barbara Pluta, 5 Tigo
Park, Antigonish, B2G 2M6
(902) 863-5696
Off-season (902) 863-5259
Hwy 104, Exit 32 to Hwy 245, two
blocks up, left to Tigo, left to first
lane • Renovated Victorian
Presbyterian manse, on 3/4 acre lot
in quiet residential area • Five o/n
units, three private B&S, one shared
B&S, one two-bedroom suite with
living room and kitchen • Colour
cable TV in lounge • Cots available
FEATURES: Gift area •
Fly-fishing in trout pond, canoeing
in estuary
*RATES: $30 (1), $40-$55 (2), suite
$80, $10 add'l person • Full
breakfast 7-10 • Open June 1-
Sept. 3 • Weekly rates available •
NSRS Member*

Antigonish
Shebby's Bed & Breakfast (c. 1854) ★★★½
Mary MacDonald, 135 Main Street,
Antigonish, B2G 2B6
(902) 863-1858
Toll free 1-800-863-1858
Three o/n units, one queen with
private B and whirlpool tub, one
queen, and one twin, shared B&S •
Colour cable TV in rooms and
living room • Clock radio in rooms
FEATURES: Downtown location
*RATES: $37.50-$55 (1), $45-$60
(2) (STC) • Full breakfast 7:30-9 •
Open May 15-Oct.15 • Off-season
by reservation • NSRS Member*

Antigonish
White Lights Bed & Breakfast
Anne Wowk, 77 Hawthorne Street,
Antigonish, B2G 1A6
(902) 863-9374
Hwy 104, Exit 32 to Rte. 245 (left
at lights to Hawthorne St.) • Four
o/n units, one B&S • Colour cable
TV in lounge • Small pets permitted
• Non-smoking only
*RATES: $35 (1), $40-$50 (2) • Full
breakfast 7:30-9:30 • Open June 1-
Sept. 4 • NSRS Member*

Ardoise
Eastwood Farm Bed & Breakfast
Anne Soper, Ardoise, RR 1,
Ellershouse, B0N 1L0
(902) 757-2702
Hwy 101, Exit 4 on Rte. 1 east
approx. 8.5 km (5.5 mi) • Dutch
colonial house with antiques and
collectibles • Two o/n units, shared
B&S • TV and VCR • Clock radio •
Not suitable for children under 10
yrs • No smoking in rooms
FEATURES: Pool • Walking trails
• Cross-country skiing
*RATES: $45 (1), $50 (2) • Full
breakfast 7:30-9:30 • Open
year-round • NSRS Member*

Auburn
Sweet Dreams Bed & Breakfast
Barbara & Arthur Leduc, 1733 Hwy
1, Box 1928, Greenwood, B0P 1N0
(902) 847-1822
From Hwy 101, Exit 16 (Aylesford)
or 17 (Kingston) • Three o/n units,
one B&S • Colour cable TV in lounge
FEATURES: Kitchen facilities

RATES: $35 (1), $40 (2) • Full breakfast 7-10 • Open year-round • NSRS Member

Auld's Cove
Bluefin Bed & Breakfast
Gardiner & Linda Burton, Box 119, Port Hastings, B0E 2T0
Tel & Fax (902) 747-2010
In Auld's Cove at Canso Causeway; enter at Cove Motel • Four o/n units, two shared B, one B&S, 1 S • Satellite TV • No pets, please
FEATURES: Licensed dining room at Cove Motel 7 a.m.-10 p.m. • Ocean swimming • Canoes and fishing charters available • Lake nearby • Gift shop
RATES: $43 (1), $48-$53 (2), $10 add'l person • Full breakfast • Open May-Nov. • AE, MC, Visa accepted • NSRS Member

Aylesford
Reborn Farm Bed & Breakfast
Eleanor Witter
(902) 847-3689
Hwy 101, Exit 16, proceed north, turn left at first crossroad, .5 km (0.2 mi) on right • Working mini-farm with small animals • Three o/n units, private and shared B&S • Non-smoking only
RATES: $32 (1), $37 (2), $55 (suite) • Full breakfast 9 • Open year-round

Baddeck
Breezy Brae Bed & Breakfast
Michael & Patricia Woodford, 1163 Baddeck Bay Road, Box 566, Baddeck, B0E 1B0
(902) 295-2618/1700
Fax (902) 295-1020

Hwy 105, Exit 9 or 10, Rte. 205, 3 km (2 mi) east of village • One hundred-year-old summer estate with 90 ft. veranda overlooking Bras d'or Lakes • Three o/n units, two shared B • No pets, please • Non-smoking only
RATES: $40 (1), $45-$50 (2), taxes incl. (STC) • Substantial continental breakfast 7:30-9 • Open June 15-Sept. 15 • TIANS Member

Baddeck
Broad Water Inn & Cottages (c. 1794)
Gail Holdner, Box 702, Baddeck, B0E 1B0
(902) 295-1101
2.2 km (1.5 mi) east of town on Bay Road (Rtc. 205) • Overlooking Bras d'Or Lakes • Three o/n units, private B&S • No pets, please • Non-smoking only
FEATURES: Manicured gardens • Local art • Cottages available • Craft shop
RATES: $65-$95 (2) (STC) • Generous continental breakfast 7-9 • Open year-round • DIS, MC, Visa accepted

Baddeck
Clan Cameron Bed & Breakfast
Darlene Cameron, 282 Shore Road, Box 27, Baddeck, B0E 1B0
(902) 295-2725
Fax (902) 295-2725
Hwy 105, Exit 8, Rte. 205 (Shore Rd.) • Three o/n units, one B&S • Colour cable TV • Clock radio • Playpen available • No pets, please • Non-smoking only
RATES: $40 (1), $50 (2), $15 add'l person (STC) • Full breakfast 7:30-9:30 • Open year-round • Visa accepted NSRS Member

Baddeck
Dunlop Guest House ★★★
Pat Dunlop, 552 Chebucto Street,
Baddeck, B0E 1B0
(902) 295-1100
Register at the Telegraph House –
479 Chebucto St. • Historic
Victorian home on shore of Bras
d'Or Lake • Four o/n units, private
and shared B&S • Colour cable TV
and VCR in living room •
Non-smoking only
FEATURES: Kitchen facilities •
Private beach
*RATES: $69 (1), $79 (2) • Open
year-round • Please call Telegraph
House for information and
reservations*

Baddeck
Duffus House Inn
(c. 1830)
John & Judy Langley, Water Street,
Box 427, Baddeck, B0E 1B0
(902) 295-2172
Off-season (902) 928-2878
Quiet waterside inn • Eight o/n
units in two houses, private and
shared B, one suite with sitting
room • No pets, please •
Non-smoking only
FEATURES: Antique furnishings •
English gardens • Private dock
*RATES: $55-$65 (1), $65-$95 (2),
$90-$110 (suite), $15 add'l person
(STC) • Open mid-June to mid-Oct.
• Visa accepted*

Baddeck
Eagle's Perch
Bed & Breakfast
Gail Holdner, Box 425, Baddeck,
B0E 1B0
(902) 295-2640
Hwy 105, Exit 9 at stop sign turn
north away from Baddeck and

follow Margaree Rd. to Baddeck
Bridge 4 km (2.5 mi), cross bridge
and turn left (west); 1 km from
bridge on left • Log home on
Baddeck River • Three o/n units,
one private B, one shared B •
Non-smoking only
FEATURES: Canoe rentals,
bicycle rentals
*RATES: $32-$47 (1), $40-$55 (2),
$10 add'l person (STC) • Full
breakfast 7-9 • Open May 15-Oct.
15 • MC, Visa accepted •
Off-season by appointment •
CBBBA; NSRS Member*

Baddeck
Flying Squirrel
Bed & Breakfast
Linda Murphy, Box 185, Baddeck,
B0E 1B0
(902) 295-2904
Hwy 105, Exit 9 north to Baddeck
Bridge 4 km (2.5 mi), left towards
Hunter's Mountain 2 km (1.5 mi) •
Log house with mountain view •
One o/n unit, private B&S • TV in
living room • No pets, please • No
smoking in rooms
FEATURES: Room on ground floor
*RATES: $40 (1), $50 (2) • Open
May 15-Oct. 31*

Baddeck
Lynwood Country
Inn ★★★
Daryl MacDonnell & Louise
DesRochers, 23 Shore Road,
Baddeck, B0E 1B0
(902) 295-1995
Fax (902) 295-3084
Century-old home located in the
heart of town • Three o/n units,
private B&S, two overlook lake •
Non-smoking only
FEATURES: Licensed dining room
(wheelchair accessible) overlooking

Bras d'Or Lake • Quiet living room
Large deck • Whirlpools • Lake view
*RATES: $80-$100 (1), $90-$110
(2), $10 add'l person • Continental
breakfast • Open year-round •
Off-season rates Sept. 18-June 30
$60-$80 (1), $65-$85 (2) • Seasonal
rates available • NSRS Member*

Baddeck
MacNeil House ★★★★
Warren Janes, Box 399, Baddeck,
B0E 1B0
(902) 295-2340
Fax (902) 295-2484
Toll free 1-800-565-VIEW (8439)
Hwy 105, Exit 8, Rte. 205 to Shore
Rd. • Six suites, private B&S •
Colour cable TV in rooms • Radio
in room • Telephone in rooms
FEATURES: Suites have living
room, fireplace, kitchen, Jacuzzi, and
balcony • Live Scottish entertainment
Licensed dining room • Picnic lunches
• Playground • Air-conditioning •
Outdoor heated swimming pool •
Lakeside beach • Walking trails • Chip
and putt area • Bicycles, boat rentals •
Craft and gift shop
*RATES: $125-$225 • Open May
15-Oct. 31 • AE, ER, MC, Visa
accepted • Packages available •
NSRS Member*

Baddeck
M and V
Bed & Breakfast
Mack & Viola Garland, Box 284,
Baddeck, B0E 1B0
(902) 295-2668
Hwy 105, Exit 9 to Baddeck Bridge
Rd. • Three o/n units, one private
B&S, one shared B&S, one private
1/2 B • No pets, please •
Non-smoking only
*RATES: $35-$45 (1), $40-$50 (2),
taxes incl. (STC) • Substantial*

*continental breakfast 7-8:30 • Open
May 1-Oct. 31*

Baddeck
Restawyle
Bed & Breakfast
Peter & Patti MacAulay, 321 Shore
Road, RR 3, Baddeck, B0E 1B0
(902) 295-2500
Hwy 105, Exit 8 • Four o/n units,
two shared B&S • Colour cable TV
in living room • Non-smoking only
*RATES: $40-$55 (2), $5 add'l
person • Continental breakfast
7:30-9 • Open June 15-Oct. 15*

Baddeck
Sealladh Aluinn
Bed & Breakfast
Shelage Fraser, 251 Shore Road,
Box 59, Baddeck, B0E 1B0
(902) 295-1160
Hwy 105, Exit 8 • Overlooking
Bras d'Or Lakes • Three o/n units,
one shared B&S • Colour cable TV
• Clock radio • Non-smoking only
*RATES: $35 (1), $45 (2) •
Continental breakfast 7:30-9 •
Open May 15-Oct. 31*

Baddeck
The Bay Tourist Home
Bed & Breakfast
Patricia & Harold Edwards, Box 24,
Baddeck, B0E 1B0
(902) 295-2046
Hwy 105, Exit 10 to Rte. 205, 1.5
km (1 mi) west of Baddeck • Three
o/n units, full B • TV in lounge •
No pets, please • Non-smoking only
FEATURES: Very quiet location •
Evening coffee/tea
*RATES: $30 (1), $35 (2) • Light
breakfast 7:30-9 • Open
May 1-Oct. 31*

Barrington
MacMullen House
Bed & Breakfast
(c. 1882) ★★★
Margaret Doane, 2456 Hwy 3,
Barrington, B0W 1E0
(902) 637-3892
Site of oil skin factory in early
1900s • Three o/n units, two full B
• Cable TV • Families welcome,
special rates • Non-smoking only
FEATURES: Three-story barn is
provincially designated heritage
property • Kitchen facilities •
Barbecue • Cottage available July and
Aug.
*RATES: $35 (1), $45 (2), $10 add'l
person (STC) • Full breakfast 7-9 •
Open year-round • NSRS Member*

Barrington
Schooner Lane
Bed & Breakfast
Carol & John Oss, 2149 Rte. 3, RR
1, Barrington, B0W 1E0
(902) 637-1546
Fax (902) 637-1547
Three o/n units, one B&S, one
queen bed • Cable TV in library
and living room • Crib available •
No pets, please • Designated
smoking area
FEATURES: Living room • Library
*RATES: $40 (1), $45 (2) • Full
breakfast 7-9 • Open year-round •
AE, MC, Visa accepted • NSRS
Member*

Barrington Passage
Old School House Inn
& Cottages
Nellie Gorham, Box 303,
Barrington Passage, B0W 1G0
(902) 637-3770
Fax (902) 637-3563

Rte. 3, Barrington Passage • Six o/n
units, two shared S • No smoking in
rooms
FEATURES: Licensed dining room
11 a.m.-8 p.m. • Lounge 9 p.m.-1
a.m. • Cottages available
*RATES: $35-$45 (1-2) • Open
year-round • AE, MC, Visa
accepted • NSRS Member*

*Barss Corner
(close to Mahone Bay and
Lunenburg)*
100 Acres and an Ox
Bed & Breakfast
Ardythe Wildsmith, RR 2, Barss
Corner, B0R 1A0
(902) 644-3444
Fax (902) 644-3912
Hwy 103, Exit 11, 19 km (12 mi)
inland toward Barss Corner Large
acreage with lake and river frontage
• Three o/n units, all with private B
• No pets, please • Non-smoking
only
FEATURES: Traditional Gothic
Revival reproduction filled with

antiques •
Meals and
box lunches
on request •
Rural retreat
with hiking,
salmon and
trout fishing,
canoeing,
swimming and campfires • Close to
Mahone Bay and Lunenburg
*RATES: $55 (1), $65 (2) (STC) •
Full breakfast • Open year-round •
MC, Visa accepted • Please call
ahead • Off-season by reservation •
NSRS Member*

Barton
Barton House B&B
Laurette Deschenes, RR 1, Box 33, Barton, B0W 1H0
(902) 245-6695
Three o/n units, one private and one shared B
FEATURES: Outdoor hot tub
RATES: $35 (1), $45 (2) • Full breakfast until 10 • Open May 1-Oct. 31 • NSRS Member

Barton
Bellview
Bed & Breakfast ★★½
Beverly Bell, Box 71, Barton, B0W 1H0
(902) 245-2225
Hwy 101, 8 km (5 mi) west of Digby • Four o/n units, one private B&S, one full B • Colour cable TV in all rooms • Non-smoking only
FEATURES: Mini park with fish pond, walking trails
RATES: $35-$50 (1), $40-$60 (2), $10 add'l person • Full breakfast 7-9 • Open June 1-Oct. 31 • Visa accepted • Off-season by reservation • Family room sleeps three • NSRS Member

Bass River
King's Rest Beach
Bed & Breakfast
George Fulton, Clarice Fulton, 300 Birch Hill Road, Bass River, B0M 1B0
(902) 647-2672
Recently renovated home situated on Cobequid Bay • Three o/n units, double beds, private B&S, private entrance • Not suitable for small children • Non-smoking only
FEATURES: Three sitting rooms and viewing decks overlooking the bay • World's highest tides, explore the ocean floor before the tide comes in • Clam digging, bass fishing, bird watching • Steps to beach for swimming and beachcombing
RATES: $48-$55 (1-2), suite $70, $10 add'l person (STC) • Full breakfast 7-9 • Open year-round

Bay St. Lawrence
Buchanan's
Bed & Breakfast
Wilma Buchanan, Box 17, St. Margaret's Village, B0C 1R0
(902) 383-2075/2597
Fax (902) 383-2995
Turn off Cabot Trail at Cape North, 16 km (10 mi) to Bay St. Lawrence • Two o/n units, shared B • TV and VCR in lounge Clock radio • No pets, please • No smoking in rooms
RATES: $32 (1), $40 (2) • Breakfast 7:30-9 • Open May-Oct. • Off-season by arrangement

Bay St. Lawrence
Highlands By the Sea
B&B
Susanne MacDonald & Reginald MacDonald, St. Margaret's Village, B0C 1R0
(902) 383-2537
Turn on Cabot Trail at Cape North, 13 km (8 mi) • Century-old rectory house, surrounded by mountains • Three o/n units, shared B&S • TV and VCR in lounge • Clock radio • No pets, please • No smoking in rooms
FEATURES: Hiking trails • Horseshoes • Mountain bikes for rent • Whale-watching and deep-sea fishing arranged
RATES: $35 (1), $40 (2), $8 add'l person (STC) • Full breakfast 7:30-9

Bayfield
Sea 'Scape
Bed & Breakfast
and Cottages ★★★
Frank & Lelia (O'Rourke) Machnik,
Box 94, Heatherton, B0H 1R0
(902) 386-2825
Hwy 104, Exit 36, north 7 km (4.5
mi). 26 km (16 mi) east of
Antigonish • 150 acre coastal
property with panoramic view • Pay
phone
FEATURES: Laundromat •
Barbecues • Playground • Cottages
available • Sandy beach and dunes,
walking trails, bird-watching,
fishing, boat tours, boats and canoes
available • Babysitting
*RATES: $45 (2), $5 add'l person •
Breakfast • Open May 1-Oct. 31 •
CAA; NSRS Member*

Bear River
House on the Hill ★★½
C. Gene Samson, Riverview Road
719, Bear River, B0S 1B0
(902) 467-3933
Historic settler's farm house (c. 1760)
• Three o/n units, one shared B&S
FEATURES: Rural countryside
setting • Art gallery • Walking and
hiking trails nearby/adjoining • Tent
sites available
*RATES: $32 (1), $42 (2) • Full
breakfast 7:30-9:30 Open
June-Sept. • NSRS Member*

Bear River
Inn Bear River B&B
Doug Dockrill & Zoë Onysko, Box
142, Bear River, B0S 1B0
(902) 467-3809
Hwy 101, Exit 24, Upper River Rd.
• Gothic Revival (1860) known
locally as the Millionaire's House •
Three o/n units, one private and one

shared B • Reading room with
TV/VCR
FEATURES: Collection of
antiques, vintage quilts, hats, period
clothing, hooked rugs, original art
Piano, fireplace in lounge • Library
• Stained glass windows • Verandas
• Bicycles available
*RATES: $30 (1), $30-$34 (2), $8
add'l person • Full breakfast • Open
Jan.-Nov. • MC, Visa accepted • Cats
on premises • NSRS Member*

Bear River
Lovett Lodge Inn B&B
Adrian Potter, Main Street, Box
119, Bear River, B0S 1B0
(902) 467-3917
Hwy 101, Exit 24 or 25, 10 min.
east of Digby • Victorian doctor's
residence (1892) • Four o/n units,
family suite, two private, one
shared B • Colour cable TV/VCR,
radio in lounge • Pets welcome
FEATURES: Antiques • Art and
music • Medical library •
Laundromat • Evening tea • Located
on tidal river in "Switzerland of
Nova Scotia" • Alpine tea garden,
hiking trails • Whale-watching
arranged
*RATES: $35 (1), $43-$46 (2-3), $8
add'l person, private B $6 extra •
Full breakfast • Open May 20-Oct.
31 • MC, Visa accepted • NSRS
Member*

Beaver River
Duck Pond Inn & Space
Barn Museum ★★★½
Harry & Tina Taylor, RR 1, Box
2495, Beaver River, Yarmouth,
B5A 4A5
(902) 649-2249
Fax (902) 649-2421
Just off Evangeline Trail, Rte. 1 on
Beaver River Rd. at Yarmouth/

Digby county line • Historic sea captain's home • Three o/n units, queen beds, one with private B, two with shared B • TV in lounge • No pets, please • Non-smoking only
FEATURES: Ceiling fans throughout • Complimentary show in unique museum by space scientist host • Walk to beach
RATES: $70 (1), $80 (2), $90 (Suite), taxes incl. Full breakfast • Open May-Oct. • Packages available • NSRS Member

Berwick
Berwick Inn
Bruce & Anne Drummond, 160 Commercial Street, Berwick, B0P 1E0
(902) 538-8532
Victorian century home • Five o/n units, two shared B&S, private entrance • TV in lounge
FEATURES: Kitchen facilities • Air-conditioning
RATES: $43 (1), $53 (2) • Breakfast 8-10 • Open year-round • MC, Visa accepted • NSRS Member

Berwick
Fundy Trail Farms B&B
Marie & Derill Armstrong, 2986 McNally Road (Burlington), RR 5, Berwick, B0P 1E0
(902) 538-9481
Fax (902) 538-7934
Hwy 101, Exit 15, north on Rte. 360 to stop sign, Hwy 221 left to Viewmont sign, right 6.5 km (4 mi), to four-way intersection, left 1.3 km (0.8 mi), 10 minutes total • Century-home overlooking Bay of Fundy • Three o/n units, 1 1/2 shared B&S
RATES: $35 (1), $40 (2), $8 add'l person • Full breakfast 8-8:30 • Open year-round • NSRS Member

Berwick
North Haven Bed & Breakfast
Jennie Mahar, RR 5, Berwick, B0P 1E0
(902) 538-8441
Hwy 101, Exit 15 to Rte. 360 north, approx. 8 km (5 mi) over North Mountain toward Harbourville, second house on left in Garland • Georgian home • Three o/n units, one private 1/2 B, one shared full B with whirlpool • Not suitable for children • No pets, please • Non-smoking only
FEATURES: Evening tea • Patio overlooking formal gardens
RATES: $40 (1), $45 (2) • Full breakfast 7:30-8:30 • Open May 15-Oct. 15 • Off-season by reservation • NSFCV; NSRS Member

Bible Hill
At the Organery
Akke & Jan Van der Leest, 53 Farnham Road, Bible Hill, B2N 2X6
(902) 895-6653
Hwy 102, Exit 14A • Three o/n units, one queen suite with private B, TV and pull-out bed, one double and one twin with shared B&S • Colour cable TV/VCR in family room • Clock radio and ceiling fan in rooms • Non-smoking only
FEATURES: Private collection of over 100 antique reed organs for viewing or playing • Piano in family room • Ceiling fans in all rooms
RATES: $40 (1), $45-$55 (2), $10 add'l person Full breakfast 8-9:30 Open May 15-Nov. 15 • Pets on premises • Visa accepted • Off-season by reservation • NSFC; NSRS Member

Bible Hill
Eleanor's
Bed & Breakfast ★★★
Eleanor & Richard Humby, 348
Pictou Road, Truro, B2N 2T7
(902) 893-7637
Hwy 104, Exit 17, Bible Hill, 3 km
(2 mi); or Hwy 102, Exit 14A,
drive east (right) through Onslow to
2nd set of lights, turn left onto
Pictou Rd. for 3 km (2 mi) • Three
o/n units, two queen beds, two
shared B&S, one private B • Colour
cable TV in rooms • VCR and
telephone in lounge • Clock radio
and fans in rooms • Cot available •
School-age children welcome •
Non-smoking only
FEATURES: Evening tea and
conversation • Fans in rooms
*RATES: $35 (1), $40-$50 (2),
$10-$15 add'l person • Full breakfast
7:30-8:30 • Open year-round • MC,
Visa accepted • Off-season by
reservation, lower rates Oct. 30-
Apr. 30 • NSRS Member*

Bickerton West
By the Sea
Bed & Breakfast ★★★
Bruce & Dolores Kaiser, Box 39,
Port Bickerton West, B0J 1A0
(902) 364-2575
Rte. 7 to Sherbrooke to Rte. 211,
east for 26 km (16 mi) • Three o/n
units, double and twin beds, shared
B, queen with private B • Colour
cable TV in lounge • Cot & crib
available • No pets, please •
Non-smoking
FEATURES: Harbour, ocean &
lighthouse view from deck • Private
road to scenic shore
*RATES: $40 (1), $45-$55 (2), $10
add'l person (STC) • Full breakfast
7:30-9:30 • Open May 15-Oct. 15 •
Visa accepted • Off-season by*
*reservation • ESTA; NSFC; NSRS
Member*

Big Harbour
The Roost B&B
Lal Coleman, RR 2, Baddeck,
B0E 1B0
(902) 295-2722
Off Hwy 105, 3 km (2 mi) on Big
Harbour Rd. • Quiet location Three
o/n units, 1 1/2 shared B&S • Clock
radios • Adults only • Non-smoking
only
FEATURES: Picnic table/patio
deck • Zoned electric heat • Garden
• Birding
*RATES: $40 (1), $50-$60 (2), taxes
incl. • Full breakfast • Open June
15-Oct. 15 • Check in after 4 p.m. •
NSRS Member*

Big Pond
Big Pond
Bed & Breakfast
Keith & Pat Nelder, RR 1, East Bay,
B0A 1H0
(902) 828-2476
Fax (902) 828-3065
Three o/n units, one private B, one
shared B
FEATURES: Lake swimming •
Walking trail • 9 m (30 ft) sailboat
for charter
*RATES: $36-$40 (1), $46-$50 (2) •
Full breakfast 7-10 • Open May
1-Nov. 1 • Packages available •
NSRS Member*

Big Pond
MacIntyre's
Bed & Breakfast
Ed & Ann MacIntyre, 7903 Hwy 4,
Big Pond, RR 1, East Bay, B0A 1H0
(902) 828-2184
Three o/n units, shared B&S, clock
radio • Non-smoking only

FEATURES: Saltwater frontage •
Walking trails
*RATES: $35 (1), $42 (2) • Full
breakfast 7:30-10 • Open May-Oct.
• Off-season by arrangement •
NSRS Member*

Blandford
Blownaway
Bed & Breakfast
Michelle Cordeiro, 5206 Hwy 329,
Blandford, B0J 1C0
(902) 228-2041
Hwy 103, Exit 6 or 7 • Three o/n
units, shared B • TV in lounge •
Radio in lounge • Telephone •
Small dogs permitted • No smoking
in rooms
FEATURES: Piano • Library
*RATES: $50 (1-2), $10 add'l
person • Breakfast 7-9 • Open May
1-Oct. 31 • Visa accepted •
Off-season by reservation*

Blockhouse
Bedspread
(le Couvre-Lit)
Bed & Breakfast
Mrs. Pat Marleau, 96 Cornwall Road,
Box 136, Blockhouse, B0J 1E0
(902) 624-8192
Rte. 324 from Hwy 103, Exit 11 •
Three o/n units, three full B&S •
TV in lounge
*RATES: $40 (1), $45-$50 (2), $15
add'l person • Full breakfast • Open
year-round • MC, Visa accepted*

Blockhouse
By-Way Guest House
B&B
Bill & Shirley Murphy, RR 3,
Blockhouse, Mahone Bay, B0J 2E0
(902) 624-9636
  Hwy 103, Exit 11, 1.5 km (1 mi)
towards New Cornwall • Three o/n

units, shared B • TV in lounge •
Radio in lounge
*RATES: $35 (1), $45 (2) $10 add'l
person • Full breakfast • Open
May-Nov. • Visa accepted • NSRS
Member*

Boisdale
Lakeview
Bed & Breakfast
Leona O'Handley, Boisdale, RR 2,
Christmas Island, B0A 1K0
(902) 871-2808
Cellular (902) 565-7290
Hwy 105, Exit 6, at Little Narrows,
follow Rte. 223 to Boisdale • Two
o/n units, shared B&S • TV in
living room • Non-smoking only
*RATES: $40 (1), $45 (2) • Full
breakfast 8 • Open year-round •
NSRS Member*

Bras d'Or
Annfield Manor
Country Inn (c.1893)
Denise & Bill Mulley, RR 3, Bras
d'Or, B0C 1B0
(902) 736-8770
Off Hwy 105, 1.5 km (1 mi), Exit
18 west • Historic mansion • Seven
o/n units, private and shared B
FEATURES: Lunch, 12 noon,
dinner, 7:30 p.m.
*RATES: $45-$70, $15 add'l person
• Full breakfast • Open year-round
• MC, Visa accepted • Reservations
required • NSRS Member*

Bras d'Or
Dollie's Bed and Breakfast
RR 1, Bras d'Or, B0C 1B0
(902) 736-9945
Hwy 105, past Exit 16, left at
Irving station • Three o/n units,
shared B • TV and telephone in
lounge • Children under 3 yrs free
*RATES: $30 (1), $40 (2), $10 add'l
person • Full breakfast 8-10 • Open
year-round*

Bras d'Or
Gilead Bed & Breakfast
Aileen & Eugene Devoe, Box 809,
RR 1, Bras d'Or, B0C 1B0
(902) 674-2412
Hwy 105, Exit 14 at Bras d'Or, first
driveway on left • Two o/n units,
private B • Non-smoking only
FEATURES: View of Kelly's
Mountain and Great Bras d'Or
Channel from veranda • Sitting
room with stone fireplace •
barbecue • Bird-watching • 15
minutes to Nfld ferry, 20 minutes to
Cabot Trail
*RATES: $38-$45 (1), $45-$52 (2),
$8 add'l person • Full breakfast 7-9
• Open year-round • Visa accepted*

Bridgetown
Bush's by the Bay Bed & Breakfast
Cora & Bill Bush, RR 2, Hampton,
B0S 1L0
(902) 665-2048
Hwy 101, Exit 20 to Church St. in
Bridgetown (becomes Hampton
Mountain Rd.) to Hampton, East on
Shore Rd. 1.6 km (1 mi) • Two o/n
units, shared B • TV and VCR in
lounge • Radio in rooms
FEATURES: Walking trails,
horseshoe pit

*RATES: $35 (1), $45 (2), taxes
incl. • Breakfast 7-9:30 • Open
June-Oct.*

Bridgetown
Chesley House Bed & Breakfast
Lorelei Robins & David Shepherd,
304 Granville Street, Bridgetown,
B0S 1C0
(902) 665-2904
Three o/n units, shared B&S •
Colour cable TV, telephone, reading
room • Cot available • Families
welcome, children under 5 yrs free
• Non-smoking only
FEATURES: French and Spanish
spoken • Deck
*RATES: $30 (1), $40 (2), $42 (3),
$6 add'l person • Full breakfast
7:30-9:30 • Open April 15-Oct. 31*

Broad Cove
South Shore Country Inn ★★★½
Avril Betts, Rte. 331, Broad Cove,
B0J 2H0
(902) 677-2042
Hwy 103, Exit 15 from Halifax or
Exit 17 from Yarmouth, follow
signs • Two two-bedroom suites
with private B, four o/n units with
shared B, two other suites, clock
radio and hair dryer • Colour cable
TV in rooms • Telephone in rooms
• Not suitable for small children
FEATURES: Licensed dining room
8 a.m.-9 p.m. • Kitchenette available •
Two minute walk to ocean beach
*RATES: $55 (1), $69 (2), $99-$135
(suite), $12 add'l person •
Breakfast $3.99 • Open
Easter-October • AE, MC, Visa
accepted • Off-season retreat
programs • Packages available •
IGNS; NSRS; TNS Member*

Brookfield
Anglers Arm
Bed & Breakfast

Verlie Grant, 13 Crystal Lake Road,
Brookfield, B0N 1C0
(902) 673-2590
Hwy 102, Exit 12, Rte. 289 East
over railroad track through flashing
lights, 1st left past two schools
(Brookfield Rd.) to Crystal Lake
Rd. (left), five minutes off hwy •
Landscaped country property •
Three o/n units, two shared B&S,
rooms on one level, no stairs •
Colour cable TV in rec room •
Ceiling fan in rooms • Pets, if
caged, crates & kennels available •
Non-smoking only
FEATURES: Quiet • Lawn games
• Private trout pond for fly fishing
*RATES: $35 (1), $50 (2) (STC) •
Full breakfast 7-9 • Open May 1-
Oct. 31 • Visa accepted • Check out
10 a.m. • NSRS Member*

Bucklaw
Castle Moffett ★★★★

Mr. & Mrs. Desmond Moffett, Box
678, Baddeck, B0E 1B0
(902) 756-9070
Fax (902) 756-3399
Hwy 105, Bucklaw 19 km (12 mi)
west of Baddeck • Castle on 185-acre
wooded mountainside • Centrally
located on the Bras d'Or Lakes • Three
o/n suites, all with Jacuzzi baths,
four-poster beds • Not suitable for
children • Non-smoking only
FEATURES: Views of lakes •
Living area with fireplace • Art
gallery in Great Hall • Grand piano
• Air-conditioning
*RATES: $130-$200 per suite (STC)
• Complimentary breakfast • Open
year-round • MC, Visa accepted •
Honeymoon package • NSRS;
TIANS Member*

Caledonia
Whitman Inn ★★★

Bruce & Nancy Gurnham, RR 2,
Caledonia, B0T 1B0
(902) 682-2226
Fax (902) 682-3171
#12389 Rte. 8, in Kempt, 4 km (2.5
mi) south of Kejimkujik National Park
• Ten o/n units, private B, honeymoon
suite with Jacuzzi • No pets, please •
Non-smoking rooms available
FEATURES: Licensed dining room
(by reservation) • Picnic lunches •
Lounge area • Indoor heated pool,
sauna, whirlpool • Housekeeping
unit available
*RATES: $45-$50 (1), $50-$60 (2),
$80 (suite), $110 (housekeeping
suite), $5 add'l person, $21 MAP
Breakfast 8-9:30 • Open year-round •
AE, ER, MC, Visa, personal cheques
accepted • Packages available •
CAA; NSRS; TNS; UCI Member*

Canning
Farmhouse Inn
B&B ★★★½

Ellen & Doug Bray, 1057 Main
Street, Box 38, Canning, B0P 1H0
(902) 582-7900
Toll free 1-800-928-4346
Hwy 101 (Exit 11) or Rte. 1 to Rte.
358 • Seven o/n units, private B,
luxury suite • Colour cable TV • Crib
available • Children under 6 yrs free •
No pets, please • Smoking outside only
FEATURES: Two parlours with
fireplaces • Book collection • Afternoon
tea • Antiques and handmade quilts
Exercise room • Sleigh rides
*RATES: $49-$99 (1), $59-$109 (2),
$10 add'l person • Full breakfast •
Open year-round • MC, Visa
accepted • Senior Citizens' rates,
weekend packages, off-season rates
available • CAA; IGNS; NSRS;
TIANS Member*

Canning
Tree Tops
Bed & Breakfast
Eleanor & Bernard Mason, RR 3,
Canning, B0P 1H0
(902) 582-7470
Hwy 101, Exit 11 to Rte. 1 to Rte. 358
at Irving station, follow it for 16.3 km
(10.1 mi) towards Look Off, turn left
at sign 1.2 km (0.8 mi) on left • View
of Annapolis Valley • Two o/n units,
shared B&S • Cot available • No
pets, please Non-smoking only
FEATURES: Sitting room • View
of world's highest tides
*RATES: $40 (1), $45-$50 (2), $12
add'l person (cot)*

Canso
Pendletons'
Bed & Breakfast
Alice Pendleton, 95 Union Street,
Box 371, Canso, B0H 1H0
(902) 366-3055
Hwy 104, Exit 37 to Exit 16, or from
Sherbrooke, Marine Drive • Three
o/n units, shared B&S • Colour cable
TV in lounge • No pets, please
*RATES: $35 (1), $45 (2) (STC) •
Breakfast 7:30-9 • Open year-round*

Canso
Whale's Tail
Bed & Breakfast ★★½
Myrna Livingston, 3 Sterling Street,
Canso, B0H 1H0
(902) 366-2271
Hwy 104, Exit 37 or from
Sherbrooke, follow Marine Drive
Three o/n units, two B&S • Colour
cable TV in living room • No pets,
please • Non-smoking only
FEATURES: Ici on parle français •
Collection of Elvis memorabilia
*RATES: $40 (1), $50 (2) • Open
year-round • NSRS Member*

Cape d'Or
Cape d'Or Guest House
Cape d'Or, RR 3, Parrsboro, B0M 1S0
(902) 664-2108
5.5 km (3.5 mi) from Advocate,
follow signs • Lighthouse site on
Minas Channel • Three o/n units,
shared B&S
FEATURES: Lunch room 8 a.m.-
8 p.m.
*RATES: $25 (1), $35-$40 (2), $10
add'l person • Open May 15-Oct. 15*

Cape North
Oakwood Manor ★★★
Sharon McEvoy, RR 1, Box 1,
Comp 9, Dingwall, B0C 1G0
Tel & Fax (902) 383-2317
1.5 km (1 mi) on Bay St. Lawrence
Rd., 1.5 km (1 mi) on North Side
Rd. • Country estate 200 acres •
Three o/n units, two shared Bs, sink
in rooms • TV/VCR and free
movies in lounge • Pay telephone •
No pets, please • Non-smoking only
*RATES: $35 (1), $45-$52 (2), $7
add'l person (STC) • Full breakfast
7:30-9:30 • Open May 1-Oct. 31 •
Visa accepted • IGNS; NSRS
Member*

Catalone
Camilla Peck's Tourist
Home Bed and Breakfast
Mrs. Camilla Peck, 5353 Highway
22, Louisbourg, B0A 1M0
(902) 733-2649
On Rte. 22 at Catalone, 8 km (5 mi)
from Louisbourg, 22.5 km (14 mi)
from Sydney, Exit 8 to Rte. 22 •
Farm house (c. 1902) on scenic
hilltop away from traffic • Three
o/n units, shared B • TV and radio
in lounge • Children under 5 yrs free
FEATURES: Coffee/tea • Variety
of animals to view •
Complimentary tea/coffee anytime

*RATES: $35 (1), $40-$42 (2),
$10-$12 add'l person (STC) • Full
country breakfast 7:30-9:30 • Open
June 1-Oct. 30*

Catalone
MacLeod's
Bed & Breakfast ★★½
Ramona MacLeod, 5247 Hwy 22,
RR 1, Louisbourg, B0A 1M0
(902) 733-2456
Hwy 125, Exit 8 on Rte. 22, 10 km
(6 mi) before Louisbourg • Three
o/n units, one private B, one shared
B&S • TV and radio in lounge • No
pets, please • Non-smoking only
*RATES: $30-$35 (1), $45-$50 (2),
$10-$20 add'l person (STC) • Full
breakfast 7-9 • Open May 1-Sept.
30 • Visa accepted • NSRS Member*

Central Port Mouton
Apple Pie
Bed & Breakfast
John & Judy Adams, Box 32,
Central Port Mouton, B0T 1T0
(902) 683-2217
Fax (902) 683-2216
One mile off Hwy 103 (1.5 km) at
Exit 21 • Three o/n units, one
shared B • Colour cable TV in
lounge • Non-smoking only
*RATES: $40 (1), $50 (2), $5 add'l
person • Full breakfast • Open
year-round • NSRS Member*

Charlos Cove
Seawind Landing
Country Inn ★★★½
Lorraine & Jim Colvin, Charlos
Cove, B0H 1T0
Toll free 1-800-563-INNS (4667)
Secluded 20-acre coastal property •
Twelve o/n units, private B&S or S,
six whirlpools, ten seaside rooms •
Non-smoking only

FEATURES: Ocean beaches,
sheltered coves and nature trails •
Licensed seaside dinning room •
Antique furnishings • barbecue •
Lawn games • Picnic tables • Gardens
Sailing, motor boating, canoeing,
mountain biking, ocean swimming,
seal-watching, clam digging
*RATES: $60-$75 (1), $70-$85 (2),
$190 (suite) (STC) • Breakfast 7-9 •
Open year-round • MC, Visa
accepted Packages available •
CAA; IGNS; NSRS; UCI Member*

Chegoggin
Gateway Farms
Bed & Breakfast
Lloyd & Joy Sweeney, RR 3, Box
2020, Yarmouth, B5A 4A7
(902) 742-9786/5787
From Rte. 1, Chegoggin Rd. 4 km
(2.5 mi) to yield sign, turn right •
Three o/n units, two shared Bs • TV
in lounge • Infants free
*RATES: $30 (1), $40 (2), $5 add'l
person • Full breakfast 7-8:30 •
Open May 1-Nov. 1*

Chester
Captain's House Inn
Nicki Butler & Jane McLoughlin,
29 Central Street, Chester, B0J 1J0
(902) 275-3501
Fax (902) 275-3502
C. 1822 • Four o/n units, private B&S
FEATURES: Large waterfront
decks • Licensed dining room and
lounge, breakfast 8-10, lunch 11:30
a.m.-3 p.m., dinner 5:30-10 p.m.
*RATES: $70 (1), $75 (2) (STC) •
Continental breakfast • Open
year-round • AE, ER, MC, Visa
accepted*

Chester
Casa Blanca Guest House and Cabins B&B
Mrs. Margaret I. Marshall, 23 Duke Street, Box 70, Chester, B0J 1J0
(902) 275-3385
Eight o/n units, four private and two shared B, sink in rooms • Private and centrally located TVs • No pets, please
FEATURES: Cabin available
RATES: $44 (1), $10 add'l person, no GST (STC) • Breakfast 8-9:15 • Open year-round • Visa accepted

Chester
Gray Gables Bed & Breakfast
David & Jeanette Tomsett, 19 Graves Island Road, RR 1, Chester, B0J 1J0
(902) 275-3983
Hwy 103, Exit 7 or 8, off Hwy 3 in East Chester • Three o/n units, private B&S • Colour cable TV and VCR in sitting room • No pets, please • Non-smoking only
FEATURES: View of Mahone Bay and Graves Island Park • Dutch spoken • Afternoon or evening refreshments • Fireplace • Whirlpool • Bicycles available
RATES: $50 (1), $60-$70 (2), $20 add'l person • Full breakfast 7-9 • Open May 15-Oct. 31 • MC, Visa accepted • Off-season by arrangement

Chester
Haddon Hall Inn ★★★★½
Cynthia O'Connell, 67 Haddon Hill Road, Box 640, Chester, B0J 1J0
(902) 275-3577
Fax (902) 275-5159
Hilltop 35-ha (85-acre) country estate with ocean view • Seven o/n units, all suites with private B&S and Jacuzzi or fireplace • Colour cable TV in rooms • Telephone in rooms • No pets, please
FEATURES: Professionally designed interiors • Licensed restaurant with gourmet dining • Life-size chess game • Heated outdoor swimming pool • Tennis court • Boat rentals and charter service • Recreational private island
RATES: From $175, $15 add'l person (STC) • Open Apr. 1-Jan.1 • AE, MC, Visa accepted • IGNS; NSRS Member

Chester
Mecklenburgh Inn ★★★
Suzi Fraser, 78 Queen Street, Box 350, Chester, B0J 1J0
Tel & Fax (902) 275-4638
Located in the heart of the village  next to the post office Four o/n units, two shared full B&S, clock radio in rooms, down duvets • TV/VCR in living room • Smoking on balcony only
FEATURES: Registered heritage property • Living and dining rooms with fireplaces • Hostess is a Cordon Bleu chef • Bicycles available
RATES: $50 (1), $59-$65 (2), $20 add'l person • Full breakfast 8-9:30 • Open May 17-Nov. 17 • Visa accepted • Theatre/dinner/cruise packages available • CAA; IGNS, NSRS; SSTA Member

Chester
Stoney Brook
Bed & Breakfast ★★★
Jeanne & Ned Nash, Box 716,
Chester, B0J 1J0
(902) 275-2342
On Rte. 3 at
Chester •
Registered
heritage
property •
Four o/n
units, shared
B&S •
Children

over 10 yrs welcome • Smoking on
balcony only
FEATURES: French spoken •
Fireplace • Gardens
RATES: $40 (1), $50 (2) •
Breakfast 8-9 • Open May 1-Oct. 15
• Visa accepted • Golf packages
available • NSRS; SSBBA; SSTA
Member

Chester Basin
The Sword & Anchor
Arthur & Jane McLaughlin, Nicki
Butler, 5306 Rte. 3, Chester Basin,
B0J 1K0
(902) 275-2478/3501
Sister inn to The Captain's House,
Chester • Waterfront property •
Nine o/n units, private B&S
FEATURES: Large deck
RATES: $70 (1), $75 (2) (STC) •
Continental breakfast • Open
year-round

Cheticamp
Blue Island
Bed & Breakfast
Betty Gunther, 107 Cheticamp
Island Road, Box 675, Cheticamp,
B0E 1H0
(902) 224-3077

Log house with view of town and
harbour • Two o/n units, shared
B&S • TV in living room •
Children under 7 yrs free
RATES: $37 (1), $42 (2), $10 add'l
person • Continental breakfast
7:30-9:30 • Open June 15-Oct. 15

Cheticamp
Cheticamp Outfitters
Bed & Breakfast
Veronica & Gilles Hache, Point
Cross, Box 448, Cheticamp,
B0E 1H0
(902) 224-2776
Three o/n units, one B&S •
TV/VCR in living room • Clock
radio • No smoking in rooms
FEATURES: Guest decks and
barbccuc • Great ocean view •
Complete licensed outfitting
guiding service
RATES: $40 (1), $45 (2) (STC) •
Full breakfast at guests'
convenience • Open May 1-Dec. 31
• AE, MC, Visa accepted •
Off-season by reservation • NSRS
Member

Cheticamp
dejeuner de soleil Inn
Anne & Armand St. Jean, Box 974,
Cheticamp, B0E 1H0
(902) 224-1373
Turn at post office on Belle March
Rd., follow signs • Three o/n units,
shared B&S • Colour cable TV in
living room • No smoking in rooms
FEATURES: Peaceful countryside
• Bilingual • Berry-picking in season
RATES: $36 (1), $45-$50 (2) • Full
breakfast 7-10 • Open year-round •
MC, Visa accepted

Cheticamp
Germaine's Bed & Breakfast ★★½
Germaine & Roland Doucet, Box 275, Cheticamp, B0E 2R0
(902) 224-3459
Located in Point Cross, 8 km (5 mi) from Cheticamp • Three o/n units, one B&S • Colour cable TV in living room • Non-smoking only • No pets, please
FEATURES: Bilingual (Acadian family) • Panoramic view of sunsets • Walking trail
RATES: $35 (1), $42 (2), $15 add'l person (STC) • Full breakfast 7-9 • Open April 1-Nov. 30 • MC, Visa accepted • Off-season by reservation only • CBBBA; NSFC; NSRS Member

Cheticamp
L'Auberge Doucet Inn ★★★
Adele & Ronnie Doucet, Box 776, Cheticamp, B0E 1H0
(902) 224-3438
Fax (902) 224-2792
Toll free 1-800-646-8668
Eight o/n units, full B&S • Wheelchair accessible • TV in rooms • Colour cable TV in lounge • Children under 12 yrs free
RATES: $70 (1), $75 (2), $8 add'l person (STC) • Continental breakfast 7:30-10 • Open May 1-Nov. 1 • AE, MC, Visa accepted • NSRS Member

Cheticamp
Laurence Guest House
Judy Wakefield & Sylvia LeLievre, 15408 Main Street, Cheticamp, B0E 1H0
(902) 224-2184
In centre of town • Three o/n units, two B&S • Clock radio • Not suitable for children • Non-smoking only
FEATURES: French spoken
RATES: $40 (1), $48 (2), $8 add'l person • Full breakfast 7-9 • Open May 1-Oct. 31 • Off-season by arrangement

Cheticamp
Overnight Country Log Home B&B
Adrienne Deveaux, Belle March Road, Box 337, Cheticamp, B0E 2R0
(902) 224-2816
Turn at post office, 1.4 km (0.9 mi) on right • Rustic log home in quiet countryside • Two o/n units, shared B • Colour cable TV in living room • No smoking in rooms
RATES: $40 (1), $45 (2) • Continental breakfast 8-9:30 • open June 1-Sept. 30 • NSRS Member

Cheverie
Studio Vista Bed & Breakfast
Karen & Ted Casselman, 2018 New Cheverie Road, Cheverie, B0N 1G0
(902) 633-2837
Hwy 101, Exit 4 or 5 to Brooklyn, Rte. 215 to Cheverie, follow signs • One o/n unit, private B • TV in room • Telephone in room • No smoking inside
FEATURES: 40 km (25 mi) view overlooking three beaches and world's highest tides • Gardens • Safe walking • Bird-watching •

Fossils • Handwoven blankets for sale
RATES: $45 (1), $58 (2) • Hearty breakfast • Open May-Oct. • NSRS Member

Church Point
Chez Benoit Stuart B&B
Benoit Stuart, Box 23, Church Point, B0W 1M0
(902) 769-2715
Three o/n units, two shared B • Colour cable TV & radio in kitchen • Non-smoking only
RATES: $20 (1), $30-$35 (2), $10 add'l person • Full breakfast 7-9:30 • Open year-round

Clark's Harbour
Cape Island Bed & Breakfast
Sheila Evans, Box 9, Clark's Harbour, B0W 1P0
(902) 745-1356
On Rte. 330, from Hwy 103 to Barrington Passage to Rte. 3 to Rte. 330, 13 km (8 mi) on Rte. 330 • Three o/n units, one S • Colour cable TV in living room
RATES: $35 (1), $45 (2), $5 add'l person (STC) • Full breakfast 7-9 • Open year-round • Off-season by reservation • NSRS Member

Clementsport
Olde Port of Clements (c. 1827) Bed & Breakfast
James & Christine Povah, 8 Clementsport Road, Clementsport, B0S 1E0
(902) 638-8120
Hwy 101, Exit 23, 5 km (3 mi) east on Rte. 1 to Clementsport Colonial home • Three o/n units, Two private

B&S • TV in rooms • Smoking on patio only
FEATURES: Situated on mouth of Moose River French spoken • Antiques throughout • Canoeing • Art gallery
RATES: $20-$40 (1), $45 (2), $5 add'l person, no GST (STC) • Full breakfast 7-9 • Open June-Sept. • NSRS Member

Cole Harbour
Cole Harbour Bed & Breakfast
Doug & Audrey Uloth, Cole Harbour RR 2, Larry's River, B0H 1T0
(902) 358-2889
Toll free 1-800-565-9144
On Rte. 316, 30 km (18 mi) west of Canso, 42 km (26 mi) from Guysborough • Two o/n units, shared B&S
FEATURES: View of harbour and sunsets • Evening snack • Host is lobster fisherman with 10 m (34 ft.) boat to view seals
RATES: $30 (1), $45 (2) (STC) • Full breakfast 8 • Open year-round

Coxheath (near Sydney)
Edna's Bed & Breakfast
Edna & Charlie Ponée, 17 Andrews Avenue, Sydney, B1R 2G8
(902) 567-2239
Quiet residential setting • Three o/n units, two shared B&S • Colour cable TV in rooms and living room • No pets, please • Non-smoking only
RATES: $32 (1), $40 (2), $16 add'l person (STC) • Full breakfast 7-8:30 • Open year-round • Please call for reservations • NSRS Member

Creignish
Creignish
Bed & Breakfast
Sandra Kuzminski, Creignish, Port
Hastings, B0E 2T0
(902) 625-3336
Rte. 19, 10 km (6 mi) north of
Canso Causeway • Three o/n units,
one B&S
FEATURES: Ocean swimming,
fishing, hiking trails, geological
tours, sea cliffs, canoeing, kayaking,
children's activities and workshops
*RATES: $35 (1), $40 (2) • Full
breakfast at guests' convenience •
Open May 1-Oct. 31*

Cribbons Point
Cribbons Cottages and
Bed & Breakfast
Paul & Laureen Boyd, Cribbons
Point, B2G 2L2
(902) 863-6320/2936
20 km (12.5 mi) from town of
Antigonish on Rte. 337 North •
Two o/n units in new facility,
shared B&S • No pets, please
FEATURES: Ocean view •
Playground and picnic tables •
Bicycles • Ocean swimming at
sandy beach • Walking trails,
horseshoes • Hunting, deep-sea
fishing arranged • Cottages
available • Boats available
*RATES: $30 (1), $40 (2), $10 add'l
person • Open May-Nov. • Visa
accepted • Off-season rates*

Darling Lake
Churchill Mansion
Country Inn
Bob Benson, RR 1, Yarmouth,
B5A 4A5
(902) 649-2818
Off-season (902) 467-3549

Rte. 1, 14.5 km (9 mi) northeast of
Yarmouth at Darling Lake Heritage
property with widow's walk • Eight
o/n units, private B • Colour cable
TV in lounge • Children under 6 yrs
free
FEATURES: Meals available •
Lake swimming • Canoeing
*RATES: $35-$49 (1), $44-$59
(2-3), $10 add'l person • Breakfast
7-10 • MC, Visa accepted •
Off-season rates available • NSRS
Member*

Debert
Berry Farm
Bed & Breakfast
John & Sophie Esau, 433 Plains
Road, Debert, B0M 1G0
Tel & Fax (902) 662-2389
2 km (1.5 mi) from Hwy 104,
Debert/Belmont intersection •
Operating farm surrounded by
hardwood forest • One o/n unit,
private B • No pets, please •
Non-smoking only
FEATURES: Evening snack
*RATES: $25 (1), $40 (2), $10 add'l
person • Full breakfast • Open
June 1-Oct. 15*

D'Escousse
D'Escousse
Bed & Breakfast
Sara & Al McDonald, RR 1,
D'Escousse, B0E 1K0
(902) 226-2936
Hwy 104, Exit 46, Rte. 320 East
toward Arichat to Rte. 320 South •
Three o/n units, one shared B&S •
TV in lounge • Crib available •
Non-smoking only
FEATURES: Ocean swimming
*RATES: $32 (1), $42 (2), $12 add'l
person • Full breakfast at guests'
convenience • Open May 15-Oct. 15*

Digby
Admiral's Landing (c. 1890)
Darlene Hersey, 115 Montague Row, Box 459, Digby, B0V 1A0
(902) 245-2247
Toll free 1-800-651-2247
Waterfront view • Eight o/n units, three private B, two shared B, sinks in rooms • Colour cable TV • Small pets permitted
FEATURES: Kitchen facilities
RATES: $40-$45 (1), $45-$50 (2), $5 add'l person • Open year-round • MC, AE, DC, Visa accepted • Off-season rates • IGNS; NSRS Member

Digby
Mary's Waterview Bed & Breakfast
Mary Harvieux, 34 Carleton Street, Box 1314, Digby, B0V 1A0
(902) 245-4949
Two o/n units, shared full B • Colour cable TV in living room • No smoking in rooms
FEATURES: View of Fundy tides from deck • Whale-watching arranged
RATES: $35 (1), $50 (2), $10 add'l person • Breakfast 8-9 • Open year-round • NSRS Member

Digby
Ocean Hillside Bed & Breakfast
Maria & Bob Cabana, RR 3, Shore Road, Digby, B0V 1A0
(902) 245-5932
Shore Rd. minutes from Digby ferry • Overlooks Annapolis Basin • Three o/n units, one  private B&S • Non-smoking only
FEATURES: Laundry facilities • Afternoon tea • Victorian antiques, handmade quilts and crafts • Flower gardens • Whale-watching arranged
RATES: $45-$60 • Full candlelight breakfast • Open May 1-Oct. 31 • Visa accepted • Off-season by reservation only NSRS Member

Digby
Salt & Light Bed & Breakfast
John & Jill Bonham, 189 King Street, Box 493, Digby, B0V 1A0
(902) 245-4562
Hwy 101, Exit 26, Rte. 303 to Warwick St., second street on the left past Victoria • Victorian home, c.1870s, veranda overlooks Annapolis Basin • Four o/n units, one B&S, one S • No pets, please • No alcohol permitted • Non-smoking only
FEATURES: Our mandate: Joshua: 24:15
RATES: $35-$40 (1), $45-$50 (2) (STC) • Full breakfast 7:30-8:30 • Open year-round • Visa accepted • ETTA; NSRS Member

Digby
Summer's Country Inn
Herbert & Gloria Robicheau, 6
Warwick Street, Digby, B0V 1A0
(902) 245-2250
Fax (902) 245-6694
Centrally located restored 1800s
country inn • Seven o/n units, five
queen, two double, private B •
Colour cable TV and VCR in lounge
FEATURES: Candlelight Maritime
home-cooked dinners for guests
only, 6-8 p.m. • Evening coffee/tea
• High poster and brass beds •
barbecue • Two-bedroom suite with
kitchen and living room available •
Bicycle rentals • Whale-watching
arranged
RATES: $50-$59, $99 (suite for 2),
$10 add'l person (STC) • Full
breakfast • Open May 1-Oct. 30 •
MC, Visa accepted • IGNS, NSRS,
UCI Member

Digby
Thistle Down
Country Inn ★★★½
Ed Reid & Lester Bartson, 98
Montague Row, Box 508, Digby,
B0V 1A0
(902) 245-4490
Fax (902) 245-6717
Toll free 1-800-565-8081
Historic 1904 home on Digby
Harbour with view of fishing fleet
and Annapolis Basin • Six o/n units,
king or queen, private B • Colour
cable TV and VCR in lounge •
Public telephone in lobby •
Non-smoking only
FEATURES: On parle français •
Candlelight dinners for guests only
in Queen Alexandra dining room, 7
p.m. • Bicycle rentals
RATES: $55-$60 (1), $65-$75 (2),
$15 add'l person • Full breakfast
7:30-8:30 • Open May 1-Oct. 12 •

AE, DC, MC, Visa accepted • NSRS
Member

Digby
Westway House B&B
Keith & Evelyn Burnham, 6
Carleton Street, Box 1576, Digby,
B0V 1A0
Tel & Fax (902) 245-5071
Heritage Property c. 1839 • Five o/n
units, one private B, two shared B
• Colour cable TV/VCR in rooms •
Cot and crib available
FEATURES: Panoramic view of
8.5 m (28 ft.) tides • Evening tea •
Library • Antiques and handcrafted
quilts • Barbecue and picnic table •
Golf and whale-watching arranged •
Quiet location
RATES: $30-$36 (1), $37-$41
(2-3), private B $41-$46, $8 add'l
person • Full breakfast 8-9:30 •
Open May 15-Oct.31 • MC, Visa
Accepted • NSRS Member

Dingwall
The Inlet
Bed & Breakfast
Brian Fitzgerald, Box 18, Dingwall,
B0C 1G0
(902) 383-2112
From Cabot Trail 2.5 km (1.5 mi)
on Dingwall Harbour • Three o/n
units, two B&S • TV in living room
• No pets, please • Non-smoking
only
RATES: $35 (1), $42-$45 (2), $9
add'l person (STC) • Full breakfast
7:30-9 • Open May 1-Oct. 31 •
Off-season by reservation •
CBBBA; IGNS; NSRS Member

Durham
Rose Cottage
Bed & Breakfast
(c. 1814) ★★★
Judy & Sonny Campbell, RR 2,
Pictou, B0K 1H0
(902) 485-6733
Hwy 104, Exit 20 to Rte. 376, 4.5
km (3 mi) east from Exit 20; or Rte.
376, 12.5 km (8 mi) west from
Pictou Rotary on the West River •
18 km (11 mi) from PEI ferry •
Three o/n units, king, queen and
double beds, shared B&S • Colour
cable TV in lounge • Non-smoking
only
FEATURES: Fireplace, games,
piano in lounge • Gift shop
*RATES: $35 (1), $45-$55 (2)
(STC) • Full breakfast 7:30-9:30,
continental breakfast available
earlier • Open year-round • NSRS
Member*

East Bay
East Bay
Bed & Breakfast
Audrey Ryan, Box 13, East Bay,
B0A 1H0
(902) 828-3140
Rte. 4, in East Bay, halfway
between Big Pond and Sydney •
Three o/n units • King or Queen,
two shared B&S, clock radio
Colour TV and VCR in guests'
lounge • Not suitable for young
children • No pets, please •
Non-smoking only
FEATURES: Fitness equipment
*RATES: $45-$55 (1), $50-$55 (2),
$15 add'l person Full breakfast
7-9:30 • Open May-Oct. • MC, Visa
accepted • Off-season by
reservation • NSRS Member*

East Chester
East Chester Inn B&B
Jess & Ross Davis, 3280 Hwy 3,
East Chester, B0J 1J0
(902) 275-3017/4790
On Rte. 3, 1.5 km (1 mi) east of
Chester • Six o/n units, one full
B&S, one B • Colour cable TV and
radio in lounge
*RATES: $34 (1), $44-$59 (2) • Full
breakfast 8 • Open May-Oct. •
NSRS Member*

East LaHave
Tradewinds
Bed & Breakfast ★★★
Walter & Edna Lomertin, 4952 East
LaHave, RR 3, Bridgewater,
B4V 2W2
(902) 766-4020
On Rte. 332, 3 km (2 mi) upriver
from LaHave Ferry • Three o/n
units, two with queen bed, one with
two double beds, private B&S,
ceiling fans • TV and telephone in
lounge • Radio • No pets, please
FEATURES: German spoken •
Upper sun deck overlooking river •
Bicycles • Lunenburg or
Bridgewater 15 minutes away
*RATES: $47-$55 (1), $52-$60 (2),
$10 add'l person Full breakfast
until 9 • Open May-Oct. • Cat on
premises • MC, Visa accepted •
Off-season by reservation • NSRS
Member*

East Margaree
Margaree Inn
Bed & Breakfast
Julia & Dianne LeBlanc, Box 19,
Margaree Harbour, B0E 2B0
(902) 235-2524/2935
Off Cabot Trail 1 km (0.5 mi) •
Four o/n units, private B&S TV
RATES: $40 (1), $50 (2), $10 add'l
person • Full breakfast 7-8:30 •
Open May-Oct. 31 • MC, Visa
accepted • Off-season by
arrangement • NSRS Member

Economy
Thompson's
Bed and Breakfast
Kathleen Thompson, Lower
Economy, B0M 1J0
(902) 647-2777
On Rte. 2, 29 km (18 mi) east of
Parrsboro • Three o/n units, shared
B • TV, radio • Piano in lounge
FEATURES: Overlooking world's
highest tides
RATES: $40 (1-2), taxes incl.
(STC) • Full breakfast 7-10 • Open
May-Dec.

Fall River
The Arbour
Bed and Breakfast
Evangeline Brown, 1303 Fall River
Road, Fall River, B2T 1E6
(902) 861-2324
Hwy 102, Exit 5 to Rte. 2, north to
Fall River Rd. • One o/n unit,
private B • Colour cable TV and
VCR in guest lounge • Children
over 13 welcome • Non-smoking
only
FEATURES: Guest lounge with
mini-fridge Sunroom
RATES: $50 (1), $55 (2), $10 add'l
person • Full breakfast 7-8:30 •
Open May-Oct. • Visa accepted •
Off-season by arrangement

Fall River
Avril's Place B&B ★★★
Avril Betts, 23 Scout Camp Road,
Fall River, Box 44208, Bedford,
B4A 3Z8
Tel & Fax (902) 861-1066
Toll free 1-800-565-8183
Hwy 102, Exit 5, proceed towards
Hwy 118/Dartmouth, follow signs;
from Dartmouth take Hwy 118, Exit
14, follow signs One o/n unit, private
B • TV, radio, clock, coffee machine
in room • No smoking in room
FEATURES: View of Miller Lake
• Laundry facilities • Fridge
available • Fax, photocopier
available • Pedal boat
RATES: $45 (1), $49.95 (2) •
Self-serve continental breakfast •
Open year-round • AE, MC, Visa
accepted • NSRS Member

Fall River
Milligan Home
Bed & Breakfast ★★½
Charles & Hester Milligan, 2093 Porto
Bello Road, Waverley, B0N 2S0
(902) 861-1142
Hwy 102, Exit 5, Rte. 318 to
Waverley, 4 km (2.5 mi) on the
right • Three o/n units, one B&S •
No pets, please • Non-smoking only
FEATURES: Lake swimming •
Paddle boat • Free parking
RATES: $40 (1), $45 (2), $10 add'l
person (STC) • Full breakfast 7-9 •
Open May 15-Oct. 31 • NSRS
Member

Fall River
Nap 'n Nibble
Bed & Breakfast ★★★
Judith Church, 20 Beaverbank Rd.,
Lower Sackville, B4E 1G5
(902) 865-9100
Rte. 102, Exit 4B then Exit 2 to
Beaverbank Rd. • Three o/n units,
two shared B&S • TV/VCR, radio
and telephone in lounge • No pets,
please • Non-smoking only
FEATURES: Laundry facilities •
Close to major highways and
Halifax Airport • Transportation
to/from airport and/or city provided
at hosts' convenience
RATES: *$35 (1), $40-$45 (2) $5
add'l person • Breakfast 8-9 • Open
year-round • Special rates for
families and long-term stays •
MATA; NSRS Member*

Fall River
Ye Olde Manor House
Bed & Breakfast
Launa Lunn, 1380 Rocky Lake Drive,
P.O. Box 323, Waverley, B0N 2S0
(902) 861-1800
Hwy 102, Exit 5, or Hwy 118, Exit
14, across
from Post
Office •
Victorian
house (1847)
• Three o/n
units, one
shared B
with

hand-held S, one private B&S • TV
and videos • Cot and crib available
• Non-smoking only
FEATURES: Antiques, library of
local books • Music parlour • Two
fireplaces • Barbecue • Indoor hot
tub in sunroom • Swimming,
canoeing • Next to Lake William •
Ten minutes from airport,

transportation arranged • Twenty
minutes from downtown Halifax
RATES: *$39-$55 (1), $45-$59 (2),
$55-$69 (3), $9 add'l person • Full
breakfast 7-10:30 • Open
year-round • 48 hour cancellation
notice required • Off-season, long
stay and seniors' 5% discount •
NSFBBA; NSRS Member*

Falmouth
Apple Valley Inn B&B
Mary Dinner, 98 Town Road, Box
3, Falmouth, B0P 1L0
(902) 798-8169
Hwy 101, Exit 7, left on Rte. 1 then
first right on Town Rd. • Renovated
older home • Two o/n units, shared
B&S • Colour cable TV in sunroom
• Not suitable for younger children
Non-smoking only
RATES: *$45 (1), $55 (2) • Full
breakfast 8-10 Open May 24-
Sept. 30*

Folly Lake
Winnet House B&B
Angela L. Younger, RR 1,
Londonderry, B0M 1M0
(902) 662-4197
On Hwy 104 at Folly Lake • Three
o/n units, one B&S • TV/VCR in
living room • Non-smoking only
FEATURES: Piano in living room
• Evening snack • Deck with view
of lake and mountain • Lake
swimming
RATES: *$35-$40 (1), $40-$45 (2) •
Full breakfast 7:30-10 • Open
year-round • Packages available •
NSRS Member*

Forks Baddeck
Auld Manse B&B
Marj Theriault, RR 1, Forks,
Baddeck, B0E 1B0
(902) 295-2362
1-800-254-7982
East on Hwy 105, Exit 9, turn left
then right to Baddeck Forks. Stay on
paved road, first laneway on right
after second iron bridge. Eleven km
(7 mi) north of village • Three o/n
units, one private B, one shared B&S
• TV in lounge • Non-smoking only
*RATES: $35 (1), $40-$45 (2), $50
(private bath), $7-$10 add'l person
(STC) • Full breakfast 6:30-8:30 •
Open March 1-Nov. 30*

Garden of Eden
Edein Gardens
Bed & Breakfast
Ron & Glenda Fraser, 3595
Kerrogare Road, Garden of Eden,
RR 5, New Glasgow, B2H 5C8
(902) 922-2739
Hwy 104, Exit 26 to Rte. 347 south
(between New Glasgow and
Sherbrooke Village); or from Rte 7,
at Aspen, Rte. 347 north • Family
blueberry farm • Three o/n units,
shared B&S, fan • TV and VCR •
Clock radio • Cot available •
Children under 5 yrs free •
Non-smoking only
FEATURES: Evening tea • Piano •
Fireplace
*RATES: $35 (1), $45 (2), $10 add'l
person • Open June 15-Oct. 15 •
Visa accepted*

Gilbert Cove
Gilbert's Cove Farm
Bed and Breakfast
Hope & John Spencer, RR 3,
Weymouth, B0W 3T0
(902) 837-4505
Fax (902) 837-4409
Off Lighthouse Rd. in Gilbert Cove,
Rte. 1, 8 km (5 mi) east of
Weymouth, 19 km (12 mi) west of
Digby • Century-old waterfront
farm on St. Mary's Bay • Three o/n
units, two double, one twin, 1 1/2
shared Bs
*RATES: $30 (1), $45 (2) • Full
breakfast 7-9 • Open July 1-Sept. 1*

Glace Bay
Blossoms & Lace
Bed & Breakfast ★★★
Linda Aucoin, 127 Haulage Road,
Reserve Mines, B0A 1V0
(902) 849-3550
From Reserve St. turn onto Haulage
Rd. just before the "Welcome to
Glace Bay" sign • Three o/n units,
two shared B&S • Colour cable TV,
radio, stereo, telephone in lounge •
Non-smoking only
*RATES: $32 (1), $40 (2), $15
add'l person (STC) Full breakfast
8-10 • Open year-round • MC, Visa
accepted CBBBA; CBTA; NSFC;
NSRS; TIANS Member*

Glace Bay
Justamere
Bed & Breakfast
Angus & Brenda MacDonald, 2489
Tower Road, RR 1, Glace Bay,
B1A 5T9
(902) 849-0218
Just off Marconi Trail, at end of
Brookside St. • Three o/n units, two
private and one shared B&S, clock
radio • Colour cable TV and VCR
in lounge
*RATES: $32-$36 (1), $40-$44 (2),
$10 add'l person • Full breakfast
7-9 • Open May-Oct. • Visa
accepted • NSRS Member*

Glace Bay
Will-Bridg House B&B ★★★

Eileen Curry, 322 King Edward
Street, Glace Bay, B1A 3W3
(902) 849-6585
Four o/n units, one private and one
shared B&S • Colour cable TV in
lounge • Non-smoking only
FEATURES: Housekeeping suite
available
*RATES: $40-$50 (1), $45-$55 (2),
$10 add'l person • Full breakfast
7:30-9 • Open year-round • Visa
accepted • NSRS Member*

Glen Margaret
Shore Gardens Bed & Breakfast

Pat & Paul Freake, RR 1, Tantallon,
B0J 3J0
Tel & Fax (902) 823-3093
Hwy 103, Exit 5 on Rte. 333
(#10502) • Overlooking St.
Margaret's Bay, 2.3 acres • Two o/n
units, one with private entrance, one
shared 4-piece B • TV in living
room • Non-smoking only
FEATURES: Campfire area and
picnic table on beach
*RATES: $35 (1), $45 (2), $10 add'l
person • Substantial continental
breakfast 7:30-9 • Open July-Aug. •
Special rates available for 2 or
more nights*

Gold River
Pictor's Place Bed & Breakfast

Nell Schilder, 5950 Hwy 3, Gold
River, B0J 1K0
(902) 627-2989
Fax (902) 627-1252
Two o/n units queen, shared B&S •
Children welcome • Non-smoking
only

FEATURES: French and Dutch
spoken • Coffee room garden
*RATES: $45 (1-2) (STC) • Full
breakfast • Open year-round • Cats
on premises*

Grand Narrows
Bras d'Or Lakes Hideaway Bed & Breakfast ★★★

Jane & John Worton, 601 Derby
Point Road, RR 1, Grand Narrows,
Christmas Island, B0A 1C0
(902) 622-2009
Fax (902) 622-2365
Hwy 105, Exit 6, Rte. 223 east 29
km (18 mi) or Hwy 125, Exit 3 to
Rte. 223 west 51.5 km (32 mi) •
Centrally located with panoramic
lake view • Three o/n units, one
private B&S, one shared B&S •
TV/VCR in lounge • Not suitable
for children • Non-smoking only
FEATURES: Fridge and stone
fireplace in lounge • Fishing •
Cycling • Patio • Central
Air-conditioning • Garden • Access
to beach
*RATES: $44-$55 (1), $55-$60 (2)
(STC) • Full breakfast 7:30-10 •
Open May 1-Oct. 31 • Visa
accepted • Off-season by
reservation • NSRS Member*

Grand Pré
Gowan Brae B&B
c. 1770
June Robertson, Box 42, Grand Pré,
B0P 1M0
(902) 542-4277
Hwy 101, Exit 10 to Hwy 1, turn
right on Grand Pré Road, right
again, 0.3 km (0.2 mi) to 273 Old
Post Rd. • Registered 18th-century
Heritage home • Three o/n units,
one with king bed, one with double
and one with twin, 1 1/2 B shared •
No pets, please • Non-smoking only
FEATURES: Fresh fruit in season,
home-baked bread • Tea upon
arrival • Piano • Antiques •
Fireplaces • Shaded lawns, orchards
• Lawn games and picnic table •
Spacious grounds, beautiful view
*RATES: $40 (1), $50-$65 (2), $15
add'l person • Full country
breakfast • Open May-Oct.*

Grand Pré
Inn the Vineyard
B&B c. 1779 ★★★
John Halbrook & Cally Jordan, 264
Old Post Road, Box 66, Grand Pré,
B0P 1M0
(902) 542-9554
Fax (902) 542-1248
Restored Provincial Heritage Home
in owners' family since 1779 •
Three o/n units, two with fireplaces,
one with private B&S • VCR in
common room • Babysitting • Pets
welcome
FEATURES: French spoken •
Antiques • Games in common room
• Nova Scotia art displayed •
Barbecue • Bicycles • Bay of Fundy
view
*RATES: $46-$60 (1), $45-$65 (2),
$10 add'l person • Full breakfast •
Open June 1-Sept. 30 • Visa
accepted • NSRS Member*

Granville Beach
Nicci's Bed & Breakfast
Nicci Thompson, 42 McKenzie
Mountain Road, Granville Beach,
B0S 1K0
Tel & Fax (902) 532-2143
At turnoff from Hwy 1, 8 km (5
mi) toward Port Royal • Three o/n
units, one full B&S • Colour cable
TV in living room • No smoking in
rooms
FEATURES: Beautiful view over
Annapolis Basin • German spoken •
Walking and hiking trails
*RATES: $35 (1), $45 (2) • Full
breakfast at guests' convenience •
Open year-round • Pets on premises
• Visa accepted • Special weekend
and weekly rates • NSRS Member*

Granville Centre
Mount Nod
Bed & Breakfast
Clare J. Burrow, RR 1, Box 1079A,
Granville Ferry, B0S 1K0
(902) 532-7461
On Hwy 1 (#6047) in Granville
Centre • Three o/n units, one B&S •
Colour cable TV/VCR in living
room • Crib available •
Non-smoking only
*RATES: $32 (1), $40 (2-3), $10
add'l person • Full breakfast 7:30-9
• Open May 15-Oct. 15 • Off-season
by reservation • Pets on premises •
NSRS Member*

Granville Ferry
Briny Breezes Bed &
Breakfast
Brian Dyer & Susan Stopford,
Karsdale, RR 2, Granville Ferry,
B0S 1K0
(902) 532-5563
Four km (2.5 mi) past Habitation •
Two o/n units, shared B&S and

shared S • TV and VCR in living room • No pets, please • Non-smoking only
FEATURES: Nova Scotia art for sale • Evening snack
RATES: $45 (1), $55 (2), $10 add'l person • Full breakfast 7-9 • Open June 1-Sept. 30 • Pet-free environment • Visa accepted • NSRS Member

Granville Ferry
Moorings
Bed & Breakfast
Susan & Nathaniel Tileston, 5287 Granville Street, Box 118, Granville Ferry, B0S 1K0
Tel & Fax (902) 532-2146
From Rte. 1, 1.5 km (1 mi) on road to Port Royal Habitation • Built in 1881 by Capt. Joseph Hall • Three o/n units, one 1/2 private B, two shared B&S
FEATURES: Antiques • Contemporary art • Bicycles • Waterfront picnic area • Rooms overlook historic Fort Anne and the Annapolis Basin • Fireplace, tin ceilings
RATES: $38 (1), $44-$50 (2), $10 add'l person • Full breakfast 8-9:30 • Open May-Oct. • Visa accepted Off-season by reservation • NSRS Member

Granville Ferry
Nightingale's Landing
Bed & Breakfast
Sandra & Jim Nightingale, Box 30, Granville Ferry, B0S 1K0
Tel & Fax (902) 532-7615
From Rte. 1, 1.5 km (1 mi) in village of Granville Ferry Historic Victorian house with gingerbread trim (1870) and large veranda overlooking Annapolis River and Fort Anne • Three o/n units, suite

with private B&S, two rooms with one shared B • Non-smoking only
FEATURES: Antique furnishings • German spoken • Fireplace • Gardens • Antiques/craft shop on premises
RATES: $40 (1), $45-$60 (2), $50 (3)$10 add'l person • Full country breakfast 8-9:30 • Open May-Oct. • Visa accepted • Off-season by reservation • Packages available (write or call for details) • NSRS Member

Granville Ferry
White Raven Inn
Hans & Jeanne Denee, 5345 Granville Street, Granville Ferry, B0S 1K0
(902) 532-5595
From Rte. 1 on road to Habitation • Registered Heritage Property, early 1800s • Three o/n units, private B&S or S • No pets, please • Non-smoking only
FEATURES: Dutch, German and French spoken • Restaurant with Cordon Bleu chef
RATES: $45-$60 (1), $55-75 (2) • Breakfast 8-9 • Open Apr. 1-Jan. 1 • AE, MC, Visa accepted • Off-season packages available • NSRS Member

Great Village
Windflower Coach House Bed & Breakfast ★★★
Richard Michaud, RR 1, Great Village, B0M 1L0
(902) 668-2780
Hwy 104, Exit 11, 5 km (3 mi), turn left on Balamore Loop and continue left • Original stagecoach stop (late 1700s) • Three o/n units, suite has private B, fireplace and hide-a-bed, one shared B&S • TV in den • Non-smoking only
FEATURES: Tea/lemonade on arrival • Heated swimming pool • Cross-country skiing and walking trails
RATES: $40-$50 (1-2), $65 (Suite, queen), $10 add'l person (STC) • Full breakfast 7-9 • Open year-round • Visa accepted • Please call for reservations • NSRS Member

Guysborough
Carritt House Bed & Breakfast (c. 1842)
Buster & Sharon Jarvis, 20 Pleasant Street, Box 297, Guysborough, B0H 1N0
(902) 533-3855
On Rte. 16 • Three o/n units, shared B&S • TV and VCR in common area • Non-smoking only
RATES: $40 (1), $50 (2), $10 add'l person • Continental or full breakfast 7-9:30 • Visa accepted • Open year-round

Guysborough
Morgan's Point Bed & Breakfast
Charlotte Morgan, Box 201, Guysborough, B0H 1N0
(902) 533-3813
Fax (902) 533-2895

Hwy 104, Exit 37 to Rte. 16 to Guysborough • Two shared rooms, shared B&S • TV & VCR in lounge • Radio • Non-smoking only
FEATURES: Private saltwater beach • Kennels
RATES: $50 (1-2) • Breakfast 8-9:30 • Open year-round • Visa accepted

Hackett's Cove
Havenside Bed & Breakfast
Shelley & Karl Webb, 225 Boutilier's Cove Road, Hackett's Cove, B0J 3J0
Tel & Fax (902) 823-9322
Hwy 103, Exit 5, Rte. 333 to Hackett's Cove, turn right on Boutilier's Cove Rd. • Luxury accomodation in spacious new home on scenic cove • Three o/n units, two queen, one bed-sitting room, private B&S • Colour cable TV/VCR in sitting room • No pets, please • Non-smoking only
FEATURES: Games room with Brunswick pool table • Picnic site with barbecue • Salt water swimming • Complimentary canoe use • 10 m (32-ft.) yacht for charter
RATES: $55-$75, $15 add'l person • Full breakfast 7:30-9 • Open May 1-Oct. 15 • MC, Visa accepted • Off-season by reservation • Special "Land & Sea" package available • IGNS; MATA; NSRS; SMBBA; TIANS Member

Halifax, Dartmouth, Bedford
Autumn Leaves Bed & Breakfast
Audrey J. Brown, 12 Evans Court, Dartmouth, B2X 2T5
(902) 435-3980
Rte. 111, Exit 6, Rte. 318 N (Braemar, Waverley Rd. Exit),

1 km (0.5 mi) turn right on Evans Court • Three o/n units, one B&S, hair dryers and clock radios in rooms • Colour cable TV/VCR in living room • Non-smoking only *RATES: $35 (1), $45 (2)* • *Full breakfast 8:30-9:30, earlier on request* • *Open Apr. 1-Oct. 31* • *NSRS Member*

Halifax, Dartmouth, Bedford
Beautiful Bedford
Bed & Breakfast ★★½
Lynda & Richard Downing, 512 Basinview Drive, Bedford, B4A 1T4 **(902) 835-2110**
Hwy 102, Exit 3, turn towards Bedford, 3rd street on the left • Two queen rooms, private B&S • No pets, please • Non-smoking only *FEATURES:* Private tours arranged *RATES: $55-$60 (STC)* • *Full breakfast 7-9* • *Open May 1-Oct. 31* • *Pet on premises* • *Off-season by arrangement NSRS Member*

Halifax, Dartmouth, Bedford
Bobs' Bed & Breakfast
Robert Grandfield, Robert Woods & Evelyn Nichol, 2715 Windsor Street, Halifax, B3K 5E1 **(902) 454-4374**
Old-home charm • Three o/n units, two shared and one private B • Non-smoking only *FEATURES:* Original Nova Scotian art throughout Whirlpool • Patio • Garden *RATES: $55-$75 (2)* • *Open May 1-Oct. 31* • *NSRS Member*

Halifax, Dartmouth, Bedford
Caribou Lodge B&B
Bruce & Anna Ellis, 6 Armada Drive, Halifax, B3M 1R7 **(902) 445-5013**

Three o/n units, private and shared B, fan • Colour cable TV • Telephone • Cot available • Non-smoking only *FEATURES:* Working art studio/gallery with wildlife studies by A.J. Scanlan-Ellis *RATES: $50 (2), $65 (suite), $10 add'l person* • *Continental breakfast 7-9* • *Open year-round* • *Visa accepted* • *NSRS Member*

Halifax, Dartmouth, Bedford
Caroline's
Bed & Breakfast ★★
Caroline McCully, 134 Victoria Road, Dartmouth, B3A 1V6 **(902) 469- 4665**
Uphill from the Angus L. Macdonald bridge • Three o/n units, two shared B •  Colour cable TV in lounge • Non-smoking only *RATES: $30 (1), $35-$40 (2)* • *Continental breakfast 8-9:30* • *Open Apr. 1-Nov. 30* • *NSRS Member*

Halifax, Dartmouth, Bedford
Centretown/
Ville Guest House
Stephen Parsons, 2016 Oxford Street, Halifax, B3L 2T2 **(902) 422-2380**
Three o/n units, private and shared B *RATES: $50-$60 (1-2)* • *Open year-round*

Halifax, Dartmouth, Bedford
Do Duck In ★★★
Jeanette Romkey, 14 Cathy Cross
Drive, Dartmouth, B2W 2R5
(902) 434-4358
Hwy 111 in Dartmouth to Exit 7E
(Cole Harbour/Woodlawn Rd), left
on Woodlawn through 2 sets of
lights, right on Day to stop sign,
right on Clifford to Cathy Cross •
Four o/n units, two private B&S,
one shared B&S, TV and clock
radio • Colour cable TV/VCR in
lounge • Cots and crib available •
Non-smoking only
FEATURES: Coffee/tea • Outdoor
swimming pool
*RATES: $35-$45 (1), $40-$60 (2),
$10 add'l person • Full breakfast
7:30-9:30 • Open May 15-Oct. 31 •
Jan. 1-May 14 by reservation only •
Children 5-16 yrs $5 • NSRS
Member*

Halifax, Dartmouth, Bedford
Fountain View
Guest House ★★
Helen Vickery, 2138 Robie Street,
Halifax, B3K 4M5
(902) 422-4169
**Toll free 1-800-565-4877 evenings
& weekends**

Opposite
Halifax
Commons,
near the
Citadel •
Seven o/n
units, four
shared B •
TV, clock
radio and ceiling fan in rooms • No
pets, please • Non-smoking rooms
available
FEATURES: Tours arranged
*RATES: $24-$28 (1), $30-$40
(2-4) • Light breakfast (extra) on*

*request • Open year-round •
Off-season rates • MATA; IGNS
Member*

Halifax, Dartmouth, Bedford
Four Marks
Bed & Breakfast
Mrs. Emma K. Creese, 306 Portland
Street, Dartmouth, B2Y 1K4
(902) 466-6929
Exit 7W off Hwy 111 to Rte. 207
(Portland St.) • Three o/n units, two
shared B&S, TV and clock radio •
No pets, please
FEATURES: Guest lounge •
Coffee/tea in rooms • Deck •
Basketball hoop and lawn games in
backyard
*RATES: $36.04 (1), $45.04 (2),
$9.01 add'l person • Full breakfast
7:30-9 • Open year-round • NSRS
Member*

Halifax, Dartmouth, Bedford
Fresh Start
Bed & Breakfast
Innis & Sheila MacDonald, 2720
Gottingen Street, Halifax, B3K 3C7
(902) 453-6616
Fax (902) 453-6617
Eight o/n units, two private B&S, 2
1/2 shared B&S • Colour cable TV
and telephone in lounge • Clock
radio • Non-smoking only
FEATURES: Laundry facilities •
Off-street parking
*RATES: $50-$70 (1), $55-$70 (2),
$10 add'l person (STC) • Full
breakfast at guests' convenience •
Open year-round • AE, DC, ER,
MC, Visa accepted • Off-season
rates IGNS; NSRS Member*

Halifax, Dartmouth, Bedford
Galloway
Bed & Breakfast
Margaret Galloway, 1760 Vernon Street, Halifax, B3H 3N2
(902) 422-1110
Central location • Three o/n units, shared B • Colour cable TV in living room • Non-smoking only
RATES: $44-$49 (1), $49-$54 (2) • Continental breakfast 8-9 • Open May 15-Oct. 7

Halifax, Dartmouth, Bedford
The Garden Inn
Karen Jamieson, 1263 South Park Street, Halifax, B3J 2K8
(902) 492-8577
Conveniently located in downtown Halifax off Spring Garden Rd. • Registered Heritage Home • Nine o/n units, two shared B, 1 1/2 private Bs • Colour cable TV • Telephone in porch
RATES: $50-$70 (1-2), $10 add'l person (STC) • Continental breakfast • Open year-round • Off-season rates $40-$60 (no breakfast) • NSRS Member

Halifax, Dartmouth, Bedford
Halliburton
House Inn ★★★★
Robert Pretty, 5184 Morris Street, Halifax, B3J 1B3
(902) 420-0658
Fax (902) 423-2324
Http://www.newedge.net/holiday/halhouse
Registered heritage property • 25 o/n units, three suites, private B&S or S, down duvets • Colour cable TV, radio and telephone in rooms • Children under 16 yrs free
FEATURES: Antique furnishings • Full-service dining room and garden cafe • Air-conditioning
RATES: From $110, $15 add'l person • Continental breakfast • Open year-round • AE, DC, ER, MC, Visa accepted CAA; IGNS, NSRS; TNS Member

Halifax, Dartmouth, Bedford
Marie's
Bed & Breakfast
Marie Wilson, 3440 Windsor Street, Halifax, B3K 5G4
(902) 453-4987
Three o/n units, shared B&S • TV in lounge • Radio • No pets, please • Non-smoking only
RATES: $30 (1), $40 (2), taxes not incl. Breakfast 8-9 • Open May 15-Oct. 31 • NSRS Member

Halifax, Dartmouth, Bedford
Martin House
Bed & Breakfast
Helmuth & Medlinda Wiegert, 62 Pleasant Street, Dartmouth, B2Y 3P5
(902) 463-7338
Fax (902) 466-2857
Overlooking Halifax/Dartmouth Harbour • Three o/n units, one shared B&S
FEATURES: Furnished with antiques
RATES: $45 (1), $48-$58 (2) • Continental breakfast 8-9 • Open May 15-Oct. 31 • NSRS Member

Halifax, Dartmouth, Bedford
Nova's Place
Bed & Breakfast ★★★
Nova Rochford, 27 Portland Estates
Boulevarde Dartmouth, B2W 6A1
(902) 435-2935
Hwy 111, Exit 7E to Rte. 207
(Portland St.) to Portland Estates •
Two o/n units, shared B • Colour
cable TV and VCR in lounge •
Radio • Telephone • No pets, please
• Non-smoking only
RATES: $45 (1), $55 (2) •
Breakfast 7:30-9:30 • Open
Apr.-Nov. • Visa accepted •
Off-season by arrangement • NSRS
Member

Halifax, Dartmouth, Bedford
Queen Street Inn ★★
Alfred J. Saulnier, 1266 Queen
Street, Halifax, B3J 2H4
(902) 422-9828
Registered Heritage Property • Six
o/n units, shared B • Not suitable
for children • No pets, please •
Non-smoking only
FEATURES: Decorated in Nova
Scotia antiques • Apartment
available (summer only) • Free
parking
RATES: $40-$45 (1), $45-$50 (2),
$5 add'l person (STC) • Open
year-round • NSRS Member

Halifax, Dartmouth, Bedford
Rankin
Bed & Breakfast ★★½
Harvey & Linda Pardy, 45 Rankin
Drive, Lower Sackville, B4C 3A7
(902) 865-3151
E-mail pardylg@atcon.com
Hwy 101 Exit 1K, turn right on
Cobequid Rd., left on Glendale,
first street on the right past three
sets of lights • Two o/n units,

shared S and shared Jacuzzi B •
Colour cable TV and VCR • Stereo
• Telephone • Crib available
Children under 12 yrs free • Small
pets permitted • Smoking in lounge
area
FEATURES: Kitchen facilities •
Barbecue • New 36 ft. indoor pool •
Shuttle service to Halifax airport
RATES: $45, $12 add'l person •
Continental breakfast • Open
year-round

Halifax, Dartmouth, Bedford
Rebecca's
Bed & Breakfast
Rebecca Lampshire, 2719 Windsor
Street, Halifax, B3K 5E1
(902) 455-5802
Charming older home centrally
located • Three o/n units, two with
double beds, one with twin, one
shared B&S
FEATURES: Fireplace in living
room • Tea & biscuits on arrival •
Canopy bed • Formal dining room •
Patios off one room and in backyard
RATES: $45-$50 (1-2), $10 add'l
person • Full breakfast • Open
year-round • NSRS Member

Halifax, Dartmouth, Bedford
Riverdell Estate
Bed & Breakfast ★★★½
Clare & Isabel Christie, 68 Ross
Road, RR 3, Dartmouth, B2Z 1B4
(902) 434-7880
Three km (2 mi) east of Dartmouth
via Hwy 107 and 7, 13 km (9 mi)
from centre of Halifax, 20 minutes
from airport • Three o/n units, two
private and shared B, two suites
with double whirlpool • Colour
cable TV • Clock radio • Not
suitable for children under 10 yrs •
Non-smoking only

FEATURES: Whirlpool in suite • Suite has fireplace, feather bed and full kitchen • Honeymoon/Escape suite
RATES: $50-$65 (1), $65-$85 (2), $100-$150 (suite) • Full breakfast in sunroom 7:30-9 • Open year-round Package available • CAA; NSRS Member

Halifax, Dartmouth, Bedford
Seawatch
Bed & Breakfast
Elaine E. Hatfield, 139 Ferguson's Cove Road, Box 135, Site 14, RR 5, Armdale, B3L 4J5
(902) 477-1506
On Halifax Harbour, near York Redoubt • One o/n unit, private bath, private entrance • Colour cable TV and VCR • Radio • No pets, please • Non-smoking only
FEATURES: Light housekeeping facilities
RATES: $55 (1), $65 (2), taxes incl. (STC) • Continental breakfast 7:30-9:30 • Open year-round • NSRS Member

Halifax, Dartmouth, Bedford
Sterns Mansion Inn ★★★½
Bill de Molitor, 17 Tulip Street, Dartmouth, B3A 2S5
(902) 465-7414
Fax (902) 466-2152
Toll free 1-800-565-3885
Victoria Rd. south, left onto Tulip • Restored century home • Five o/n units, private B, two with Jacuzzi spa • Colour cable TV/VCR and telephone • No pets, please • Non-smoking only
FEATURES: Complimentary sherry in rooms • Player piano in sitting room • Air-conditioning
RATES: $65-$75 (1), $75-$130 (2), $10 add'l person (STC) • Four-
course breakfast • Open year-round • MC, Visa accepted • Off-season rates and honeymoon packages available • MATA; NSRS; TIANS Member

Halifax, Dartmouth, Bedford
Top Floor
Bed & Breakfast ★★★
Ina Kelson & Vikki Sweeney, 1379 St. Margaret's Bay Road, Lakeside, B3T 1A8
(902) 876-7587
At Halifax city limits, Hwy 103, Exit 4 through Timberlea corner of Raines Mill Rd., Hwy 102, Exit 2A through Beechville, second house on right after Lakeside sign • Two o/n units, private B • TV and VCR • Clock radio
FEATURES: Evening snack • Patio • Picnic table • Barbecue • Lawn games • Locked bicycle garage
RATES: $55 (1), $65 (2), $110 (suite) (STC) • Open May 15-Sept. 30 • NSRS Member

Halifax, Dartmouth, Bedford
Virginia Kinfolks ★★★
Lucy & Dick Russell, 1722 Robie Street, Halifax, B3H 3E8
Tel & Fax (902) 423-6687
Toll free 1-800-668-7829
One block from Public Gardens • Three o/n units, one private B, 1 1/2 shared B&S • Colour cable TV • Not suitable for children • Non-smoking only
FEATURES: Antique furnishings • Library
RATES: $35-$50 (1), $45-$60 (2), $10 add'l person (STC) • Full country/gourmet breakfast • Open year-round Discount for three nights or more, senior citizens' discount available • MATA Member

Halifax Entry Area
Forevergreen
Bed & Breakfast
Joanna Howell, 18 Garden Road,
Elmsdale, B0N 1M0
(902) 883-4445
Fax (902) 883-1456
Hwy 102, Exit 8, 2.5 km (1.5 mi)
towards Windsor • On 2 ha (5
acres) of grounds and gardens •
Three o/n units, private B • Colour
cable TV, VCR and stereo in guest
sitting room • Smoking on deck only
FEATURES: Evening snack
*RATES: $45 (1), $55 (2), $65
(suite) (STC) • Full breakfast
7:30-9:30 • Open year-round*

Hantsport
Magnolia Tree
Bed & Breakfast
Valerie & Alain St. Amour, 10
William St., Box 427, Hantsport,
B0P 1P0
(902) 684-3450
Hwy 101, Exit 8, second street on
right of Main Street • Restored
older home • Two o/n units, shared
S • Colour cable TV and VCR in
living room • Non-smoking only
FEATURES: French spoken
*RATES: $45 (1-2) • Full breakfast
at guests' convenience • Open
year-round • Cats on premises •
MC, Visa accepted • NSRS Member*

Harbourville
Fundy Tides
Bed & Breakfast
Lynne & George Spicer, 385 Russia
Road, Harbourville, RR 5, Berwick,
B0P 1E0
(902) 538-3922
Hwy 101, Exit 15, Rte. 360 North
12 km (7.5 mi) to Russia Road •
View of Bay of Fundy, access to

rocky shoreline • Two o/n units,
shared B&S • TV in living room •
Non-smoking only
*RATES: $35 (1), $40 (2) • Full
breakfast 7-9 • Open May 15-Oct.
15 • Off-season by reservation*

Hebron
Eaton's Cottages, Motel
& Tourist Home
Kelvin & Brenda French, Box 40,
Hebron, B0W 1X0
(902) 742-2007
Hwy 101, Exit 34, Rte. 1. On
Doctor's Lake, 4 km (2.5 mi)
northeast of Yarmouth • Three o/n
units, 1 1/2 shared B • Pay phone •
No pets, please
FEATURES: Picnic area • Beach •
Lake swimming • Boating • Fishing
*RATES: $30-$60 (1-2), $5 add'l
person • Open Mar. 15-Nov. 1 •
MC, Visa accepted • Off-season
rates • NSRS Member*

Hebron
Manor Inn ★★★
Bev & Terry Grandy, Box 56,
Hebron, B0W 1X0
(902) 742-2087
Fax (902) 742-8094
E-mail manorinn@fox.nstn.ca
Hwy 101, Exit 34, Rte. 1. Eight km
(5 mi) northeast of Yarmouth •
Nine o/n cable units, private B •
Colour cable TV in rooms •
Telephone in rooms
FEATURES: Dining room •
Whirlpool • Outdoor heated
swimming pool • Lawn games,
horseshoes • Bicycles, canoes,
tennis • Motel units available
*RATES: $45-$139 • Open
year-round • AE, DIS, ER, MC,
Visa accepted • Packages available
• NSRS Member*

Hilden
Ann's Farmhouse Bed & Breakfast ★★★
Ann & David Pullen, 2627 Irwin Lake Road, Hilden RR 1, Brookfield, B0N 1C0
(902) 897-0300
Toll free 1-800-603-7887
From Truro, take Hwy 2 to Hilden, turn right at flashing light for 4 km (2.5 mi), or from Hwy 102, Exit 12 to Brookfield and Hilden and turn left at flashing light • Old farm house in pastoral setting • Three o/n units, two B&S TV, telephone and radio in lounge • Non-smoking only *RATES: $35 (1), $50 (2) • Full breakfast 7:30-9 • Open Apr. 1-Oct. 31 • NSRS Member*

Hilden
Julaine's Tourist Home B&B
Judith Castell, 31 Edwards Road, Hilden, B0N 1C0
(902) 897-4450
Exit 12 or 13 off Hwy 102, follow sign to Hilden • Three o/n units, two shared B • Non-smoking only *FEATURES: Evening snack RATES: $30 (1), $35-$40 (2), $7 add'l person • Breakfast • Open May 1-Oct. 31 • Dog and cats on premises • NSRS Member*

Horne's Road
Jennifer's Bed & Breakfast
Jennifer Thomas, 33 Wilford Place, Horne's Road, Mira, B0A 1P0
(902) 564-0589/737-5184
Horne's Road off Sydney-Louisbourg Highway • Three o/n units, one B&S • TV in living room • Families welcome • Non-smoking only

FEATURES: Evening tea • Horse stables on property (children can ride in paddock, but no trail riding) *RATES: $35 (1), $45 (2), $10 add'l person • Full breakfast 7-9 • Open May 15-Oct. 15 • CBBBA; NSRS Member*

Hubbards
Dauphinee Inn ★★★
Rhys & Kim Harnish, 167 Shore Club Road, Hubbards, B0J 1T0
(902) 857-1790
Fax (902) 857-9555
Toll free 1-800-567-1790
Hwy 103, Exit 6 • On the shore of Hubbards Cove • Six o/n units, private B&S, two suites with Jacuzzi • Colour cable TV in lounge • No pets, please • Designated smoking area
FEATURES: Licensed dining room and sun deck, 5:30-10 p.m., lunch on weekends, 12-4 p.m., lounge 6 p.m.-midnight • Herb garden • Wharf • Rowboat, canoe, fishing rods, bikes • Bird-watching, deep-sea fishing, geneology • View *RATES: $74-$115 (1-2) • Breakfast • Open May 1-Oct. 30 • AE, DC, DIS, MC, Visa accepted • CAA; IGNS; NSRS; TNS; UCI Member*

Hubbards
Just Inn Tyme Bed & Breakfast
Gary & Julia Dorey, 1539 Hwy 329, RR 1, Hubbards, B0J 1T0
(902) 857-3298
Hwy 103, Exit 6, south on Rte. 329, five minutes from village • Secluded country inn overlooking St. Margaret's Bay • Three o/n units, shared B&S
FEATURES: Recreation area with fireside atmosphere, stereo • Pool table *RATES: $55 (1), $65 (2) • Full breakfast • Open year-round*

Hubbards
Kay's Bed & Breakfast
Kay McOnie, 10384 Hwy 3, Box 178, Hubbards, B0J 1T0
(902) 857-3021
One-hundred-and-sixty-year-old home overlooking Hubbards Cove • Two o/n units, shared B&S • Non-smoking only
RATES: $35 (1), $45 (2) • Full breakfast 6:30-9 • Open July 1-Sept. 30 • Pets on premises

Hubbards
Wyndecrest Bed & Breakfast
Terri Harnish, 247 Shore Club Road, Hubbards, B0J 1T0
(902) 857-3191
Hwy 103, Exit 6 • Traditional country home on the shore of Hubbards Cove • Three o/n units, shared B&S • No pets, please • Non-smoking only
FEATURES: Rooms have cove view • Library • Local land and sea tours arranged
RATES: $50 (1), $60 (2), $75 (3) (STC) • Breakfast 8-9:30 • Open year-round • Reservations preferred

Indian Brook
Piper's Guest House
James & Lucy Piché, Indian Brook, Englishtown, B0C 1H0
(902) 929-2339
Fax (902) 929-2067
Five o/n units, two shared B • TV in lounge
FEATURES: Whirlpool
RATES: $30 (1), $36 (2), $5.50 add'l person (STC) • Open June 1-Nov. 15

Indian Point
Bayview Pines Country Inn
Adolf & Elisabeth Sturany, Indian Point, RR 2, Mahone Bay, B0J 2E0
(902) 624-9970
From Hwy 103, right at Exit 10 towards Mahone Bay, left at Indian Point sign for 6 km (3.5 mi) • Six o/n units, private B&S, two suites with whirlpool • Colour cable TV • Pay phone • Children under 3 yrs free
FEATURES: Vienna restaurant, licensed, breakfast and dinner • Housekeeping units available
RATES: $58 (1), $68 (2), $15 add'l person, $100 (suite), $500 (suite, weekly) (STC) • Continental breakfast 8-10 • Open May 1-Oct. 31 • MC, Visa accepted • IGNS; NSRS Member

Indian Point
Marline Spike Guest House B&B
Tricia Barr, RR 2, Indian Point, Mahone Bay, B0J 2E0
(902) 624-8664
Hwy 103, Exit 10 to Indian Pt. 6.5 km (4 mi) • Sea captain's house overlooking ocean and islands • Three o/n units, two 1/2 shared Bs • TV, telephone and radio in lounge • Children under 5 yrs free • No pets, please • Non-smoking only
FEATURES: Afternoon tea • Canoe
RATES: $35 (1), $45 (2), $10 add'l person • Continental breakfast 7:30-9 • Open June 25-Oct. 1 • NSRS Member

Ingonish Beach
The Island Inn B&B
Paula & Perry MacKinnon, Box 116, Ingonish Beach, B0C 1L0
(902) 285-2404
Off-season 285-2684

On Cabot Trail, in Ingonish Beach •
Eleven o/n units, eight private and
three shared B • TV in lounge • Pay
phone • Children under 2 yrs free •
Pets with permission
FEATURES: View of ocean and
lake • Licensed • Lobster suppers,
June 22-Oct. 12 • Fireplace in
lounge • Sailboat tours available
*RATES: $42-$49 (1), $49-$56 (2),
$10 add'l person • Breakfast 8-10 •
Open year-round • Off-season rates
Sept. 20-June 20, all rooms $49 • AE,
MC, Visa accepted • NSRS Member*

Ingonish Beach
Knotty Pine Cottages & Tourist Home ★★
Roland & Patricia MacKinnon, RR
1, Ingonish Ferry, B0C 1L0
(902) 285-2058
Three o/n units, shared and private
B&S • Black & white TV
FEATURES: Cottages available
*RATES: $35-$38 (1-2), $5 add'l
person • Open year-round • MC,
Visa accepted • Off-season rates
available • NSRS Member*

Inverness
MacLeod Inn ★★★
Alistair MacLeod, RR 1, Inverness,
B0E 1N0
(902) 258-3360
Approx. 5 km (3 mi) north of the
town of Inverness, off Rte. 19 on
Broad Cove Rd. • Panoramic view
of Northumberland Strait & Mabou
Highlands • Five o/n units, queen
beds, full B&S, three with Jacuzzi,
three with hide-a-beds • TV in
rooms • Smoking area provided
FEATURES: Displays by local
artists • Reading and sitting room •
Air-conditioning in three rooms •
Bicycle rentals • Boat tours •
Horseback riding • Small gift shop

*RATES: $60-$90 (STC) •
Continental breakfast 7:30-9:30 •
Open May 1-Oct. 31 • MC, Visa
accepted • Off-season package
available • NSRS Member*

Kentville
Grand Street Inn
Richard & Sandra Snow, 160 Main
Street, Kentville, B4N 1J8
(902) 679-1991
Century home • Four o/n units,
three shared B • Designated
smoking area
FEATURES: Front and back deck •
Outdoor swimming pool
(chemical-free) • Beautiful home with
fine examples of carpentry and oak
*RATES: $45 (1), $50 (2), $70
(family), $10 add'l person, taxes
not incl. • Full breakfast • Open
year-round Visa accepted • ETTA;
NSRS; TIANS Member*

Kentville
Wickwire House Bed & Breakfast (c. 1895)
Darlene & Jim Peerless, 183 Main
Street, Kentville, B4N 1J6
(902) 679-1188
Fax (902) 679-5196
Elegant and cozy Victorian home
close to downtown • Two o/n units,
one king, one double, private B&S,
ceiling fans • TV in lounge •
Telephone • Not suitable for
children • Designated smoking area
FEATURES: Antiques •
Veranda/gazebo • Tastefully
decorated, extensive teak panelling,
princess grand piano • View of
Cornwallis River
*RATES: $73-$78 (2), $15 add'l
person • Full breakfast 8-9:30 •
Open May 1-Oct. 31 • MC, Visa
accepted • Off-season by
reservation • ETTA Member*

Lakeville
Hutten Family Farm B&B

Anne van Arragon Hutten, 161 Thorpe Road, Lakeville, B4N 3V7 **(902) 678-7088**
From Kentville, take Rte. 359 to Centreville, west of Rte. 221 for 6.5 km (4 mi), right on Lamont Rd. to T, left on Thorpe to first farm • Working farm under the North Mountain • One o/n unit, shared B • No pets, please • Non-smoking only
RATES: $39 (1), $45 (2), $5 add'l person • Full breakfast • Reservations preferred

LaHave
Court Yard Garden Bed & Breakfast ★★

Jean & James Campbell, 3562 Hwy 331, Box 51, LaHave, B0R 1C0 **(902) 688-1926**
Century-old house • Three o/n units, 1 1/2 shared B&S • No smoking in rooms
FEATURES: Decorated in Victorian style • Veranda overlooking LaHave River • Courtyard garden
RATES: $40 (1), $50 (2) (STC) • Full breakfast 8-10 • Open May 1-Oct. 31 • Pets on premises • NSRS Member

LaHave
Hove-To Inn B&B

Patricia Hamilton, RR 1, Pleasantville, B0R 1G0 **(902) 688-1025**
Thirteen minutes from Bridgewater on Rte. 331, west side of LaHave River • Old sea captain's house on the banks of the LaHave • Two o/n units, shared B&S • Children welcome • Pets welcome
RATES: $35 (1), $45 (2) (STC) • Full breakfast 7-9 • Open June 15-Oct. 15

LaHave
Keeper's Bed & Breakfast ★★★

Phil & Carol Kenny, 38 Fort Point Road, LaHave, B0R 1C0 **(902) 688-2399**
Located on historic Fort Point on LaHave River • Peaceful, secluded property • Three o/n units, two shared B&S • TV in lounge • No pets, please
FEATURES: Beautiful view • Gardens
RATES: $45-$50 (1), $50-$55 (2), $10 add'l person (STC) • Full breakfast 7-9 • Open May 1-Oct. 31 • Call for reservations • Pets on premises • NSRS Member

Lawrencetown
Alberta's Place Bed & Breakfast (c.1858) ★★★½

Alberta Dumas, 670 Main Street West, RR 1, Lawrencetown, B0S 1M0 **(902) 584-7222**
Hwy 101, Exit 19, Rte. 1 between Bridgetown and Middleton • Three o/n units, one shared B&S, one two-bedroom family unit with private B • TV, clock radio in rooms • Cot or crib $5 • Smoking area
FEATURES: Outdoor swimming pool • Family unit has connecting rooms
RATES: $30-35 (1), $40-$45 (2), $55 (family), $7 add'l person • Full breakfast 8-9 • Open May 18-Aug. 31 • NSRS Member

Lawrencetown
Cricket's Harp Inn

Ingrid Jahn & Michel Jodoin, 7165 Hwy 201, RR 1, Lawrencetown, B0S 1M0 **(902) 584-3388**
Fax (902) 584-3389

Hwy 101, Exit 19 to Rte. 1, towards Lawrencetown. Right on Lawrencetown Lane, left on Rte. 201 East, 2.5 km (1.5 mi) • Renovated homestead (c. 1867) on 93 acres with apple and fruit orchards • Three o/n units, large shared B&S • TV and VCR • No pets, please • Non-smoking only
FEATURES: Wrap around porch with valley view • French, German, Spanish and Portuguese spoken • Dinner available • Play area • Farm animals • Babysitting available
RATES: $50 (1), $55 (2), $10 add'l person • Full breakfast 8:30 • Open year-round • Pets on premises • MC, Visa accepted • NSRS Member

Lawrencetown
Marian's Bed & Breakfast
Berend & Marian Pietersma, 469 Main Street, Box 101, Lawrencetown, B0S 1M0
Tel & Fax (902) 584-3649
E-mail berend@atcon.com
Exit 19 from Hwy 101, turn left twice • Restored 18th century home • Three o/n units, two B&S • TV/VCR, radio and telephone in lounge • Children under 12 yrs $12.50
FEATURES: Laundry facilities • Kitchen facilities • Playroom • Veranda • Lawn games • Bicycles
RATES: $35 (1), $55 (2), PST incl. • Full breakfast on veranda 7-10 • Open June 1-Sept. 1 • Visa accepted • NSRS Member

Lawrencetown Beach
Seaboard Bed & Breakfast ★★★
Sheila & Barrie Jackson, RR 2, Porters Lake, B0J 2S0
(902) 827-3747
Toll free 1-800-732-6566

Hwy 107 to Rte. 207 (Marine Drive) at foot of Porters Lake Three o/n units, two B, one S • Colour cable TV/VCR in lounge • Non-smoking only
FEATURES: Evening snack • Barbecue and picnic table • Ceiling fans • Porch with sea and lake view • Walk to beach
RATES: $40-$45 (1), $50-$55 (2), $15 add'l person (STC) • Full breakfast 7:30-9 • Open year-round • Visa accepted Oct.-June by reservation only • ESTA; NSFC; NSRS Member

Lawrencetown Beach
Moonlight Beach Inn
Calvin & Jane Dominie, 2 Wyndenfog Lane, RR 2, Porters Lake, B0J 2S0
(902) 827-2712
Toll free 1-800-SEA-0191 (732-0191)
Hwy 7 or 107 to Rte. 207 to Wyndenfog Lane, 16 km (10 mi) east of Dartmouth • Overlooking ocean, beach and sand dunes • Three queen o/n units, two suites, private B&S, separate entrance, deck • Colour cable TV in rooms • Clock radio • Cot and crib available • No pets indoors
FEATURES: Other meals on request • Seaside lounge • Fireplace • Pool table • Exercise equipment • VCR available • Hot tub • Suites have fireplace, Jacuzzi • Walking and cycling trails • Ocean and lake swimming, surfing, windsurfing, boating, fishing, cross-county skiing, sledding, skating
RATES: $85-$150 (1-2), $10 add'l person Breakfast • Open year-round • MC, Visa accepted • Special packages, discounts • NSRS Member

Little Harbour
Chestnut Lane Bed & Breakfast
Joye Taylor-Ross, Site 4A, RR 1,
New Glasgow, B2H 5C4
(902) 755-4202
Hwy 104, Exit 22 to Hwy 106, Exit
1A toward Trenton, 11 km (7 mi),
left on Rte. 289, 4 km (2 1/2 mi).
From Pictou Rotary, Hwy 106, Exit
1A • Three o/n units, one B&S •
Non-smoking only
FEATURES: Evening tea
*RATES: $40 (1), $50 (2) • Full
breakfast 7:30-9:30 • Open
year-round • Off-season rates
available • NSRS Member*

Liverpool
Hopkins House Bed & Breakfast
Michiline Hines, 120 Main Street,
Liverpool, B0T 1K0
(902) 354-5484
Across from Perkins Museum •
Loyalist home, pre-1812 • Three o/n
units, two shared B • TV in lounge •
Cots available • Children under 2 yrs
free
FEATURES: Eight years in
business • French and English
spoken
*RATES: $40 (1), $50 (2), $10 add'l
person, taxes incl. • Full breakfast
at guests' convenience • Open
year-round • Cash only*

Liverpool
Joseph Burnaby House B&B
Mary MacDonald, 58 Main Street,
Liverpool, B0T 1K0
(902) 354-5588
On Liverpool Bay • Three o/n units,
shared B, clock radios • Colour

cable TV in living room • No pets,
please • Non-smoking only
FEATURES: Garden
*RATES: $50 (STC) • Full breakfast
8-9 • Open June 1-Oct.31*

Liverpool
Lane's Privateer Bed & Breakfast ★★★
Ron & Carol Lane, 33 Bristol Avenue,
Box 509, Liverpool, B0T 1K0
(902) 354-3456
Fax (902) 354-7220
Hwy 103, Exit 19, right on Rte. 3
into Liverpool, on Mersey River,
annex to Lane's Privateer Inn •
Three o/n units, two shared full
B&S • Colour cable TV, telephone
and fan in rooms • Radio • No pets,
please • Non-smoking only
FEATURES: Meals available 7
a.m.-noon
*RATES: $40 (1), $45 (2) (STC) •
Continental breakfast • Open
year-round • AE, MC, ER, DC, CB
& Visa accepted • IGNS; NSRCSA;
NSRS; SSTA; TIANS Member*

Liverpool
MacPherson House Bed & Breakfast ★★★
Leona Farrow, 41 MacPherson Street,
Box 223, Liverpool, B0T 1K0
(902) 354-2565
Restored 200-yr-old home • Two
o/n units, shared B&S • Colour
cable TV in living room • Radio in
rooms • Non-smoking only
FEATURES: Hand-hooked wool
mats available
*RATES: $35 (1), $45 (2) • Full
breakfast 7-9 • Open year-round*

Liverpool
Royal Bed & Breakfast
Reg & Carole Thompson, Box 285, Liverpool, B0T 1K0
(902) 354-5368
Hwy 103, Exit 18 or 19 • Three o/n units, one shared B • Families welcome • Non-smoking only
FEATURES: Outdoor swimming pool
RATES: $40 & up (2) (STC) • Open May-Oct • NSRS Member

Lochiel Lake (Aspen)
Lochiel Lake Bed & Breakfast
Lainie & Maggie Jo Landry, RR 5, Antigonish, B2G 2L3
(902) 783-2309
At Lochiel Lake, 26 km (15.5 mi) from historic Sherbrooke Village on Rte. 7, or 35 km (22 mi) from Antigonish or 3.2 km (2 mi) from Aspen on Rte. 7 • Three o/n units, one with queen bed, one with double bed, shared B&S, one with twin beds, private B&S • TV in lounge • Non-smoking only
FEATURES: Sitting room • Sundeck overlooking lake • Lake swimming • Private dock and boating (complimentary)
RATES: $40 (1), $45-$55 (2) (STC) • Full breakfast • Open July and August • NSRS Member

Lockeport
Hillcrest Bed & Breakfast ★★½
Pam Decker, 5 Crest Street, Lockeport, B0T 1L0
(902) 656-3300
Three o/n units, one full B • Colour cable TV/VCR in living room • Clock radio • No smoking in rooms

FEATURES: Registered Municipal Heritage Property, run as a hotel from late 1800s to 1958 and again in the mid-1960s • Two living rooms, one with stereo • Five minute walk to Crescent Beach, other businesses
RATES: $40 (1), $50 (2), $7 add'l person • Full breakfast 7:30-9:30 • Open year-round

Lockeport
Locke's Island Lodging & Licensed Dining
Linda Balish, 17 North Street, Box 238, Lockeport, B0T 1L0
(902) 656-3222
From Hwy 103, Exit 23 or 24, 16 km (10 mi) • Three o/n units, shared S • Colour cable TV in lounge
FEATURES: Dining room, 7 days a week, 10 a.m.-9 p.m.
RATES: $45 (1), $55 (2), $10 add'l person Continental or full country breakfast 8-9:30 • Open year-round • Visa accepted • NSRS member

Lockeport
Seventeen South Bed & Breakfast
Margaret Mitchell, 17 South Street, Lockeport, B0T 1L0
(902) 656-2512
Cape cod house by the sea • Three o/n units, one private, one shared B&S • Colour cable TV/VCR in living room • Children welcome • No pets, please • Non-smoking only
FEATURES: Ocean view • Cyclists welcome and workshop available • Ocean swimming
RATES: $45 (1), $55 (2), $7 add'l person • Full breakfast 8-9 • Open year-round • Visa accepted

Lorneville
Amherst Shore Country Inn ★★★★
Donna Laceby, Box 839, Wolfville,
B0P 1X0
(902) 661-4800
Toll free 1-800-661-2724
At Lorneville, 32 km (20 mi) from
Amherst on Rte. 366, on
Northumberland Strait • Four o/n
units, private B, four suites with
fireplace, Jacuzzi and private B •
No pets, please • Non-smoking only
FEATURES: Licensed dining room
• Four-course gourmet dinner by
reservation only • Beach swimming
*RATES: $69-99 (2), $129 (suite,
2), $7 add'l person • Breakfast 8,
8:30 or 9 • Open May 1-Oct. 13 •
MC, Visa accepted • Cancellation
policy • Special rates May 1-June
15, Sun.-Thurs., 20% off • CAA;
TNS Member*

Lorneville
Goodwin's Chat & Chew Bed & Breakfast
Fraser & Arleen Goodwin, RR 2,
Amherst, B4H 3X9
(902) 661-0282
At Lorneville, about 32 km (20 mi)
from Amherst on Rte. 366 on
Northumberland Strait • Three o/n
units, one full B&S, ceiling fan in
rooms • TV in living room • Radio
• Non-smoking only
FEATURES: Piano and organ in
living room • Orchard with variety
of fruit trees • Outdoor games,
horseshoes, tether ball and
badminton • Access to beach,
swimming and walking trail
*RATES: $40 (1), $50 (2) •
Substantial continental breakfast
7:30-9:30 • Open May 15-Oct. 15 •
NSRS Member*

Louisbourg
Ashley Manor Bed & Breakfast ★★½
Stacy Simpson, Main Street,
Louisbourg, B0A 1M0
(902) 733-3268
Three o/n units, two shared B&S •
Colour cable TV in lounge • Adults
only • No pets, please
FEATURES: Walking distance to
Fortress Louisbourg
*RATES: $35 (1), $45-$49 (2)
(STC) • Full breakfast at guests'
convenience • Open year-round •
NSRS Member*

Louisbourg
Cranberry Cove Inn
Carole Swander, 17 Wolfe Street,
Louisbourg, B0A 1M0
(902) 733-2171
Renovated turn-of-the-century home
close to Fortress Louisbourg
entrance • Seven o/n units, private
B&S, some with Jacuzzi, gas
fireplaces and ocean view •
Children 10 yrs and older welcome
• Non-smoking only
FEATURES: Licensed dining •
Walk to town
*RATES: $85-$135 • Full breakfast
• Open year-round • AE, MC, Visa
accepted • IGNS; NSRS Member*

Louisbourg
Evensong Bed & Breakfast
Margaret Marshall, 30 Upper
Warren Street, Box 272,
Louisbourg, B0A 1M0
Tel & Fax (902) 733-3691
Turn up at post office • Restored
Victorian home • Two o/n units,
shared B&S • Colour TV in living
room • Crib available •
Non-smoking only

RATES: $40 (1), $45 (2) (STC) •
Full breakfast 7:30-9 • Open
May 1-Oct. 31

Louisbourg
Grandmother's Place Bed & Breakfast
Jennifer Pope, 15 Brittanic Street,
Louisbourg; Box 185, Sydney,
B1P 6H1
(902) 733-2375
Off-season (902) 562-1130
Off Main St. • Three o/n units,
shared B&S • Colour cable TV in
lounge
RATES: $40 (1-2), $10 add'l
person • Breakfast 7:30-9 • Open
Apr.-Oct. • MC, Visa accepted

Louisbourg
Greta Cross Bed and Breakfast ★★½
Greta Cross, 81 Pepperell Street,
Box 153, Louisbourg, B0A 1M0
(902) 733-2833
Three o/n units, two shared B •
Colour cable TV and radio in
lounge • Telephone and clock radio
in rooms • Children welcome •
Children under 5 yrs free •
Non-smoking only
FEATURES: Scenic view •
Laundry facilities • Kitchen
privileges • Electric organ in lounge
RATES: $32 (1), $40 (2) (STC) •
Full breakfast at guests'
convenience • Open May 1-Nov. 1

Louisbourg
Levy's Bed & Breakfast
Annie Levy, 7 Marvin Street, Box
175, Louisbourg, B0A 1M0
(902) 733-2793
Three o/n units, 1 1/2 shared B&S •
Colour cable TV and radio in
lounge • Non-smoking only

RATES: $32 (1), $40 (2) (STC) •
Full breakfast 7:30-8:30 • Open
May-Oct.

Louisbourg
Louisbourg Harbour Inn
Parker Bagnell, 9 Warren Street,
Louisbourg, B0A 1M0
(902) 733-3222
Century-old sea captain's house •
Eight o/n units, queen, five with
Jacuzzi • Not suitable for children •
No pets, please • Non-smoking only
FEATURES: Balconies overlook
harbour and Fortress • Honeymoon
suite available
RATES: $75-$105 (2), $120 (2,
suite) • Open May 1-Oct. 31 • AE,
DC, MC, Visa accepted • NSRS
Member

Louisbourg
Lupine Tours Bed & Breakfast
Susan Stevens, 7394 Main Street,
Louisbourg, B0A 1M0
(902) 733-2122
Three o/n units, one B&S • Colour
cable TV in living room •
Non-smoking only
FEATURES: Stereo in living room
• Kitchen facilities
RATES: $40 (1), $45 (2) • Full
breakfast • Open year-round • MC,
Visa accepted • Packages available
• NSRS Member

Louisbourg
The Manse
Bed & Breakfast ★★½
Dorothy Brooks, 10 Strathcona
Street, Louisbourg, B0A 1M0
(902) 733-3155
Victorian home overlooking harbour
• Three o/n units, two shared B&S •
Children over 12 yrs welcome
*RATES: $35 (1), $45 (2) (STC) •
Full breakfast • Open Apr. 1-Oct.
31 • Off-season by appointment •
NSRS Member*

Louisdale
Seal Cove
Bed & Breakfast
Vivian Sampson, 341 Main Street,
RR 1, Louisdale, B0E 1V0
(902) 345-2155
From Hwy 104, Exit 46, left at
caution light, 1.5 km (1 mi).
Twenty-five km from causeway •
Three o/n units, one shared B&S
FEATURES: Ocean view from
decks • Coffee/tea • Evening lunch
6-9 p.m. • Dining room • Snacks •
Cleanliness
*RATES: $35 (1), $45 (2), $5 add'l
person over 13 yrs, taxes incl.
(STC) • Full breakfast • Open
May-Oct. 31 CBBBA; NSRS Member*

Lower South River
Peggy's
Bed & Breakfast
Margaret Halloran, RR 3, St.
Andrews, B0H 1X0
(902) 863-3805
Hwy 104, Exit 35 to Rte. 316
South, 8.5 km (5.5 mi) • Three o/n
units, one B&S • TV in living room
• Non-smoking only
*RATES: $30 (1), $40 (2) • Full
breakfast at guests' convenience •
Open May 1-Oct. 31*

Lunenburg
Arbor View Inn
Daniel & Rose Orovec, 216
Dufferin Street, Lunenburg, B0J 2C0
(902) 634-3658
Turn-of-the-century home (c.1907)
on large estate • Six o/n units,
private B • Non-smoking only
FEATURES: Private dining rooms
• Library • Garden paths
*RATES: $75-$125 • Full breakfast
at guests' convenience • Open
year-round • Gourmet weekend
packages and cooking classes
available*

Lunenburg
Blue Rocks Road
Bed and Breakfast
Merrill & Al Heubach, 579 Blue
Rocks Road, RR 1, Lunenburg,
B0J 2C0
Tel & Fax (902) 634-8033
Toll free 1-800-818-3426
Hwy 103, Exit 11. Travel 10 mi left
at stop sign (follow sign to Blue
Rocks); left at next stop sign, 3rd
driveway on left • On Lunenburg Bay
• Three o/n units, one private B, one
shared B&S • Smoking outdoors
FEATURES: English and German
spoken • Library • Veranda •
Full-service bicycle shop with
quality rentals on premises
*RATES: $45-$55 (1), $55-$65 (2),
$15 add'l person • Awesome
breakfast • Open April 1-Oct. 15 •
MC, Visa accepted • Off-season by
reservation • NSFC; SSBBA Member*

Lunenburg
Boscawen Inn &
McLachlan House ★★★½
Michael & Ann O'Dowd, 150
Cumberland Street, Box 1343,
Lunenburg, B0J 2C0

(902) 634-3325
Fax (902) 634-9293
Toll free 1-800-354-5009
Two Registered Heritage Properties
(c.1888, 1905) overlooking harbour
• Twenty-one o/n units
FEATURES: Licensed dining room
• Meeting rooms • Outdoor sundeck
RATES: $40-$120 (2), MAP
available • Open Easter to year-end
• Off-season by arrangement for
groups • AE, ER, MC and Visa
accepted • NSRS; TNS Member

Lunenburg
Commander's
Bed & Breakfast ★★★½
Tom & Judy Jennings, 56 Victoria
Road, Box 864, Lunenburg, B0J 2C0
Tel & Fax (902) 634-3151
Located at intersection of Hwy 3
(Victoria Road) and Hwy 324
(Green St.) • Turn-of-the-century
home • Three o/n units, two shared
B&S • Colour TV/VCR in lounge •
Clock radio in rooms • Junior adults
(over 12) welcome
FEATURES: Three lounges with
books and games • Sundeck and
patio • Interesting naval
memorabilia, ship and train models
and a unique "pig" collection
RATES: $45 (1), $50-$60 (2), $10
add'l person, no GST • Full
breakfast 8-9:30 • Open year-round
• AE, MC and Visa accepted •
NSRS; SSTA Member

Lunenburg
Compass Rose Inn ★★★
Rodger & Suzanne Pike, 15 King
Street, Box 1267, Lunenburg, B0J 2C0
Toll free 1-800-565-8509
Historic Captain's house (c.1825) •
Four o/n units, private B&S •
Children under 2 yrs free

FEATURES: Licensed dining room
• Guest lounge • Outdoor garden
patio • Gift shop
RATES: $60-$75 (1-2) •
Continental breakfast 8:30-9:30,
hot breakfast available • Open mid
Feb.-Dec. • AE, ER, MC and Visa
accepted • Off-season rates •
Packages available • NSRS; UCI
Member

Lunenburg
Daniel Rudolf House
Bed & Breakfast ★★★
Jane & Jack Rowberry, 325 Lincoln
Street, Lunenburg, B0J 2C0
Tel & Fax (902) 634-4110
Historic Home • Three o/n units,
queen with private B, queen & twin
with shared B, clock radio • Colour
cable TV and VCR in lounge • No
pets, please
RATES: $50-$70 (STC) • Open
June-Oct. • Cats on premises •
NSRS Member

Lunenburg
Kaulbach House
Historic Inn ★★★½
Enzo & Karen Padovani, 75 Pelham
Street, Box 1348, Lunenburg, B0J 2C0
Toll free 1-800-568-8818
Registered Heritage Inn (c.1880)
overlooking water • Eight o/n
units, six with private B • Colour
cable TV in rooms • No pets, please
• Non-smoking only
FEATURES: Antique furnishings •
Licensed dining for guests • Room
service • Off-street parking
RATES: $55-$85 (1), $60-$90 (2)
(STC) • Elaborate 3-course
breakfast 8-9:15 • Open year-round
• AE, MC and Visa accepted •
Nov. 1-Apr. 30 by chance or
reservation, off-season rates • CAA;
NSRS; UCI Member

Lunenburg
Lamb & Lobster
Bed and Breakfast
William & Hilary Flower, 619 Blue
Rocks Road, RR 1, Lunenburg,
B0J 2C0
(902) 634-4833
From Lunenburg, 1.3 km (.75 mi)
on Blue Rocks Rd., 0.5 km (0.3 mi)
beyond flashing light • Working
sheep farm with beautiful ocean
view • Three o/n units, 1 1/2 shared
B&S • Colour cable TV in lounge •
Telephone • Not recommended for
small children • Smoking outdoors
FEATURES: Border Collie
demonstrations on request • Fishing
and scuba diving charters
*RATES: $40 (1), $50 (2) • Full
breakfast 7:30-9:30 • Open
June-Oct. 31 • Visa accepted*

Lunenburg
Lincoln House
Bed & Breakfast
Tony & George Morris, 130 Lincoln
Street, Box 322, Lunenburg, B0J 2C0
(902) 634-7179
Restored Victorian home (c. 1860)
located in historic "old town"
over-looking the harbour • Three
o/n units, private S, shared B&S,
sinks in rooms • No pets, please •
Non-smoking only
FEATURES: Victorian tea room
on premises
*RATES: $45-$55 (1), $50-$55 (2),
$10 add'l person • Gourmet
breakfast 8-9:30 • Open May 1-Oct.
31 • Off-season by arrangement*

Lunenburg
Lion Inn
Bed & Breakfast
George, Lois & Mindi Morin, 33
Cornwallis Street, Box 487,
Lunenburg, B0J 2C0
(902) 634-8988
Georgian home (c. 1835) located in
National Historic district • Three
o/n units, private B&S, two rooms
have two double beds • Clock radio
FEATURES: Two separate licensed
dining rooms, one non-smoking •
Fishing and scuba diving charters
*RATES: $60 (1), $65 (2), $10 add'l
person • Full country breakfast •
Open year-round • AE, MC, ER,
Visa accepted • Off-season rates •
NSRS Member*

Lunenburg
Lunenburg Inn
Gail & Don Wallace, 26 Dufferin
Street, Box 1407, Lunenburg, B0J 2C0
(902) 634-3963
Fax (902) 634-9419
Toll free 1-800-565-3963
Registered Heritage Inn (c.1893) •
Seven o/n units, private B&S, two
suites with whirlpool • Colour cable
TV in rooms • Cot available •
Designated smoking area
FEATURES: Full liquor license for
guests • Sitting room • Sundeck •
Covered veranda
*RATES: $65-$100 (1-2), $10 add'l
person • Full breakfast 8-9:30 •
Open year-round • AE, DC, MC,
Visa accepted CAA; IGNS; NSRS;
UCI Member*

Lunenburg
Mainstay Country Inn
Elisabeth & Hubert Gieringer, 167
Victoria Road, Box 1510, Lunenburg,
B0J 2C0

(902) 634-8234
Toll free 1-800-616-4411
Three o/n units, private B
FEATURES: Whirlpool tub
RATES: $50-$60 (1-2) (STC) •
Breakfast 8-10:30 • Open June 15-
Oct. 15 • ER, MC, Visa accepted

Lunenburg
1826 Maplebird House B&B
Dean & Gail Westbrook, 36 Pelham
Street, Box 493, Lunenburg, B0J 2C0
(902) 634-3863
Central location • Three o/n units,
shared B&S • Colour cable TV in
living room • Non-smoking only
FEATURES: Stereo in parlour •
Swimming pool • Parking
RATES: $45 (1), $50 (2), taxes
incl. • Continental breakfast 8-10 •
Open May-Oct. • Cats on premises
• Visa accepted • NSRS Member

Lunenburg
Margaret Murray Bed & Breakfast
Margaret Murray, 20 Lorne Street,
Box 1197, Lunenburg, B0J 2C0
(902) 634-3974
Three o/n units, one shared B&S •
Non-smoking only
RATES: $35 (1), $45-$50 (2)
(STC) • Full breakfast from 7 •
Open year-round • Visa accepted

Lunenburg
Old Hammett Hotel (c.1790)
Wayne & Carolyn Bowser, 120
Montague Street, Box 220,
Lunenburg, B0J 2C0
(902) 634-8165
Harbourside location • Seven
one-bedroom suites, private B&S,
ceiling fan, clock radio, sofa-bed •

Colour cable TV in rooms • Not
recommended for small children •
No pets, please • Designated
smoking area
FEATURES: Housekeeping units
available
RATES: $75-$90 (1-2), $15 add'l
person, weekly $450-$540 • Open
May 1-Oct. 31 • MC, Visa accepted
• Off-season by arrangement •
NSRS Member

Lunenburg
Pelham House Bed & Breakfast ★★★
Geraldine Pauley, 224 Pelham Street,
Box 358, Lunenburg, B0J 2C0
(902) 634-7113
Fax (902) 634-7114
Century sea captain's home 1906 •
Three o/n units, private B, one with
queen and twin beds, two have
queen • Colour TV/VCR in parlour
• Clock radios, hair dryers and fans
on request • Not recommended for
small children • No pets, please •
Vented smoking room
FEATURES: Period decorating
throughout, large collection of
books and periodicals about the sea,
sailing and wooden boats • Laundry
facilities • Kitchen facilities
Afternoon tea • Picnic lunches
available • Sitting room with books
and games • Veranda overlooking
harbour • Restaurants nearby •
Close to downtown and harbour •
Telephone, fax and word processing
services available
RATES: $65-$105 • Full 5-course
breakfast 8-10 • Open year-round •
Cats in owner's quarters • Visa
accepted • Off-season rates •
Special dietary needs
accommodated • NSRS Member

Lunenburg
Rous Brook Landing B&B
Judy & Merrill Strong, 311 Pelham Street, Lunenburg, B0J 2C0
(902) 634-9274
Three o/n units, two full B&S •
Colour cable TV in lounge
FEATURES: Veranda overlooking harbour
RATES: $40 (1), $45-55 (2), $10 add'l person (STC) • Full breakfast 7:30-9 • Open June-Oct. • NSRS Member

Lunenburg
Seaside Tourist Home
Bernice Croft, 24 Hopson Street, Lunenburg, B0J 2C0
(902) 634-8256
One o/n unit, private B • Centrally located colour cable TV •
Non-smoking only
FEATURES: Breakfast area •
Guests' living room
RATES: $50 (STC) • Self-serve continental breakfast • Open June 15-Sept. 15

Lunenburg
Smuggler's Cove Inn
Yvonne Tanner, 139 Montague Street, Box 1090, Lunenburg, B0J 2C0
(902) 634-9200
Fax (902) 634-4822
Check in at Rum Runners Inn, 66-70 Montague Street • Four o/n units, private B&S, clock radio, hide-a-bed • Colour cable TV in rooms • Telephone in rooms
FEATURES: Licensed dining room, 8 a.m.-9 p.m. • Elevator •
Patio off three units
RATES: $100-$125 (2), $5 add'l person • Open year-round • AE, DC, MC, Visa accepted

Lunenburg
Westhaver Haus Bed & Breakfast
Barbara Eisenhauer, 102 Dufferin Street, Lunenburg, B0J 2C0
(902) 634-4937
Three o/n units, one full B&S, one with queen bed and private deck •
Colour cable TV in queen room & living room • Non-smoking only
RATES: $50 (1), $60-$65 (2) • Distinctive breakfast 8 • Open June 1-Oct. 31 • NSRS Member

Mabou
Beaton's Bed & Breakfast
Mrs. Anne Beaton, Box 78, Mabou, B0E 1X0
(902) 945-2806
On Rte. 19, just south of Mabou •
Three o/n units, shared B&S •
Colour cable TV • No pets, please •
Non-smoking only
RATES: $40 (1), $50-$55 (2), $20 add'l person • Full breakfast 8-9 • Open year-round • NSRS Member

Mabou
Clayton Farm Bed & Breakfast
Isaac & Bernadette Smith, Box 33, Mabou, B0E 1X0
Tel & Fax (902) 945-2719
On Rte. 19 just south of Mabou •

 Large old-fashioned farmhouse and working farm on 185-acre peninsula •
Three o/n units, one shared B&S • Non-smoking only

FEATURES: Municipal Registered Heritage Property (c. 1835), furnished with antiques • Close to sandy beach, traditional Scottish square dances, hiking trails and restaurant
RATES: $40 (1), $55-$60 (2), $25 add'l person, no GST • Full breakfast • Open May 1-Oct. 31 • NSFC, NSRS Member

Mabou
Duncreigan Country Inn ★★★½
Eleanor & Charles Mullendore, Box 59, Mabou, B0E 1X0
(902) 945-2207
Toll free 1-800-840-2207
New facility on harbour, antique furnishings • Three o/n rooms, queen beds, one king suite with whirlpool, private B&S • Colour cable TV in rooms • Non-smoking only
FEATURES: Licensed dining room (wheelchair accessible) • Canoe, bikes, eagles • Gift shop and gallery
RATES: $75-$100, $15 add'l person (STC) • Open year-round • Off-season rates available • MC, Visa accepted NSRS; TNS Member

Mabou
Glendyer Mills Bed & Breakfast
Kathy McIntyre, RR 4, Mabou, B0E 1X0
(902) 945-2455
Follow signs from Mabou Village • Older comfortable home • Three o/n units, two double, one two-bedroom suite, two B&S
FEATURES: Heritage Property (c. 1848) filled with antique furniture • Deck with great view of gardens • Donkeys, geese and brook

RATES: $40-$50 (1), $50-$60 (2), $20 add'l person • Full breakfast • Open year-round • NSRS Member

Mabou
Rankins Bed & Breakfast
Donald & Mary Rankin, RR 3, Mabou Harbour, B0E 1X0
(902) 945-2375
Rte. 19 to Mabou Village, turn onto Mabou Harbour Road, 5.5 km (3.5 mi) from St. Mary's Church • Three o/n units, two shared B&S
FEATURES: Magnificent sunrises and sunsets
RATES: $35 (1), $40 (2) (STC) • Full breakfast NSRS Member

Mahone Bay
Abundance Inn B&B
Mimi Findlay, 403 West Main Street, Mahone Bay, B0J 2E0
(902) 624-9943
Award-winning Historic Property • Three o/n units, private B&S, hair dryer and clock radio
FEATURES: Fruit, flowers, chocolates, robes, and toiletries provided • Fireplace • Antiques and folk art • Cooking classes on request
RATES: $80 • Full breakfast at guests' convenience Open year-round by chance or reservation • NSRS Member

Mahone Bay
Amber Rose Inn
Faith & John Piccolo, 319 West
Main Street, Box 397, Mahone Bay,
B0J 2E0
(902) 624-1060
Hwy 103, Exit 11, left at four-way
stop, 2 km (1.5 mi) from Mahone
Bay Harbour, straight up from
monument at main intersection, 1
km (0.5 mi) • Restored Heritage
House (c. 1891), originally J.E.
Lantz General Store • Three queen
suites, private B&S, whirlpool,
clock radio, hair dryer, robes,
fridge, coffee maker • Colour cable
TV in rooms • Telephone on
request • No pets, please • No
smoking in rooms
FEATURES: Lawns and gardens •
Air-conditioning • Craft shop with
locally-made apparel
*RATES: $95-$110 (1-2), $15 add'l
person • Generous breakfast • Open
May-Oct. • Major credit cards
accepted*

Mahone Bay
Bay Abode Bed and
Breakfast & Gallery ★★★
Ger ry & Chris Nolan, 1486
Oakland Road, RR 2, Mahone Bay,
B0J 2E0
(902) 624-1439
In Mahone Bay, 1.7 km (1 mi) from
intersection of Hwy 3 and Oakland
Rd. • Restored farm house (c.
1898), 20-acre landscaped and
forested property • Three o/n`units,
one full B&S • Colour cable
TV/VCR and telephone in living
room • Playpen and cot available •
Children welcome, under 6 yrs free
• No pets, please • Smoking area
FEATURES: Furnished in country
antiques • Extensive library • Large
screened porch • Gardens

Horseshoes, croquet, walking and
ungroomed cross-country ski trail •
Vistas of Mahone Bay and harbour
• Small art gallery (oils)
*RATES: $45-$60, $10 add'l person
• Full breakfast 8-9 • Open
year-round • Visa accepted •
Reservations preferred MBBA;
NSRS; SSTA Member*

Mahone Bay
Dory Inn
Bed & Breakfast
Tillie & John Biebesheimer, 404
Main Street, Box 130, Mahone Bay,
B0J 2E0
(902) 624-6460
Restored Victorian home • Two o/n
units, shared B&S • Colour cable
TV and VCR in parlour •
Designated smoking area
FEATURES: Furnished with
country antiques and early Nova
Scotian collectibles • Books and
games • Rowboat available for
guests at government wharf
*RATES: $40 (1), $45 (2) • Full
country breakfast until 9:30 • Open
year-round*

Mahone Bay
Echo Bay House
Irmtraut Schoen, 335 Sunnybrook
Road, Mahone Bay, B0J 2E0
(902) 624-4853/3735
Between Mahone Bay and
Lunenburg, please call for
directions • Located on an inlet of
Mahone Bay • Two o/n units,
private B Colour cable TV in rooms
• Cot available
FEATURES: Large private garden
• English and German spoken •
Kitchen facilities • Barbecue •
Housekeeping units • Swimming,
sailing • Private wharf • Power boat
tours

RATES: $45-$65 (STC) $10 add'l person Open year-round

Mahone Bay
Edgewater
Bed & Breakfast ★★★
Betty & Dave Hess, 44 Mader's Cove Road, Mahone Bay, B0J 2E0
(902) 624-9382
Fax (902) 624-8733
Just off Rte. 3, enroute to Lunenburg • Restored century home with  waterfront view • Three o/n units, one shared B, one king suite with private B, one double with powder room • TV in lounge • Clock radio and ceiling fan in rooms • Cots available • Children under 10 yrs free • No pets, please • Non-smoking only
FEATURES: TV lounge with games • Sun deck
RATES: $45 (1), $60-$65 (2), $10 add'l person • Full breakfast 8-9 in dining room or on deck • Open year-round • MC, Visa accepted • Off-season rates Nov.-Apr. • MBBA; NSRS; SSBBA; SSTA Member

Mahone Bay
Fairmont House B&B
Thomas Hill & Michael McNair, 654 Main Street, Mahone Bay, B0J 2E0
(902) 624-6173
Toll free 1-800-565-5971
Victorian home (c. 1857) • Three o/n units, private B&S • Colour cable TV/VCR in parlour • Smoking area

FEATURES: Dinners available • Room service available 8-9:30 • Games in parlour
RATES: $50 (1), $60 (2), no GST (STC) • Full breakfast 8-9:30 • Open May 15-Oct. 10 • MC, Visa accepted

Mahone Bay
Heart's Desire
Bed & Breakfast
Jean & Mort Lohnes, 686 Main Street, Mahone Bay, B0J 2E0
(902) 624-8766
Victorian home • Two o/n units, private B&S, one queen bed and balcony, one with two beds and sitting room • Colour cable TV • Ceiling fan in rooms • No pets, please • Non-smoking only
FEATURES: Veranda overlooking bay • Piano, books, games in lounge
RATES: $68 (1-2) • Full breakfast • Open May 1-Oct. 31 • MC, Visa accepted • NSRS Member

Mahone Bay
MacDonald's
Bed & Breakfast
Huguette MacDonald, 397 Main Street, Mahone Bay, B0J 2E0
(902) 624-9365
Hwy 103, Exit 10 or 11 • Three o/n units, shared B • Private and centrally located TVs • Telephone in lounge • Radio in lounge • No pets, please • Non-smoking only
RATES: $35 (1), $50 (2), $10 add'l person • Breakfast 8-9 • Open June 1-Nov. 30 • MC, Visa accepted

Mahone Bay
Once Upon a Time B&B
Lise & Denis Corcoran, 40 Pleasant Street, Box 233, Mahone Bay, B0J 2E0
(902) 624-6383

Elegant secluded Victorian home • Four o/n units, private B&S Centrally located TV • Children 16 yrs and under $14
FEATURES: English and French spoken • Parlour with piano, games • Five minute walk to shore or downtown
RATES: $50-$55 (1), $60-$70 (2), $20 add'l person (STC) • Gourmet breakfast • Open year-round • MC, Visa accepted • Off-season rates $10 less Oct. 15-June 15 • MBBA; NSRS; SSTA Member

Mahone Bay
Sou'Wester Inn ★★★½
Ron & Mabel Redden, 788 Main Street, Box 146, Mahone Bay, B0J 2E0
(902) 624-9296
Victorian shipbuilder's home • Four o/n units, private B&S • Non-smoking only

FEATURES: Antique furniture • Evening tea Parlour with piano and games • Veranda overlooking waterfront • Picnic table • Touring and hiking maps
RATES: $62 (1), $72 (2), $15 add'l person • Full breakfast • Open May 1-Oct. 15 • MC, Visa accepted • CAA, NSRS Member

Mahone Bay
Threadneedle Bed & Breakfast ★★★½
Donald & Mary Gillies, Indian Point Road, Mahone Bay, B0J 2E0
(902) 624-8310
Fax (902) 624-1203
Hwy 103, Exit 10, 5 km (3 mi) from Rte. 3 • Three o/n units, private B • Colour cable TV and VCR in lounge • Radio in rooms • No pets, please
FEATURES: Laundry facilities • Guest kitchenette • Sauna • Private beach • Needlepoint shop
RATES: $60 (1), $70 (2), $15 add'l person (STC) • Breakfast 8-9 • Open May-Mar. • MC, Visa accepted

Mahone Bay
Westhavers Beach Bed & Breakfast
Dorothy & Milton Dorey, 268 Mader's Cove Road, Box 436, Mahone Bay, B0J 2E0
(902) 624-9261/9211
Three o/n units, shared B&S, clock radio, one queen suite with private whirlpool B&S • Colour cable TV in rooms • Smoking outdoors only
FEATURES: View of Mahone Bay's outer harbour and some of its 365 islands from indoors or from the decks
RATES: $45 (1), $55 (2), $70-$80 (suite) • Full breakfast 7:30-9 • Open May 1-Nov. 15 • Visa accepted • NSRS Member

Maitland
Foley House Inn B&B
Lucy Maidment, Box 86, Maitland,
B0N 1T0
(902) 261-2844
From Halifax, Hwy 102, Exit 10 to
Rte. 215. From Truro, Hwy 102,
Exit 14 to Rte. 236 to Rte. 215 •
Three o/n units, shared and private
B • Colour cable TV in lounge •
Children under 12 yrs $6
FEATURES: Licensed dining room
*RATES: $40-$45 (1), $48-$55 (2),
$15 add'l person • Full breakfast •
Open year-round • Visa accepted •
NSRS Member*

Margaree Centre
Browns' Bruaich na H'Aibhne
Bed & Breakfast ★★★
Alice Brown, Box 88, Margaree
Valley, B0E 2C0
(902) 248-2935
Toll free 1-800-575-2935
Off Cabot Trail 6.5 km (4 mi) on
the banks of the Margaree River •
Four o/n units, private B • Colour
cable TV in lounge
FEATURES: Laundry facilities •
Cottage available • Salmon, trout
fishing, river swimming,
cross-country skiing, snowmobiling,
walking trail to eagles' nest
*RATES: $32 (1), $40-$50 (2), $10
add'l person (STC) • Full breakfast
7-9 • Open year-round • MC, Visa
accepted • NSRS Member*

Margaree Forks
Harrison Hill
Bed & Breakfast ★★★
Robin & Marilyn Harrison, Box
561, Margaree Forks, B0E 2A0
(902) 248-2226

Three o/n units, two shared B&S •
TV and VCR in lounge • No pets,
please • Non-smoking only
FEATURES: Music room soirees •
Live theatre • Gift corner
*RATES: $55 (1-2) (STC) •
Breakfast 8-9:30 • Open May
24-Oct. 31 • NSRS Member*

Margaree Forks
McDaniel
Bed & Breakfast
Eleanor & Neil McDaniel, Box 532,
Margaree Forks, B0E 2A0
(902) 248-2734
Century-old home • Two o/n units,
one shared B&S • TV in living
room • No pets, please •
Non-smoking only
FEATURES: Valley scenery •
Salmon pools
*RATES: $40 (1), $50 (2) • Full
breakfast 7-9 • Open May 1-Oct. 31
• Reservations preferred • NSRS
Member*

Margaree Forks
Old Miller Trout Farm
B&B
Pat Wood & John Stinson, 402 Doyles
Road, Margaree Forks, B0E 2A0
(902) 248-2080
250 acre property • Two o/n units,
private B&S • TV in lounge •
Non-smoking only
FEATURES: U-fish farm • Nature
trails
*RATES: $50 (2) • Full breakfast •
Open May 24-Oct. 15*

Margaree Harbour
Chimney Corner
Bed & Breakfast ★★★
Jan & Bob Wheeler, Margaree
Harbour, B0E 2B0
Tel & Fax (902) 235-2104
Shore Rd., Rte. 219, 7 km (4.5 mi)
south of Margaree Harbour • Three
o/n units, one private B&S, one
shared B&S, each room on separate
level • Centrally located TV • Adult
accommodation • Non-smoking only
FEATURES: Evening snack •
Barbecue • Housekeeping cottages
available • Ocean swimming at
private beach • Fax available
*RATES: $45 (1), $55 (2), PST
extra • Full breakfast at 9 • Open
May 15-Oct. 15 • Visa accepted •
Packages available, will cater to
dietary needs • IGNS; NSFC;
NSRS; TIANS Member*

Margaree Harbour
Harbour View Inn
Connie Jennex, Box 52, Margaree
Harbour, B0E 2B0
(902) 235-2314
At junction of Cabot and Ceilidh
Trails • Three o/n units, 1 1/2 B
shared • Colour cable TV in lounge
FEATURES: Ocean swimming
*RATES: $34 (1), $42-$67 (2), $10
add'l person (STC) • Full compli-
mentary breakfast • Open year-round
• MC accepted • NSRS Member*

Margaree Harbour
Mill Valley Farm Bed
& Breakfast ★★★½
Stu & Slawa Lamont, Mill Valley,
Margaree Harbour, B0E 2B0
Tel & Fax (902) 235-2834
From Cabot Trail, turn off at Scotch
Hill, Mill Valley Hwy sign and
keep right • Three o/n units, one B

with Jacuzzi, hand-held shower •
Colour cable TV in living room •
Non-smoking only
FEATURES: View of mountains,
acres of softwood and apple trees •
English, French, German, Russian
and Polish spoken • Olympic gym •
Walking and hiking trails • Cabins
available • Entire property is smoke
free
*RATES: $50 (1), $55 (2) • Full
breakfast 7-10 Open June 1-Oct. 31
• MC, Visa accepted • Call for
reservations • Packages available •
CAA; IGNS; NSRS; TIANS Member*

Margaree Harbour
Ocean Haven
Bed & Breakfast
Joan & Peter Sheehan, Box 54,
Margaree Harbour, B0E 2B0
(902) 235-2329
Off-season (613) 837-4954
Three o/n units, two shared B&S •
Colour TV in lounge • No pets,
please • Non-smoking only
FEATURES: Overlooking ocean
with unobstructed view • Beaches
*RATES: $35 (1), $45 (2), $10 add'l
person • Full breakfast 7:30-8:30 •
Open June 15-Oct. 15 • Cancellation
policy • Reservations recommended*

Margaree Harbour
Taylor's
Bed & Breakfast
Francis & Mary Taylor, RR 1,
Margaree Harbour, B0E 2B0
(902) 235-2652
Approx. 1.5 km (1 mi) south of
Margaree Harbour Bridge •
Century-old house overlooking
Margaree River and Gulf of St.
Lawrence • Three o/n units, one
B&S • TV in living room
*RATES: $32 (1), $40 (2) (STC) • Full
breakfast 8-9 Open May 1-Oct. 31*

Margaree Valley
Normaway Inn ★★★
David MacDonald, Box 101,
Margaree Valley, B0E 2C0
(902) 248-2987
Fax (902) 248-2600
Toll free 1-800-565-9463
On Egypt Rd., 3 km (2 mi) off
Cabot Trail • Tranquil 1920s inn on
250 acres • Nine o/n units, private
B&S
FEATURES: Country gourmet
dining room • Nineteen cabins
available, most with fireplace,
woodstove, some with Jacuzzi
*RATES: MAP $117 (1), $159-$199
(2), $50 add'l person, EP $75 (1),
$75-$115 (2) • Open June 17-Oct.
15 • MC, Visa accepted • IGNS;
NSRS; TNS; UCI Member*

Margaree Valley
Portree
Bed & Breakfast ★★½
Maryon L. Ross, RR 1, Margaree
Valley, B0E 2C0
(902) 248-2728
Cabot Trail to Northeast Margaree,
10 km (6 mi) to Portree Working
farm • Three o/n units, two B&S •
Non-smoking only
FEATURES: Walking trails,
salmon fishing
*RATES: $32 (1), $40-$42 (2), $15
add'l person Breakfast 7:30-9 •
Open May-Oct. • MC, Visa
accepted • Off-season by
reservation • CBBBA; NSFC; NSRS
Member*

Margaree Valley
Valley Bed & Breakfast
Angela Stepaniak, Margaree Valley,
B0E 2C0
(902) 248-2651
Off the Cabot Trail 2 km (1.5 mi),
1 km from Margaree Airport •

Three o/n units, one B&S • TV in
living room • Non-smoking only
*RATES: $35 (1), $40 (2) (STC) •
Full breakfast at guests'
convenience • Open May 15-Oct. 15
• MC, Visa accepted • Off-season
by arrangement*

Marion Bridge
L'il Bit of Heaven
Bed & Breakfast
Bruce & Carol Butts, 371 Trout Brook
Road, Marion Bridge, B0A 1P0
(902) 727-2936
Hwy 125, Exit 7 to Marion Bridge,
left 2.5 km (1.5 mi) on Trout Brook
Rd. • Two o/n units, private and
shared B&S, clock radio • TV in
rooms
FEATURES: Barbecue • River
swimming, boating, fishing
*RATES: $40-$55 (1), $55 (2), $10
add'l person • Full breakfast 7-9 •
Open May-Oct. • Off-season by
arrangement*

Marion Bridge
Riverside
Bed & Breakfast
Lorraine Ferguson, 1818 Hillside
Road, Box 140, Marion Bridge,
B0A 1P0
(902) 727-2615
Hwy 125, Exit 7 to Rte. 327, 14 km
(9 mi) to Marion Bridge, left on
Hillside Rd. 4.5 km (3 mi) • Three
o/n units, shared B • No pets, please
• Non-smoking only
FEATURES: Swimming, boating,
fishing
*RATES: $35 (1), $45 (2), $16 add'l
person, taxes extra (STC) • Full
breakfast 7-9 • Open May 1-Oct. 31
• Visa accepted • NSRS Member*

Marshville
Lazy Lamb Inn B&B
Collette Lunn, Marshville, RR 3,
River John, B0K 1N0
(902) 351-3296
Toll free 1-800-286-1566
On Rte. 6, 15 minutes east of
Tatamagouche, five minutes from
River John • Working hobby farm
with a variety of animals • Three
o/n units, 1 1/2 B&S •
Non-smoking only
FEATURES: Tea room • Sun deck
• Craft shop
*RATES: $45 (1), $50-$55 (2) • Full
breakfast 7-10 • Open May 1-Oct.
31 • Off-season by arrangement •
Packages available*

Masstown
Mingo's
Bed & Breakfast
Jennie & Keith Mingo, Masstown,
RR 1, Debert, B0M 1G0
(902) 662-2561
Hwy 104, Exit 12, 1 km (0.5 mi) on
Rte. 2, from Hwy 102, Exit 14A,
14 km (9 mi) • Three o/n units, 1
1/2 shared B&S Colour cable
TV/VCR in lounge
FEATURES: Den
RATES: *$30 (1), $40 (2) • Full
breakfast • Open year-round • MC,
Visa accepted • NSRS Member*

Masstown
Shady Maple
Bed & Breakfast ★★★
James & Ellen Eisses, RR 1,
Masstown, B0M 1G0
(902) 662-3565
Toll free 1-800-493-5844
Hwy 104, Exit 12, 3 km (2 mi) on
Rte. 2, from Hwy 102, Exit 14A,
12 km (7 mi) in Masstown •
Operating farm, century home •

Three o/n
units, two
shared B&S,
one with
double bed
and daybed,
one with
queen bed,
deluxe suite with waterbed TV in
lounge • Cots and crib available •
Children under 3 yrs free •
Non-smoking only
FEATURES: Fireplace in lounge •
Evening snack • Heated swimming
pool • Whirlpool in suite, outdoor spa
• View of bay from upstairs balcony
*RATES: $32-$40 (1), $40-$65 (2),
$5-$10 add'l person • Full
breakfast • Open year-round • Visa
accepted • Packages available •
NSFC; NSRS Member*

Meteghan
Anchor Inn B&B
Marie & Hans deMan, 8755 Rte. 1,
Box 19, Meteghan Centre, B0W 2K0
(902) 645-3390
On Rte. 1, 2 km (1.5 mi) north of
Meteghan • Three o/n units, shared
B • Colour cable TV in lounge •
Non-smoking only
*RATES: $22.20 (1), $33.30-$38.50
(2), $11.10 add'l person, taxes incl.
• Open May 15-Oct. 15*

Middle Ohio
Five Acres
Bed & Breakfast
Linda & David Ferretti, Middle
Ohio, RR 1, Shelburne, B0T 1W0
(902) 875-4175
Hwy 103, Exit 26 to Rte. 203, 18.5
km (11.5 mi) • Country setting on
MacKay's Lake • Two o/n units,
shared S • No pets, please
FEATURES: Outdoor swimming
pool

RATES: $40 (1), $45 (2), $6 add'l person, taxes incl. • Full breakfast 6-9 • Open year-round • Visa accepted

Middle River
Seven Springs Farm Bed & Breakfast

Kevin & Linda Scherzinger, RR 3, Baddeck, B0E 1B0
Tel & Fax (902) 295-2094
From Margaree turn right at 1st Middle River W sign and 1.6 km (1 mi), from Baddeck take Cabot Trail Exit 7, 13.8 km (8.6 mi) and turn left at MacLennan's Cross, turn right after crossing river, 3.5 km (2.2 mi) to 4th farm on left • Restored 1839 farm house nestled against green hills • Three o/n units, two suites and one single, private B&S • Pets outside only • Smoking outside only
FEATURES: Icelandic horse and working farm with cattle and horses • Gas fireplaces • Trail riding from Sept. 15 to Nov. 1
RATES: $35-$55 (1), $55 (2) • Full breakfast • Open July 1-Nov. 1

Middleton
Fairfield Farm Inn (c. 1886) ★★★

Richard & Shae Griffith, 10 Main Street, Box 1287, Middleton, B0S 1P0
Tel & Fax (902) 825-6989
Toll free 1-800-237-9896
Rte. 1 West • Restored century-old farmhouse on working fruit and vegetable farm within the town of Middleton • Five o/n units, private B, king and queen beds • Colour cable TV and VCR in parlour • Not suitable for children under 16 yrs • No pets, please • Non-smoking only
FEATURES: 110-acre property bordered by Annapolis River • Laundry facilities • Kitchen facilities • Air-conditioning • Nature trails, on-site putting green • Car rentals available
RATES: $45-$55 (1), $50-$60 (2) • Full breakfast • Open year-round • AE, DC, ER, MC, Visa accepted • Nov. 1-Mar. 31 by reservation only • CAA; IGNS; NSRS; UCI Member

Middleton
Falcourt Inn (c. 1920) ★★★½

LeGard family, 8979 Hwy 201 East, RR 3, Middleton, B0S 1P0
(902) 825-3399
Fax (902) 825-3422
Hwy 101 Exit 18 or 18A, Rte. 1 to Rte. 10 to Rte. 201 East Restored 1920 fishing lodge on the Nictaux River with river and mountain view • Six o/n units, private B, one suite Wheelchair accessible • TV and clock radio in rooms • Non-smoking rooms available
FEATURES: 50 m (150 ft) veranda • Laundry facilities • Licensed dining room • Common area • Suite has living room, fireplace and jet tub • River fishing on property
RATES: $70 (1), $75 (2), suite extra • AE, MC, Visa accepted • Packages available • NSRS Member

Middleton
Mount Hanley Austria Inn ★★★
Family Schnetzer, Mount Hanley Road, RR 1, Middleton, B0S 1P0
(902) 825-3744
Hwy 101, Exit 18 to Mount Hanley • Nine o/n units, private B&S, incl. three suites, one with Jacuzzi • TV in rooms • No pets please
FEATURES: Licensed dining room 5-10 p.m. • Austrian and German meals served • Private balconies • Chalet available
RATES: $44 (1), $59 (2), suite extra • Open Easter-Oct. 31 • CAA; IGNS Member

Middleton
Victorian Inn B&B
Gary Hannam, 145 Commercial Street, Box 1065, Middleton, B0S 1P0
(902) 825-6464
Five o/n units, one B&S • TV in lounge • Children under 12 yrs free
FEATURES: Outdoor swimming pool • Craft shop
RATES: $36 (1), $40-$44 (2), $4 add'l person • Continental and full breakfast 8-9:30 • Open year-round • Visa accepted • NSRS Member

Milton
Morton House Inn B&B
Valerie & Jay Blondahl, 147 Main Street, Box 351, Milton, B0T 1P0
(902) 354-2908
Less than two minutes north of Liverpool on Rte. 8, 1 km (0.5 mi) from Exit 19, Hwy 103 • Empire-style mansion (1864) Six o/n units, private B&S • Colour cable TV and radio in lounge • Telephone • No pets, please

FEATURES: Award-winning gardens • Hiking • Canoes • Marina • Bicycles • River swimming • Veranda viewing Mersey River
RATES: $59-$69 (1) (STC) • Full breakfast 7:30-9 • Open year-round • MC, Visa accepted • Off-season rates Oct. 16-May 15 • NSRS Member

Milton
Second Home Bed & Breakfast
Sally Kaulback, 380 Main Street, Milton, B0T 1P0
(902) 354-3573
From Hwy 103, Exit 19 to Rte. 8, 10 minutes from Liverpool Borders the Mersey River • Three o/n units, one full bath • Non-smoking only
RATES: $30 (1), $35 (2) (STC) • Self-serve continental breakfast • Open May 1-Nov. 1 • NSRS Member

Musquodoboit Harbour
Camelot Inn ★★★
Ms. P.M. "Charlie" Holgate, Box 31, Musquodoboit Harbour, B0J 2L0
(902) 889-2198
On Hwy 7E • Five acres (2 hectares) of woodland overlooking river rapids and salmon pool • Five o/n units, one B&S, two S • No pets, please • Non-smoking only
FEATURES: Lounge with fireplace and library • River swimming
RATES: $34-$45 (1), $52-$60 (2), $70-$80 (Family rooms 3-4) • Breakfast extra 7:30-9 • Open year-round • MC, Visa accepted • NSRS Member

Musquodoboit Harbour
Murphy's
Bed & Breakfast
Ralph & Judith Murphy, 1843
Ostrea Lake Road, RR 1,
Musquodoboit Harbour, B0J 2L0
(902) 889-2779
On Ostrea Lake Rd. 213 m (233 yd)
off Hwy 7 • Three o/n units, two
shared B • Non-smoking only
FEATURES: Lounge
*RATES: $30 (1), $39 (2) $5 add'l
person (STC) • Open May 1-Oct. 31
• Off-season by reservation • NSRS
Member*

Musquodoboit Harbour
Seaview Fisherman's
Home B&B
Mildred & Ivan Kent, Pleasant
Point, RR 1, Musquodoboit
Harbour, B0J 2L0
(902) 889-2561
Off Rte. 7, Ostrea Lake-Pleasant
Point Rd. to Kent Rd. 13 km (8
mi.) • House (c. 1861) on a 20-acre
island (causeway) with lighthouse •
Three o/n units, two shared B&S
and 1/2 B • TV in lounge • No pets,
please • Non-smoking rooms
FEATURES: Fifteen years in
business • Antiques • Small
housekeeping cottage available
(couples only) • Ocean view and
beach area, walking trails • Fishing
stand. boats nearby
*RATES: $35 (1), $40-$45 (2), $10
add'l person • Full breakfast 7-9 •
Open Apr. 1-Oct. 31 • Visa
accepted • Off-season by
reservation • NSFC; NSRS; Pantel
Member*

Musquodoboit Harbour
Tea & Treats
Cafe & Inn
Jens & Renate Ziemsen,
Musquodoboit Harbour, B0J 2L0
(902) 889-2880
Toll free 1-800-565-0828
Three o/n units, private B&S •
Colour cable TV in rooms
FEATURES: Licensed restaurant,
Canadian and German cuisine •
Patio deck • Playground •
Babysitting • Outdoor above-ground
swimming pool • Hiking, biking
*RATES: $45 (1), $55-$65(2), $10
add'l person (STC) • Continental
breakfast 8-10:30 • Open May
15 Oct. 15 AE, MC, Visa accepted •
NSRS Member*

Musquodoboit Harbour
Wayward Goose Inn
★★★
Judy & Randy Skaling, 343 West
Petpeswick Road, Musquodoboit
Harbour, B0J 2L0
Tel & Fax (902) 889-3654
Rte. 7, then road to West
Petpeswick, 1.7 km (1 mi) on left •
Three o/n units, private B, one
whirlpool • Colour cable TV/VCR
in lounge • No pets, please •
Non-smoking only
FEATURES: Stereo and fireplace
in lounge • Fishing • Barbecue •
Pool table, canoe, sailboat and
rowboat free for guests • Swimming
• Walking trail and cross-country
skiing • Small boat docking/
deep-water anchorage
*RATES: $40-$60 (1), $49-$69 (2),
$10 add'l person (STC) • Full
breakfast 7:30-9 • Open year-round
• Visa accepted Nov.-Apr. by
reservation • Honeymoon suite and
packages available • ESTA; NSFC;
NSRS Member*

Newburn
Country Homestead B&B
Karsa Veinotte, 126 Veinotte Road,
Newburn, RR 1, Barss Corner,
B0R 1A0
(902) 644-2196
Hwy 103, Exit 11, Rte. 324 North
25 km (15.5 mi) • Three o/n units,
shared B&S • TV in living room •
Radio in living room • Pets
permitted, usually on leash •
Smoking in designated areas only
FEATURES: French spoken
*RATES: $40 (1), $45 (2) • Full
breakfast 7:30-9 • Open May 1-Oct.
31 • Cats on premises • Off-season
by arrangement • NSRS Member*

Newburn
Hackmatack Farm Bed & Breakfast
Heather Sanft & Janet Southwell,
RR 3, Mahone Bay, B0J 2E0
(902) 644-2415
Fax (902) 644-3614
From Hwy 103, Exit 11, 24 km (15
mi) inland through the Cornwalls to
Newburne, right on Walburne Rd. •
Two o/n units, one shared B •
Non-smoking only
FEATURES: Cottage available
*RATES: $35 (1), $40 (2), $10 add'l
person (STC) • Full breakfast • Open
May-Oct. • Visa accepted •
Off-season rates by arrangement •
NSRS Member*

New Germany
Oakwood Inn B&B
Rosemary & David Furlong, 5175
Hwy 10, RR 2, New Germany,
B0R 1E0
(902) 644-1291
Hwy 103, Exit 12, 23 km (14.5 mi)
on Rte. 10 • Three o/n units, shared

B&S • Colour cable TV in living
room • Non-smoking only
*RATES: $40 (1), $50 (2), $10 add'l
person • Continental breakfast 7-9 •
Open year-round • Visa accepted
NSRS Member*

New Glasgow
MacKay's Bed & Breakfast
Mrs. Evelyn MacKay, 44 High
Street, New Glasgow, B2H 2W6
(902) 752-5889

Hwy 104,
Exit 25 •
Three o/n
units, shared
B • Colour
cable TV in
lounge •
Radio
*RATES: $35
(1), $45-$50 (2), $10 add'l person •
Breakfast 7:30-9 • Open June 15-
Sept. 15 • No credit cards •
Off-season by reservation • NSRS
Member*

New Glasgow
Wynward Inn B&B
Dorothy Leahy Walsh, 71 Stellarton
Road, New Glasgow, B2H 1L7
(902) 752-4527
Hwy 106, Exit 2 to Abercrombie;
Hwy 104, Exits 23 or 24 • Six o/n
units, three shared B&S, one private
B&S • Colour cable TV and radio in
lounge
FEATURES: Radio in lounge •
Picnic table • Swings • Swimming
pool
*RATES: $30-$40 (1), $36-$45 (2),
$5 add'l person • Continental
breakfast 5-11 • Open year-round •
MC, Visa accepted*

Newport Landing
Highfield House
Bed & Breakfast

Allen & Judith Tamsett, 249
Belmont Road, Box 17, Newport,
Avondale, B0N 2A0
(902) 757-3739
Hwy 101, Exit 5 to Rte. 14 to
Brooklyn & follow signs • Three
o/n units, all with private B&S • No
pets, please • Non-smoking only
*RATES: $52 (1), $62 (2) • Full
breakfast 8-9 • Open year-round •
Please call for reservations • NSRS
Member*

Newport Station
Wavertree Inn ★★★

Jane Reid Stevens, 5178 Hwy 1,
Newport Station, B0N 2B0
(902) 798-5864
On Rte. 1 between St. Croix &
Windsor • Victorian country home •
Three o/n units, one shared B •
Colour cable TV in lounge •
Children under 5 yrs free
FEATURES: Furnished with
antiques • Den with woodstove and
games • Library • Sun room •
Barbecue • Landscaped gardens, 3
acres
*RATES: $40 (1), $50 (2), $8 add'l
person • Full breakfast 7:30-9:30 •
Open year-round • Visa accepted
Packages available • NSRS Member*

Nictaux Falls
Country Charm and
Comfort Break
Bed & Breakfast

Ilene Orr, 2305 Bloomington Road,
Nictaux Falls, Box 259,
Greenwood, B0P 1N0
(902) 825-2566
From Middleton, five minutes from
junction of Rte. 1 and Hwy 10;

from Greenwood, 10 mins. (Ward
Rd. to 201 W left on Hwy 10), Hwy
10 left at Bloomington sign keep left
0.6 km to Nictaux Falls Bridge and
then 0.1 km to first left • Restored
Queen Anne Revival century home •
Three o/n units, two with queen beds
and private B, one with single bed,
shared B • Colour TV and telephone
• Cot available • No pets, please •
Not suitable for children under 16 •
Non-smoking only
FEATURES: Evening tea, coffee •
Herb and vegetable gardens •
Hiking, cycling, cross-country
skiing, tubing, nature trails and
picnic site • Crafts for sale
*RATES: $45 (1), $49-$55 (2), $12
add'l person (STC) • Breakfast •
Open year-round • Nov.-April
reservations preferred •
Weekly/monthly rates, packages and
day trips available*

North East Margaree
Heart of Harts ★★★

Brooks Hart & Ethna Gillis, Box
21, North East Margaree, B0E 2H0
(902) 248-2765
Fax (902) 248-2606
Off Cabot Trail, 0.4 km (0.2 mi) •
1880s farmhouse furnished with
antiques and coloured glass • Five
o/n units, two shared B • Satellite
TV • Smoking outside only
FEATURES: Landscaped grounds,
including annuals and Heritage
Farm perennials • Dinner by
reservation at 7 p.m., $30/person
*RATES: $40-$50 (1), $55-$65 (2) •
Full Scottish breakfast • Open
year-round • MC, Visa accepted •
NSRS Member*

North East Point
(Cape Sable Island)
Penney Estate
Bed & Breakfast Ltd.
Lois & Herbert Atkinson, Box 57,
Barrington Passage, B0W 1G0
(902) 745-1516
On Rte. 330 (Cape Sable Island) off
Rte. 3, 4 Penney Beach Rd., North
East Point • Three o/n units, two
shared B&S • Colour cable TV
*RATES: $40 (1), $50 (2), $10 add'l
person • Full breakfast 7-9 • Open
year-round • MC, Visa accepted*

North Ingonish
Bear Cove
Bed & Breakfast
Jean & Gerald Brown, Box 41,
North Ingonish, B0C 1K0
(902) 285-2699
Two o/n units, shared B&S • No
pets, please • Non-smoking only
FEATURES: View of Cape
Smokey from balcony
*RATES: $40 (1), $45 (2), $10 add'l
person (STC) • Open June 1-Oct. 15*

North River Bridge
Stephen's
Bed & Breakfast
Murdena & Bob Stephen, 279
Murray Road, North River Bridge
RR 4, B0E 1B0
(902) 929-2860
Hwy 105, Exit 11, 19 km (12 mi)
north on Cabot Trail • Restored
country home overlooking North
River • Three o/n units, shared B&S
• TV and VCR in living room •
Non-smoking only
FEATURES: Movies available
*RATES: $50 • Full breakfast 8 •
Open May 15-Oct. 15 • NSRS
Member*

North Sydney
Alexandra Shebib's
Bed & Breakfast
Mrs. Alexandra Shebib, 88 Queen
Street, North Sydney, B2A 1A6
(902) 794-4876
Approx. 2 km (1.5 mi) west of
Newfoundland ferry terminal • Five
o/n units, four with washbasin, 2 1/2
shared B • TV in lounge • Children
under 5 yrs free
*RATES: $35 (1), $45-$50 (2), $10
add'l person Full breakfast 7:30-9 •
Open year-round • Visa accepted
Off-season rates Oct. 15-Apr. 15 •
NSRS Member*

North Sydney
Dove House
Bed & Breakfast
Helene Reashore, 108 Queen Street,
North Sydney, B2A 1A6
(902) 794-1055
Hwy 125, Exit 2 • Three o/n units,
private and two shared B• TV in
rooms • Non-smoking only
FEATURES: View of Sydney
Harbour from large veranda and
upper deck • Near Newfoundland
ferry
*RATES: $50 (shared B), $60 (private
B), $10 add'l person • Full breakfast
6:30-9:30 • Open May 1-Oct. 31 •
MC, Visa accepted • Off-season by
arrangement • NSRS Member*

North Sydney
Heritage Home
Bed & Breakfast
Juana Moreland, 110 Queen Street,
North Sydney, B2A 1A6
(902) 794-4815
Hwy 125, Exit 2 • Victorian home
(c. 1860) with commanding view of
harbour from all rooms • Four o/n

units, private B&S • Colour cable
TV in family room
FEATURES: Antiques • Local
artwork • Library • Housekeeping
unit available • Two minutes from
Newfoundland ferry
RATES: $45 (1), $50-$70 (2), $10
add'l person (STC) • Full breakfast
7:30-9 • Open year-round • MC,
Visa accepted • Check out 10 a.m. •
IGNS; TIANS Member

North Sydney
Scottland Farm
Bed & Breakfast
Scott & Pamela Andrews, 2189
Shore Road, Point Edward, RR 1,
North Sydney, B2A 3L7
(902) 564-0074
Hwy 105, Exit 4 or 5 to Rte .239,
approx. 10 km (6 mi) • Working
dairy farm • Two o/n units, shared
B&S • Colour cable TV and VCR in
lounge • Children welcome • No
smoking in rooms
RATES: $38.35 (1), $44.40 (2),
taxes incl. • Breakfast 7-9 • Open
May-Oct.

Nyanza
Don-El-Mar
Bed & Breakfast
Brian Plant, Nyanza, RR 3,
Baddeck, B0E 1B0
(902) 295-1142/2564
Hwy 105, 17 km (10.5 mi) west of
Exit 8 • Three o/n units, shared B&S
RATES: $30 (1), $40 (2) • Full
breakfast 7:30-9:30 • Open May
15-Oct.31

Old Barns
Yuill's
Bed & Breakfast ★★★
Florence M. Yuill & sons, RR 1,
Truro, B2N 5A9

(902) 893-3797, 895-1847
Hwy 102, Exit 14, Rte. 236, 8 km
(5 mi) to Old Barns, flashing amber
light • Three o/n units, king, double,
twin, one shared B&S
RATES: $35 (1), $45 (2) • Full
breakfast 7:30-9 • Open June
1-Sept. 30 • Visa accepted • NSRS
Member

Oxford
Lea Side
Bed & Breakfast ★★★
J. Wallace, 177 Water Street,
Oxford, B0M 1P0
(902) 447-3039
Hwy 104, Exit 6, turn north into
town • Comfortable, restored "turn-
of-the-century" home • Three o/n
units, 1 1/2 shared B&S, two with
queen, one with twin beds • Colour
cable TV in lounge • Smoking areas
provided
FEATURES: Tastefully furnished
with antiques • Five-course
candlelight dinner by reservation •
Evening lunch • Electronic organ and
stereo in lounge • Works of art on
display • Picnic tables and barbecue •
Play, game area
RATES: $40-$45 (1), $45-$50 (2),
$10 add'l person, no GST • Full
breakfast • Open year-round • MC,
Visa accepted • IGNS; NSRS
Member

Paradise
Paradise Inn B&B
Claude & Kim Grimard, 116
Paradise Lane, Box 24, Paradise,
B0S 1R0
(902) 584-3934
Hwy 101, Exit 19, just off Rte. 1 •
Three o/n units, private & shared B
• Not suitable for children • No
pets, please • Non-smoking only
FEATURES: Evening refreshments
• Outdoor seating • Lawn games
RATES: $40-$50 (1), $45-$55 (2) •
Full breakfast 8-9 • Open
year-round

Paradise
Paradise Tourist Haven
Elizabeth Greenlaw, Box 35,
Paradise, B0S 1R0
(902) 584-3749
On Rte. 1, 8 km (5 mi) east of
Bridgetown • Three o/n units, 2 1/2
shared B • Colour cable TV in
lounge • Non-smoking only
FEATURES: Laundry facilities •
Kitchen facilities • Complimentary
evening beverage
RATES: $30 (1), $40 (2), $5 add'l
person • Continental breakfast 7-9 •
Open June 1-Aug. 30

Parrsboro
Gillespie House
Bed & Breakfast
Shirley Cormier, 64 Main Street,
Box 464, Parrsboro, B0M 1S0
(902) 254-3196
Three o/n units, 2 1/2 B&S • Cable
TV and telephone in lounge • Radio
in rooms
RATES: $40 (2), $10 add'l person
(STC) • Breakfast 7-10 • Open
May-Oct. • Off-season by
reservation

Parrsboro
Knowlton House
Bed & Breakfast
Keith & Joyce Knowlton, 21 Western
Avenue, Parrsboro, B0M 1S0
(902) 254-2773
Three o/n units, Three shared B&S
• Colour cable TV in lounge • No
pets, please • Non-smoking only
FEATURES: Bird watching
RATES: $40 (1), $45-$50 (2), $10
add'l person (STC) • Full breakfast
7:30-8:30 • Open June 23-Sept. 18
• NSRS Member

Parrsboro
Maple Inn
Trevor & Anne McNelly, 17
Western Avenue, Box 457,
Parrsboro, B0M 1S0
(902) 254-3735
Eight o/n units, six private and two
shared B, one two-bedroom suite
with king-size canopied bed and
Jacuzzi • Colour cable TV in lounge
• Radio • Pay phone • Infants free
No pets, please • Non-smoking only
RATES: $45-$70 (1-2), $80 (suite),
$10 add'l person • Full breakfast
7:30-8:30 • AE, MC, Visa accepted
NSRS Member

Parrsboro
Parrsboro Mansion
B&B ★★★
Anita & Wolfgang Mueller, 15
Eastern Avenue, Box 579,
Parrsboro, B0M 1S0
(902) 254-3339
Fax (902) 254-2585
Decorated with original European
modern art • Three o/n units, shared
B&S, ceiling fan • Colour cable TV
• Clock radio • No pets, please • No
smoking

FEATURES: Laundry facilities • Large bay windows • Bicycles available • Copying service
RATES: $49-$55 (1), $54-$59 (2), $10 add'l person • Full European breakfast 8-10 • Season June 1-Sept. 30 • MC, Visa accepted • Off-season by arrangement • NSRS Member

Parrsboro
White House
Muriel McWhinnie, Upper Main Street, Box 96, Parrsboro, B0M 1S0
(902) 254-2387
Five o/n units, 1 1/2 shared B • Private and centrally located TVs • Radio • Children under 12 yrs free
RATES: $30 (1), $45 (2), $5 add'l person

Peggy's Cove
Breakwater Inn
Bed & Breakfast
Crystal Crooks, Peggy's Cove, B0J 2N0
(902) 823-2440
Completely renovated fisherman's home in Peggy's Cove • Three o/n units, private B&S, whirlpool • TV in rooms • No pets, please • Non-smoking only
RATES: $85 (STC) • Continental breakfast • Open year-round • MC, Visa accepted

Peggy's Cove
Peggy's Cove
Bed & Breakfast
Audrey O'Leary, 19 Church Road, Peggy's Cove, B0J 2N0
(902) 823-2265
Spectacular view from large downstairs front and rear decks • Five o/n units, one private and two shared full B • TV/VCR in lounge, two rooms • Non-smoking only

FEATURES: Four rooms feature patio doors opening onto large shared balcony overlooking Peggy's Cove
RATES: $60-$70 (2), $15 add'l person • Full breakfast • Open May 15-Oct. 15 • AE, MC, Visa accepted Weekly $350-$425 • Off-season by chance or reservation only • NSRS Member

Petite Riviere
Little River
Bed & Breakfast ★★★
Joan Patterson, 5666 Rte. 331, Box 2A-4, Petite Riviere, B0J 2P0
(902) 688-1339
Hwy 103, Exit 15 to Italy Cross, to Petite Riviere Rte. 331 • Three o/n units, one shared B, one private bath (Jacuzzi tub, queen bed) • Non-smoking only
FEATURES: Large deck • Barbecue • Nature walks, bird-watching
RATES: $40 (1), $50 (2), $65 (Queen) • Full breakfast • Open year-round • NSRS Member

Pictou
Braeside Inn ★★★½
Michael & Anne Emmett, 126 Front
Street, Box 810, Pictou, B0K 1H0
(902) 485-5046
Fax (902) 485-1701
Toll free 1-800-613-7701
Twenty o/n units, mostly private B
• TV in rooms • Telephone in
rooms • Children under 2 yrs free
FEATURES: Licensed A/C dining
rooms overlooking harbour •
Summer deck dining • Casual dress
code • Conference and banquet
facilities
*RATES: $55-$95 (1), $55-$100 (2),
$6 add'l person • Open year-round
• AE, MC, Visa accepted •
Packages available • CAA; IGNS,
NSRS; TNS Member*

Pictou
Consulate Inn ★★★
Floyd & Claudette Brine, 157
Water Street, Pictou, B0K 1H0
(902) 485-4554
Four o/n units, private B&S •
Colour cable TV in all rooms
*RATES: $50-$80 (2) (STC) •
Continental breakfast 8-9 • Open
year-round • AE, MC, Visa
accepted • CAA; IGNS; NSRS
Member*

Pictou
Customs House Inn
David & Douglas DesBarres, 38 Depot
Street, Box 1542, Pictou, B0K 1H0
(902) 485-4546
Brick and sandstone building (c.
1870) with antique furnishings • Nine
o/n units, private B&S, most with
original fireplaces • Colour cable TV
in rooms • Telephone in rooms •
Non-smoking rooms available
FEATURES: On Pictou waterfront
with view of harbour • Licensed

restaurant • Lounge •
Air-conditioning • Kitchenette
available • Walking distance to all
attractions
*RATES: $69-$109 (STC) •
Continental breakfast • Open
year-round • MC, Visa accepted •
Off-season rates*

Pictou
Jardine's Bed & Breakfast
Debbie Jardine, 202 Faulkland
Street, Box 1642, Pictou, B0K 1H0
(902) 485-8580
One suite, private B • TV and
stereo in room
FEATURES: Afternoon tea
*RATES: $65 • Continental
breakfast 8-9 • Cats on premises*

Pictou
Linden Arms Bed & Breakfast ★★½
Earle & Nadine Maskell, 62 Martha
Street, Pictou, B0K 1H0
(902) 485-6565
Three o/n units, one shared B&S •
Cable TV in rooms • Radio • Crib
available • Non-smoking only
*RATES: $30 (1), $40 (2), $10 add'l
person • Continental breakfast 7-9 •
Open June 1-Sept. 30 • Off-season
by reservation • NSRS Member*

Pictou
Strathyre House Bed & Breakfast
Jean & Hugh McCrome, 2713 West
River Road, Lyons Brook, Pictou,
B0K 1H0
(902) 485-3495
On Rte. 376, 8 km (4 mi) from PEI
ferry • Two o/n units, shared B&S •
Non-smoking only

FEATURES: Living area •
Walking trails on 45 acres
*RATES: $45-$50 (2), $10 add'l
person (STC)* • *Full breakfast* •
Open year-round • *Visa accepted*

Pictou
Walker Inn (c. 1865) ★★★
Felix & Theresa Walker, 34
Coleraine Street, Pictou, B0K 1H0
(902) 485-1433
Registered Historic Property in
historic Pictou • Ten o/n units,
private B, honeymoon room •
Colour cable TV in rooms • No
smoking in rooms
FEATURES: Licensed dining room
• Meeting room and library
*RATES: $55 (1), $69-$75 (2), $10
add'l person* • *Open year-round* •
Continental breakfast 7:30-9 • *AE,
MC, Visa accepted* • *Off-season
rates Oct. 16-May 31* • *CAA;
HIAC; NSRS Member*

Pictou
W.H. Davies House
Bed & Breakfast
(c. 1855) ★★½
Cathy & Brian MacKinnon, 90 Front
Street, Box 423, Pictou, B0K 1H0
(902) 485-4864
Located on Pictou waterfront •
Large Victorian home decorated
with period furniture • Three o/n
units, one private B&S, one shared
B&S • Colour cable TV in two
rooms • No pets, please • Children
welcome • Non-smoking only
*RATES: $35-$45 (1), $40-$50 (2),
$5-$10 add'l person* • *Continental
breakfast 8-10* • *Open year-round* •
Visa accepted • *NSRS Member*

Pictou
Willow House Inn
(c. 1840)
Robert & Arvell Cormier, 11
Willow Street, Pictou, B0K 1H0
(902) 485-5740
Registered Historic Property in
downtown area • Ten o/n units, six
private and two shared B • Colour
cable TV in rooms • No smoking in
rooms
FEATURES: Dinner available
*RATES: $40-$60 (1), $45-$70 (2),
$5-$10 add'l person* • *Full breakfast
7:30-9* • *Open year-round* • *MC, Visa
accepted* • *CAA; NSRS Member*

Pleasantville
Blue Waters
Bed & Breakfast
Joyce & Don Goodspeed, 178 Pentz
Road, RR 1, Pleasantville, B0R 1G0
(902) 688-1007
Rte. 331 south 15 km (9 mi) from
Bridgewater, on LaHave River •
Newly renovated house • Two o/n
units, shared B&S • Non-smoking
only
FEATURES: Cottage available
*RATES: $45, $65 (2 - cottage), $10
add'l person* • *Full breakfast* •
Open June 1-Sept. 30

Pleasantville
Harrises' Bed & Breakfast
Bob & May Harris, 1056 Mt.
Pleasant Road, RR 1, Pleasantville,
B0R 1G0
(902) 688-2234
Hwy 103, Exit 15 to Petite Riviere,
turn left to West Dublin, left again
at West Dublin to Mt. Pleasant (3.5
km) or Exit 12 (Hwy 103) to Rte.
331 in Bridgewater, left to West
LaHave, turn right to Mt. Pleasant
(5 km) • Renovated 1910 house
overlooking Huey Lake • Three o/n
units, one full B&S, fans and hair
dryers in each room • Clock radios
• Non-smoking only
*RATES: $35-$40 (1), $43-$45 (2) •
Full breakfast 7-8:30 • Open May
15-Oct. 15 • Reservations preferred
• NSFC; NSRS; SSTA Member*

Plympton
Japanese Inn
(MOKUSHI-DO
RYOKAN)
Tom Haynes-Paton, 7213 Rte. 1,
Box 44, Plympton, B0W 2R0
(902) 837-5692
Beach front of St. Mary's Bay •
Three o/n units, two shared B
FEATURES: Japanese interior
including two hori-gotatsu (sunken
tables) • Japanese spoken • Kitchen
Fireplace • Two large Japanese
decks • Zen garden • Shuffleboard •
Whale-watching • Japanese
language and cultural immersion
courses available
*RATES: Weekends $450, week
$1000, month $3000 (2) • Open
year-round • Call for details*

Plympton
Stagecoach Inn B&B
Alma & Frank Havenga, Hwy 101,
Plympton, B0W 2R0
(902) 837-7335/7276
Registered Heritage Property (1798)
• Five o/n units, one private and 1
1/2 shared B • Colour cable TV/
VCR in lounge
FEATURES: Super Nintendo in
lounge • Library • Overlooking St.
Mary's Bay
*RATES: $29 (1), $36-$40 (2), $7
add'l person • Full breakfast
7:30-9:30 • Open June 1-Oct. 30 •
Visa accepted • Off-season by
reservation • NSRS Member*

Pomquet
Porter's
Bed and Breakfast ★★
George & Margaret Porter, 32
Pomquet Road, RR 7, Upper
Pomquet, Antigonish, B2G 2L4
(902) 386-2196
Hwy 104, 16 km (10 mi) east of

Antigonish;
from
Pomquet/St.
Andrews
intersection,
north 3 km
(2 mi) to
Pomquet
Point Rd. •
Large farm house • Four o/n units,
two shared Bs • TV in lounge
FEATURES: Separate guest lounge
*RATES: $30 (1), $40 (2), $10 add'l
person • Breakfast at guests'
convenience • Open May 1-Oct. 30
Off-season by reservation only •
NSFC Member*

Port Clyde
MacLaren Inn B&B
Mrs. Eva Haeghaert, Port Clyde,
Shelburne, B0W 2S0
(902) 637-3296
Hwy 103, Exit 28 • Victorian
house, waterfront, great view •
Three o/n units, one shared B
FEATURES: Coffee
*RATES: $35 (1), $45 (2) (STC) •
Full breakfast • Open June 1-Oct. 31*

Port Greville
Greville Bay
Bed & Breakfast
Douglas & Edith Allen, 24
Fletcher's Hill Loop, Box 32, Port
Greville, B0M 1T0
(902) 348-2418
West of Parrsborro, 16 km (10 mi) on
Rte. 209 • Three o/n units, 1 1/2 B&S
• TV, radio and telephone in lounge
*RATES: $30 (1), $40 (2) •
Breakfast 7-10 • Open May 31-
Oct. 1 • Off-season by reservation •
NSRS Member*

Port Hawkesbury
Harbourview
Bed & Breakfast
Marlene Pase, 209 Granville Street,
Port Hawkesbury, B0E 2V0
(902) 625-3224
From Causeway approx. 5 km (3 mi)
on Rte. 4 to Port Hawkesbury, take
Granville St. exit • Ferry captain
James Embree House (c.1880), a
restored Provincial Heritage Property
on the waterfront • Three o/n units,
one private and one shared B&S • No
pets, please • Non-smoking only
FEATURES: Evening tea and
conversation in parlour • Parking in
rear
*RATES: $43-$53 (2) (STC) • Full
breakfast at guests' convenience •*

*Open May 1-Oct. 15 • NSRS
Member*

Port Hood
Gillis' Bed & Breakfast
C.B. Gillis, RR 2, Port Hood, B0E 2W0
(902) 787-3037
Rte. 19 to Hawthorne Road, 0.8 km
(0.5 mi) • Quiet country home
FEATURES: Two o/n units, shared
B&S • No smoking in rooms
*RATES: $32 (1), $40 (2) • Full
breakfast 8-9 • Open June 1-Oct. 31*

Port Howe
The Apple Inn B&B
Edward & Linda Benoit, 7675 Rte.
6 (Sunrise Trail), Box 28, Port
Howe, B0K 1K0
(902) 243-2814
Off-season (508) 627-5493
Restored antique farm house
(c.1885) • Three o/n units, one
queen room, one twin room, family
room with queen, two single and
crib, 2 1/2 shared B • TV/VCR in
lounge • No pets, please • Children
welcome • Non-smoking only
FEATURES: Overlooks 45 scenic
acres and saltwater inlet •
Prize-winning breads & muffins at
breakfast • Library with stereo •
barbecue • Picnic table and play
area • Movies nightly (over 300 to
choose from), many children's
movies
*RATES: $40 (1), $50 (2), $70
(family room) • Full breakfast •
Open June 26-Aug. 29 • IGNS;
NSRS Member*

Port Howe
Eagle Roost B&B
Ed & Diane Hanlon, 8903 Hwy
321, Port Howe, Rockley, B0K 1K0
(902) 447-3359
From New Brunswick border, 42
km (26 mi) east on Rte. 6 to Rte.
321, then 2 km south; 7 km (4.5
mi) west of Pugwash • 35 acres on
tidal river • Two o/n units, two
shared B&S • Cot available • Pets
permitted • Smoking area
FEATURES: Evening snack •
Lawns and gardens • Fish pond •
Walking trails
*RATES: $35 (1), $45 (2), $10 add'l
person (STC) • Full country
breakfast • Hunting and fishing
packages available in season • Visa
accepted*

Port Royal
Auberge Sieur de Monts Inn
Leona & Stefan Straka, Port Royal,
Box 2055, RR 2, Granville Ferry,
B0S 1K0
(902) 532-5852
Seven o/n units, private and shared
B&S, one two-bedroom suite •
Children under 16 yrs free
FEATURES: Kitchen facilities •
Fireplaces
*RATES: $39-$55 (2), $85 (suite),
(STC) • Breakfast available • Open
May-Oct. • MC, Visa accepted •
NSRS Member*

Port Royal
Thorne Cove Farm Bed & Breakfast
Lynne Mason & Jim Morrissey,
Karsdale, Box 2111, RR 2,
Granville Ferry, B0S 1K0
Tel & Fax (902) 532-7871

Hwy 101, Exit 22 to Hwy 8 to
Annapolis Royal, right to Hwy 1,
left after causeway 14 km (9 mi) to
Karsdale • Three o/n units, shared B
• TV and VCR in lounge • Radio in
rooms • Non-smoking only
FEATURES: Walking trails •
Horseback riding
*RATES: $30-$45, $10 add'l person
• Full breakfast 8:30-10 • Open
June-Oct. • MC, Visa accepted •
NSRS Member*

Port Williams
Carwarden Bed & Breakfast ★★★
Mary McMahon, 640 Church Street,
RR 1, Port Williams, B0P 1T0
(902) 678-7827
From Hwy 101, Exit 11 to Rte. 1,
right to Rte. 358, left 4.4 km on Rte.
358 to Church St., left 2.3 km on

Church St.
Registered
Heritage
Property
with
sweeping
view of
dykelands
from
veranda • Three o/n units, two with
vanity basin, one private and one
shared B&S • No pets, please •
Non-smoking only
FEATURES: Quiet and peaceful •
Evening tea • Antique furnishings •
Drawing room for guest use •
Shady lawns • U-Pick orchard • Ten
minutes to Atlantic Theatre Festival
*RATES: $45 (1), $55 (2), $15 add'l
person • Full breakfast 8-9 • Open
May 1-Oct. 31 • Off-season by
reservation • NSFC; NSRS; TIANS
Member*

Port Williams
Country Squire Bed and Breakfast
J. Earl & Rose Doyle, 990 Main
Street, Port Williams, B0P 1T0
(902) 542-9125
Fax (902) 542-1522
On Rte. 358 • Victorian home •
Four o/n units, two shared B&S •
TV in living room
FEATURES: Antique furnishings •
Piano in living room • Library •
Swimming pool • Sauna
RATES: $35 (1), $45 (2), $15 add'l
person • Full breakfast 7-9 • Open
May 27-Nov. 30 • Visa accepted •
NSRS Member

Port Williams
Newcomb House Bed & Breakfast (c. 1881)
John Newcombe, 997 Main Street,
Hwy 341, Upper Dyke, B0P 1J0
(902) 678-7486
Hwy 101, Exit 11 to Rte. 358 North
5 km (3 mi) through Port Williams
then left at Jawbone Corner (Rte.
341), 4.5 km (2 mi) on the right •
Working farm, Georgian style home
overlooking Canard (Wellington)
dykeland • Three o/n units, one
B&S • Colour cable TV/VCR in
living room • Smoking outside
RATES: $35-$45 (1), $45 (2), $55
(Queen) • Full breakfast at guests'
convenience • Open May 1-Oct. 31
• Visa accepted • Off-season by
arrangement • NSFC; NSRS
Member

Port Williams
Old Rectory Bed and Breakfast ★★★
Ron & Carol Buckley, 1519 Hwy
358, RR 1, Port Williams, B0P 1T0
(902) 542-1815
Fax (902) 542-2346
Hwy 101, Exit 11 to Rte. 1 to Rte.
358, 3 km (2 mi) beyond Port
Williams •
Recently
renovated
Century
home •
Three o/n
units, two
shared B&S
• Colour

cable TV in living room • No pets,
please • Non-smoking only
FEATURES: Evening tea •
Gardens and orchard U-Pick and
cider-making in season • Geological
field trips available
RATES: $45-$50 (1), $55-$60 (2),
$15 add'l person Full breakfast
7:30-9 • Open May 1-Oct. 31 •
Off-season by appointment • $5
less for second night • ETTA;
NSFC; NSRS Member

Port Williams
Planters' Barracks Country Inn ★★★★
Allen & Jennie Sheito, 1468 Starr's
Point Road, Port Williams, B0P 1T0
(902) 542-7879
Fax (902) 542-4442
Toll free 1-800-661-7879
Hwy 101, Exit 11, Rte. 358, turn
right at flashing lights in Port
Williams • Oldest building in Nova
Scotia restored as a Country Inn •
Nine o/n units, private B&S, family
and honeymoon suites • Centrally
located TV • Non-smoking only
FEATURES: French spoken •
Licensed • Acacia Croft Tearoom
serves lunch and afternoon tea •
Parlour • Gathering room • Heritage
gardens and patios • Barbecue •
Tennis
RATES: $59-$99 (1), $69-$109 (2)
• Breakfast • Open year-round • AE,
MC, Visa accepted • CAA; NSRS;
UCI Member

Portapique
Teacups & Flowers Bed & Breakfast
Cliff & Emily Lane, Portapique, RR
1, Bass River, B0M 1B0
(902) 668-2235
Hwy 104, Exit 11, 13.5 km (8.5 mi)
• Renovated 150-year old
farmhouse • Two o/n units, shared
B&S • Clock radio • Non-smoking
only
FEATURES: Evening snack •
Reading room for guests
RATES: $30 (1), $40 (2) • Full
breakfast 7:30-9:30 • Open May
1-Oct. 31 • Pets on premises •
NSRS Member

Prospect
Prospect Bed & Breakfast ★★★
Helena Prsala, Box 68, Prospect,
B0J 2V0
(902) 852-4493
Toll free 1-800-725-8732 (1-800-
SALTSEA)
Hwy 333, Prospect Exit (halfway
between Halifax & Peggy's Cove) •
Historic
Victorian
home • Four
o/n units,
private
B&S, one
room with
fireplace •
Colour cable
TV and free movie channel in room
• Children under 10 yrs free •
Non-smoking only
FEATURES: Ocean swimming •
Sandy beach • Canoe • Walking
trail • Island picnics
RATES: $60-$75 (1-2), $10 add'l
person (STC) • Continental
breakfast • Open year-round • MC,
Visa accepted • Off-season rates •
NSRS Member

Pubnico
Chez Marie Bed and Breakfast
Marie d'Entremont, Box 66, West
Pubnico, B0W 3S0
(902) 762-2107
On Rte. 335, 4 km (2.5 mi) off Rte.
3, 5.5 km (3.5 mi) off Hwy 103,
Exit 31 • Quiet rural setting • Three
o/n units, one shared B&S
FEATURES: French and English
spoken • Barbecue • Bicycle shelter
• Large lawn • View of harbour
RATES: $30 (1), $36-$40 (2), $6
add'l person Generous continental
breakfast • Open April-Oct. 31 •

Sandy Cove
Olde (1890) Village Inn ★★★½
Dixie & Bob Van, Sandy Cove,
Digby Neck, B0V 1E0
(902) 834-2202
Fax (902) 834-2927
Toll free 1-800-834-2206
Sandy Cove, Rte. 217 • Restored
buildings (c. 1830-1890) with ocean
view • Sixteen o/n units, private
B&S, some with fireplace, most
with balcony • Colour cable TV in
lounges • Pay telephone • No pets,
please • Non-smoking only
FEATURES: Antique furnishings •
French spoken • Licensed dining
room • Wicker sunroom • Cottages
available • Lawn games, hiking trails,
chip/putt, lake and ocean beach
swimming • Crafts, gifts, art, gift shop
*RATES: $60-$85 (2), $10 add'l
person • Breakfast 8-9:30 • Open
May 15-Oct. 15 • Off-season rates •
Packages available • DC, DIS, MC,
Visa accepted • CAA; NSRS Member*

Sandy Cove
Sandy Cove Bed & Breakfast
Joyce & Louis Morin, 6363 Rte.
217, Sandy Cove, B0V 1E0
(902) 834-2031
On main hwy, Digby Neck • Three
o/n units, two shared B&S • Colour
cable TV in lounge • Children 3 yrs
and under free
FEATURES: French spoken •
Kitchen facilities • Separate
entrance for guests • Lake/ocean
swimming • Whale-watching
arranged
*RATES: $30.10 (1), $45 (2), $8
add'l person, children $5 • Full
breakfast 8-10 • Open
June 1-Oct. 1 • Visa accepted •
Weekly rates available*

Sandy Cove
Wingberry House (c. 1850) B&B
Shirley Nelson, Sandy Cove, Digby,
B0V 1E0
(902) 834-2516
Digby Neck Rte. 217 W • Sea
captain's home with antique decor •
3 o/n units, 1/2 private B, one
shared full B • TV in den
FEATURES: Fireplace • Piano •
Fresh and salt water swimming •
Whale watching
*RATES: $35 (1), $45 (2) •
Breakfast 8-9 • Open June 1-Nov. 1*

Saulnierville
Bayshore Bed and Breakfast
Ted & Connie Murphy, Box 176,
Saulnierville, B0W 2Z0
(902) 769-3671
On Rte. 1 at Saulnierville/
Comeauville line • Farm house c.
1830 • Three o/n units, one shared
B&S, one suite with private B&S •
Colour cable TV in lounge •
Smoking area provided
FEATURES: Bay frontage
*RATES: $30 (1), $35-$40 (2) $50
(suite) • Full breakfast • Open
July 1-Sept. 1 • Off-season by
reservation • Cats on premises •
NSRS Member*

Seabright
The Mermaid's Garden Bed & Breakfast ★★★
Sara Ellis, 139 McDonald Point
Road, Box 695, RR 1, Seabright,
B0J 3J0
(902) 823-2227
Hwy 103, Exit 5 to Rte. 333, 9 km
(5.5 mi) • Three o/n units, shared B
• Colour cable TV and VCR in

MC, Visa accepted • Off-season by
reservation • NSRS Member

Pubnico
Yesteryear's Bed & Breakfast ★★★
Richard & Deborah Donaldson,
Box 16, Pubnico, B0W 2W0
Tel & Fax (902) 762-2969
Hwy 103, Exit 31 to intersection of
Rte. 335 & Rte. 3 • Majestic
Victorian home with antique
furnishings •
Two o/n
units, 1 1/2
B&S •
Remote
colour cable
TV •
Telephone in
rooms •
Radio • Non-smoking only
FEATURES: Owner is captain of a
lobster fishing vessel • Bicycle
shelter • Walking trails
*RATES: $40 (1), $50 (2), $10 add'l
person • Continental breakfast 7-9 •
Open year-round • MC, Visa
accepted • NSRS Member*

Pugwash
Blue Heron Inn B&B ★★★
David & Anne Gouldson, Durham
Street, Box 405, Pugwash, B0K 1L0
(902) 243-2900
Five o/n units, three private, 1 1/2
shared B • Colour cable TV/VCR in
lounge • Children under 10 yrs free
FEATURES: Piano in lounge •
Bilingual • Picnic table • One room
with private bath and kitchenette
*RATES: $40-$60 (2), $48-$54
(Queen), $8 add'l person (STC) •
Continental breakfast • Open
year-round • Visa accepted • NSRS
Member*

Pugwash
Maple Leaf Inn B&B
Sheila Ley, 10363 Durham Street,
Box 245, Pugwash, B0K 1L0
(902) 243-2560
Directly off Rte. 6 (Sunrise Trail) •
Three o/n units, two with shared
B&S, one family suite of two
rooms, private B • TV in lounge •
Radio in lounge • No pets, please •
Non-smoking only
FEATURES: Close to beaches and
golf
*RATES: $40 (1), $50 (2), $60
(suite), $10 add'l person • Full
breakfast 8 • Open May 15-Oct. 15
• NSRS Member*

Queensland
Surfside Inn B&B ★★½
Michelle & Bill Batcules, 9609 St.
Margaret's Bay Road (Rte. 3), RR
2, Hubbards, B0J 1T0
(902) 857-2419
Toll free 1-800-373-2417
Fax (902) 857-2107
Hwy 103, Exit 5 or 6 to Rte. 3,
access from Queensland beach •
Four o/n units, private B (three
whirlpool), ceiling fan • Colour
cable TV and VCR in rooms •
Radio in rooms • Non-smoking only
FEATURES: Swimming pool •
Craft/antique shop
*RATES: $67-$100 (1), $72-$105
(2), $10 add'l person • Full
breakfast 8-9:30 • Open year-round
• MC, Visa accepted • NSRS
Member*

Queensport
Queensport House Bed & Breakfast
Joyce Conrad, RR 2, Guysborough, B0H 1N0
(902) 358-2402
Off-season (902) 454-5020
In Queensport, on Rte. 16 • Quiet view overlooking Chedabucto Bay • Three o/n units, all with B&S • No pets, please • Non-smoking only
RATES: $45 (1), $55 (2), $10 add'l person • Full breakfast 7:30-9:30 • Open July 1-Labour Day (weekends until Oct. 31) • Visa accepted

Reserve Mines
Becky's Bed & Breakfast
Lou & Rebecca Oliver, 208 Main Street, Reserve Mines, B0A 1V0
(902) 849-2974
Located between Sydney & Glace Bay, Hwy 105 to Rte. 4, 3 km from Sydney Airport turn left on Main Street, across from Reserve Mines Fire Hall • Three o/n units, one B&S, one B • Colour cable TV in two living rooms • Clock radio • Non-smoking rooms
FEATURES: Light lunch in evening • Kitchen facilities • Apartment available
RATES: $32 (1) $40 (2), $10 add'l person (STC) • Full breakfast 7:30-9:30 • Open year-round • Cash only • NSRS Member

River Bourgeois
Grandma's House Bed & Breakfast
Rose & Tom Scott, RR 1, River Bourgeois, B0E 2X0
(902) 535-2512
Fax (902) 535-3717

Hwy 104, Exit 47, to Rte. 4, turn right, approx. 1 km (0.5 mi) on the right • Victorian house from early 1900s • Three o/n units, one with private patio overlooking river, one shared B&S • No pets, please • Children over 12 yrs welcome • Non-smoking only
FEATURES: Coffee/tea • Dining room overlooks river • Antique furnishings • Gift and antique shop on premises
RATES: $35 (1), $45 (2) (STC) • Full country breakfast 7-9 • Open May 15-Oct. 15 • NSRS Member

River John
Mountain Farm Bed & Breakfast ★★½
John & Margaret Minney, RR 2, River John, B0K 1N0
(902) 351-2821
From Rte. 6, 5 km (3 mi) on Mountain Rd., from Rte. 326, 7 km (4.5 mi) on Mountain Rd. • Working farm with abundant wildlife • Three o/n units, one full B&S • TV/VCR in living room • No pets, please • Non-smoking only
FEATURES: Evening snack
RATES: $33 (1), $45 (2), $12 children 12 and under • Full breakfast at guests' convenience • Open May 1-Oct. 15 • Lower rate for three or more nights • NSFC; NSRS Member

Riverport
(near Lunenburg)
Barrett's Bed & Breakfast ★★★
Bill & Sheila Barrett, 723 Feltzen South, RR 1, Riverport, B0J 2W0
(902) 766-4655
Fifteen minutes from Lunenburg, next to Ovens Park • Quiet ocean-front captain's house with

view of Lunenburg town and harbour • Four o/n units, two shared B&S • Non-smoking only
FEATURES: Hooking/braiding artisans • Filled with antiques • Reading room • Fishing • Bicycles • Ocean swimming • Hiking • Boats • Close to The Ovens Park
RATES: $45 (1), $55 (2) • Full country breakfast • Open year-round • MC, Visa accepted • NSRS Member

Ross Ferry
Dreamland Bed & Breakfast
Melena & Alan Rea, 9078 Ross Ferry Road, RR 1, Box 619, Bras d'Or, B0C 1B0
(902) 674-2083
Fax (902) 674-2991
Hwy 105, Exit 13 at Bras d'Or, 16 km (10 mi) on Ross Ferry-Kempt Head Rd. • Three o/n units, one private B&S, one shared B&S • TV in family room • Cot available • Children welcome • No pets, please • Non-smoking rooms
FEATURES: Screened in porch and deck overlooking Bras d'Or Lakes • Swimming pool • Canoeing
RATES: $36 (1), $46 (2), $50 (private B), $15 add'l person (STC) • Full breakfast 7-8:30 • Open year-round CBBBA; NSRS Member

Sable River
Pillar & Post Bed & Breakfast
June Williams, Sable River, B0T 1V0
(902) 656-2695
Hwy 103, in Sable River • Two o/n units, one private and one shared B • Colour cable TV/VCR in lounge
RATES: $40-$50 (1), $45-$55 (2) • Continental breakfast 7-9 • Open May-Nov. • Off-season by reservation NSRS Member

Salmon River Bridge
Dock'n'Launch Bed & Breakfast
Susan L. Fader, 12 Myers Point Road, Salmon River Bridge, Head of Jeddore, B0J 1P0
(902) 889-3420
From Hwy 107, Hwy 7, 10 km (6 mi), exit at Head of Jeddore to Myers Point Rd. • Three o/n units, two shared B • TV and VCR in lounge • No smoking in rooms
FEATURES: Barbecue • Horseshoes • Canoe, boat • Saltwater shore
RATES: $45 (1), $55 (2), $10 add'l person • Breakfast 7-9 • Open year-round • Visa accepted

Salmon River Bridge
Salmon River House Country Inn ★★★½
Adrien & Norma Blanchette, 9931 #7 Hwy, Salmon River Bridge, B0J 1P0
(902) 889-3353
Fax (902) 889-3653
Toll free 1-800-565-3353
Wheelchair accessible • Historic Inn (c. 1855) • Six o/n units, private B&S, family suite, honeymoon suite with Jacuzzi • Colour cable TV in four rooms and lounge • No pets, please • No smoking
FEATURES: Licensed dining room • Sundeck overlooking water • Lawn games • Bicycles • Saltwater fishing, boating, swimming, hiking • Thirty-five minutes from Halifax/Airport
RATES: $52.50-$65 (1), $68.25-$99.75 (2), $12.50 add'l person (STC) • Breakfast 7:30-9 • Open year-round • Off-season rate Jan.-Apr. by reservation only • CAA; IGNS; NSRS; UCI Member

lounge • Stereo in lounge • Pets with permission • Non-smoking only *RATES: $50-$60 (1-2) (STC) • Full breakfast 8-9 Open May-Oct. • Off-season by arrangement • IGNS; NSRS Member*

Selma
The Cobequid Inn B&B
Jim & Nancy Cleveland, RR 1, Maitland, B0N 1T0
(902) 261-2079
Hwy 102, Exit 10, Rte. 215 West to Selma. From Truro, Exit 14 to Rte. 236, then Rte. 215 West. From Hwy 101, Exit 5 to Rte. 14, then Rte. 215 East • Three o/n units, two shared B • Colour cable TV in lounge • Children under 3 yrs free *FEATURES:* Licensed dining room • Board games • Lawn chess, horseshoes • Outdoor swimming pool • Bicycles
RATES: $38 (1), $48 (2), $10-$15 add'l person • Full breakfast • Open May-Oct. • MC, Visa accepted • NSRS Member

Selma
Terranita Bed & Breakfast
Terry & Anita Duckenfield, 8098 Hwy 215, RR 1, Maitland, B0N 1T0
Tel & Fax (902) 261-2102
From Truro, Hwy 102, Exit 14 to Rte. 236, then Rte. 215 West to Selma; from Windsor, Hwy 101, Exit 5 to Rte. 14, then Rte. 215 East to Selma • Restored country heritage home (c. 1825) situated on five acres overlooking Cobequid Bay • Two o/n units, shared S • No pets, please • Non-smoking only
RATES: $35 (1), $45-$50 (2) • Full breakfast 7:30-9 • NSRS Member

Sheet Harbour
Black Duck Seaside Inn B&B
Al & Gloria Horne, 25245 Hwy 7, Port Dufferin. Mailing address: Box 26, Sheet Harbour, B0J 3B0
Tel & Fax (902) 885-2813
Three o/n units, one shared B&S, one room with queen bed, private whirlpool and TV • Colour cable TV in lounge • Smoking on deck only  *FEATURES:* Evening meal by reservation • Cottage available *RATES: $60 (1), $65-$85 (2), $10 add'l person • Full breakfast 8-9:30 • Open year-round • Visa accepted Off-season by reservation • ESTA; IGNS; NSRS Member*

Shelburne
Bear's Den
Elizabeth J. Atkinson, Box 883, Shelburne, B0T 1W0
(902) 875-3234
Corner of Water & Glasgow Sts. • Three o/n units, one shared B • Colour cable TV in lounge and one room • Telephone in rooms • Pets welcome
FEATURES: Upstairs patio • Bicycle shed • Collector bears available
RATES: $35 (1), $45 (2) • Full breakfast 7:30-9:30 • Open year-round • Visa accepted

Shelburne
Harbour House
Bed & Breakfast
Wolfgang Schricker, 187 Water
Street, Box 362, Shelburne, B0T 1W0
Tel & Fax (902) 875-2074
Hwy 103, Exit 26 to Water St. corner
of Water St. & Harbourview Lean •
Three o/n units, one full B&S • Cot
available • Children under 12 yrs free
• Non-smoking only
FEATURES: English & German
spoken • Coffee/tea Piano •
Air-conditioning
*RATES: $45 (1), $55 (2), $10 add'l
person, no GST • Full breakfast
7-9:30 • Open June 15-Sept. 30 •
Visa accepted • Senior citizens'
discount • NSRS Member*

Shelburne
Mill Stones Country Inn
Julie & Gary Jeschke, 2 Falls Lane,
Box 758, Shelburne, B0T 1W0
(902) 875-3958
Three o/n units, private B, family
suite • Colour cable TV in lounge
FEATURES: Licensed dining room
Wed.-Sun.
*RATES: $48 (1-2), $58-$78 (suite)
• Full breakfast 8-10 • Open Apr.
15-Jan. 1 • Visa accepted • NSRS
Member*

Shelburne
Toddle Inn Dining
Room Bed & Breakfast
Tony Caruso, 63 Water Street, Box
837, Shelburne, B0T 1W0
(902) 875-3229
Hwy 103, Exit 25 or 26 • Four o/n
units, private and shared B&S •
Children under 6 yrs free •
Non-smoking only
FEATURES: Dining room open to
public 8 a.m. to closing

*RATES: $60-$70 (1-2), $10 add'l
person • Full breakfast • AE, DIS,
MC, Visa accepted • NSRS Member*

Sherbrooke
Days-a-go
Bed & Breakfast
Randy & Linda Peck, 15 Cameron
Road, Box 71, Sherbrooke, B0J 3C0
(902) 522-2983
Rte. 7, west side • Older home (c.
1920), recently renovated • Two o/n
units, one double, one double and
single, shared B&S • Not suitable
for children • No pets, please •
Non-smoking only
FEATURES: Quiet rural setting,
mini farm, fresh eggs • Antique
furniture • Enclosed sunporch with
view of Sherbrooke Village and St.
Mary's River • Professional guide
available for hunting and fishing
*RATES: $40 (1), $48-$54 (2), $8
add'l person (STC) • Full breakfast
7:30-9:30 • Open May-Sept. •
Off-season by arrangement*

Shubenacadie
White House
Guest Home
Robert & Rosalita MacMillan,
Shubenacadie, B0N 2H0
(902) 758-3784
Rte. 224, 15 minutes from airport •
Three o/n units, private and shared
B, private entrance • Colour cable
TV • Not suitable for children
*RATES: $30 (1), $40 (2) (STC) •
Breakfast $3.50*

Smith's Cove
Harbourview Inn ★★★
Mona & Philip Webb, Box 39,
Smith's Cove, B0S 1S0
(902) 245-5686
Fax (902) 245-4828

5 km (3 mi) east of Digby, Exit 24/25 off Hwy 101 • Turn-of-the-century country inn and annex • Nine o/n units including two suites, private B&S • Wheelchair accessible Colour cable TV in suites and lounge • No pets, please • Non-smoking rooms available
FEATURES: Laundromat • Dining room • Playground • Tennis court • Outdoor swimming pool • House-keeping unit available • Tidal beach
RATES: $55 (1), $59-$89 (2), $79-$149 (suite) • Open June-Oct. 15 • MC, Visa accepted • Packages available UCI; NSRS Member

South Haven
An Seanne Mhanse B&B

Laverne Drinnan, South Haven, RR 2, Baddeck, B0E 1B0
(902) 295-2538
Hwy 105, 12 km (7.5 mi) east of Baddeck, 2 km (1.5 mi) west of Exit 11 • Three o/n units, two with sinks, one shared B • Non-smoking only
FEATURES: Bicycle storage
RATES: $35 (1), $45-$50 (2), $15 add'l person (STC) • Full breakfast • Open Apr.-Nov. • Family rates available • NSRS Member

Spencer's Island
Spencer's Island Bed & Breakfast

Margaret Griebel, RR 3, Parrsboro, B0M 1S0
(902) 392-2721
Rte. 209 to Spencer's Island, turn off at Spencer's Beach sign • Three o/n units, two B&S • TV and radio in library • Non-smoking only
RATES: $25 (1), $35 (2) • Full breakfast 7-10 • Open June-Sept.

Springfield
Frog Pond Bed & Breakfast

Larry Richardson, RR 3, Springfield, B0R 1H0
(902) 547-2359
Hwy 101, Exit 18, 40 km (24 mi) on Rte. 10 • Two o/n units, one shared B&S • Cot available • No smoking in rooms
FEATURES: Lawn, garden, frog pond • Lake swimming, walking trails • Cross-country skiing, skating
RATES: $35 (1), $40 (2), $10 add'l person • Full breakfast 7-9 • Open year-round

St. Ann's
McGovern's of Hummingbird Hill Bed & Breakfast

Jean & Jim McGovern, St. Ann's, RR 4, Baddeck, B0E 1B0
(902) 929-2880
Hwy 105, Exit 11, 9 km (5.5 mi) north on Cabot Trail Overlooking St. Ann's Harbour and North Harbour • Two o/n units, shared B • TV and VCR in living room
FEATURES: French spoken • Movies available
RATES: $35 (1), $50 (2) • Full breakfast 8 • NSRS Member

St. George's Channel
Marble View Bed & Breakfast

Anne Martin, The Points, RR 2, West Bay, B0E 3K0
(902) 345-2281
Twenty-four km (15 mi) from St. Peter's on the Bras d'Or Trail in Richmond County • Secluded setting on the shores of the Bras d'Or Lake • Two o/n units, shared B
RATES: $35 (1), $45 (2) (STC) • Open May 15-Oct.15 • MC Visa accepted

St. Joseph du Moine
Conti's Bed & Breakfast
Arthur & Jacqueline Conti, 309
Bazile Road, St. Joseph du Moine,
B0E 3A0
(902) 224-2697
Three o/n units, shared B&S • TV
in living room
FEATURES: Panorama of ocean,
islands, lakes, mountains, sunsets •
French spoken • Arrangements for
whale-watching, deep-sea fishing
*RATES: $32 (1), $40 (2), $10-$15
add'l person • Full breakfast 8 •
Open May 15-Oct. 15 • MC, Visa
accepted*

St. Joseph du Moine
Pilot Whale Bed & Breakfast
Cheryl Power, Bazile Road, St.
Joseph du Moine, B0E 3A0
(902) 224-2592
New log home • Three o/n units,
private & shared B&S • TV in
living room
FEATURES: Double fireplace
*RATES: $60-$85 (1-2) • Full
breakfast 7:30-9:30 • May 15-
Oct. 31*

Stellarton
MacDonalds Bed & Breakfast
James & Rena MacDonald, 292
South Foord Street, Box 831,
Stellarton, B0K 1S0
(902) 752-7751
From Hwy 104, Exit 24, 10 minutes
from New Glasgow • Three o/n
units, one shared B
*RATES: $30 (1), $40 (2), $10 add'l
person (STC) • Full breakfast •
Open year-round • NSRS Member*

Stewiacke
Interval Pines Bed & Breakfast
Joyce & Len Barak, 487 St.
Andrews Street, Box 415,
Stewiacke, B0N 2J0
(902) 639-2835
Hwy 102, Exit 11 • Large home,
secluded and private, in the St.
Andrew's River valley • One o/n
unit, shared B • Private and
centrally located TVs
FEATURES: Trout fishing •
Family unit available
*RATES: $45 (1-2) taxes incl. •
Continental breakfast 7-9 • Open
July 1-Aug. 31*

Summerville Beach
Summerville Beach Retreat
June Lohnes-Davis, RR 1, Port
Mouton, Queen's County, B0T 1T0
(902) 683-2874
Toll-free 1-800-213-5868
From Hwy 103, Exit 20, 2 km (1
mi) • Three o/n units, one shared B
• Colour cable TV in two rooms •
Clock radio • Non-smoking only
FEATURES: Outside deck •
Screened spa • Three new deluxe
two-bedroom chalets available • Two
minutes from beach with lots of
privacy • Call for a vacation video
*RATES: $45 (1), $50-$60 (2), $10
add'l person • Full breakfast • B&B
open May 1-Sept. 30, chalets
year-round Visa accepted •
Off-season rates available for
chalets NSFCV; NSRS Member*

Sydney
Anne's Bed & Breakfast
Anne & Bob Gaetz, 34 Amelia
Street, Sydney, B1P 6C2
(902) 539-3536

Turn-of the-century home • Three
o/n units, two shared B&S • Colour
cable TV in rooms • No smoking in
rooms
FEATURES: Furnished with
antiques
RATES: $35 (1), $40 (2), $10 add'l
person (cot) (STC) • Full breakfast
7-9 • Open year-round

Sydney
Gathering House
Bed & Breakfast ★★½
Jean & Ken Phillips, 148 Crescent
Street, Sydney, B1S 2Z8
(902) 539-7172
Easy access from Kings Rd. (Hwy
104 & 105) George St. (Rte. 125)
overlooking Wentworth Park •
Three o/n units, two shared B&S •
Centrally located TV
FEATURES: Antiques • Veranda
therapy • Sunday park concerts
RATES: $40 (1), $45-$55 (2), $15
add'l person • Full breakfast 7:30-9
• Open year-round • Off-season by
reservation • Long-term rates
available • NSRS Member

Sydney
Old Country Post
Office B&B
Dr. Pushpa Rathor, 3 Strathcona
Street, Sydney, B1R 1X7
(902) 539-8033
Two o/n units, shared B&S, suite
with private B • Non-smoking only
FEATURES: A unique experience
• Palm reading and stress reduction,
meditation available with hostess,
who is also an artist, writer and
musician
RATES: $45 (1), $50 (2), $60
(suite) • Breakfast (vegetarian,
non-vegetarian, Indian) 7-9 • Open
May 1-Oct. 31 • Off-season by
arrangement

Sydney
Park Place
Bed & Breakfast
Evanel McEwen, 169 Park Street,
Sydney, B1P 6W7
(902) 562-3518
Exit 8 from Hwy 125, take George
St. to second traffic lights, right onto
Cottage Rd. left onto Park St. •
Victorian house • Three o/n units, one
shared B&S • Colour cable TV and
radio • Non-smoking only
RATES: $35 (1), $40 (2) (STC) •
Full breakfast 7-9 • Open
May-Oct. • MC, Visa accepted •
Off-season by reservation • NSRS
Member

Sydney
Rockinghorse Inn ★★★
Margaret Glabay, 259 Kings Road,
Sydney, B1S 1A7
(902) 539-2696
Registered Heritage Property •
Eight o/n units, six private and two
shared B • Colour cable TV in
common area • No smoking in
rooms
FEATURES: Decorated with
antiques • Dinner by reservation •
Library of steelworkers and miners
of Cape Breton • Sunroom •
Honeymoon suite available
RATES: $55-$100 (2), $10 add'l
person • Full breakfast 8-9 • Open
year-round • MC, Visa accepted •
NSRS Member

Sydney
White Maples
Bed & Breakfast
Pamela Roberts, 72 Curry Street,
Box 6036, Sydney, B1P 5G5
(902) 564-4674
Hwy 125, Exit 6 to Rte. 4, 5 km (3
mi) to Howie Centre; or Rte 4, 6
km (3.5 mi) past Sydney River
Tourist Bureau • One o/n unit,
shared B&S • Colour cable TV in
room • No pets, please • No
smoking in room
*RATES: $32-$35 (1), $40 (2)
(STC) • Full breakfast 7-9 • Open
May 15-Oct. 15*

Sydney Forks
Christie's
Bed & Breakfast
Olive Christie, 2486 Kings Road,
Sydney Forks, B1L 1A1
(902) 564-9364
Hwy 125, Exit 6, 7 km (4.5 mi)
towards St. Peter's • Three o/n
units, shared B&S • Colour cable
TV and VCR in recreation room •
Non-smoking only
FEATURES: Pool table, games
available • Model ship display
*RATES: $30 (1), $45 (2), $8 add'l
person • Full breakfast 8-10 • Open
June 1-Nov. 15*

Sydney Mines
Annandale Bed &
Breakfast ★★★
Meg Sargent & Scott Phillips, 157
Shore Road, Sydney Mines, B1V 1A9
(902) 544-1052
Hwy 105, Exit 21 to Rte. 305 N, 3
km (2 mi) • Victorian house (c.
1880) • Four o/n units, one B&S •
TV/VCR and telephone in lounge •
Pets with permission •
Non-smoking only

FEATURES: Antiques • Veranda
with ocean view • Croquet • Five
minutes from Newfoundland ferry
*RATES: $38-$48 (1), $45-$60 (2)
(STC) • Full breakfast 7:30-9 •
Open year-round • MC, Visa
accepted Dec.-March by reservation*

Sydney Mines
Garland Stubbert's
Bed & Breakfast ★★★
Garland Stubbert, 117 Shore Road,
Sydney Mines, B1V 1A5
(902) 736-8466
Hwy 105, Exit 21 to Rte. 305
North, 2.5 km (1.5 mi) from
Newfoundland ferry • Three o/n
units, one B&S • Colour cable TV
in lounge • Non-smoking only
FEATURES: Large deck
overlooking harbour • Barbecue &
camp stove
*RATES: $40 (2), $16 add'l person
(STC) • Full breakfast 7-9 • Open
May 1-Oct. 31 • NSRS Member*

Sydney Mines
Gowrie House Country
Inn ★★★
C.J. Matthews & K.W. Tutty, 139
Shore Road, Sydney Mines, B1V 1A5
(902) 544-1050
Hwy 105, Exit 21 to Rte. 305 North,
3 km (2 mi) • Historic Georgian
house • Six o/n units, two shared B,
four bed-sitting rooms, private B,
fireplace • Colour cable TV in some
rooms • No smoking in rooms
FEATURES: Antiques showcase •
Dinner 7:30 p.m., reservations
required • English gardens •
Veranda and decks
*RATES: $55-$115 (1), $65-$125
(2), $15 add'l person, MAP $35
extra • Breakfast 7:30-9:30 • Open
May 1-Oct. 30 • MC, Visa accepted
• IGNS; NSRS; UCI Member*

MC, Visa accepted • Off-season by reservation • NSRS Member

Pubnico
Yesteryear's Bed & Breakfast ★★★
Richard & Deborah Donaldson, Box 16, Pubnico, B0W 2W0
Tel & Fax (902) 762-2969
Hwy 103, Exit 31 to intersection of Rte. 335 & Rte. 3 • Majestic Victorian home with antique furnishings •

Two o/n units, 1 1/2 B&S • Remote colour cable TV • Telephone in rooms • Radio • Non-smoking only
FEATURES: Owner is captain of a lobster fishing vessel • Bicycle shelter • Walking trails
RATES: $40 (1), $50 (2), $10 add'l person • Continental breakfast 7-9 • Open year-round • MC, Visa accepted • NSRS Member

Pugwash
Blue Heron Inn B&B ★★★
David & Anne Gouldson, Durham Street, Box 405, Pugwash, B0K 1L0
(902) 243-2900
Five o/n units, three private, 1 1/2 shared B • Colour cable TV/VCR in lounge • Children under 10 yrs free
FEATURES: Piano in lounge • Bilingual • Picnic table • One room with private bath and kitchenette
RATES: $40-$60 (2), $48-$54 (Queen), $8 add'l person (STC) • Continental breakfast • Open year-round • Visa accepted • NSRS Member

Pugwash
Maple Leaf Inn B&B
Sheila Ley, 10363 Durham Street, Box 245, Pugwash, B0K 1L0
(902) 243-2560
Directly off Rte. 6 (Sunrise Trail) • Three o/n units, two with shared B&S, one family suite of two rooms, private B • TV in lounge • Radio in lounge • No pets, please • Non-smoking only
FEATURES: Close to beaches and golf
RATES: $40 (1), $50 (2), $60 (suite), $10 add'l person • Full breakfast 8 • Open May 15-Oct. 15 • NSRS Member

Queensland
Surfside Inn B&B ★★½
Michelle & Bill Batcules, 9609 St. Margaret's Bay Road (Rte. 3), RR 2, Hubbards, B0J 1T0
(902) 857-2419
Toll free 1-800-373-2417
Fax (902) 857-2107
Hwy 103, Exit 5 or 6 to Rte. 3, access from Queensland beach • Four o/n units, private B (three whirlpool), ceiling fan • Colour cable TV and VCR in rooms • Radio in rooms • Non-smoking only
FEATURES: Swimming pool • Craft/antique shop
RATES: $67-$100 (1), $72-$105 (2), $10 add'l person • Full breakfast 8-9:30 • Open year-round • MC, Visa accepted • NSRS Member

Queensport
Queensport House Bed & Breakfast
Joyce Conrad, RR 2, Guysborough, B0H 1N0
(902) 358-2402
Off-season (902) 454-5020
In Queensport, on Rte. 16 • Quiet view overlooking Chedabucto Bay • Three o/n units, all with B&S • No pets, please • Non-smoking only
RATES: $45 (1), $55 (2), $10 add'l person • Full breakfast 7:30-9:30 • Open July 1-Labour Day (weekends until Oct. 31) • Visa accepted

Reserve Mines
Becky's Bed & Breakfast
Lou & Rebecca Oliver, 208 Main Street, Reserve Mines, B0A 1V0
(902) 849-2974
Located between Sydney & Glace Bay, Hwy 105 to Rte. 4, 3 km from Sydney Airport turn left on Main Street, across from Reserve Mines Fire Hall • Three o/n units, one B&S, one B • Colour cable TV in two living rooms • Clock radio • Non-smoking rooms
FEATURES: Light lunch in evening • Kitchen facilities • Apartment available
RATES: $32 (1) $40 (2), $10 add'l person (STC) • Full breakfast 7:30-9:30 • Open year-round • Cash only • NSRS Member

River Bourgeois
Grandma's House Bed & Breakfast
Rose & Tom Scott, RR 1, River Bourgeois, B0E 2X0
(902) 535-2512
Fax (902) 535-3717

Hwy 104, Exit 47, to Rte. 4, turn right, approx. 1 km (0.5 mi) on the right • Victorian house from early 1900s • Three o/n units, one with private patio overlooking river, one shared B&S • No pets, please • Children over 12 yrs welcome • Non-smoking only
FEATURES: Coffee/tea • Dining room overlooks river • Antique furnishings • Gift and antique shop on premises
RATES: $35 (1), $45 (2) (STC) • Full country breakfast 7-9 • Open May 15-Oct. 15 • NSRS Member

River John
Mountain Farm Bed & Breakfast ★★½
John & Margaret Minney, RR 2, River John, B0K 1N0
(902) 351-2821
From Rte. 6, 5 km (3 mi) on Mountain Rd., from Rte. 326, 7 km (4.5 mi) on Mountain Rd. • Working farm with abundant wildlife • Three o/n units, one full B&S • TV/VCR in living room • No pets, please • Non-smoking only
FEATURES: Evening snack
RATES: $33 (1), $45 (2), $12 children 12 and under • Full breakfast at guests' convenience • Open May 1-Oct. 15 • Lower rate for three or more nights • NSFC; NSRS Member

Riverport
(near Lunenburg)
Barrett's Bed & Breakfast ★★★
Bill & Sheila Barrett, 723 Feltzen South, RR 1, Riverport, B0J 2W0
(902) 766-4655
Fifteen minutes from Lunenburg, next to Ovens Park • Quiet ocean-front captain's house with

view of Lunenburg town and harbour • Four o/n units, two shared B&S • Non-smoking only
FEATURES: Hooking/braiding artisans • Filled with antiques • Reading room • Fishing • Bicycles • Ocean swimming • Hiking • Boats • Close to The Ovens Park
RATES: *$45 (1), $55 (2) • Full country breakfast • Open year-round • MC, Visa accepted • NSRS Member*

Ross Ferry
Dreamland Bed & Breakfast
Melena & Alan Rea, 9078 Ross Ferry Road, RR 1, Box 619, Bras d'Or, B0C 1B0
(902) 674-2083
Fax (902) 674-2991
Hwy 105, Exit 13 at Bras d'Or, 16 km (10 mi) on Ross Ferry-Kempt Head Rd. • Three o/n units, one private B&S, one shared B&S • TV in family room • Cot available • Children welcome • No pets, please • Non-smoking rooms
FEATURES: Screened in porch and deck overlooking Bras d'Or Lakes • Swimming pool • Canoeing
RATES: *$36 (1), $46 (2), $50 (private B), $15 add'l person (STC) • Full breakfast 7-8:30 • Open year-round CBBBA; NSRS Member*

Sable River
Pillar & Post Bed & Breakfast
June Williams, Sable River, B0T 1V0
(902) 656-2695
Hwy 103, in Sable River • Two o/n units, one private and one shared B • Colour cable TV/VCR in lounge
RATES: *$40-$50 (1), $45-$55 (2) • Continental breakfast 7-9 • Open May-Nov. • Off-season by reservation NSRS Member*

Salmon River Bridge
Dock'n'Launch Bed & Breakfast
Susan L. Fader, 12 Myers Point Road, Salmon River Bridge, Head of Jeddore, B0J 1P0
(902) 889-3420
From Hwy 107, Hwy 7, 10 km (6 mi), exit at Head of Jeddore to Myers Point Rd. • Three o/n units, two shared B • TV and VCR in lounge • No smoking in rooms
FEATURES: Barbecue • Horseshoes • Canoe, boat • Saltwater shore
RATES: *$45 (1), $55 (2), $10 add'l person • Breakfast 7-9 • Open year-round • Visa accepted*

Salmon River Bridge
Salmon River House Country Inn ★★★½
Adrien & Norma Blanchette, 9931 #7 Hwy, Salmon River Bridge, B0J 1P0
(902) 889-3353
Fax (902) 889-3653
Toll free 1-800-565-3353
Wheelchair accessible • Historic Inn (c. 1855) • Six o/n units, private B&S, family suite, honeymoon suite with Jacuzzi • Colour cable TV in four rooms and lounge • No pets, please • No smoking
FEATURES: Licensed dining room • Sundeck overlooking water • Lawn games • Bicycles • Saltwater fishing, boating, swimming, hiking • Thirty-five minutes from Halifax/Airport
RATES: *$52.50-$65 (1), $68.25-$99.75 (2), $12.50 add'l person (STC) • Breakfast 7:30-9 • Open year-round • Off-season rates, Jan.-Apr. by reservation only • CAA; IGNS; NSRS; UCI Member*

Sandy Cove
Olde (1890) Village Inn ★★★½
Dixie & Bob Van, Sandy Cove,
Digby Neck, B0V 1E0
(902) 834-2202
Fax (902) 834-2927
Toll free 1-800-834-2206
Sandy Cove, Rte. 217 • Restored
buildings (c. 1830-1890) with ocean
view • Sixteen o/n units, private
B&S, some with fireplace, most
with balcony • Colour cable TV in
lounges • Pay telephone • No pets,
please • Non-smoking only
FEATURES: Antique furnishings •
French spoken • Licensed dining
room • Wicker sunroom • Cottages
available • Lawn games, hiking trails,
chip/putt, lake and ocean beach
swimming • Crafts, gifts, art, gift shop
RATES: $60-$85 (2), $10 add'l
person • Breakfast 8-9:30 • Open
May 15-Oct. 15 • Off-season rates •
Packages available • DC, DIS, MC,
Visa accepted • CAA; NSRS Member

Sandy Cove
Sandy Cove Bed & Breakfast
Joyce & Louis Morin, 6363 Rte.
217, Sandy Cove, B0V 1E0
(902) 834-2031
On main hwy, Digby Neck • Three
o/n units, two shared B&S • Colour
cable TV in lounge • Children 3 yrs
and under free
FEATURES: French spoken •
Kitchen facilities • Separate
entrance for guests • Lake/ocean
swimming • Whale-watching
arranged
RATES: $30.10 (1), $45 (2), $8
add'l person, children $5 • Full
breakfast 8-10 • Open
June 1-Oct. 1 • Visa accepted •
Weekly rates available

Sandy Cove
Wingberry House (c. 1850) B&B
Shirley Nelson, Sandy Cove, Digby,
B0V 1E0
(902) 834-2516
Digby Neck Rte. 217 W • Sea
captain's home with antique decor •
3 o/n units, 1/2 private B, one
shared full B • TV in den
FEATURES: Fireplace • Piano •
Fresh and salt water swimming •
Whale watching
RATES: $35 (1), $45 (2) •
Breakfast 8-9 • Open June 1-Nov. 1

Saulnierville
Bayshore Bed and Breakfast
Ted & Connie Murphy, Box 176,
Saulnierville, B0W 2Z0
(902) 769-3671
On Rte. 1 at Saulnierville/
Comeauville line • Farm house c.
1830 • Three o/n units, one shared
B&S, one suite with private B&S •
Colour cable TV in lounge •
Smoking area provided
FEATURES: Bay frontage
RATES: $30 (1), $35-$40 (2) $50
(suite) • Full breakfast • Open
July 1-Sept. 1 • Off-season by
reservation • Cats on premises •
NSRS Member

Seabright
The Mermaid's Garden Bed & Breakfast ★★★
Sara Ellis, 139 McDonald Point
Road, Box 695, RR 1, Seabright,
B0J 3J0
(902) 823-2227
Hwy 103, Exit 5 to Rte. 333, 9 km
(5.5 mi) • Three o/n units, shared B
• Colour cable TV and VCR in

lounge • Stereo in lounge • Pets
with permission • Non-smoking only
*RATES: $50-$60 (1-2) (STC) • Full
breakfast 8-9 Open May-Oct. •
Off-season by arrangement • IGNS;
NSRS Member*

Selma
The Cobequid Inn B&B
Jim & Nancy Cleveland, RR 1,
Maitland, B0N 1T0
(902) 261-2079
Hwy 102, Exit 10, Rte. 215 West to
Selma. From Truro, Exit 14 to Rte.
236, then Rte. 215 West. From
Hwy 101, Exit 5 to Rte. 14, then
Rte. 215 East • Three o/n units, two
shared B • Colour cable TV in
lounge • Children under 3 yrs free
FEATURES: Licensed dining room
• Board games • Lawn chess,
horseshoes • Outdoor swimming
pool • Bicycles
*RATES: $38 (1), $48 (2), $10-$15
add'l person • Full breakfast •
Open May-Oct. • MC, Visa
accepted • NSRS Member*

Selma
Terranita
Bed & Breakfast
Terry & Anita Duckenfield, 8098
Hwy 215, RR 1, Maitland, B0N 1T0
Tel & Fax (902) 261-2102
From Truro, Hwy 102, Exit 14 to
Rte. 236, then Rte. 215 West to
Selma; from Windsor, Hwy 101,
Exit 5 to Rte. 14, then Rte. 215 East
to Selma • Restored country
heritage home (c. 1825) situated on
five acres overlooking Cobequid
Bay • Two o/n units, shared S • No
pets, please • Non-smoking only
*RATES: $35 (1), $45-$50 (2) • Full
breakfast 7:30-9 • NSRS Member*

Sheet Harbour
Black Duck Seaside Inn B&B
Al & Gloria Horne, 25245 Hwy 7,
Port Dufferin. Mailing address: Box
26, Sheet Harbour, B0J 3B0
Tel & Fax (902) 885-2813
Three o/n units, one shared B&S,
one room
with queen
bed, private
whirlpool
and TV •
Colour cable
TV in
lounge •
Smoking on
deck only

FEATURES: Evening meal by
reservation • Cottage available
*RATES: $60 (1), $65-$85 (2), $10
add'l person • Full breakfast 8-9:30
• Open year-round • Visa accepted
Off-season by reservation • ESTA;
IGNS; NSRS Member*

Shelburne
Bear's Den
Elizabeth J. Atkinson, Box 883,
Shelburne, B0T 1W0
(902) 875-3234
Corner of Water & Glasgow Sts. •
Three o/n units, one shared B •
Colour cable TV in lounge and one
room • Telephone in rooms • Pets
welcome
FEATURES: Upstairs patio •
Bicycle shed • Collector bears
available
*RATES: $35 (1), $45 (2) • Full
breakfast 7:30-9:30 • Open
year-round • Visa accepted*

Shelburne
Harbour House Bed & Breakfast
Wolfgang Schricker, 187 Water
Street, Box 362, Shelburne, B0T 1W0
Tel & Fax (902) 875-2074
Hwy 103, Exit 26 to Water St. corner
of Water St. & Harbourview Lean •
Three o/n units, one full B&S • Cot
available • Children under 12 yrs free
• Non-smoking only
FEATURES: English & German
spoken • Coffee/tea Piano •
Air-conditioning
*RATES: $45 (1), $55 (2), $10 add'l
person, no GST • Full breakfast
7-9:30 • Open June 15-Sept. 30 •
Visa accepted • Senior citizens'
discount • NSRS Member*

Shelburne
Mill Stones Country Inn
Julie & Gary Jeschke, 2 Falls Lane,
Box 758, Shelburne, B0T 1W0
(902) 875-3958
Three o/n units, private B, family
suite • Colour cable TV in lounge
FEATURES: Licensed dining room
Wed.-Sun.
*RATES: $48 (1-2), $58-$78 (suite)
• Full breakfast 8-10 • Open Apr.
15-Jan. 1 • Visa accepted • NSRS
Member*

Shelburne
Toddle Inn Dining Room Bed & Breakfast
Tony Caruso, 63 Water Street, Box
837, Shelburne, B0T 1W0
(902) 875-3229
Hwy 103, Exit 25 or 26 • Four o/n
units, private and shared B&S •
Children under 6 yrs free •
Non-smoking only
FEATURES: Dining room open to
public 8 a.m. to closing

*RATES: $60-$70 (1-2), $10 add'l
person • Full breakfast • AE, DIS,
MC, Visa accepted • NSRS Member*

Sherbrooke
Days-a-go Bed & Breakfast
Randy & Linda Peck, 15 Cameron
Road, Box 71, Sherbrooke, B0J 3C0
(902) 522-2983
Rte. 7, west side • Older home (c.
1920), recently renovated • Two o/n
units, one double, one double and
single, shared B&S • Not suitable
for children • No pets, please •
Non-smoking only
FEATURES: Quiet rural setting,
mini farm, fresh eggs • Antique
furniture • Enclosed sunporch with
view of Sherbrooke Village and St.
Mary's River • Professional guide
available for hunting and fishing
*RATES: $40 (1), $48-$54 (2), $8
add'l person (STC) • Full breakfast
7:30-9:30 • Open May-Sept. •
Off-season by arrangement*

Shubenacadie
White House Guest Home
Robert & Rosalita MacMillan,
Shubenacadie, B0N 2H0
(902) 758-3784
Rte. 224, 15 minutes from airport •
Three o/n units, private and shared
B, private entrance • Colour cable
TV • Not suitable for children
*RATES: $30 (1), $40 (2) (STC) •
Breakfast $3.50*

Smith's Cove
Harbourview Inn ★★★
Mona & Philip Webb, Box 39,
Smith's Cove, B0S 1S0
(902) 245-5686
Fax (902) 245-4828

5 km (3 mi) east of Digby, Exit 24/25 off Hwy 101 • Turn-of-the-century country inn and annex • Nine o/n units including two suites, private B&S • Wheelchair accessible Colour cable TV in suites and lounge • No pets, please • Non-smoking rooms available
FEATURES: Laundromat • Dining room • Playground • Tennis court • Outdoor swimming pool • House-keeping unit available • Tidal beach
RATES: $55 (1), $59-$89 (2), $79-$149 (suite) • Open June-Oct. 15 • MC, Visa accepted • Packages available UCI; NSRS Member

South Haven
An Seanne Mhanse B&B
Laverne Drinnan, South Haven, RR 2, Baddeck, B0E 1B0
(902) 295-2538
Hwy 105, 12 km (7.5 mi) east of Baddeck, 2 km (1.5 mi) west of Exit 11 • Three o/n units, two with sinks, one shared B • Non-smoking only
FEATURES: Bicycle storage
RATES: $35 (1), $45-$50 (2), $15 add'l person (STC) • Full breakfast • Open Apr.-Nov. • Family rates available • NSRS Member

Spencer's Island
Spencer's Island Bed & Breakfast
Margaret Griebel, RR 3, Parrsboro, B0M 1S0
(902) 392-2721
Rte. 209 to Spencer's Island, turn off at Spencer's Beach sign • Three o/n units, two B&S • TV and radio in library • Non-smoking only
RATES: $25 (1), $35 (2) • Full breakfast 7-10 • Open June-Sept.

Springfield
Frog Pond Bed & Breakfast
Larry Richardson, RR 3, Springfield, B0R 1H0
(902) 547-2359
Hwy 101, Exit 18, 40 km (24 mi) on Rte. 10 • Two o/n units, one shared B&S • Cot available • No smoking in rooms
FEATURES: Lawn, garden, frog pond • Lake swimming, walking trails • Cross-country skiing, skating
RATES: $35 (1), $40 (2), $10 add'l person • Full breakfast 7-9 • Open year-round

St. Ann's
McGovern's of Hummingbird Hill Bed & Breakfast
Jean & Jim McGovern, St. Ann's, RR 4, Baddeck, B0E 1B0
(902) 929-2880
Hwy 105, Exit 11, 9 km (5.5 mi) north on Cabot Trail Overlooking St. Ann's Harbour and North Harbour • Two o/n units, shared B • TV and VCR in living room
FEATURES: French spoken • Movies available
RATES: $35 (1), $50 (2) • Full breakfast 8 • NSRS Member

St. George's Channel
Marble View Bed & Breakfast
Anne Martin, The Points, RR 2, West Bay, B0E 3K0
(902) 345-2281
Twenty-four km (15 mi) from St. Peter's on the Bras d'Or Trail in Richmond County • Secluded setting on the shores of the Bras d'Or Lake • Two o/n units, shared B
RATES: $35 (1), $45 (2) (STC) • Open May 15-Oct.15 • MC Visa accepted

St. Joseph du Moine
Conti's Bed & Breakfast
Arthur & Jacqueline Conti, 309
Bazile Road, St. Joseph du Moine,
B0E 3A0
(902) 224-2697
Three o/n units, shared B&S • TV
in living room
FEATURES: Panorama of ocean,
islands, lakes, mountains, sunsets •
French spoken • Arrangements for
whale-watching, deep-sea fishing
*RATES: $32 (1), $40 (2), $10-$15
add'l person • Full breakfast 8 •
Open May 15-Oct. 15 • MC, Visa
accepted*

St. Joseph du Moine
Pilot Whale
Bed & Breakfast
Cheryl Power, Bazile Road, St.
Joseph du Moine, B0E 3A0
(902) 224-2592
New log home • Three o/n units,
private & shared B&S • TV in
living room
FEATURES: Double fireplace
*RATES: $60-$85 (1-2) • Full
breakfast 7:30-9:30 • May 15-
Oct. 31*

Stellarton
MacDonalds
Bed & Breakfast
James & Rena MacDonald, 292
South Foord Street, Box 831,
Stellarton, B0K 1S0
(902) 752-7751
From Hwy 104, Exit 24, 10 minutes
from New Glasgow • Three o/n
units, one shared B
*RATES: $30 (1), $40 (2), $10 add'l
person (STC) • Full breakfast •
Open year-round • NSRS Member*

Stewiacke
Interval Pines
Bed & Breakfast
Joyce & Len Barak, 487 St.
Andrews Street, Box 415,
Stewiacke, B0N 2J0
(902) 639-2835
Hwy 102, Exit 11 • Large home,
secluded and private, in the St.
Andrew's River valley • One o/n
unit, shared B • Private and
centrally located TVs
FEATURES: Trout fishing •
Family unit available
*RATES: $45 (1-2) taxes incl. •
Continental breakfast 7-9 • Open
July 1-Aug. 31*

Summerville Beach
Summerville Beach
Retreat
June Lohnes-Davis, RR 1, Port
Mouton, Queen's County, B0T 1T0
(902) 683-2874
Toll-free 1-800-213-5868
From Hwy 103, Exit 20, 2 km (1
mi) • Three o/n units, one shared B
• Colour cable TV in two rooms •
Clock radio • Non-smoking only
FEATURES: Outside deck •
Screened spa • Three new deluxe
two-bedroom chalets available • Two
minutes from beach with lots of
privacy • Call for a vacation video
*RATES: $45 (1), $50-$60 (2), $10
add'l person • Full breakfast • B&B
open May 1-Sept. 30, chalets
year-round Visa accepted •
Off-season rates available for
chalets NSFCV; NSRS Member*

Sydney
Anne's Bed & Breakfast
Anne & Bob Gaetz, 34 Amelia
Street, Sydney, B1P 6C2
(902) 539-3536

Turn-of the-century home • Three o/n units, two shared B&S • Colour cable TV in rooms • No smoking in rooms
FEATURES: Furnished with antiques
RATES: $35 (1), $40 (2), $10 add'l person (cot) (STC) • Full breakfast 7-9 • Open year-round

Sydney
Gathering House Bed & Breakfast ★★½
Jean & Ken Phillips, 148 Crescent Street, Sydney, B1S 2Z8
(902) 539-7172
Easy access from Kings Rd. (Hwy 104 & 105) George St. (Rte. 125) overlooking Wentworth Park • Three o/n units, two shared B&S • Centrally located TV
FEATURES: Antiques • Veranda therapy • Sunday park concerts
RATES: $40 (1), $45-$55 (2), $15 add'l person • Full breakfast 7:30-9 • Open year-round • Off-season by reservation • Long-term rates available • NSRS Member

Sydney
Old Country Post Office B&B
Dr. Pushpa Rathor, 3 Strathcona Street, Sydney, B1R 1X7
(902) 539-8033
Two o/n units, shared B&S, suite with private B • Non-smoking only
FEATURES: A unique experience • Palm reading and stress reduction, meditation available with hostess, who is also an artist, writer and musician
RATES: $45 (1), $50 (2), $60 (suite) • Breakfast (vegetarian, non-vegetarian, Indian) 7-9 • Open May 1-Oct. 31 • Off-season by arrangement

Sydney
Park Place Bed & Breakfast
Evanel McEwen, 169 Park Street, Sydney, B1P 6W7
(902) 562-3518
Exit 8 from Hwy 125, take George St. to second traffic lights, right onto Cottage Rd. left onto Park St. • Victorian house • Three o/n units, one shared B&S • Colour cable TV and radio • Non-smoking only
RATES: $35 (1), $40 (2) (STC) • Full breakfast 7-9 • Open May-Oct. • MC, Visa accepted • Off-season by reservation • NSRS Member

Sydney
Rockinghorse Inn ★★★
Margaret Glabay, 259 Kings Road, Sydney, B1S 1A7
(902) 539-2696
Registered Heritage Property • Eight o/n units, six private and two shared B • Colour cable TV in common area • No smoking in rooms
FEATURES: Decorated with antiques • Dinner by reservation • Library of steelworkers and miners of Cape Breton • Sunroom • Honeymoon suite available
RATES: $55-$100 (2), $10 add'l person • Full breakfast 8-9 • Open year-round • MC, Visa accepted • NSRS Member

Sydney
White Maples
Bed & Breakfast
Pamela Roberts, 72 Curry Street,
Box 6036, Sydney, B1P 5G5
(902) 564-4674
Hwy 125, Exit 6 to Rte. 4, 5 km (3
mi) to Howie Centre; or Rte 4, 6
km (3.5 mi) past Sydney River
Tourist Bureau • One o/n unit,
shared B&S • Colour cable TV in
room • No pets, please • No
smoking in room
*RATES: $32-$35 (1), $40 (2)
(STC) • Full breakfast 7-9 • Open
May 15-Oct. 15*

Sydney Forks
Christie's
Bed & Breakfast
Olive Christie, 2486 Kings Road,
Sydney Forks, B1L 1A1
(902) 564-9364
Hwy 125, Exit 6, 7 km (4.5 mi)
towards St. Peter's • Three o/n
units, shared B&S • Colour cable
TV and VCR in recreation room •
Non-smoking only
FEATURES: Pool table, games
available • Model ship display
*RATES: $30 (1), $45 (2), $8 add'l
person • Full breakfast 8-10 • Open
June 1-Nov. 15*

Sydney Mines
Annandale Bed &
Breakfast ★★★
Meg Sargent & Scott Phillips, 157
Shore Road, Sydney Mines, B1V 1A9
(902) 544-1052
Hwy 105, Exit 21 to Rte. 305 N, 3
km (2 mi) • Victorian house (c.
1880) • Four o/n units, one B&S •
TV/VCR and telephone in lounge •
Pets with permission •
Non-smoking only

FEATURES: Antiques • Veranda
with ocean view • Croquet • Five
minutes from Newfoundland ferry
*RATES: $38-$48 (1), $45-$60 (2)
(STC) • Full breakfast 7:30-9 •
Open year-round • MC, Visa
accepted Dec.-March by reservation*

Sydney Mines
Garland Stubbert's
Bed & Breakfast ★★★
Garland Stubbert, 117 Shore Road,
Sydney Mines, B1V 1A5
(902) 736-8466
Hwy 105, Exit 21 to Rte. 305
North, 2.5 km (1.5 mi) from
Newfoundland ferry • Three o/n
units, one B&S • Colour cable TV
in lounge • Non-smoking only
FEATURES: Large deck
overlooking harbour • Barbecue &
camp stove
*RATES: $40 (2), $16 add'l person
(STC) • Full breakfast 7-9 • Open
May 1-Oct. 31 • NSRS Member*

Sydney Mines
Gowrie House Country
Inn ★★★
C.J. Matthews & K.W. Tutty, 139
Shore Road, Sydney Mines, B1V 1A5
(902) 544-1050
Hwy 105, Exit 21 to Rte. 305 North,
3 km (2 mi) • Historic Georgian
house • Six o/n units, two shared B,
four bed-sitting rooms, private B,
fireplace • Colour cable TV in some
rooms • No smoking in rooms
FEATURES: Antiques showcase •
Dinner 7:30 p.m., reservations
required • English gardens •
Veranda and decks
*RATES: $55-$115 (1), $65-$125
(2), $15 add'l person, MAP $35
extra • Breakfast 7:30-9:30 • Open
May 1-Oct. 30 • MC, Visa accepted
• IGNS; NSRS; UCI Member*

Tantallon
Stillwater Lake Bed & Breakfast
Elaine MacInnis, 40 Stillwater Lake Drive, Tantallon, B0J 3J0
(902) 826-1105
Fax (902) 826-2435
Hwy 103, Exit 5, or Hwy 102, Exit 3, Hammonds Plains Rd. to Stillwater Lake Dr. • Two o/n units, shared B&S • Colour cable TV and VCR in living room • No pets, please • Non-smoking only
FEATURES: Sundeck overlooking lake • Bonfire pit • Lake swimming, fishing, skating, cross-country skiing, snowshoeing • Canoe available
RATES: $45 (1), $55 (2) • Full breakfast 7-9 • Open year-round

Tantallon
Teddy Bear Trail Bed & Breakfast
Thomas Betts, 2 Whynacht's Point Road, Box 2548, RR 2, Tantallon, B0J 3J0
(902) 826-7960
Hwy 103, Exit 5, follow Peggy's Cove signs to Rte. 333, proceed approx. 4 km (2.5 mi) on Rte. 333 to Whynacht's Point Road • Overlooking a quiet cove • Three o/n units, shared B&S, suite with queen, private B, living room • Colour cable TV and VCR in common room • Telephone • Children under 12 yrs free • No pets, please • Non-smoking only
FEATURES: Rooms at ground level for easy access, ideal for asthmatics or sensitive individuals
RATES: $50 (1), $60 (2), $75-$85 (suite), $10 add'l person • Full breakfast 8 • Open year-round • No strong scents, please • NSRS Member

Tarbotvale
Greer's Cabot Trail Bed & Breakfast
Bob & Ann Greer, RR 4, Tarbotvale, B0E 1B0
(902) 929-2115
Turn in at Tarbotvale, cross bridge and up the hill. Close to Gaelic College, 1/2 hr. from Baddeck • Three o/n units, two B&S • No pets, please • No smoking inside
FEATURES: Special diet needs considered
RATES: $40 (1), $50 (2) (STC) • Full breakfast • Open June 15-Sept. 15 • MC, Visa accepted • CBBBA; NSFC; NSRS Member

Tatamagouche
Mountain Breeze Farm Bed &Breakfast
Hannelore & Herbert Deffren, RR 4, Tatamagouche, B0K 1V0
Tel & Fax (902) 657-3193
Hwy 6 to Maple Ave. in Tatamagouche, then take first left onto Truro Rd. for approx. 3 km (2 mi) • Three o/n units, one B&S • Non-smoking only
FEATURES: Deck • Barbecue • Sauna and whirlpool
RATES: $40 (1), $45 (2) • Full breakfast 7-10 Open year-round • Packages available • NSRS Member

Tatamagouche
Train Station Inn ★★★
Shelley & James LeFresne, Station Rd, Box 67, Tatamagouche, B0K 1V0
(902) 657-3222
Restored century-old train station with railway cars • Five o/n units in station, private B&S, two mini suites in train cars, private B • Private and centrally located TVs and VCRs • Cots available
FEATURES: Laundry facilities • Kitchen facilities • Air-conditioning (suites) • Outdoor skating, nature walks on old rail bed, bicycles
RATES: $40-$55 (1), $45-$68.75 (2), $98 (railway cars), $5-$10 add'l person • Continental breakfast 8-10 • Open year-round • AE, DIS, MC, Visa accepted

Trenton
Three Flags
Bed & Breakfast
Carolyn Duncan, RR 1, Trenton, B0K 1X0
(902) 755-6289
From west on Hwy 104, Exit 22 to Hwy 106, Exit 1A toward Trenton, 7 km (4.3 mi) to flashing light (Rte. 348), left 17 km (10 mi) to Black Point Rd., 1 km (0.5 mi), left hand side. From Pictou Rotary (PEI ferry) Hwy 106, Exit 1A, same as above. From east on Hwy 104, exit 27A, follow Melmerby Beach signs, 8 km (5 mi) to stop sign, left 5 km (3 mi) to Black Point Rd., 1 km (0.5 mi) left hand side • Three o/n units, one private and two shared B&S • Colour cable TV centrally located • Clock radio • No pets, please • Non-smoking only
FEATURES: Great waterfront view
RATES: $40-$50 (1), $50-$60 (2) (STC) • Full breakfast • Open year-round • Reservations only

Truro
Blue House Inn B&B
Doug & Enid Jennings, 43 Dominion Street, Truro, B2N 3P2
(902) 895-4150
Two o/n units with vanity basin, full B&S • Colour cable TV, radio and fan in rooms • Colour cable TV/VCR in living room • No alcohol • Non-smoking only
FEATURES: Kitchen facilities • Piano in living room
RATES: $39 (1), $47 (2), $8 add'l person (STC) • Full breakfast • Open July 1-Aug. 31

Truro
Elizabeth House
Bed & Breakfast ★★★
Betty Kelly, 401 Robie Street, Truro, B2N 1L9
(902) 893-2346
Hwy 102, Exit 14 • Three o/n units, one B&S • Colour cable TV in lounge • Non-smoking only
FEATURES: Deck off guest rooms • Evening tea • Homemade sweets
RATES: $35 (1) $40 (2) (STC) • Full breakfast 7-9 • Open year-round

Truro
Silver Firs
Bed & Breakfast ★★★½
Bev & Grant Richardson, 397 Prince Street, Truro, B2N 1E1
Tel & Fax: (902) 897-1900
Three o/n units, private B, one suite with TV and clock radio • Colour cable TV in lounge • Children over 12 yrs welcome • Non-smoking only
FEATURES: Air-conditioning • Suite has twin and hide-a-bed
RATES: $50 (1), $75 (2), $95 (suite), $10 add'l person • Full breakfast 8-9:30 • Open May

15-Oct. 15 • *Off-season by request* •
IGNS Member

Truro
Suncatcher
Bed & Breakfast
Ruth & Gerry Mailloux, 25 Wile
Crest Avenue, North River, RR 6,
Truro, B2N 5B4
(902) 893-7169
Near Hwys 102 and 104, please call
for directions • Two o/n units,
shared B • Colour cable TV in
family room • Cot available • No
pets, please • Non-smoking only
FEATURES: French spoken
*RATES: $30 (1), $40 (2), $8 add'l
person* • *Full breakfast at guests'
convenience* • *Open year-round*

Tusket
Plum Tree
Bed & Breakfast ★★★
Jill & Larry Trask, Box 115, RR 1,
Tusket, B0W 3M0
(902) 648-3159
Hwy 103, Exit 33, follow signs •
Three o/n units, shared B&S •
Colour cable TV in living room
FEATURES: Deck with barbecue •
Picnic tables • Garden • Walking trails
*RATES: $35 (1), $40-$45 (2), $10
add'l person* • *Continental
breakfast* • *Open May 1-Nov. 1* •
NSRS Member

Tusket
Vaughn Lake
Bed & Breakfast
George & Dale Duncanson, Box 88,
Gavelton, Tusket, Yarmouth, B0W 3M0
(902) 648-3122
Fax (902) 648-0012
At Gavelton, 15 minutes from
Maine ferries; from Hwy 103, exit
33 at Tusket, follow signs 3.5 km

(2.5 mi) • Four o/n units, 1 1/2
B&S • Cable TV in living room •
Children welcome
FEATURES: Kitchen facilities •
Sun deck • Swimming
*RATES: $35 (1), $40 (2), $100
(whole house)* • *Full breakfast 7-10*
• *Open Apr.-Nov.* • *NSRS Member*

Upper Clements
Cheshire Cat B&B
Betty McKaigue, RR 2, Annapolis
Royal, B0S 1A0
Tel & Fax (902) 532-7655
Three o/n units, private S, five
housekeeping suites, private S,
some private entrances • Colour
cable TV in lounge and suites •
Radio • Children under 10 yrs free
FEATURES: View over Annapolis
River • Twenty wooded acres with
hiking trails • Bird-watching
*RATES: $35 (1), $40 (2), $45 (3),
$50 (queen), $40-$70 (suite), $10
add'l person* • *Full breakfast 7-9* •
Open May 15-Oct. 15 • *NSRS
Member*

Victoria Beach
Golden Anchor Inn B&B
Bertha & Bill Titus, Victoria Beach,
RR 2, Granville Ferry, B0S 1K0
(902) 532-2960
25 km (15 mi) west of Annapolis
causeway • Three o/n units, family
room with one double and one twin,
one with twin and private 1/2 B, one
with double, two shared B&S • TV in
lounge • Clock radio • Cots available
FEATURES: View of Bay of
Fundy and sunsets • Kitchen
facilities • Ceiling fan • Picnic tables
*RATES: $30 (1), $35 (2), $45
(family), $10 add'l person* •
Continental breakfast 8-9 • *Open
May 15-Oct. 15* • *Visa accepted* •
NSFC; NSRS Member

Vogler's Cove
Shorebirds B&B
Judy & Len Brown, 8728 Rte. 331,
Vogler's Cove, B0J 2H0
(902) 677-2056
Fax (902) 677-2184
Hwy 103, Exit 16 from Halifax, 9.5
km (6 mi), turn left at T junction on
to Rte. 331, Exit 17 from Yarmouth
• Three o/n units, shared B&S, one
with queen bed, one with twin and
one with double • Children 12 or
older welcome • No pets, please •
Non-smoking only
FEATURES: Sitting room for
reading, games or music • Scenic
view of harbour
*RATES: $35 (1), $45-$50 (2), $12
add'l person • Full breakfast •
Open June 15-Sept. 15 • MC, Visa
accepted • NSRS Member*

Wallace
Crumpetty Tree
Bed & Breakfast ★★★
Joyce Langille, 1154 Wallace River
West Road, RR 3, Wallace, B0K 1Y0
(902) 257-2610
Three km (2 mi) west of Wallace •
Three o/n units, one shared B&S,
one shared full B • Colour cable TV
in lounge • Cots and crib available •
Children under 3 yrs free
FEATURES: Piano in lounge •
Canoe available • Bicycles available •
Picnic table and barbecue • Ceiling fans
*RATES: $30 (1) $40 (2), $5-$10 add'l
person • Full breakfast • Open June
1-Sept. 30 • Visa accepted • Senior
citizens' discount • IGNS; NSRS Member*

Wallace
Drysdale's
Bed & Breakfast
Nancy & Ira Drysdale, Rte. 6,
Wallace, B0K 1Y0

(902) 257-2440
Turn-of-the-century home beside
Wallace Harbour • Two o/n units,
shared B • Colour cable TV in guests'
sitting room Non-smoking only
FEATURES: Barbecue • Picnic
table in garden • Swimming, hiking
and bird-watching
*RATES: $35 (1), $40 (2),
$210-$240 (weekly) • Open June
15-Sept. 15*

Wallace
Jubilee Cottage
Country Inn
Les & Daphne Dominy, Hwy 6,
Wallace, B0K 1Y0
Tel & Fax (902) 257-2432,
Off-season (506) 529-1912
On Rte. 6 • Three o/n units, one
with fireplace, full B&S • Colour
cable TV/VCR in parlour •
Non-smoking only
FEATURES: Ocean view •
Five-course dinner for guests only
by reservation • Evening snack •
Ceiling fans • Horseshoes, croquet •
Migratory stopover for Great Blue
Herons and Canada Geese
*RATES: $60 (2), $7 add'l person •
Full breakfast • Open June 1-Oct.
14 • MC, Visa accepted •
Cancellation policy • Packages
available*

Waterville
Orchard Hill House
Country Inn ★★★½
Kim & Norma Banks, RR 1,
Waterville, NS, B0P 1V0
(902) 538-9750
Hwy 101, Exit 14, 12 km (7.5 mi)
west toward Berwick, or Hwy 101,
Exit 15, south on Rte. 360 to Rte. 1,
then turn left 2.5 km (1.5 mi) • One
hundred-acre produce and dried
flower century farm • Three o/n units,

private B&S • Colour cable TV in lounge • No pets, please • No smoking in rooms
FEATURES: Dining room • Guest living room with fireplace • Garden • Walking trails • Volleyball • Bird-watching • Farm market
RATES: $53 (1), $58 (2), $8 add'l person • Full breakfast • Open Apr. 1-Oct. 31 • MC, Visa accepted Cancellation policy • NSRS Member

West Arichat
Maison Emile Mouchet B&B
Maurice D. LeBlanc, General Delivery, West Arichat, B0E 3J0
(902) 226-9740
Hwy 104, Exit 46 to Rte. 320, follow to Rte. 206 to West Arichat • Three o/n units, shared B&S • No pets, please
FEATURES: Salt water shoreline
RATES: No rates available • Full breakfast 7-9 • Open May-Oct. • Off-season by reservation

West Dover
Joanne's Bed & Breakfast
Joanne Publicover, 6922 Rte. 333, West Dover, B0J 3L0
(902) 823-3006
View of West Dover Harbour from deck • Two o/n units, shared B&S • Private and centrally located TVs • Non-smoking only
RATES: $50 (1-2) taxes incl. • Full breakfast 7-9

West Dover (Middle Village)
Oceanside Inn Bed & Breakfast ★★★
Tom & Dorothy Code, General Delivery, Peggy's Cove, B0J 2N0
Tel & Fax (902) 823-2765

On Rte. 333, 5 km (3 mi) east of Peggy's Cove at Middle Village Road, West Dover • Three o/n units, one queen suite with private whirlpool, bidet, twin Italian sinks, TV; two rooms with private B • Colour cable TV/VCR • No pets, please • Non-smoking only
FEATURES: Private nature trails • Ocean swimming • Sandy beach • Complimentary rowboats
RATES: $60-$95, $10 add'l person (STC) • Full breakfast 8 • Open year-round

West Jeddore
Jonah By The Sea B&B
Dora & Bill Jonah, 624 Lower West Jeddore Road, RR 1, Head of Jeddore, B0J 1P0
(902) 889-3516
From Rte. 7, exit at Head of Jeddore to West Jeddore Road, eight minutes to mouth of harbour • Country home (c. 1900) in quaint fishing village • Three o/n units, shared B • TV • No pets, please • Non-smoking only
FEATURES: View of ocean, Jeddore Rock and light • Private beach • Walking trails • Clam digging, bird-watching, fishing
RATES: $35 (1), $40-$45 (2), $10 add'l person (STC) • Full breakfast 8-9 • Open May-Oct. • Visa accepted • Off-season by arrangement • NSRS Member

West Jeddore
Serenity
Bed & Breakfast
Keith & Marilyn Baker, RR 1,
Head Jeddore, B0J 1P0
(902) 889-2489
Exit Rte. 7 at Head Jeddore, 8 km (5
mi) to West Jeddore Overlooking
Jeddore Harbour • Three o/n units, two
B&S, one housekeeping unit, radio in
rooms • Colour cable TV in lounge •
No pets, please • Non-smoking only
FEATURES: Salt-water swimming
*RATES: $35 (1), $40(2), $10 add'l
person, $50 (housekeeping) •
Continental breakfast 7-9 • Open
mid-June-mid-Sept. • Weekly $250 •
NSRS Member*

Westport
Brier House
Claire Leng, Westport, B0V 1H0
(902) 839-2879
Rte. 217 via two ferries to Westport •
Waterfront property • Three o/n units,
one shared B&S • TV/VCR, radio in
lounge • Children under 2 yrs free
FEATURES: Whale and bird library
*RATES: $35 (1), $45 (2), $10 add'l
person • Full breakfast • Open Apr.
1-Oct. 31 • MC, Visa accepted • Apr.,
May and Nov. by reservation only*

Westport
Westport Inn B&B
Roland & Nancy Swift, Box 1226,
Westport, Brier Island, B0V 1H0
(902) 839-2675
Fax **(902) 839-2245**
Brier Island, Rte. 217 • Three o/n
units, one private B, one shared
B&S • TV and VCR in lounge
FEATURES: Licensed dining room
*RATES: $35 (1), $45 (2), $10 add'l
person • Full breakfast • Open May
1-Oct. 31 • MC, Visa accepted*

White Point
Two Tittle
Bed and Breakfast
Cyril & Marguerite Dunphy, 2119
White Point Road, RR 2, Dingwall,
B0C 1T0
(902) 383-2817
Exit off Cabot Trail on to alternate
scenic route at Neils Harbour or at
White Point Rd. • Waterfront
property • Three o/n units, two
B&S • TV in lounge • No pets,
please • Non-smoking only
FEATURES: Patio overlooking Aspy
Bay • Hiking trails • Sandy beach
*RATES: $35 (1), $45-$48 (2)
(STC) • Full breakfast 7:30-8:30 •
Open year-round • CBBBA; NSRS
Member*

White's Lake
Inn Joy
Bed & Breakfast
Joyce & Jerry Platz, 3505 Rte. 333,
White's Lake, B3L 4J4
(902) 852-2543
Two o/n units, private B&S and S •
Colour cable TV and VCR in living
room • No pets, please • No smoking
in rooms
*RATES: $40 (1), $50 (2) • Full
breakfast 7-10 • Open June 1-Sept.
30 • MC, Visa accepted*

Whycocomagh
Mary Smith
Bed and Breakfast
Mary Smith, 21 Lakeview Drive,
Whycocomagh, B0E 3M0
(902) 756-2157
Hwy 105, turn on Main St. and
follow sign • Two o/n units, shared
B&S • TV in living room • Radio
*RATES: $35 (1), $45 (2), taxes
incl. • Full breakfast 8 • Open May
15-Oct. 15 • Cats on premises*

Windsor
Boegel's
Bed & Breakfast ★★★
Sharon & Terry Boegel, 145 Dill
Road, RR 1, Windsor, B0N 2T0
(902) 798-4183
Fax (902) 798-1063
Only minutes from Hwy 101, Exit
5, west on Rte. 14 toward Martock
to Dill Rd., or Exit 5A Wentworth
St. towards Martock to King St. to
Hwy 14 • Quiet scenic area on the
edge of town • Three o/n units, one
shared B&S • Colour cable
TV/VCR in living room • Clock
radio • Non-smoking only
FEATURES: Fax service • 8 km to
Ski Martock • Twenty minutes from
Wolfville
*RATES: $35 (1), $40-$45 (2), $10
add'l person • Full breakfast
7:30-9:30 • Open year-round • MC,
Visa accepted • Cat on premises •
Ski package available • B&B online
(bb@proton.com); NSRS Member*

Windsor
Clockmaker's Inn ★★★
Veronica & Dennis Connelly, 1399
King Street, Curry's Corner,
Windsor, B0N 1H0
Tel & Fax (902) 798-5265
Victorian home • Four o/n units,
two with
fireplaces,
one shared
B&S and
1/2 B •
Colour cable
TV in
lounge •
Crib

available • No pets, please •
Non-smoking only
FEATURES: Provincial Heritage
Property furnished with antiques •
Baby grand piano, video library of

classical music • Bicycles •
Barbecue
*RATES: $35 (1), $45-$50 (2), $10
add'l person • Full breakfast
7:30-9:30 • Open year-round • MC,
Visa accepted IGNS; NSRS Member*

Windsor
Fiddlehead Inn B&B
Lesley Crowe, 307 King Street,
Box 2550, Windsor, B0N 2T0
(902) 798-2659
Hwy 101, Exit 6, right at stop sign
then first left (between museum and
church) • Three o/n units, private
B&S • Colour cable TV and VCR in
den • No pets, please • Non-smoking
only
FEATURES: Outdoor swimming
pool
*RATES: $46 (1-2), $52-$58 (suite)
• Open year-round • NSRS Member*

Wolfville
Birchcliff
Bed & Breakfast
Leah B. Patterson, 84 Main Street,
Box 736, Wolfville, B0P 1X0
(902) 542-3391
Two o/n units, shared B&S, studio
(four people), private B • TV
*RATES: $35 (1), $40 (2), $60
(studio, 2), $10 add'l person (STC)
• Full breakfast 8-9:30 • Open May
15-Aug. 31*

Wolfville
Blomidon Inn ★★★★
Donna & Jim Laceby, 27 Main
Street, Box 839, Wolfville, B0P 1X0
(902) 542-2291
Fax (902) 542-7461
Toll free 1-800-565-2291
Restored 1877 sea captain's mansion
on four acres of terraced lawns •
Twenty-six o/n units, private B, two
with fireplace, two with Jacuzzi •
Two rooms wheelchair accessible •
33-in. colour cable TV in parlour
FEATURES: Two licensed dining
rooms and outdoor terrace,
reservations recommended •
Air-conditioning
*RATES: $69-$119 (S), $79-$119
(2), $119-$129 (suite), $12 add'l
person, $109-$159 (2, MAP) •
Continental breakfast 7:30-10 •
Open year-round • MC, Visa
accepted • Cancellation policy •
Off-season rates Nov. 1-Apr. 30 •
CAA; NSRS; TNS; UCI Member*

Wolfville
Gingerbread House Inn ★★★
Pat & Hedley Duffield, 8 Robie
Tufts Drive, Wolfville, B0P 1X0
(902) 542-1458
1990 Nova Scotia Government
Award for Excellence in House
Design • Four o/n units and one
suite, private B&S or S, clock
radios and ceiling fans • TV in
rooms • No pets, please
Non-smoking only
FEATURES: Suite has infloor spa,
fireplace, wet bar, and small
sleeping loft
*RATES:$59-$79 (1), $65-$89 (2),
$105-$135 (suite), $15 add'l person
• Full breakfast 8-9:30 • Open
year-round • Visa accepted • NSRS
Member*

Wolfville
Seaview House Bed & Breakfast
Loretta Premi, 8 Seaview Avenue,
Wolfville, B0P 1X0
(902) 542-1436
Fax (902) 542-2873
 Hwy 101, Exit 10 or 11 to Main
St., Wolfville, to Seaview Ave. •
Three o/n units, private and shared
B • Colour cable TV and VCR in
guest lounge • Non-smokng only
*RATES: $45-$65 (1-2), $10 add'l
person • Full breakfast 8-9:30 •
Open May-Sept. • Visa accepted •
Off-season by reservation • NSRS
Member*

Wolfville
Tattingstone Inn ★★★★½
Betsey Harwood, 434 Main Street,
Wolfville, B0P 1X0
Toll free 1-800-565-7696
Fax (902) 542-4427
Registered Heritage Property • Ten
o/n units, private B&S • TV in rooms
• Clock radio • Telephone in rooms •
No pets, please • Non-smoking only
FEATURES: Licensed dining room
Air-conditioning • Outdoor heated
swimming pool • Cottage available
*RATES: $78-$125 • Breakfast
8-9:30 • Open year-round • AE,
MC, Visa accepted • Cancellation
policy • Packages available • CAA;
NSRS; TNS Member*

Wolfville
Victoria's Historic Inn and Carriage House ★★★★
Urbain & Carol Cryan, 416 Main
Street, Box 308, Wolfville, B0P 1X0
(902) 542-5744
Fax (902) 542-7794
Sixteen o/n units and three suites in
inn and carriage house, private B,

suites have Jacuzzi • Colour cable TV in rooms • Telephone in rooms • No pets, please • Non-smoking only
FEATURES: Licensed dining room by reservation
RATES: $79-$125, $10 add'l person • Breakfast 8-9:30 • Open year-round • DC, MC, Visa accepted • CAA; NSRS; UCI Member

Woods Harbour
Flossie's Bed & Breakfast
Sherry Sears, RR 1, Woods Harbour, B0W 2E0
(902) 723-2496
On Rte. 3, from Hwy 103, Exit 29 from Shelburne or Exit 31 from Yarmouth • Three o/n units, one shared B • Colour cable TV
FEATURES: Kitchen facilities
RATES: $30 (1), $40 (2) • Full breakfast 7-9:30 • Open June 1- Aug. 31

Yarmouth
Clementine's Bed & Breakfast ★★★
Evelyn & Ron Gray, 21 Clements Street, Yarmouth, B5A 2B9
(902) 742-0079
Three o/n units, three shared Bs • Coloured cable TV in lounge • No pets, please • Not suitable for children • Non-smoking only
RATES: $50-$60 • Full breakfast • Open May-Nov. • Cash or cheque only

Yarmouth
Morrow Bed & Breakfast
Denny & Jennie Morrow, 481 Main Street, Yarmouth, B5A 1H4
(902) 742-9265

Historic Georgian-style home • Two o/n units, two B
FEATURES: Artist's studio • Art gallery
RATES: $40 (1), $45-$55 (2) • Full breakfast • MC, Visa accepted • NSRS Member

Yarmouth
Murray Manor (c. 1820) ★★★
George & Joan Semple, 225 Main Street, Yarmouth, B5A 1C6
Tel & Fax (902) 742-9625
Heritage property • Three o/n units, 1 1/2 shared Bs
FEATURES: Acadian French spoken • Afternoon tea 3-4 p.m. • Gardens • Close to ferry, bus, airport, shops and museums

RATES: $50 (1), $60 (2) • Full breakfast • Open year-round • Visa accepted • NSRS Member

Yarmouth
Victorian Vogue Bed & Breakfast
Dawn-Marie Skjelmose, 109 Brunswick Street, Yarmouth, B5A 2H2
(902) 742-6398
Sea captain's Queen Anne Revival historic home • Five o/n units, two shared B, one with B&S • Non-smoking only
RATES: $38 (1), $45-$60 (2) (STC) • Full breakfast • Open year-round • NSRS Member

Prince Edward Island

Alberton
Cold Comfort Farm ★★★
Marilyn Wells, Box 105, Alberton,
C0B 1B0
(902) 853-2803
Rte. 12 near Alberton • Handsome
house • Three o/n units, shared B
FEATURES: Hundreds of books •
Surrounded by gardens • Solitude or
conversation • Name is a family joke
RATES: $45 (2), $10 add'l person
• Elegant breakfast • Open June
15-Sept. 15 • Weekly $270 (2), $50
add'l person. • Breakfast

Alberton
Poplar Lane
Bed & Breakfast ★★
Dick & Gaya Dykerman, Box 257,
Alberton, C0B 1B0
(902) 853-3732
Turn left off Main St. onto Poplar St.
at end of road • Built 1912, quiet
location • Three o/n units, one B&S,
one room, verandah; two with cable
TV • Pets permitted, usually on leash
FEATURES: Dining room within
walking distance
RATES: $35 (2), $7 add'l person, no
GST • Continental breakfast, full
breakfast extra • Open June 1-Sept. 15

Albion Cross
Needles and Haystacks
Bed & Breakfast ★★½
Fred Foster, RR 2, St. Peters Bay,
C0A 2A0
(902) 583-2928

Toll free 1-800-563-2928
Rte. 327, 500 m off Rte. 4 • Large
1880s home surrounded by farm
country • Four o/n units, one B, one
S, three rooms with double bed, one
with twin singles • Pets permitted
FEATURES: Antique furnishings •
Sun deck with hot tub • Ideal for
cycling, walks, bird watching •
White beaches, restaurants, golf
nearby • Info. on eastern PEI
attractions • Winter by reservation
only
RATES: $45 (2), $5 add'l person •
Delicious homey breakfasts • Open
June 1-Oct. 31 • MC, Visa accepted
• Reservations preferred • Weekly
$275 (2), $30 add'l person •
TIAPEI Member

Augustine Cove
Shore Farm
Bed & Breakfast ★★½
Mrs. Roy Cutcliffe, Port Borden
RR 1, Augustine Cove, C0B 1X0
(902) 855-2871
Rte. 10, 8 km east of Borden ferry •
Farm, 200 acres with private beach
• Three o/n units, two B&S, 1/2 B,
Double and twin beds, private
entrance • Adults preferred • No
pets, please • Non-smoking only
FEATURES: Private beach 600 m
RATES: $40 (2), $5 add'l person •
Breakfast extra • Open May-Oct. 31

Baltic
Shady Lawn
Bed & Breakfast ★★
Florence & Burrows MacPhail,
RR5, Kensington, C0B 1M0
(902) 836-5580
Toll free 1-800-275-7972
Rte. 103, 10 km from Kensington •
Century home in farming
community with quiet, shaded,
spacious
lawns • Five
o/n units,
two shared
B&S, double
and single
beds • TV in
family room
• Cot and
crib available • Pets permitted,
usually on leash • Non-smoking only
FEATURES: Gardens • Horseshoes
• Sand box • Housekeeping unit
available • Restaurants and
attractions nearby • Five minutes to
beach
*RATES: $35-$50 (1-2), $60-$76
(suite), Weekly $390-$500 (2-5),
$8-$15 add'l person • Full
breakfast • Open year-round •
Off-season rates Oct. 1-May 30 •
Cash or travellers cheques • KATA;
LATA Member*

Bay Fortune
The Inn at Bay
Fortune ★★★½
David Wilmer, Souris RR 4, C0A
2B0 (winter: 49 Bond Street,
Hartford, CT, USA, 06114, (860)
296-1348)
(902) 687-3745
Fax: (902) 687-3540
Former summer home of Broadway
playwright Elmer Harris and late
actress Colleen Dewhurst (Marilla,
Anne of Green Gables) • Eleven o/n

units, private B&S, eight with
fireplace sitting area
FEATURES: Recommended by
Where to Eat in Canada as
"without question the best on the
Island" • Overlooking Fortune
Harbour, with the Northumberland
Strait beyond • Dinner only
*RATES: $120-$175 (2), $25 add'l
person • Full breakfast • Open May
24 to mid-Oct.*

Bay Fortune
Odds & Ends
Bed & Breakfast ★★½
June Underhay, Souris RR 4, C0A 2B0
(902) 687-2980
Quiet family home on 100-acre
farm with view of Northumberland
Strait • Three o/n units, queen and
twin beds, shared B&S
FEATURES: Flower and vegetable
gardens • Laundry facilities •
Kitchen facilities • Deck • Barbecue
• Picnic table • Lawn • Golf, fine
dining and beaches nearby
*RATES: $40-$70 • Breakfast •
Open June 15-Nov. 30*

Belle River
J.R.'s Tourist Home
Arthur & Jan Roome, Belle River
RR 1, C0A 1B0
(902) 962-2183
On Belle River Wharf Road, off
TransCanada Hwy • Century
farmhouse on three landscaped
acres • Two o/n units, double beds,
one shared B&S, 1/2 private B •
Colour TV and VCR • Pets
permitted • Non-smoking only
FEATURES: Minutes from Wood
Islands ferry
*RATES: $40 (2) • Continental
breakfast • Open May 1-Oct. 15*

Bideford
Hilltop Acres
Bed & Breakfast ★★★
Mrs. Janice (Wayne) Trowsdale,
Box 3011, Ellerslie, C0B 1J0
(902) 831-2817
Rte. 166, Lady Slipper Dr., 3 km
west of Tyne Valley • Renovated
1930s country home on 75 acres•
Four o/n units, queen, double, twin,
one B&S • Centrally located colour
TV • Pets allowed • Non-smoking
FEATURES: Living/dining room for
guests • Croquet • Whirlpool tub •
Excellent for cycling and walking •
Second-storey balcony overlooks
scenic Goodwood River and Malpeque
Bay • Bay beach • 3 km to Tyne
Valley, ten minutes to Green Park
*RATES: $30-$40 (1), $38-$40 (2),
$10-$15 add'l person • Breakfast •
Open June 1-Sept. 30 • Discount on
second and subsequent nights,
group/family rates, weekly $235 (2),
$60-90 add'l person • Off-season by
reservation • PEIBBA Member*

Birch Hill
MacLean's
Bed and Breakfast ★★½
Mrs. Esther MacLean, RR 1,
Richmond, C0B1Y0
(902) 831-2570
Toll free 1-800-288-8112
Near junction of Rtes. 131 and 12
(Lady Slipper Dr.) • Three o/n units,
two B&S, 1/2 B. One room with
double bed, two with queen beds •
Two colour TVs • Cot and crib • Pets
permitted, usually on leash
FEATURES: Dinner theatre • Green
Park, golfing nearby • Beach on
property
*RATES: $35 (1), $40 (2), $10 add'l
person • Breakfast • Open
May 1-Dec. 10 • Weekly $225-$240*

*(2), $60 add'l person • TIAPEI
Member*

Bonshaw
Lone Star
Bed & Breakfast ★★
Herbert & Marie MacDonald, RR 1
Bonshaw, C0A 1C0
(902) 675-2209
400 m off TransCanada Hwy, 20
km west of Charlottetown • Dairy
farm with beautiful view of hills •
Three o/n units, one B&S, two with
double beds, one with single • One
colour TV • Non-smoking only
FEATURES: Bilingual • Golf
course & parks nearby • Beaches
nearby
*RATES: $25-$30 (1-2), $10 add'l
adult • Continental breakfast •
Open June-Sept. • Weekly $180 (2)*

Bonshaw
Oak Lane Farm
Bed & Breakfast ★★½
Ron Skinner/Dawn MacKinley, Box
781, Cornwall, C0A 1H0
(902) 675-3945
1-800-276-5197
On TransCanada Hwy, Rte. 1, 25
minutes from Charlottetown and 15
minutes from Borden ferry •
Peaceful 26-acre hobby horse farm
and vineyard near centre of PEI,
renovated century-old Green
Gables-style home • Two o/n units,
one B&S • Telephone •
Non-smoking only • Pets permitted
FEATURES: Bicycle storage •
Nature walkways and cycling •
Easy access to all PEI has to offer
*RATES: $44 (2), $8 add'l person,
taxes incl. • Continental breakfast •
Open May 1-Oct. 31 • Reservations
recommended • Off-season rates
available*

Bonshaw
Saw & Sickle
Bed & Breakfast ★★★
Paul & Wendy Naylor, Bonshaw
RR 1, Bonshaw, C0A 1C0
(902) 675-4004
Toll free 1-800-377-5792
On Green Rd. • New home, with
balcony, wrap around deck on six
acres, hill top view • Two o/n units,
one B&S, two large rooms, queen
and single beds, firm mattresses •
Non-smoking only
FEATURES: Walking, canoeing,
fishing, skiing, snowshoeing •
Outdoor hot tub
*RATES: $42 (1), $50 (2), $10 add'l
person • Breakfast • Open
year-round • Off-season rates*

Bonshaw
Strathgartney
Country Inn
Cathi & Blair McPhail, General
Delivery, Bonshaw, C0A 1C0
(902) 675-4711
Toll free 1-800-267-4407
On TransCanada Hwy 15 minutes west
of Charlottetown • Green-gabled
132-yr-old farmhouse-turned-inn • Nine
o/n units, eight B&S, 2 S • Partial
accessibility • Non-smoking only
FEATURES: Licensed dining room
with Murder Mystery • Housekeeping
unit available • Beaches, golfing,
theatre nearby
*RATES: $49-$125 (2) • Breakfast •
Open year-round • AE, MC, Visa
accepted*

Borden-Carleton
Carleton Cove Farm
Tourist Home
Gordon & Carol Myers, Albany RR
2, Carleton Siding, C0B 1A0
(902) 855-2795

On Rte. 10, 5 km from Borden
ferry in Carleton Siding • Mixed
farm property, 96 acres • Three o/n
units, one with double bed, one
with single and double, one with
two singles, private and shared
B&S • Four colour TVs • Cots
available • Pets permitted, usually
on leash • Non-smoking only
FEATURES: Complimentary
evening snack • Restaurant 4 km •
Shed for bicycles • Tour of farm on
request • Beach 6 km
*RATES: $30 (1), $35-$40 (2), $7
add'l person • Breakfast • Open
year- round • Weekly $210-$240
(2), $42 add'l person • Off-season
rates*

Borden-Carleton
MacCallum
Bed & Breakfast
Grace MacCallum, Port Borden
P.O., Port Borden, C0B 1X0
(902) 855-2229
Three km from Borden ferry •
Quiet country home • Two o/n
units, one B, one with double bed,
one with two single beds, shared B
• TV in living room • Cot available
FEATURES: Piano in living room
• Restaurants and attractions nearby
• Bicycle storage • Beach 5 km •
Excellent for late arrivals and early
departures • Ample parking
*RATES: $40 (2), $5 add'l person •
Breakfast extra • Open June 1-Sept. 30*

Brackley
Brackley House Bed & Breakfast ★★½
Len & Carol Lang, Brackley Point
Road, RR 9, Winsloe, C1E 1Z3
(902) 566-2268
Rte. 15 (Brackley Point Road)•
Century-old country home. Guest
parlour with fireplace. Spacious
grounds, garden and sundeck •
Three o/n units: king, double,
single, shared B&S • TV and VCR
• Cot available • No pets please •
Non-smoking only
FEATURES: Complimentary tea
and coffee in evening • Private
entrance • 3 km from airport, 10
minutes from Charlottetown's theatre
district and National Park beach
*RATES: $25 (1), $40-$50 (2), $10
add'l person, taxes incl. • Full
breakfast • Open May 1-Sept. 1*

Brackley
Lenrose Farm ★★★
Leonard & Rosemary MacCormack,
Winsloe RR9, Brackley, C1E 1Z3
(902) 368-8242
Across from airport and close to
beaches and Charlottetown • Horse
farm • One o/n unit, one B&S shared
FEATURES: Furnished with
antiques • Beaches nearby • Heated
swimming pool • Apartment, one
housekeeping unit available
*RATES: $35 (2), $5 add'l person •
Continental breakfast • Open June
1-Sept. 1 • Weekly $225 (2), $25
add'l person*

Brackley Beach
Blue Waters Tourist Home ★★
Lee & Judy Seaman, Brackley
Beach, RR 9, Winsloe, C1E 1Z3
(902) 672-2720

Five o/n units, two B&S
*RATES: $36-$41 (2), $4 add'l
person • Open June-Sept. • TIAPEI
Member*

Brackley Beach
Linden Lane Guest House ★★½
Margaret McCormack-Sosnkowski,
Britain Shore Road, Brackley
Beach, C1E 1Z3
(902) 672-3091
 Built in 1820 of PEI sandstone in
secluded Linden garden • Romance
vacations • Four rooms, three with
double beds, one with queen size,
shared B&S • Children over 12 yrs
welcome • Pets permitted, usually
on leash • Non-smoking only
FEATURES: French and German
spoken • Cyclists welcome
*RATES: $30-$50 (2), $10 add'l
person • Nutritious breakfast •
Open June-Sept. 30*

Brackley Beach
Windsong Farm Bed & Breakfast ★★½
Jean & John Huck, Brackley Beach,
RR 9, Winsloe, C1E 1Z3
(902) 672-2874
**Off-season (508) 540-3244; 17
Langley Rd., Falmouth, MA,
USA 02540**
Rte. 6 • Charming 1860 farmhouse
near Rustico Bay • Four o/n units,
three with double beds, one with
double and single, two B&S •
Colour TV • Children over 12
welcome • Non-smoking only
FEATURES: Furnished with
antiques • Complimentary tea &
cookies • Common room, sun
porches • Ocean beach 4 km •
*RATES: $55-$65 (2), $15 add'l
person, minimum stay two nights
July and August • Hearty breakfast*

*• Open late June to early Sept •
Weekly $330-$390 (2), $90 add'l
person • Off-season rates June and
Sept. • TIAPEI Member*

Brooklyn
Redcliffe Farm
Bed & Breakfast
Vera Bates, RR 1, Montague, C0A 1R0
(902) 838-2476
Toll free 1-800-663-3799
On Rte. 317, ten minutes from
Wood Islands ferry • Tastefully
renovated 200-year old farmhouse
on sheep farm • Three o/n units,
shared B&S • One colour TV • Pets
permitted, usually on leash
FEATURES: Dinner with advance
notice for 2-3 night stay • Porcelain
"Anne Shirley Dolls" hand-made on
premises • Ten minutes to Wood
Islands ferry
*RATES: $42-$50 (2), $8 add'l
person • Breakfast • Open June 1-
Oct.1*

Cable Head
Cable Head
Bed & Breakfast ★★½
Doug & Elizabeth Borman, St.
Peters Bay, C0A 2A0
(902) 961-3275
Rte. 16, 2 km north of Rte. 2 •
Modern home in unique setting •

Three o/n
units, two
B&S, all
with
queen-size
beds, one
with private
B, Jacuzzi
available to
guests • Cots and crib available •
Children welcome • Pets permitted •
Non-smoking only

FEATURES: Laundry facilities •
Licensed dining room 10 km •
Barbecues, picnic tables • One mile
from beautiful sandy beach, driving
range on property, 20 minutes to
championship golf courses • 3800'
x 100 ft. airstrip on property for
fly-in guests
*RATES: $40-$50 (2), $8 add'l
person • Continental breakfast •
Open year-round • MC accepted •
$225-$275 weekly, $35 add'l
person • Off-season rates Sept. 3-
June 23 • PEIBBA*

Cape Traverse
Glennhaven
Bed & Breakfast
Ed Cutcliffe, RR 1, Port Borden,
C0B 1X0
(902) 855-2729
Hwy 1 until Mowatt's Tourist Mart,
turn right for 1 km to where paved
road bears left • Christian home •
Three o/n units, one B&S •
Non-smoking only
FEATURES: 4 km from ferry and
new bridge, 2 km to safe tidal beach
*RATES: $18-$25 (1), $25-$50 (2),
$10 add'l person • Continental
breakfast • Open April-Nov. • Visa
accepted • Weekly $150-$300 (2),
$50 add'l person*

Cape Traverse
MacWilliams' Tourist Home & Cottages ★★
Mrs. Donald MacWilliams,
Borden-Carleton RR1, C0B 1X0
(902) 855-2855
Off Rte. 10 • Country setting
overlooking Northumberland Strait
• Two o/n units, double beds, one
B&S • Adults preferred •
Non-smoking only
FEATURES: Verandas • Picnic
tables • Flower gardens • Beach on
premises • Cottage and mobile
home available • Strait crossing,
tourism restaurant, stores nearby
*RATES: $35 (1-2), $7 add'l person
• Open May 15-Oct. 15*

Cavendish
Chinny-Chin-Chin
Elaine Miller, Forest Hills Park
Road, Cavendish, C0A 1N0
(902) 963-2377
One mi west on Rte. 6 from Rte. 6
& Rte. 13 traffic lights, turn left
opposite small white church on to
Forest Hill
Park Rd.,
first house
on left •
Located in
centre of
Cavendish •
Two o/n
units, shared
B&S • TV • Telephone •
Non-smoking

FEATURES: Large grounds •
Picnic table • Bicycle storage •
Cottage available • One mi to beach
• Two golf courses next door •
Horseback riding
*RATES: $25-$35 (1), $40-$50 (2) •
Deluxe continental breakfast • Open
May 1-Oct. 15 • Cats on premises •
Weekly $325 (2)*

Cavendish
Country House Inn
Ruth Brewer & Dede
Brewer-Wilson, Gulf Shore Road,
Cavendish National Park, Hunter
River, RR 2, C0A 1N0
(902) 963-2055
Toll free 1-800-363-2055
Overlooking Gulf of St. Lawrence •
Century country home furnished
with antiques, quilts • Five o/n
units, double or twin, private and
shared B&S • Non-smoking only
FEATURES: Piano • Breakfast sun
porch • Two living rooms • Guest
fridges • Housekeeping units
available • Bicycling • Walk on
cliffs or beaches
*RATES: $45-$50 (2), $10 add'l
person • Buffet continental breakfast •
Two night minimum stay • Weekly
$300-$330 (2), 50 add'l person*

Cavendish
Kindred Spirits Country Inn and Cottages ★★★½
Al & Sharon James, Cavendish,
C0A 1N0
Tel & Fax (902) 963-2434
E-mail: ajames@peinet.pe.ca
Rte. 6, Memory Lane • Country
estate beside Green Gables House
and Golf Course, decorated with
antiques and crafts • Fourteen o/n
units, priate B&S, three with
jacuzzi • Colour cable TV in rooms
• Non-smoking only
FEATURES: Bilingual •
Laundromat • Parlour lobby with
fireplace • Maid service •
Air-conditioned • Pool and
whirlpool • Beach 800m • Suites
available • Cottages available
*RATES: $65-$135 (2), $10 add'l
person, suites $115-$150 (2), $10
add'l person • Continental Plus*

breakfast buffet • Open May
15-mid-Oct. • MC, Visa accepted •
Off-season rates Labour Day-June
16, weekly and family rates
available • CAA Member

Cavendish
Marco Polo Inn ★★½
Dr. K.G. Ellis, Box 9, Hunter River,
C0A 1N0
(902) 963-2352, winter (902) 964-2960
Toll free 1-800-665-2652
Rte. 13, 2 km south of Cavendish
Beach • Six o/n units, private B&S,
double, single and twin-single beds
• Colour TV in rooms
FEATURES: Licensed restaurant •
Heated swimming pools • Marco
Polo Land facilities available
RATES: $54-$60 (2), $4 add'l
person • Breakfast included • Open
June 10-Sept. 2 • MC, Visa
accepted • Off-season rates before
June 23 • TIAPEI Member

Cavendish
Our Lady of the Way
Tourist Lodge ★½
Les Rogerson, 12 Maple Avenue,
Charlottetown, C1A 6C9
(902) 963-2024/894-4489
On Rte. 13, 1.5 km south of
Cavendish Beach • Ten o/n units,
double, single and two double beds,
five B&S, 3 S • Colour TV in
rooms • Cot available • Pets
permitted, usually on leash
FEATURES: Bilingual • Tea,
coffee • Sun-deck for lodge guests •
Picnic area • Housekeeping unit
available • Licensed dining 1 km
RATES: $35-$70 (1-4), no GST •
Open June 15-Sept. 30 • MC, Visa
accepted • Off-season and weekly
rates available

Cavendish
Parkview Farm Tourist
Home and Cottages ★★½
Alvin & Eleanor MacNeill, Cavendish,
Hunter River RR 2, C0A 1N0
(902) 963-2027
Rte. 6, 2 km east of Cavendish
intersection • Active 420-acre dairy
farm overlooking ocean • Four o/n
units, 2 B&S, 1/2 B, one or two
double beds • Two colour TVs •
Cots available • Pets permitted,
usually on leash • Non-smoking only
FEATURES: Ocean view •
Cottages available • Golf,
restaurant, Green Gables nearby •
Walk to beach 360m
RATES: $35-$45 (2), $5 add'l
person • Light breakfast extra •
Open year round • MC, Visa
accepted • Off-season rates Labour
Day-June 21 • TIAPEI Member

Cavendish
Shining Waters
Country Inn ★★★
Peter, Linda & Jennifer Steele,
Cavendish, C0A 1N0
(902) 963-2251/2758
Rte. 13 • Historic Inn overlooking
ocean • Ten o/n units, private B&S
• Colour TV in rooms •
Non-smoking only
FEATURES: Traditionally Rachel
Lynde's house (*Anne of Green
Gables*) • Licensed dining • Parlour
• Fireplaces • Antiques • Deck •
Exercise equipment • Pool,
whirlpools • Beach nearby
RATES: $75-$85 (2), $10 add'l
person • Continental breakfast •
Open May-Oct. • Off-season rates
available

Cavendish
Sunrise Farm
Tourist Home ★★
Garth & Donna MacNeil, Cavendish,
Hunter River RR 2, C0A 1N0
(902) 963-3088
On Rte. 6, 2 km east of Cavendish
intersection • New Cape Cod home
overlooking the ocean • Two o/n
units, one B&S • Cable TV •
Non-smoking only
FEATURES: Active dairy farm •
Barbecue • Picnic table • Five
minutes walk to beach • Close to
attractions, restaurants, golf course
and Green Gables
*RATES: $35-$45, $5 add'l person •
Light breakfast on weekends extra •
Open year-round • Off-season rates
Labour Day-June 21*

Cavendish
Willow Cottage Inn ★★★
Edward & Anne Morris, Cavendish,
C0A 1N0
(902) 963-3385
Memory Lane, on Rte. 6 •
Family-owned inn beside Green
Gables House and golf course •
Five o/n units, private B&S •
Colour TV and VCR in sitting
room • Non-smoking only
FEATURES: Maid service • Sitting
room with books and fireplace • Air
conditioning • Cottages available •
800m to beach
*RATES: $60-$80, $10 add'l person
• Full breakfast • Open May
15-Oct. 1 • MC, Visa accepted •
Off-season rates available*

Central Bedeque
Pine-Lawn
Bed & Breakfast ★★½
George & Marina Campbell, Box
3944, Central Bedeque, C0B 1G0

(902) 887-2270
1 km off Rte. 1A • Comfortable
quiet home overlooking acres of
farmland • Three large rooms with
queen and single beds, fans, shared
and private B&S • TVand VCR •
Cot available • Wheelchair
accessible • No pets, please •
Non-smoking only
FEATURES: Spacious deck,
barbecue • Picnic table, piano •
Panoramic view of Bedeque Bay
*RATES: $30-$40 (2), $8 add'l
person • Open May 1-Oct. 31 • Visa
accepted • Weekly $180-$240 (2),
breakfast extra*

Central Lot 16
Joppe Potato Farm
Tourist Home ★★½
Jenny Joppe, RR1, Mìscouche,
C0B 1T0
(902) 436-6472
On Rte. 12, 6.5 km off Rte. 2 west
• Modern home • Two o/n units,
shared B&S • One colour TV • No
pets, please • Non-smoking only
FEATURES: Evening tea/coffee •
Close to beaches, cycling, hiking
*RATES: $25 (1), $38-$43 (2), $15
add'l person • Continental
breakfast • Open June 1-Sept. 15 •
Weekly $230-$260 (2), $90 add'l
person*

Charlottetown Area
Abegweit Tourist
Home ★★
Gail Jenkins, 19 Blythe Crescent,
Charlottetown, C1A 8C7
(902) 892-2793
Three o/n units, double and single
beds, one B&S • Pets permitted,
usually on leash
FEATURES: Close to shopping
and restaurants

RATES: $25-$30 (2), $7 add'l person • Open May 15-Oct. 15

Charlottetown Area
Abide Awhile Tourist Home ★★
Bruce & Evelyn Younker, 256 Mt. Edward Road, Charlottetown, C1A 5T7
(902) 892-8811
Three o/n units, single, double and queen beds, one B&S • One colour TV • Partial accessibility • Pets permitted
FEATURES: Close to shopping, restaurants and downtown
RATES: $25-$30 (2), $5 add'l person • Open May 15-Sept. 5

Charlottetown Area
Allix's Bed & Breakfast ★★★
Rita Allix, 11 Johnson Avenue, Charlottetown, C1A 3H7
(902) 892-2643
Quiet residential area • Two o/n units, one B&S, one with double bed, one with twin singles • Colour TV in living room • Non-smoking only
FEATURES: Use of living room • Restaurants nearby • Close to shopping, churches and Victoria Park
RATES: $45(2), $12 add'l person • Full breakfast • Open year-round • Weekly $270 (2), $72 add'l person • Off-season rates Sept. 1-Apr. 30 • TIAPEI Member

Charlottetown Area
Aloha Tourist Home
Maynard MacMillan, 234 Sydney Street, Charlottetown, C1A 1H1
(902) 892-9944

Century home facing Hillsborough day park • three o/n units, double and single beds, one B&S • TV in rooms
FEATURES: Two fully equipped kitchens • Garage for bicycles and pets • Bus, airport pickup can be prearranged • Close to all amenities
RATES: $30 (1), $32-$38 (2), $4 add'l person • Open year-round • Off-season rates Oct. 1-May 14 (25% off)

Charlottetown Area
Altavista Bed & Breakfast ★★½
Ada & Stuart Drummond, 2 Altavista Crescent, Charlottetown, C1E 1M9
Tel or Fax (902) 894-4248
Beautiful waterfront home • Two o/n units, room and luxury suite, queen beds, private B • No pets, please • Non-smoking only

FEATURES: Canoeing on premises • Biking area • Waterfront deck • Five minutes to downtown • Fifteen minutes to beaches
RATES: $60-$70 (1), $65-$75 (2), $15 add'l person • Breakfast • Open May 15-Oct. 30

Charlottetown Area
Amanda's Tourist Home
Laura MacLauchlan, 130 Spring
Park Road, Charlottetown, C1A 3Y6
(902) 894-9909
Two o/n units, double beds, shared
B&S • Cot available
FEATURES: Close to restaurants •
Downtown shopping and
Confederation Centre ten minute
walk
*RATES: $30 (2), $10 add'l person,
no GST • Open year-round •
Off-season rates available*

Charlottetown Area
Ambrose Tourist Home ★★
Nora McLeod, 17 Passmore Street,
Charlottetown, C1A 2B8
(902) 566-5853
Toll free 1-800-665-6072
Off University Ave. • Large duplex
in city centre • Five o/n units, double
and single beds, three shared B&S •
Colour TV in rooms • Pets permitted
FEATURES: Housekeeping unit
available • Transportation provided
from bus station, airport
*RATES: $30-$38 (2), $5 add'l
person • Breakfast extra • Open
May-Oct. • AE, MC, Visa accepted
• Off-season rates before July 1
and after Sept. 6*

Charlottetown Area
An Island Rose ★★★
Steve & Nora Stephenson, 285
Kinlock Road, Charlottetown RR 1,
C1A 7J6
(902) 569-5030
Toll free 1-800-775-5030
Seven minutes from Charlottetown
on beautiful Bellevue Cove •
Pastoral setting with superb view of
Northumberland Strait • Three o/n
units, one B&S, one 1/2 B, two
with queen beds, one with twin
beds • Colour TV • No pets, please
• Adults preferred • Non-smoking
only
FEATURES: Guest lounge with
balcony • Bicycles • Fully equipped
two bedroom apartment available •
Beach and clam digging
*RATES: $45-$55 (2), $10 add'l
person • Continental-plus breakfast
• Open May 1-Oct. 15 other times
by reservation • Visa accepted •
TIAPEI Member*

Charlottetown Area
Anchor's Aweigh ★★½
Mary Y. Hopgood, 45 Queen
Elizabeth Drive, Charlottetown,
C1A 3A8
(902) 892-4319
Near Victoria Park, directly across
from Viceroy Ave. • Waterfront
property overlooking North River •
Two o/n units, one with double bed,
one with twin singles, one B&S •
Colour TV • Non-smoking only
FEATURES: Use of living room •
Large deck • Two km from amenities
*RATES: $45 (2) • Breakfast • Open
year-round • TIAPEI Member*

Charlottetown Area
Anne's Ocean View Haven Bed & Breakfast
R. Anne Olson, Kinlock, P.O. Box
2044, Charlottetown, C1A 7N7
(902) 569-4644
Toll-free 1-800-665-4644
Six minutes east of Charlottetown
off Rte. 1 • Peaceful countryside/
seascape setting • Four o/n units,
private B&S, private entrance •
Colour cable TV and fridges in
rooms • Wheelchair accessible •

Trained pets permitted •
Non-smoking only
FEATURES: Views of fields,
countryside and seascape • Packed
lunches on request • Sun room •
Garden patio • Maid service • Guest
kitchen, stove, microwave • Suite
also available, sleeps five • North
shore beaches 20 minutes
*RATES: $65-$95 (2), $120 (suite),
$10 add'l person • Full
home-cooked breakfast • Open
year-round • Packages available •
ATOPEI; CAA Member*

Charlottetown Area
Beairsto Tourist Home ★★
Mrs. Ralph Beairsto, 42 Greenfield
Avenue, Charlottetown, C1A 3N4
(902) 894-8055
Quiet residential area • One o/n
unit, double bed, private B • No
pets, please • Non-smoking only
FEATURES: Walking distance to
downtown Charlottetown, theatres,
shopping, Confederation Centre,
park boardwalk and bus stop
*RATES: $28 (2) • Open year-round
• Off-season rates Sept. 1- May 1*

Charlottetown Area
Binstead Bed & Breakfast ★★★
Susan E. Partridge, 251 Keppoch
Rd., Kinlock RR 1, Charlottetown,
C1A 7J6
(902) 569-5412
Toll free 1-800-333-5412
On Rte. 1A, six minutes to
Charlottetown • Overlooking
Northumberland Strait in peaceful
landscaped setting • Four o/n units,
one B&S, one S, one Jacuzzi,
queen, double and twin beds • Suite
available • Cable TV • Cots

available • No pets, please •
Non-smoking only
FEATURES: Balcony and veranda •
Central to most attractions. Friendly
family service • Beach 500 m
*RATES: $48-$78 (2), $10 add'l
person • Continental plus breakfast
• Open June 1-Oct. 1 • MC, Visa
accepted • Reservations
recommended • TIAPEI Member*

Charlottetown Area
Birchill Bed & Breakfast ★★½
Bob & Yvonne Santer, 14 Birch Hill
Drive, Charlottetown, C1A 6W5
(902) 892-4353
Three o/n units, 2 1/2 B&S,
queen-size bed, double bed, large
room with two single beds • TV •
Telephone • Non-smoking only
FEATURES: Sun room • Lock-up
for bicycles • Close to shopping,
theatre, university, city centre
*RATES: $45 (2), $7 add'l person •
Homemade breakfast in sunroom •
Open June 1-Oct. 1 • Weekly $270
(2), $42 add'l person • PEIBBA*

Charlottetown Area
Blanchard Heritage Home ★★
Florence Blanchard, 163 Dorchester
Street, Charlottetown, C1A 1E4
(902) 894-9756
 Three o/n units, one B&S
*RATES: $18-$30 (1-2) • Open
May-Oct. 31 • Off-season rates
available*

Charlottetown Area
Bye-The-Shore Tourist Home ★★½
Mrs. Veronica Kennedy, 77 East
River Drive, Stratford, C1A 7H6
(902) 569-2548
Off TransCanada Hwy and Rte. 21
• Tranquil setting with mature trees
• Two o/n units with double beds,
one B&S • TV lounge for guests •
Cots available • No pets, please
FEATURES: Evening tea/coffee •
Sun deck • Shed for bicycles • Four
minute drive to shopping and
theatre in downtown Charlottetown
*RATES: $32 (2), $8 add'l person •
Continental breakfast • Open
year-round • Weekly $200 (2), $50
add'l person • Off-season rates
available • TIAPEI Member*

Charlottetown Area
Cairns' Tourist Home
Helen Cairns, 18 Pond Street,
Charlottetown, C1A 2P2
(902) 368-3552
Three o/n units, one B&S •
Non-smoking only
*RATES: $24-$26 (1-2), $8 add'l
person • Continental breakfast extra •
Open year-round • TIAPEI Member*

Charlottetown Area
Callaghan Tourist Home
Mary J. Callaghan, 51 Dorchester
Street, Charlottetown, C1A 1C8
(902) 894-3502
Two o/n units, one B&S
*RATES: $25 (2) • Open year-round
• Off-season rates available*

Charlottetown Area
Campbell's Maple Bed & Breakfast ★★★
Mrs. Maida Campbell, 28 Maple
Avenue, Charlottetown, C1A 6E3

(902) 894-4488
Toll free 1-800-276-5288
Comfortable home, living room & deck
available to guests • Four o/n units, two
B&S, queen, double and single beds,
family unit • Non-smoking only
FEATURES: Five minutes from
airport, ten from downtown, 15
from north shore beaches
*RATES: $45 (2), $10 add'l adult,
$5 add'l child • Full breakfast,
fresh fruit, muffins • Open May
24-Oct. 31 • TIAPEI Member*

Charlottetown Area
Century House Bed & Breakfast
Diane Vickerson, 53 Fitzroy Street,
Charlottetown, C1A 1R4
(902) 566-2395
Newly restored century home in
downtown Charlottetown • Three
o/n units, shared B&S
FEATURES: Suite available •
Walking distance to theatre, dining,
shopping and churches • Fifteen
minutes to beaches and tourist
attractions
*RATES: $55, $95 (suite), tax
included • Continental breakfast •
Open year-round*

Charlottetown Area
Century Kennels and Farm Bed & Breakfast ★★★
Gene & Francis Wertman, Cornwall
RR 4, C0A 1H0
(902) 566-2110
Toll free 1-800-393-2110
Century farmhouse on 13 acres
bordering on North River, ten
minutes from Charlottetown • Three
o/n units, queen, double and single
beds, one B&S, one S • Pets
welcome • Non-smoking only
FEATURES: Evening tea or coffee
• Guest sitting room

RATES: $25-$40 (1-2), $8 add'l person • Full breakfast • Open year-round • Weekly/family rates available • TIAPEI Member

Charlottetown Area
Chez-Nous (A Tender Treasure) Bed & Breakfast ★★★½

Paul & Sandi Gallant, Ferry Road, Cornwall RR 4, C0A 1H0
(902) 566-2779
Fax (902) 628-3852
Toll free 1-800-566-2779
On Rte. 248 • Five o/n units, queen, double and twin beds, three B&S, sink in rooms • Cable TV in rooms • Telephone in rooms • Pets permitted
FEATURES: Picnics • Solarium-enclosed dining room • Veranda • Bicycles • Suites available
RATES: $60-$75 (2) • Full breakfast • Open year-round

Charlottetown Area
Colonial Charm Inn

Gary MacDougall, 9 Euston Street, Charlottetown, C1A 1V5
(902) 892-8934
Toll free 1-800-239-5127
Colonial home • Four o/n units, 1S, 1B • Colour TV in rooms • Non-smoking only
FEATURES: VCR rentals available • Close to downtown shopping, restaurants, tennis courts, bike rentals, Victoria Park, Confederation Centre of the Arts and waterfront
RATES: $55 (2), $8-$12 add'l person • Open year-round • MC, Visa accepted • Off-season rates Sept. 30-May 31 • Weekly $330 (2), $90-$140 add'l person

Charlottetown Area
Cosy Country Bed & Breakfast ★★½

Paul & Carolyn Whelan, 8 Ferguson Drive, Stratford, C1B 1B7
(902) 569-3748
Quiet, spacious home with a view of Charlottetown • Two o/n units, queen and single beds, shared B&S, 1/2 B • Pets permitted • Non-smoking only
FEATURES: Minutes to restaurants, theatre or beaches
RATES: $30-$50 (1-2) • Light breakfast • Open June 22-Sept. 15

Charlottetown Area
A Country Home (Halls) ★★★½

Phyllis Hall, Winsloe RR 10, West Royalty, C1E 1Z4
(902) 368-2340, Fax (902) 892-4511
Toll free 1-800-265-4255
Off Rte. 1 (Upton Road) just west of Charlottetown • Restored heritage home nestled among mature trees and flowers on spacious grounds • Three o/n units, private B&S, three rooms with vanities,  double, twin and queen beds, ceiling fans
FEATURES: Spacious deck, water view • Guest sitting room • Horses • Guest sitting room • Piano • Five minutes to airport and downtown • Short drive to all attractions • Meet on request
RATES: $45-$65 (2), $25 add'l person, no GST • Gourmet breakfast • Open year-round • Weekly $295-$390 (2) • Nov.-Apr. by reservation only • Off-season rates available • PEIBBA Member

Charlottetown Area
Court
Bed & Breakfast ★★
Sheila Grant, 68 Hutchinson Court,
Charlottetown, C1A 8H7
(902) 894-5871
Two o/n units, one B&S, one S, one
with double bed, one with twin beds
FEATURES: Living room and sun
deck • Shopping, Charlottetown
Festival and restaurants nearby
*RATES: $43 (2) • Full breakfast •
Open May 1-Sept. 7 • Weekly $258
(2) • TIAPEI Member*

Charlottetown Area
Cutcliffe's
Bed & Breakfast ★★½
Sibyl Cutcliffe, 3 Birchwood Street,
Charlottetown, C1A 5B4
(902) 894-9361
Three o/n
units,
one
B&S,
one with
queen
size and
single bed and two with two single
beds
FEATURES: Restaurant 5-10
minutes • Shed available for bicycles
• Confederation Centre is 15-minute
walk, shopping five to ten minutes
*RATES: $30-$45 (1-2), $8 add'l
person • Full breakfast • Open May
1-Oct. 31 • Weekly $227-$284 (2),
$50 add'l person • Single rate
$30-$36 • PEIBBA; TIAPEI Member*

Charlottetown Area
Duchess of Kent Inn ★★★
Sharyn Dalrymple, 218 Kent Street,
Charlottetown, C1A 1P2
(902) 566-5826
Toll free 1-800-665-5826

Heritage home (1875) in downtown
with 3-story turret corner • Seven
o/n units, three B&S, two B, five
with double beds, one with two
doubles, one with queen, 3/4 bed •
Two colour TVs and VCR •
Telephone • No pets, please •
Non-smoking only
FEATURES: Furnished with
antiques • Coffee/tea • Kitchen
available • Living room •
Laundromat nearby • Restaurants
nearby • Bicycle storage •
Confederation Centre, shopping,
museums, and churches nearby •
Suite available (air conditioned)
*RATES: $48-$60 (2), $110 (suite) •
Breakfast extra • Open year-round •
December-April by reservation only
• HIAC; PEIBBA; TIAPEI Member*

Charlottetown Area
The Edwardian ★★★½
Jordan & Judy Hill, 50 Mount Edward
Road, Charlottetown, C1A 5S3
(902) 368-1905
Fax (902) 628-1905
Corner of Confederation St. • Elegant
1850s heritage home • Two o/n units,
two housekeeping units, all units:
telephones, private B, one with Jacuzzi
• TVs in all units • Partially accessible
• No pets • Non-smoking only
FEATURES: Antiques, art, quilts,
fireplace, conservatory, perennial
garden, unique floral arrangements •
Air conditioning • Originally part of
country home of William Pope, a
Father of Confederation • Originally
owned by shipwright James Douse •
Bicycle storage • Listed in
"Frommers" • Off-street parking
*RATES: $95-$115 (2), $20 add'l
person • Breakfast • Open
year-round • MC, Visa accepted •
Off-season rates • HIAC; TIAPEI
Member*

Charlottetown Area
Elmwood Heritage Inn ★★★★

Carol, Jay, Megan & Ross
Macdonald, Box 3128,
Charlottetown, C1A 7N8
(902) 368-3310
North River Rd. • 1880s Victorian
home built by architect W.C. Harris
for Island premier with elm-lined
drive • Three o/n units, queen beds,
private B&S, one whirlpool •
Colour cable TV and VCR in
rooms • Telephone in rooms •
Non-smoking only
FEATURES: Eight working
fireplaces • Private balcony
overlooking park-like setting •
Antiques, quilts, artwork •
Air-conditioning • Housekeeping
unit available • Bicycles • Four
blocks to Victoria Park and harbour,
twelve blocks to downtown
*RATES: $90-$150 (2), $15 add'l
person • Breakfast • Open
year-round • DC, ER, MC, Visa
accepted • TIAPEI Member*

Charlottetown Area
Evergreen Bed & Breakfast ★★★

Don & Sheila Sinclair, 34 Admiral
Street, Charlottetown, C1A 2E6
(902) 892-7652
One o/n unit, private B&S with
Jacuzzi • Smoking permitted
outdoors
FEATURES: Bell and luggage
service available • Colour TV •
Two-minute walk to Victoria Park
boardwalk
*RATES: $70 (2), taxes incl. • Full
breakfast • Open year-round • Cat
and dog on premises*

Charlottetown Area
Fitzroy Hall ★★★

Helen & Reg Doucette, 45 Fitzroy
Street, Charlottetown, C1A 1R4
(902) 368-2077
Recently restored Victorian
mansion (1872) • Six o/n units,
private B&S • Colour cable TV in
rooms • No pets, please •
Non-smoking only
FEATURES: Bilingual • Antique
furnishings • Suite available •
Walking distance to Province
House, Confederation Centre,
Beaconsfield and waterfront
*RATES: $85-$120 (2), $18 add'l
person • Full breakfast • Open
year-round • MC, Visa accepted •
Off-season rates Oct. 1-June 1 •
Weekly rates • TIAPEI Member*

Charlottetown Area
Gallant's Tourist Home

Mrs. St. Clair Gallant, 196
Kensington Road, Charlottetown,
C1A 7S3
(902) 892-3030
Four o/n units, two B&S, 1/2 B,
one with double and single beds •
Non-smoking only
FEATURES: Free transportation
from airport, bus station and return
trip into city • Large backyard
*RATES: $20-$25 (2), $10 add'l
person • Breakfast extra • Open
year-round • Weekly $140-$165 (2),
$70 add'l person • TIAPEI Member*

Charlottetown Area
Great George Inn ★★★
Kevin Murphy, 455 University
Avenue, Charlottetown, C1A 4N8
(902) 892-0606
Fax: (902) 368-3806
Restored inn at 68 Great George
St., a National Historic Site • Five
o/n units, private B&S • Colour TV
in rooms • Partial accessibility • No
pets, please • Non-smoking only
FEATURES: Air-conditioning •
Housekeeping suites available in
Carriage House
*RATES: $100-$165 (2) • Continental
Breakfast • Open year-round • Major
credit cards accepted • Off-season
rates Oct. 1-May 30*

Charlottetown Area
Heart's Content ★½
Joan Cumming, 236 Sydney Street,
Charlottetown, C1A 1H1
(902) 566-1064
In Olde Charlotte Town • 1860
heritage home overlooks tree-shaded
Hillsborough Square • Four o/n units,
two B&S, one with double bed, one
with two singles, two with one
double and one single bed, rooms
with own locks • Colour cable TV in
parlour • Non-smoking only
FEATURES: Comfortable antique
furnishings • Parlour • Bilingual •
Garage for bicycles • Short stroll to
sights, shopping and waterfront
*RATES: $39 (2), $8 add'l person •
Continental breakfast • Open
year-round • MC, Visa accepted •
Weekly $250 (2) • Off-season rates
before June 25, after Labour Day*

Charlottetown Area
Heritage Harbour
House Inn ★★★
Bonnie Hennessey Brammer, 9 Grafton
Street, Charlottetown, C1A 1K3

(902) 892-6633
Toll free 1-800-405-0066
Restored early 1900s house in quiet
area of Olde Charlotte Town • Four
o/n units, two B&S, one with
queen-size bed, one with two 3/4
beds, two with two singles • TV
and VCR in living room •
Non-smoking only
FEATURES: Restaurant two
blocks • Bicycle storage • Victoria
Park, theatre and downtown
shopping two blocks away
*RATES: $60 (2), $10 add'l person
• Continental breakfast • Open
year-round • Weekly rates available
• Off-season rates Sept. 30-June 15
• PEIBBA Member*

Charlottetown Area
Heron's Moor ★★★
Carolyn & Jim Molyneaux, Box 41,
Cornwall, C0A 1H0
(902) 566-2606
Toll free 1-800-567-2458
Three o/n units, queen, double and
twin beds, private and shared B&S,
one Jacuzzi • Two colour TVs •
Non-smoking only
FEATURES: Kitchen facilities •
Sitting room • Barbecue • Backyard
• Hot tub • Harbour view • Minutes
from Charlottetown • Scenic tours
available
*RATES: $50-$70 (1-2), $10 add'l
person • Continental breakfast •
Open May 1-Oct. 1*

Charlottetown Area
Hillhurst Inn ★★★½
Scott Stewart & Jane Toombs, 181
Fitzroy Street, Charlottetown, C1A 1S3
(902) 894-8004
Heritage property (1897) • Five o/n
units, queen and double beds, two
B&S • TV and VCR • Non-smoking
only

FEATURES: Sitting/reading room
• Period furnishings and Island art
throughout • Bicycles and
windsurfing equipment available
*RATES: $70-$130 (2), $15 add'l
person • Continental Plus breakfast
• Open year-round • MC, Visa
accepted • Off-season rates •
TIAPEI Member*

Charlottetown Area
Hillsboro Park
Bed & Breakfast ★★½
Florence Pound, 145 Southdale
Avenue, Charlottetown, C1A 6Z8
(902) 892-5569
Located off Riverside Dr., call for
directions • Quiet residential area •
Three o/n units, one B&S, 1/2 B,
one with twin singles, one with
double bed, one with 3/4 bed,
private B for guests • Small pets
permitted • Non-smoking only
FEATURES: Close to downtown
and beaches, Confederation Centre
and Confederation Park
*RATES: $20 (1), $30 (2) • Light
breakfast • Open June 27-Sept. 5 •
Weekly $120 (1), $150 (2)*

Charlottetown Area
Hillside House ★★★½
Ken & Marilyn Roper, 25 Hillside
Drive, Charlottetown, C1A 6H9
(902) 892-3640
One o/n unit, private B&S • Private
spacious suite with queen-size bed,
full B, lounge with TV/VCR and
breakfast nook • Non-smoking only
FEATURES: Laundry facilities •
Complimentary evening tray, home
baking • Bicycle storage • Off-street
parking
*RATES: $80 (2), $10 add'l person
• Continental breakfast • Open
year-round • Weekly $480 •
Off-season rates Oct. 1-May 31*

Charlottetown Area
Hilltop View Tourist
Home ★★
Mrs. Violet Maund, 10 Duncan
Heights, Charlottetown, C1A 6L7
(902) 894-8393
Three o/n units, double and twin beds,
shared B&S • Non-smoking only
FEATURES: Housekeeping unit
available • Free transportation to
and from airport and bus station •
Shopping centre, downtown, golf
course, churches and beaches nearby
*RATES: $15-$25 (1-2), $5 add'l
person • Continental breakfast •
Open year-round • Weekly $145
(2), $25 add'l person • TIAPEI
Member*

Charlottetown Area
The Hughes Tourist
Home
Mrs. Margaret Hughes, 19 Lilac
Avenue, Charlottetown, C1A 6L3
(902) 892-4400
Two o/n units, shared B&S
*RATES: $24-$27 (1-2) • Open
June 30-Sept. 30*

Charlottetown Area
Kenny's Tourist Home
John & Mary Kenny, 171 Bunbury
Road, Stratford, C1A 7G9
(902) 569-3437
Three o/n units, one B&S • One
colour TV • Pets permitted, usually
on leash
*RATES: $30 (2), $10 add'l person
• Continental breakfast • Open May
24-Sept. 30*

Charlottetown Area
Lighthouse Tourist Home ★★½

Mary Dalton, 12 Zakem Heights, Stratford, C1B 1J3
(902) 569-4466
Toll free 1-800-741-6644
In Stratford, 4 km east of Charlottetown • Three o/n units, private B&S • Non-smoking only
FEATURES: Kitchen facilities • Living room • Patio • Barbecue • Minutes to restaurants, theatre, waterfront, beaches
RATES: $40-$55 (2), $6 add'l person • Continental Plus breakfast • Open Mar. 15-Oct. 30 • Weekly $240-$330 (2), $36 add'l person, off-season rates available

Charlottetown Area
MacInnis Bed & Breakfast ★★★

Jean MacInnis, 80 Euston Street, Charlottetown, C1A 1W2
(902) 892-6725
Located in downtown Charlottetown • Elegant 1892 heritage home, decorative veranda, large elm trees • Four o/n units, two B&S, one S, one with queen bed, two with one double bed, two with twin singles • Colour TVs in all rooms • Cot available • No pets, please • Non-smoking only
FEATURES: Shed for bicycles • Beautiful flower beds • Two blocks to Confederation Centre, Province House, Olde Charlotte Town, restaurants and Victoria Park
RATES: $32 (1), $45-$65 (2), $7-$10 add'l person, no GST • Continental plus breakfast • Open year-round • Weekly rates available

Charlottetown Area
The Maples Guest Home

Mrs. Earl W.G. Foster, 124 St. Peters Road, Charlottetown, C1A 5P4
(902) 892-1383
Two o/n units, double and twin beds, shared guest B&S
FEATURES: Licensed dining room 200m • 18-hole golf course 800m, harness racing 2 km
RATES: $25 (2), $6 add'l person • Continental breakfast • Open June 25-Sept. 10 • Weekly rates available

Charlottetown Area
McNichol's Tourist Home

Florence McNichol, 20 Maplewood Crescent, Charlottetown, C1A 2X5
(902) 892-6381
Quiet waterfront location • Three o/n units, queen and double beds, private and shared B&S • Non-smoking only
RATES: $25-$35 (1-2) • Open June 15-Sept. 30

Charlottetown Area
The Mill House ★★½

Susan Mill, 89 Beach Grove Road, Charlottetown, C1E 1J3
(902) 368-3450
Three o/n units, one B&S, one with double bed, one with queen, one twin single, separate B for guests • Non-smoking only
FEATURES: Patio deck with barbecue • Large backyard • Centrally located to beaches, shopping, theatre
RATES: $30 (2), $5 add'l person • Continental breakfast • One room available year-round • Weekly $180 (2), $30 add'l person

Charlottetown Area
MacKeen's Tourist Home ★★½
Rowena MacKeen, 176 King Street, Charlottetown, C1A 1C1
(902) 892-6296
Toll free 1-800-668-6296
150-year-old home, centrally located in Olde Charlotte Town • Three o/n units, one B&S, one double bed, one twin bed, one two-room suite which sleeps five comfortably • Three colour TVs
FEATURES: Large yard • Picnic table • Sunroom • Air-conditioning • Shed for bikes • Close to downtown and waterfront
RATES: $40-$50 (2-3) • Continental breakfast • Open year-round • Weekly $240-$300 (2-3), $30 add'l person • Off-season rates • TIAPEI Member

Charlottetown Area
MacLeod's Bed & Breakfast ★★½
Mrs. Gordon E. MacLeod, 29 Esher Street, Charlottetown, C1A 5G3
(902) 892-1458
Within walking distance of downtown Charlottetown • Quiet, private, friendly, residential property on spacious treed lot • Four o/n units, two B&S, one with double bed, twin singles and a family room with twin double beds, private B for guest • TV room available • Non-smoking only
FEATURES: Sun deck • Flower gardens • Walking distance to downtown, theatre, golf, marina, waterfront park, harness racing and restaurants
RATES: $35-$50 (2), $10 add'l person • Breakfast on request • Open May 15-Oct. 31 • TIAPEI Member

Charlottetown Area
Nicholson's Bed & Breakfast
Marilyn & Frank Nicholson, 7 Crestwood Drive, Charlottetown, C1A 3H2
(902) 892-9809
One o/n unit, B&S • Colour TV • Non-smoking only
RATES: $60-$80 (2), $10 add'l person • Continental breakfast • Open year-round • Reservations recommended • Weekly rates available

Charlottetown Area
Obanlea Farm Tourist Home ★★½
Mildred MacKinley, RR 4, Cornwall, C0A 1H0
(902) 566-3067
 Off TransCanada Hwy on Rte. 248 (York Point Rd.) 3 km west of Charlottetown • Family farm, 1100+ acres, potatoes, beef cattle, donkeys • Three o/n units, 2 B&S, three large carpeted rooms, two with double beds, queen-size bed, private entrance • Non-smoking only
FEATURES: Complimentary tea/coffee • Registered Herefords have won many awards • Hosts assist planning your Island holiday • First-floor housekeeping apt. available
RATES: $30-$45 (2), $4 add'l person • Continental breakfast • Open May 1-Oct. 15 • Phone reservations welcome • Weekly rates available • PEIBBA; TIAPEI Member

Charlottetown Area
Reddin House
Paul & Joyce Newcombe, 90 Brighton Road, Charlottetown, C1A 1V1
Tel & Fax (902) 892-7269
E-mail pnewcombe@peinet.pe.ca
Historic 1915 home nestled in beautiful surroundings of Victoria Park • Two o/n units, one B&S, one S, one single, two rooms with queen-size beds
FEATURES: Bicycles, tennis racquets available • Walking trails, tennis courts, swimming pool nearby. Five blocks to downtown area, shops, churches • Twenty minute drive to beach
RATES: $45-$50 (2), no GST • Breakfast • Open year-round • TIAPEI Member

Charlottetown Area
River Winds ★★★
Mark and Betty Robertson, 9 Colonel Gray Drive, Charlottetown, C1A 2S4
(902) 892-2285
Fax (902) 566-1188
Elegant Riverside home in Brighton • One o/n unit, B&S, large bedroom with double bed, private B and Jačuzzi • Colour cable TV • Non-smoking only • Five minutes from city centre
FEATURES: Flowers abound • Breakfast of your choice on veranda
RATES: $65 (2) • Breakfast • Open year-round • Friendly collie dog on premises • Off-season rates available

Charlottetown Area
St. Avards
Bed & Breakfast
Ginny Cheverie, 97 Kensington Road, Charlottetown, C1A 5J3
(902) 894-4697
Three o/n units, one B&S
RATES: $25-$35 (2), $10 add'l person • Light breakfast • Open May 1-Sept. 30

Charlottetown Area
The Shipwright Inn
Jordan & Judy Hill, 51 Fitzroy Street, Charlottetown, C1A 1R4
(902) 368-1905
Fax: (902) 628-1905
Restored 1860s heritage home originally owned by shipwright James Douse, operated by award-winning owners of The Edwardian • Four o/n units, private B&S, duvets • TV in rooms • Telephone in rooms • No pets, please • Non-smoking only
FEATURES: Fireplaces • Antiques, art, quilts • Air-conditioning • Luxury suite available • Off-street parking
RATES: $95-$135 (2), $20 add'l person • Breakfast • Open year-round • MC, Visa available • Off-season rates available

Charlottetown Area
Southview Tourist Home
Betty & Ray Peters, 8 Shelby Court, Charlottetown, C1E 1R5
(902) 566-4719
Three o/n units, one B&S, one B • Non-smoking only
RATES: $40-$55 (2) • Open year-round

Charlottetown Area
A Taste of Home ★★½
Peggy Barnes, 33 Marianne Drive, Cornwall, C0A 1H0
(902) 566-9186
Rural setting • Four o/n units, one B&S, two S
FEATURES: Homemade muffins and bread • Patio • Private backyard • Close to golf courses, beaches and Charlottetown • Free airport pickup
RATES: $35-$45 (2), $8 add'l adult, $5 add'l child • Breakfast • Open May 31-Oct. 31 • Weekly rates available

Charlottetown Area
Tea Hill Bed & Breakfast ★★★
Jean Drake, RR 1, Charlottetown, C1A 7J6
(902) 569-2366
Rte. 1A • Two o/n units, two B&S, queen beds, guest B • Colour TV in rooms • No pets, please • Non-smokers preferred
FEATURES: Panoramic view of Hillsborough Bay • Walk to park and beach, minutes to Charlottetown
RATES: $45 (2), $16.50 add'l person, taxes incl. • Full breakfast • Open year-round • Weekly $230 (2), $100 add'l person • Off-season rates Labour Day to June 25 • TIAPEI Member

Cherry Valley
Cherry Tree House Bed & Breakfast ★★½
Elsie & Josef Scheier, RR 3, Vernon Bridge, C0A 2E0
(902) 651-2010
Just off TransCanada Hwy. on Cherry Valley Cove Rd. • Older home 1870s, quiet farming area • Three o/n units, one B&S, both rooms with double beds, full B for guests • No pets, please • Adults preferred • Non-smoking only
FEATURES: German spoken • 22 km east of Charlottetown, 30 minutes from Wood Islands ferry
RATES: $35-$40 (2) • Continental plus breakfast • Open June 1-Sept. 30 • Weekly $160-$200 (2)

Churchill
Churchill Farm Bed & Breakfast ★★½
Waldron & Jeanette MacKinnon, RR 3, Bonshaw, C0A 1C0
(902) 675-2481

On TransCanada Hwy 19 km west of Charlottetown • Five o/n units, two shared B&S, one 1/2 B, four rooms with double bed, one with twin singles • No pets, please • Non-smoking only
FEATURES: Complimentary tea, coffee, snack in evening • Less than two hours from either end of Island • Beaches, lobster suppers, golf nearby
RATES: $25-$30 (2), $5 add'l person, no GST • Full breakfast with homemade jams and muffins • Open year-round • Weekly $120-$180 (2), breakfast extra • TIAPEI Member

Charlottetown Area
Pye's Village Guest Home ★★½
Everett & Mildred Boyle, Box 87, Cornwall, C0A 1H0
(902) 566-2026
On TransCanada Hwy, west of Charlottetown • Three o/n units, one B&S, one S, double bed, two-room suite with davenport and double beds • TV in living room  • VCR in living room • Non-smoking only
FEATURES: Close to golf course • Attractions nearby • Close to beaches, restaurants, theatre
RATES: $30-$35 (2), $5 add'l person, Weekly $180 (2), no GST • Breakfast extra • Open year-round

Charlottetown Area
Tighnabruaich
Joanne & Harry Rennie, Cornwall,
C0A 1H0
(902) 566-5908
Two o/n units, one B&S
*RATES: $30 (2) • Continental
breakfast • Open year-round*

Chepstow
Bed and Breakfast
by the Sea ★★½
Anna & Frankie McIntosh, Box
223, Souris, C0A 2B0
(902) 687-1527 (winter: (902) 687-2321)
On Rte. 2, east of Souris • Spacious
house in quiet area overlooks water
• Three o/n units, double and twin
beds, one B&S • Colour TV and
VCR • Non-smoking only
FEATURES: Short walk to white,
sandy beach • Minutes to Magdalen
Islands ferry
*RATES: $45-$50 (2), $5 add'l
person • Full home-cooked breakfast
• Open May 1-Oct. 7 • Off-season
rates before July 1 and after Sept. 3 •
Weekly $270-$300 (2), $30 add'l
person*

Clinton
Red Road
Country Inn ★★★
Tom Petrofsky, Kensington, RR 6,
C0B 1M0
(902) 886-3154
Toll free 1-800-249-1344
New accomodations on 45 acres in
the heart of Lucy Maud's
inspirational setting • Eight o/n
units, private B&S, queen beds
FEATURES: Fresh-made breads,
jams • View • Verandah • Wooden
row-boat rentals • Minutes from
Green Gables, beaches, golf courses

*RATES: $85-$115 (2), $8 add'l
person • Open year-round • TIAPEI
Member*

Covehead Road
Elaine's Farm
Bed & Breakfast
Elaine Wooldridge, Little York
RR1, Covehead Road, C0A 1P0
(902) 672-2430
On Rte. 25 off Rte. 2, 14 km
northeast of Charlottetown • Horse
and cattle farm, 100 acres, quiet
surroundings • Two o/n units with
double bed, one B&S • Colour TV •
No pets please
FEATURES: Churches, golf
course, ocean and bay beaches
five-minute drive • Close to harness
racing and other Charlottetown
attractions, Confederation Centre
and services
*RATES: $30-$35 (2), no GST •
Breakfast • Open June 15-Oct. 15 •
Off-season rates after Sept. 1*

Lady Fane
Empty Nest
Bed & Breakfast ★★
Judy Gallant, Crapaud RR 2, C0A 1J0
(902) 658-2013
Just ten minutes from Borden ferry
• Spacious quiet country home •
Three o/n units, 2 B&S, queen,
double and two single beds • Two
colour TVs & VCRs • Pets
permitted, usually on leash
FEATURES: Laundry facilities •
Barbecue available • Within
walking distance of trout stream,
central to all major attractions, 25
minutes to Summerside, 35 minutes
to Charlottetown
*RATES: $45-$50 (1-2), $10 add'l
person • Continental breakfast •
Open June 1-Sept. 30 • MC, Visa
accepted • GTA; TIAPEI Member*

Crapaud
Tea Cups & Roses
Bed & Breakfast
Pamela & Peter Sorensen, Box 123,
Crapaud, C0A 1J0
(902) 658-2463
On TransCanada Hwy at Rte. 1 •
1920s country home in village
nestled in rolling farmland • Three
o/n units, one S • Non-smoking only
FEATURES: Antique china •
Afternoon cream tea and sumptuous
dinners in carriage house • Veranda
• Swimming and clam digging at
nearby beaches, minutes to theatre,
ski trails, craft shops
*RATES: $49 (2) • Breakfast • Open
year-round • Weekly $320 (2) •
Minimum two- night stay, packages
available*

Crapaud
Torfness Christian
Bed & Breakfast
Anne Abernethy, Box 4907,
Sherwood Forest, Crapaud, C0A 1J0
(902) 658-2759
Two o/n units, shared B&S
*RATES: $32-$40 (1-2) • Continental
breakfast • Open May 1-Oct. 31*

Darnley
Cal-Mar Bed & Breakfast
Carl Rogers, Kensington RR 1,
C0B 1M0
(902) 836-3058
Waterfront location • Two o/n units,
shared B&S • Colour TV •
Non-smoking only
FEATURES: Malpeque's
panoramic sunsets • Beach • Clam
digging, bird-watching
*RATES: $35-$45 (1-2) • Breakfast
• Open year-round • Off-season
rates Sept. 15-June 1, weekly
$225-$275 (1-2)*

Darnley
Fralor
Bed & Breakfast ★★½
Fraser & Lorraine MacKinnon,
Darnley, C0B 1M0
(902) 836-5300
Rte. 20 (Blue Heron Drive), 14 km
north of Kensington • Remodelled
country home, sun deck and stunning
scenery • Four o/n units: two with
two doubles, two with one, one B&S,
one 1/2 B • Colour TV • Cribs
available • Non-smoking only
FEATURES: Beaches & country
lanes • Air-conditioned home •
Awaken to aroma of coffee, perfect
in family room or on sun deck
*RATES: $40 (1), $50 (2) •
Breakfast • Open June-Sept. • MC,
Visa accepted*

Darnley
Sea Breeze
Bed & Breakfast
Fran Harding, RR 1, Kensington,
C0B 1M0
(902) 836-5275
Rte. 20 • Modern home, quiet
scenic location • Three o/n units,
one B&S, queen, double or
twin-single beds. Share B • TV in
living room • Adults preferred •
Non-smoking only
FEATURES: Homemade muffins •
Restaurants nearby • Sandy beaches
& attractions nearby • Secure
bicycle storage
*RATES: $35-$45 (1-2) • Breakfast
• Open May-Oct. • PEIBBA Member*

Dunedin
Dunedin Lodge ★★★
John & Anne Read, Cornwall RR 2,
Dunedin, C0A 1H0
(902) 675-3292
Three km from TransCanada Hwy
on Rte. 247 • Island-stone home on
West River • Two o/n units, one
queen and one twin. Separate
entrance, living area available for
guests • Cable TV • Partially
accessible • Not suitable for
children under 10
FEATURES: Laundry facilities •
Coffee • Barbecue • Deck • Golfing,
canoeing, fishing, swimming and
dining nearby • 20-25 minutes to
Cavendish and Borden, 10 minutes to
Charlottetown
*RATES: $50 (2), $5 add'l person •
Full breakfast • Open June 1-Sept. 30*

Dunstaffnage
Dunstaffnage Heights
Bed & Breakfast
Evelyn & Sol Feldstein, RR 3,
Dunstaffnage, C1A 7J7
(902) 628-1715
Winter address: Bonshaw RR1, C0A
1C0, (902) 658-2658
Rte. 2 east of Charlottetown •
Victorian Home, 130 years old,
spacious grounds • Three o/n units,
two B&S • Colour TV and VCR •
Cot and crib available • Non-smoking
only
FEATURES: Bilingual • Laundry
facilities • Piano • Barbecue •
Vegetarians welcome • Picnic table
• Air conditioning • Cottage also
available • Near world-class golf
course
*RATES: $40-$45 (1), $45-$50 (2),
$10 add'l person • Full breakfast •
Open June 15 to Labour Day •
Weekly rates available • PEIBBA
Member*

Dunstaffnage
The Little Blue Shed
Bed & Breakfast &
Cottage
Nancy MacFarlane, Dunstaffnage,
Charlottetown RR 3, C1A 7J7
(902) 892-8024
At junction of Rtes. 2 east and 6 •
Two o/n units, shared B&S •
Non-smoking only
FEATURES: Cottage available
*RATES: $45 (2) • Open year-round
• Off-season rates Sept.-May,
weekly $275 (2)*

Earnscliffe
Esther's Farm Home
and Motel ★★
Esther Mutch, RR 3, Vernon, C0A 2E0
(902) 651-2415
Off TransCanada Hwy on Rte. 267,
24 km east of Charlottetown • Quiet
country home with beef cattle and
pheasants, 300 acres • Three o/n
units, B&S, one with two double
beds and one single, two with one
double bed • Cot, crib available •
Pets permitted, usually on leash •
Non-smoking
FEATURES: Complimentary tea,
coffee • Housekeeping units
available • Clam digging on private
beach within walking distance
*RATES: $26 (2), $5 add'l person •
Breakfast extra • Open year-round •
Weekly $140 (2), $25 add'l person •
TIAPEI Member*

East Bideford
Burleigh's
Bed & Breakfast ★★½
Pauline & James Burleigh, RR 2,
Ellerslie, C0B 1J0
(902) 831-2288
Toll free 1-800-259-4054

Two km off Rte. 12 on Rte. 163 (Lennox Island Road) • Quiet relaxing location by the scenic Bideford River • Three o/n units, two with double beds, one with queen-size bed, sofa bed, private B&S • Cot available • Non-smoking only
FEATURES: Complimentary evening snack, home cooking • Living room • Screened patio • Beach • Swimming, canoeing, paddle boat for guest use • Attractions nearby
RATES: $40-$45 (2), $10 add'l person • Full breakfast • Open June 1-Oct. 15 • Reservations accepted after May 1 • Weekly $250-$275 (2), $50 add'l person • TIAPEI Member

East Point
Arrowhead Lodge
Eugene Croken, South Lake RR 1, C0A 1K0
(902) 357-2482
On Rte. 16, 5 km from eastern tip of Island • Newly built lodge in natural setting • Three o/n suites, private B&S, hardwood floors, two with king beds and marble flooring • Colour TV and VCR in rooms • Partial accessibility
FEATURES: View • Two sitting areas • Decks on upper and lower levels • Video library • Games room • Kayak excursions • Bicycles • 38 acres of groomed trails overlooking the water • Air-conditioning • Beach on premises
RATES: $165-$205 (2), $60 add'l person • Full gourmet breakfast • Open year-round • Off-season rates available

Ellerslie
Vikings Haven
Dorothy Olsen, Dystant Road, Ellerslie PO, C0B 1J0
(902) 831-3015
On Rte. 133, off Rte. 2 • One o/n unit, one B&S • Colour TV • Non-smoking only
FEATURES: Winter address: 12 Rugby Road, Nashua, NH, USA, 03063, (603) 882-5093
RATES: $45 (2), $6 add'l person • Full breakfast • Open June 15-Sept. 15

Fairfield
Campbell's Guest Home
Flora Campbell, Fairfield, Souris RR 2, C0A 2B0
(902) 357-2504
Three o/n units, one B&S
RATES: $35 (2), $5 add'l person

Fairview
McIsaac's Bed & Breakfast
Barbara McIsaac, Cornwall RR 2, Fairview, C0A 1H0
(902) 675-2567
Century farm, 20 minutes from Charlottetown, overlooking West River • Two o/n units, one B&S, both rooms with double beds
FEATURES: Near golf courses and Fort Amherst-Port LaJoie historic park • Private beach, kitchen privileges
RATES: $30 (2) • Continental breakfast • Open June 1-Sept. 30

French River
The Beach House Visual Arts Centre
Brenda & Barry Philp, Kensington RR 2, C0B 1M0 (winter: 34 Union Street, Charlottetown, C1A 3V4, (902) 894-4402)
(902) 886-2145
Off Rte. 2 on the Cape Rd. • Scenic location with views of ocean, sand dunes and coastal lighthouse • Four o/n units, 1 B&S, 1 S • Pets permitted • Non-smoking only
FEATURES: Two-day video, photo workshops available • Beach on premises
RATES: $45 (2), $10 add'l person • Open May 1-Oct. 31 • Off-season rates Aug. 21-June 30

Frenchfort
Miller's Farm Bed & Breakfast ★★
Janet Miller, Charlottetown RR 3, Frenchfort, C1A 7J7
(902) 629-1509
On Rte. 260, 3 km off Rte. 2 East • Quiet, yet centrally located • Three o/n units, double beds, one B&S • Non-smoking rooms available
FEATURES: Water view from veranda • Picnic table • Shady lawn • Thirty minutes to Cavendish, National Park, golfing • Near Charlottetown
RATES: $30 (2) • Full breakfast • Open May 15-Oct. 15 • PEIBBA Member

Greenwich
Greenwich Dunes Bed & Breakfast
Betty Lou Tilley/ Brenda Lee Doyle, St. Peters RR 1, C0A 2A0; (winter: Hunter River RR 1, C0A 1N0, (902) 621-0674)

(902) 961-3370
Fax: (902) 384-2961
On Rte. 313, off Rte. 2 east • Century home overlooking St. Peters Bay on the Island's north shore • Three o/n units, 1 1/2 B&S • Non-smoking only
FEATURES: Tea room • Quilt shop • Deck with view of bay • Close to Greenwich Dunes and miles of pristine beaches
RATES: $45-$55 (2) • Breakfast • Open June 28-Sept. 2 • Weekly $1,000 (for house)

Hampton
Beachside Bed & Breakfast
Jean & Cecil Dunbar, RR 2, Cornwall, C0A 1H0
(902) 658-2693
Two o/n units, one S • One colour TV • Beach on premises
RATES: $25 (2) • Breakfast extra • Open May 15-Sept. 30

Hampton
Bradway Inn ★★½
Helen Bradway, Hampton RR 1, C0A 1J0 (winter: 66 Carmel Lane, Feeding Hills, MA, USA, 01030, (413) 786-1282)
(902) 658-2178
Three o/n units, two with skylights, one B&S, one private S
FEATURES: View of Northumberland Strait, overlooking Victoria • Twenty-five minutes to Charlottetown, Summerside, Borden and Cavendish
RATES: $40-$50 (2), $5 add'l person • Full breakfast • Open June 1 to Labour Day • Weekly $240-$300 (2), $30 add'l person, family rates available

Hampton
Wayside
Bed & Breakfast ★★½
The Gowing Family, RR 1,
Crapaud, C0A 1J0
(902) 658-2156
TransCanada Hwy • Old Island
home in quiet rural village of
Hampton • Three o/n units, two S,
two with double bed, one with
double and single • Non-smoking
only
FEATURES: Victorian furnishings
*RATES: $45 (2), $10 add'l person
• Full breakfast • Open June
15-Sept. 6 • Weekly $250 (2), $70
add'l person • Discount for
four-night stay*

Harrington
Wilbert's
Bed & Breakfast ★★★
Herbert & Vivia Wilbert, RR 9,
Winsloe, C1E 1Z3
(902) 368-8145
Toll free 1-800-847-8145
6 km north of airport. Central, 15
minutes from Charlottetown • Quiet
home, pleasant rural setting with
ducks, chickens • Three o/n units,
one B&S, one-half B, two rooms
double beds, one with twin beds •
Cot, crib available • Non-smoking
only
FEATURES: German spoken •
Nature trails • Home-made jam,
muffins • Housekeeping unit
available • Near major attractions,
Brackley Beach, Cavendish, golf,
lobster suppers, crafts
*RATES: $30 (1), $42-$45 (2), $8
add'l person • Full breakfast •
Open June 1-Sept. 30 • MC
accepted • Weekly rates available •
TIAPEI Member*

Hunter River
Cousins Village Inn
Donald & Helen Cousins, Box 100,
Hunter River, C0A 1N0
(902) 964-3457
Beautiful spacious home on hill
overlooking scenic village of
Hunter River • Three o/n units, two
B&S, queen and double beds.
Separate guests' B • Pets permitted,
usually on leash • Non-smoking only
FEATURES: Walking trails •
Swimming pool • Central location
for touring Island
*RATES: $45-$55 (2) • Full
breakfast • Open June 30-Sept. 4 •
Weekly $300-$370 (2)*

Hunter River
The Daylily
Bed & Breakfast ★★
Susan Le Maistre/Dave Johnston,
Box 83, Hunter River, C0A 1N0
(902) 964-3177
Well decorated, larger older home •
Three o/n units with double beds,
two B&S • Colour TV • Cot, crib
and play area available • No pets •
Children welcome • Non-smoking
only
FEATURES: Bilingual • Beautiful
gardens • Located in serviced
village, surrounded by rolling hills •
Fifteen km to beaches and island
attractions
*RATES: $45-$50 (2), $5-$10 add'l
person • Breakfast with homemade
bread and preserves • Open June
10-Sept. 30 • Visa accepted •
Weekly $275-$325 (2), $25-$50
add'l person • Off-season rates
available June 10-27 and after
Labour Day*

Hunter River
Jean's Overnight Guests
Jean MacDonald, RR 2, Hunter River, C0A 1N0
(902) 964-3197/2470
On Rte. 13 (Rennies Road) • Dairy farm • Three o/n units, one B&S • Colour TV
RATES: $30 (2), $5 add'l person • Breakfast extra • Open May-Sept.

Hunter River
Just Another Farm Tourist Home ★★
Gezinus & Akkelien Vos, RR 1, Hunter River, C0A 1N0
(902) 964-3498
On Rte. 2 Central PEI • Dairy farm with beautiful view • Three o/n units, one with double bed, one with double and twin bed, one sleeps family of six, one B&S, private entrance • Pets permitted, usually on leash
FEATURES: Dutch spoken • Kitchen facilities • Microwave • Licensed dining room 1 km • Barbeque • Ocean beach 16 km • Guests are welcome to watch cows being milked
RATES: $35-$40 (2), $5 add'l person • Continental breakfast • Open May 15-Sept. 15 • TIAPEI Member

Kensington
O'Sullivan's Bed & Breakfast
Margaret Wadman, 15 Centennial Drive, Kensington, C0B 1M0
(902) 836-4636
One o/n unit, one B&S
RATES: $35 (2) • Continental breakfast • Open July-Oct.

Kensington
Pickering's Guest Home
Mrs. Heber Pickering, 4 Russell Street, Box 71, Kensington, C0B 1M0
(902) 836-3441
Two o/n units, shared B&S
RATES: $20 (2), $5 add'l person • Open Apr.-Nov. • Weekly $120 (2)

Kensington
Victoria Inn and Housekeeping Suites ★★½
Raymond O'Brien, 32 Victoria Street East, Box 717, Kensington, C0B 1M0
(902) 836-3010
Renovated turn-of-the-century home with period furniture • Two o/n units, private B&S, four-poster double beds • Colour TV in rooms
FEATURES: Sun porch • Barbecue • Picnic area • Treed lawns and gardens • Centrally located for cycling • Close to beaches, golf, attractions • Housekeeping suites available
RATES: $70 (2), $5 add'l person • Breakfast • Open June 15-Sept. 15 • MC, Visa accepted • Weekly $450 (2)

Kingsboro
The Blue Panda
Bob Evans & Jack Bryant, RR 2, Kingsboro, C0A 2B0
(902) 357-2155
Relaxed atmosphere among kindred spirits • Five o/n units, one B&S, one king-size bed, two queen-size, two twins • One colour TV
FEATURES: Spectacular views, privacy, kitchen privileges • White sandy beach at Basin Head 3 km • Winter: 35 Tress Road, Prospect, CT, USA 06712, (203) 758-6109
RATES: $45-$50 (2) • Breakfast • Open July 1-Aug. 30 • Weekly rates available • Singles slightly lower

Kingsboro
Keus' Bed & Breakfast
Anna & Michael Keus, Souris RR 2,
C0A 2B0
(902) 357-2028
Off Rte. 16 east • Two o/n units,
one B&S • Colour TV
*RATES: $35 (2), $5 add'l person,
taxes incl. • Breakfast • Open June
1-Sept. 30*

Kingsboro
Robertson's Bed & Breakfast ★★
Lorna Robertson, RR 2, Souris,
C0A 2B0
(902) 357-2026
Ten km east of Souris • Five o/n
units, two B&S, three with double
bed, one with two double beds, one
single • Non-smoking only
FEATURES: Two km from Basin
Head Fisheries Museum • White,
sandy beach
*RATES: $25-$40 (2), $5 add'l
person, taxes incl • Breakfast •
Open June 15-Sept. 30*

Kingston
Younker's Farm Bed & Breakfast ★★
Belle Younker, RR 4, Cornwall,
C0A 1H0
(902) 675-2832
Rte. 247, 10 minutes off
TransCanada Hwy • Two o/n units,
one B&S, double beds • Colour TV
in living room
FEATURES: "Cleanliness is our
motto" • Fifteen minutes to
Cavendish, 10 minutes to
Charlottetown
*RATES: $35 (2), $6 add'l person •
Breakfast extra • Open June 1-Sept.
30 • TIAPEI Member*

Knutsford
Smallman's Bed & Breakfast ★★★
Arnold & Eileen Smallman, RR1,
O'Leary, C0B 1V0
(902) 859-3469
Off Rte. 2 on Rte. 142, 7 km from
O'Leary • Split-level home in
peaceful farming community • Four
o/n units, one B, one S, two with
double beds, one with queen, one
with two singles • Welcome to use
family room & TV • Cots, crib •
Pets permitted, usually on leash •
Non-smoking only
FEATURES: Dinner on request •
Churches, stores, beaches, Mill
River Golf Course nearby
*RATES: $30-$40 (2), $8 add'l
person • Breakfast extra • Open
year-round • Weekly $180-$240 (2),
$48 add'l person*

Little Pond
Ark Inn ★★★
Souris RR 4, C0A 2B0
(902) 583-2400
Fax: (902) 583-2176
Toll free 1-800-665-2400
Off Rte. 310 • Secluded retreat in
natural surroundings • Seven o/n
units, private B&S • Partially
accessible • No pets, please
FEATURES: Dinner on request •
Views from 4 km walking trail •
Private sandy beach • Suite
available • Two world-class golf
courses nearby
*RATES: $70-$95 (2), $10 add'l
person • Breakfast • Open June
2-Sept.8, Sept. 9-Oct. 26, rooms and
breakfast only • AE, MC, Visa
accepted • Off-season rates during
June, Sept. and Oct. • Packages
available*

Little Pond
Little Pond Country Store Bed & Breakfast ★★★
Eugene E. & Jessie M. Noyes,
Souris RR 4, Little Pond, C0A 2B0
(902) 583-2892
Two km off Rte. 310 (Kings
Byway) • Lovely historic home in
tranquil countryside • Three o/n
units, one B, one S, two with one
double bed and one with two
singles • Cot and crib available •
Non-smoking only
FEATURES: Nature trails • Flower
gardens • Large Island-stone
fireplace; breakfast served in cozy
country kitchen; country store to
browse in • Beach 2 km • Famous
for Island cheese
RATES: *$40 (2), $8 add'l person •
Full breakfast • Open June 15-Sept.
30 • Weekly rates on request*

Little Sands
Bayberry Cliff Inn Bed & Breakfast ★★★
Nancy & Don Perkins, Little Sands,
C0A 1W0
(902) 962-3395
On Rte. 4, 8 km east of Wood
Islands ferry • Waterfront property,

30 ft. from
cliff • Four
o/n units,
four B&S.
Double and
single beds,
one queen,
private
porches •
Colour TV • No pets, please •
Non-smoking only
FEATURES: Rooms located in 2
remodelled post & beam barns •
Decorated with antiques • Rustic
decor and quilts • Restaurants
nearby • Large screened porch &

deck • Swimming • Seal-watching,
winery and vineyards, craft stores
close by • One housekeeping unit
available
RATES: *$60-$95 (2), $15 add'l
person • Full breakfast • Open May
15-Sept. 30 • One night's deposit
required • MC, Visa accepted •
Early reservations suggested •
Weekly rates available*

Long Creek
Alice's Meadow View ★★½
Alice Taylor, Box 55, Cornwall,
C0A 1H0
(902) 675-2358
Long Creek, Rte. 19A • Quiet
century home • Four o/n units, two
double, two queen, two shared B&S
• Two colour TVs • Pets permitted
FEATURES: Laundry facilities •
Evening snack • Kitchen facilities •
Barbeque • Flower garden • 1.6 km
off Blue Heron Drive, 20 km from
Charlottetown • Near beaches, golf,
churches and restaurants
RATES: *$23-$25 (1-2), $5 add'l
person • Breakfast with homemade
breads extra • Open May 1-Oct. 31*

Long River
Memory Lane Guest Home
Fred & Barbara Doughart, RR 2,
Kensington, C0B 1M0
(902) 886-2767
Two o/n units, one B&S • Pets
permitted, usually on leash
FEATURES: Kitchen with tea
room 1 km
RATES: *$35 (2) • Breakfast • Open
year-round • TIAPEI Member*

Lower Montague
Stonehedge-by-the-Sea Bed & Breakfast ★★★½
Brenda Brindell, St. Andrews Point, RR 2, Montague, C0A 1R0
(902) 838-2971
Waterfront property • One o/n unit, one B&S, ocean frontage executive suite, queen-size bed, bidet, room key • Colour satellite TV • Telephone • Non-smoking only
FEATURES: Private breakfast room and bar fridge • Garden • Ensuite sitting area • Whirlpool • Air-conditioned • Ocean view • Fax available
RATES: $90 (2) • Breakfast • Open May 1-Oct. 30

Lower Montague
Victorian Comfort
Brian Annear & Sheilagh Lavandier-Annear, Montague, RR 2, C0A 1R0
(902) 838-3038
Three o/n units, double beds, shared and private B&S, Jacuzzi • Non-smoking only
RATES: $45-$50 • Open July 1-Sept. 6

Malpeque
Fox House Bed & Breakfast
Greg Weeks, Box 488, Kensington, C0B 1M0
(902) 836-5371
Rte. 20 at Malpeque • Heritage home • Four o/n units, two S
FEATURES: English, French and Japanese spoken • Picnic baskets available • Mountain bikes • Close to beaches
RATES: $65 (2) • Full breakfast • Open May 1-Oct. 31 • Custom tours available • Reservations recommended • Off-season rates

May 15-June 2 aned Sept. 10-Oct. 31 • Weekly $390 (2)

Malpeque
Keir's Shore Inn ★★★½
Steve Stratos, Box 7615, Malpeque, C0B 1M0
(902) 836-3938
On Rte. 20, at Malpeque, 10 km from Kensington • Restored colonial heritage house (1790) with waterfront location on Malpeque Bay • Six o/n units, private B&S • Children over 12 yrs welcome • No pets, please • Non-smoking only
FEATURES: Library • Parlour • Sun room • Porch • Beach on premises
RATES: $85-$130 (2), $20 add'l person • Full breakfast • Open May 15-Oct. 15 • AE, MC, Visa accepted • Off-season rates available

Malpeque
Malpeque Bed & Breakfast ★★
Chris & Susan Hawkins, Box 7606, RR 1, Kensington, C0B 1M0
(902) 836-5359
Off-season (705) 789-2704
Rte. 20, Malpeque • Century home with restful flower garden • Four o/n units, private and shared B&S, double and twin beds • No pets • Non-smoking only
FEATURES: Self-contained cottage and suite • Near Cabot Beach and local attractions • One housekeeping unit with B&S available
RATES: $45-$50 (2) • Full breakfast • Cash or travellers cheques • Open June 30-Aug. 31

Margate
Thompson's Tourist Home ★★½
Don & Valerie Thompson, RR 6,
Kensington, C0B 1M0
(902) 836-4160
Toll free 1-800-567-7907
Northeast 5 km on Rte. 6 from
Kensington, exit left on Thompsons
Point Rd., 1.4 km • Large, restored
farm home, three acres, overlooking
picturesque river • Five o/n units,
one B&S • Colour TV • VCR in
family room • Pets permitted,
usually on leash
FEATURES: Period furnishings •
Near Green Gables & attractions •
Cavendish nearby
RATES: $35 (2), $5 add'l person •
Light breakfast • Open June 1-Sept.
30 • Weekly $220 (2), $35 add'l
person

Marshfield
Rosevale Farm Bed & Breakfast ★★½
Athol & Doris MacBeath, RR 3
Charlottetown, Marshfield, C1A 7J7
(902) 629-1341
Rte. 2 East, 3 km from
Charlottetown • Active dairy farm •
Two o/n units, one B&S, queen or
double bed, private B for guests' use
FEATURES: Theatre and beaches
nearby • Central location for Island
touring
RATES: $40 (2) • Full breakfast •
Open May 1-Oct. 15 • MC accepted
• Off-season rates before June 15
and after Sept. 15 • PEIBBA;
TIAPEI Member

Marshfield
Woodmere Bed & Breakfast ★★★
Doris Wood, RR 3 Charlottetown,
Marshfield, C1A 7J7
Tel & Fax (902) 628-1783
Toll free 1-800-747-1783
On Rte. 2 East, 6 km from
Charlottetown • Colonial home,
standard-bred horses grazing in

fields • Four
o/n units,
private
B&S, two
with queen
beds, two
with two
doubles,
private entrance, individually
controlled heat • Colour TV in each
room • Non-smoking only
FEATURES: Fragrant rose gardens
• Minutes to airport, golf, harness
racing, dining, theatre and beaches.
Central to all attractions
RATES: $65 (2), $10 add'l person
• Full breakfast • Open year-round
• MC, Visa accepted • Weekly rates
available • Off-season rates Sept.
1-June 30 • TIAPEI Member

Maximeville
Chez Évangéline Bed & Breakfast ★★
Évangéline Gallant, RR 3, Box 35,
Wellington, C0B 2E0
(902) 854-3097
On Rte. 11 (Lady Slipper Dr.) in
Région Acadienne • Three o/n units.
One B&S, 1/2 B, all double beds •
Three B&W TVs • Crib available •
Pets permitted, usually on leash
FEATURES: Bilingual • Barbecue
on request • Beach nearby
RATES: $30 (2), $5 add'l person •
Open June 15-Sept. 30 • Weekly
$175 (2), $25 add'l person

Meadow Bank
MacFadyen's Farm
Bed & Breakfast ★★½
Dolphie & Dingwell MacFadyen,
RR 2, Cornwall, C0A 1H0
(902) 566-2771
On Rte. 19 • Two o/n units, two
B&S, one double and single beds,
one two double beds, private
entrance • Two colour TVs • Pets
permitted, usually on leash •
Non-smoking only
FEATURES: Hostess will assist
guests in planning the perfect Island
vacation • Kitchen privileges
*RATES: $35 (2), $6 add'l person,
no GST • Continental breakfast,
home-made jams • Open May
1-Oct. 30*

Mermaid
Mermaid
Bed & Breakfast ★★½
Heidi & Elmer Swanson, Mermaid
Mini Farm, Box 5218,
Charlottetown, C1A 7J8
(902) 569-1274
Nine km from Charlottetown •
Quiet, with garden • Two o/n units,
one B&S, one with double bed, one
with twin singles • Crib • Pets
permitted
FEATURES: Complimentary tea,
coffee • Barbecue area • Heated indoor
pool • Private, safe, sandy beach
*RATES: $45 (2) • Full breakfast •
Open mid-May to mid-Dec.*

Millview
Smith's Farm
Bed & Breakfast ★★½
Louise Smith, Vernon Bridge PO,
Millview, C0A 2E0
(902) 651-2728
Toll free 1-800-265-2728

On Rte. 3, 2 km off TransCanada
Hwy • Four o/n units, two B&S,
family bedroom with two double
beds, private B • TV in living room
• Cot available • Non-smoking only
FEATURES: Complimentary tea •
Charlottetown 15 minute drive •
Walking trail • Bicycle storage •
Guests are welcome in our living
room with TV, organ and piano,
to relax and have tea with us • 30
minutes from Wood Islands Ferry
*RATES: $22 (1), $30-$35 (2), $5
add'l person • Continental plus
breakfast $3 extra • Open May
1-Nov. 15 • Weekly $180-$210 (2),
$30 add'l person • FVBB; TIAPEI
Member*

Milo
Milo Bed & Breakfast ★★
Doris Gallant, Coleman RR1, C0B 1H0
(902) 859-3419
Rte. 14 • Quiet rural setting • One
o/n unit with double bed, one B&S
• Pets permitted
FEATURES: Bilingual • Minutes
to good restaurants • Only minutes
to Elephant Rock and Mill River
Golf Course • Ocean beach nearby
*RATES: $35 (2) • Breakfast • Open
June 1-September 30 • Weekly $210
(2)*

Milton
Miltonvale
Bed & Breakfast ★★★
Verna and Ken Coles, RR 10,
Winsloe, C1E 1Z4
(902) 368-1085
On Rte. 2, 13 km west of
Charlottetown • New home, quiet

scenic
surroundings
• Two o/n
units, one
room with
two double
beds, one
with queen
bed, private
B • TV in family room
FEATURES: Golf, fishing nearby •
Beaches 20 minute drive
*RATES: $45 (1), $55 (2), $10 add'l
person • Breakfast • Open May
15-Sept. 30 • Weekly $330 (2), $60
add'l person • Off-season rates
before June 15 and in Sept.,
off-season by reservation*

Miscouche
Lecky's
Bed & Breakfast
Allen & Dorothy Lecky, Box 273,
Summerside, C1N 4Y8
(902) 436-3216
Victorian home (c. 1905) with period
furnishings • Six o/n units, two
shared B&S • Not suitable for
children under 10 yrs • No pets, please
FEATURES: Wrap-around lower
deck, upper deck overlooking
meadow
*RATES: $60-$90 (3-4), $8 add'l
person • Full breakfast • Open June
1-Oct. 30 • Off-season rates before
June 14 and after Sept. 30, weekly
$385-$550 (3-4), $56 add'l person*

Montague
Boudreault's
"White House"
Tourist Home ★★½
Zita Boudreault, RR 2, Montague,
C0A 1R0
(902) 838-2560/3417
On Rte. 17 (Kings Byway), 1 km
south of Montague • Quiet, friendly
atmosphere • Four o/n units, one
B&S, one S, two with double beds,
one with twin singles, family room
with queen-size and single bed • TV
room available • Telephone • Cots
available
FEATURES: Bicycle storage •
Restaurants nearby • Two
eighteen-hole championship golf
courses, swimming, banks, theatres,
deep-sea fishing, seal-watching
cruises nearby • Craft shop nearby
*RATES: $40-$45 (2), $8 add'l
person • Continental plus breakfast
• Open June 15-Oct. 15*

Montague
Parker's
Bed & Breakfast ★★★
Bill & Olive Parker, Box 398,
Montague, C0A 1R0
(902) 838-3663
Toll free 1-800-511-8786
At 90 Main St. south on Rte. 17 •
Nestled in small-town setting,
Montague the Beautiful • Four o/n
units, two B&S, two with twin
beds, two with queen and cots •
Partially wheelchair accessible •
Colour TV in rooms • Cot available
• No pets, please • Non-smoking
only
FEATURES: Living room and
decks available to guests • Bicycle
storage • Golf and swimming
nearby; restaurants, aquatic centre,
seal watching, and churches nearby

RATES: $45 (2), $10 add'l person
• Full home-cooked breakfast •
Open May 24-Oct. 31 • BBOL;
PEIBBA; Pantel Member

Montague
The Pines
Bed & Breakfast ★★★
Al & Anne Coneen, Box 486,
Montague, C0A 1R0
(902) 838-3675
31 Riverside Dr., off Main St. •
Century home • Four o/n units, two
B and 3 S,
one queen,
one twin,
two double,
private
entrance •
Centrally
located
colour TV •

No pets inside, please • No smoking
inside
FEATURES: Laundry facilities
available • Common room • Patio •
Barbecue • Picnic table • Croquet,
horseshoes • Bicycle storage • Close
to aquatic centre, restaurants,
churches, museum, crafts, golf,
river cruises and seal-watching
RATES: $40-$45 (2), $8 add'l
person • Full breakfast • Open May
24-Oct. 15 • Weekly $255-$290 (2),
$56 add'l person • TIAPEI Member

Montague
Robin's Nest
Guest House
Gaelene & Bobby Nicholson, 106
Main Street North, Montague, C0A 1R0
(902) 838-3274
Two o/n units, double beds, shared
B&S • Children welcome • Pets
permitted • Non-smoking only

FEATURES: Bicycle storage •
Walking distance to heart of
Montague
RATES: $40 • Open June 1-Sept. 7
• Weekly $200

Morell
A Village
Bed & Breakfast ★★★
Daphne MacAdam, Box 71, Morell,
C0A 1S0
(902) 961-2394
Located midway between
Charlottetown & Souris, on Rte. 2,
Main Street, across from Esso
station • Three o/n units, two B&S,
one with double bed, private B, one
with double bed, one with two
single beds • Non-smoking only
FEATURES: Laundry facilities •
Patio • Barbecue • Bicycle storage •
Churches, restaurants and stores
within walking distance • Short
drive to links at Crowbush Cove,
trout and deep-sea fishing
RATES: $35-$45 (2), $8 add'l
person • Breakfast • Open
year-round • Reservations preferred
between Sept. 30 and May 1 •
Weekly $210-$270 (2) • Off-season
rates available • HBDTA; PEIBBA;
TIAPEI Member

Morell
Kelly's Bed & Breakfast
Mary S. Kelly, RR 2, Morell, C0A 1S0
(902) 961-2389
On Rte. 2 • Former telephone office
still houses old magneto switchboard
and telephone memorabilia • Six o/n
units, two B&S • Pets permitted •
Non-smokers preferred
FEATURES: Laundry facilities •
Bicycle storage • Barbecue • Picnic
table • Flower gardens • Fishing •
Restaurant and stores nearby • Only 4
km to The Links at Crowbush Cove
or to Lakeside's sandy ocean beach
*RATES: $35 (2), $8 add'l person •
Breakfast • Open June 1-Oct. 31 •
Weekly $210 (2), $45 add'l person*

Mount Stewart
Cottage 'Laine Bed & Breakfast
Elaine Clark, Box 54, Mount
Stewart, C0A 1T0
(902) 676-2827
On Rte. 2, 20 km east of
Charlottetown across from Irving •
Century home overlooking the
village of Mount Stewart • Three
o/n units, shared B
FEATURES: Tea room • Craft
shop • Five minutes to Links at
Crowbush Cove, beaches
*RATES: $35 (2), $5 add'l person •
Light breakfast • Open June 1-
mid-Oct. • Weekly $210 (2), $35
add'l person*

Murray Harbour
The Morning Glory Bed & Breakfast ★★½
David & Lillian Rourke, Murray
Harbour, C0A 1V0
(902) 962-3150
Toll free 1-800-881-3150

Rte. 18A • Three acres nestled
among trees, flowers and vegetables
in scenic fishing village • Three o/n
units, 1 1/2 B&S, one with queen,
two with double and single beds •
Centrally located colour TV and
VCR • No pets, please •
Non-smoking only
FEATURES: Bicyle storage •
Seal-watching tours, churches,
Kings Castle Park; 15 minutes from
Wood Islands ferry • Five minutes
to beaches • Restaurant and gift
shop nearby
*RATES: $45 (1-2), $8 add'l
person, no GST • Light breakfast •
Open June 1-Sept. 15 • MC, Visa
accepted • TIAPEI Member*

Murray Harbour North
Lady Catherine's Bed & Breakfast ★★★
Tom Rath & Colleen Dempsey, RR
4, Montague, C0A 1R0
(902) 962-3426
Toll free 1-800-661-3426
On Rte. 17 (Kings Byway),
southeast of Montague • Large

Victorian
country
home • Four
o/n units,
one B&S,
one S, two
with
queen-size
bed, one
with double beds, one with twin
beds • Non-smoking only
FEATURES: Dietary concerns
accomodated • Handmade quilts •
Relax on verandas overlooking
Northumberland Strait • Bicycles
and fishing rods available • Beach,
craft shops, golf, seal-watching
tours nearby

RATES: $40 (1), $44-$50 (2)
Weekly $250-$315 (2), $70 add'l
person • Full breakfast • Open
year-round • MC, Visa accepted •
Off-season (Oct.-May), custom
packages with meals can be
arranged • TIAPEI Member

Murray River
Mary Catherine's Bed & Breakfast Guest Home
Catherine Mary Foley, General
Delivery, Murray River, C0A 1W0
(902) 962-3437
On Main Street, 500m past post
office • Two o/n units, shared B&S
• Colour TV in rooms • Pets
permitted • Non-smoking only
FEATURES: French spoken •
Laundry facilities • Bicycle storage
• Cottages available • Minutes from
shopping, dining, marina, seal- and
bird-watching tour, deep-sea
fishing, swimming • Close to seal
colony, mini-golf, ferry • RV
parking
RATES: $40 (2), $7 add'l person •
Full breakfast • Open May 1-Oct.
30 • Off-season rates before June 1
and after Sept. 1 • Weekly $300 (2),
$42 add'l person

New Glasgow
Clyde View Guest Home
Wanda Dickieson, Hunter River RR 2,
C0A 1N0
(902) 964-2651
Off Rte. 13, across from PEI
Preserve Co. • Three o/n units, two
with double beds, one with twn
singles, shared B&S with Jacuzzi •
Non-smoking only
RATES: $40 (2) Weekly $235 (2)•
Breakfast • Open June 1-Oct. 15 •
Off-season rates Sept. 15-Oct. 15

New Glasgow
Country View Farm Tourist Home
Ada & Richard B. Smith, New
Glasgow, Hunter River RR 2, C0A 1N0
(902) 964-2660
Three o/n units, shared B
RATES: $25 (2), $5 add'l person •
Open June 15-Oct. 15 • TIAPEI
Member

New Glasgow
My Mother's Country Inn ★★★
Nellie Andrew Ingleman & Ragnar
Ingleman, New Glasgow, Box 172,
Hunter River RR 2, C0A 1N0
(902) 964-2508
Toll free 1-800-278-2071
On Rte. 13 • Recently refurbished
historic home (c.1850) on 50 acres
of rolling hills and woodland •
Eight o/n units, four B&S • TV
FEATURES: Trout stream • Mill
pond • Trails • Fishing, boating •
Housekeeping units and cottage
available • Five minutes from
Cavendish Beach and National Park
RATES: $60-$90 (2), $15 add'l
person • Breakfast buffet • Open
June 15-Sept. 15 • Off-season rates
in June and Sept. • TIAPEI Member

New Haven
Safe Haven Guest House
Maryann Chaisson & Wayne
Campbell, Cornwall, RR 3, C0A 1H0
(902) 675-2623
On TransCanada Hwy at New
Haven • Old, refurbished farmhouse
• Three o/n units, queen and antique
3/4 bed, cot, one B&S, one B, one
S • Non-smoking only
FEATURES: Home baking,
preserves • Dinner on request •
Country walks, meditation • Close
to beach, fishing, festivals, theatre •
Fifteen minutes to Charlottetown,
twenty-five minutes to Borden and
30 minutes to Cavendish
*RATES: $35-$45 (2), $10 add'l
person • Full farm breakfast • Open
year-round • Cat on premises •
Reservations accepted • Off-season
rates available*

New Perth
Schellen's Bed & Breakfast ★★½
Sharon & Martin Schellen,
Cardigan RR 6, C0A 1G0
(902) 838-2396
Toll free 1-800-242-8367
On Rte. 3, 2 km west of Poole's
Corner • Cape Cod home on
five-acre lot • Three o/n units,
queen beds, shared B&S • Colour
TV and VCR
FEATURES: Eighteenth
century-style furniture hand-crafted
on site • Close to golfing, beaches,
scenic drives, restaurants
*RATES: $37 (2), $8 add'l person •
Full breakfast • Open June 1-Oct. 31
• Off-season rates Sept. 22-Oct. 31*

New Perth
VanDyke's Lakeview Bed & Breakfast ★★½
Lorraine & John VanDyke,
Montague RR 3, C0A 1R0
(902) 838-4408
On Rte. 3 • Overlooks man-made
lake • Six o/n units, two B&S, one
Jacuzzi, 1/2 B • Colour TV and VCR
FEATURES: Octagonal
dining/living room built in 1885 •
Large patio • Walking trails along
lake • Close to beaches, golf
courses and trail rides
*RATES: $20-$50 (2), $10 add'l
person • Continental breakfast •
Open May 1-Oct. 31 • Weekly
$120-$300 (2), $60 add'l person*

North Carleton
Captain's Lodge ★★★
Jim & Sue Rogers, Seven Mile Bay,
RR 2, Albany, C0B 1A0
(902) 855-3106
Toll free 1-800-261-3518
Off Rte. 10 down a country lane •

Sea
captain's
house, circa
1850 • Three
o/n units,
one B&S,
two with
queen-size
beds and
shared B, one ground-floor with
twin beds, en suite powder room •
Non-smoking only
FEATURES: Furnished with
antiques • Sitting room • Evening
desserts • Sun porch, veranda •
Horseshoe pit • Gardens •
Hammock • Cycling • Walk to
beach • Borden ferry 7 km
*RATES: $50 (1), $60 (2) • Gourmet
breakfast • Open June 1-Oct. 15 •*

Visa accepted • Off-season $50 (2)
• GTA, PEIBBA, TIAPEI Member

North Carleton
Muttart's
Bed & Breakfast
and Cottage ★★
Everett and Freda Muttart, Albany
RR 2, C0B 1A0
(902) 437-6403
Toll free 1-800-253-1749
Two o/n units, double beds, one
B&S
FEATURES: Camp-fire pit • Beach
• Clam digging, wind-surfing •
View of Northumberland Strait,
Borden and "The Link"
RATES: $40 (2) • Continental
breakfast • Open June 1-Oct. 30

North Granville
Hilltop House ★★
Ina & Michelle Dionne,
Breadalbane RR 1, North Granville,
C0A 1E0
(902) 886-2059
Toll free 1-800-704-8756
Charming Victorian farmhouse in
scenic hillside setting with river
view • Three o/n units, one B&S,
queen-size beds • Non-smoking only
FEATURES: Parlour available •
Beautiful area for walking,
bird-watching, cycling, golf • Near
Cavendish, lobster suppers •
Housekeeping unit available
RATES: $35 (2) • Continental
breakfast • Open June 15-Sept. 7 •
Weekly $220 (2) • TIAPEI Member

North Lake
Lakeville Bed &
Breakfast & Cottage ★★½
Mrs. Elora Rose, RR 1, Elmira,
C0A 1K0
(902) 357-2206/2811
Off Rte. 16 on North Lake Harbour
Rd. • Potato and grain farm, 200
acres overlooking North Lake •
Three o/n units two B&S, one S,
double beds • Two colour TVs •
Children welcome • Pets permitted,
usually on leash
FEATURES: Deep-sea fishing
arranged • Partially accessible
cottage available • Walk to beach
RATES: $30 (1), $35-$40 (2), $8
add'l person, no GST • Breakfast
extra • Open June 20-Nov 1 •
Weekly $210-$245 (2), $30 add'l
person

North Rustico
Orchard View Farm
Tourist Home ★★
Ronald & Heather Toombs, North
Rustico, Hunter River RR 2,
C0A 1N0
(902) 963-2302/2300
Toll free 1-800-419-4468
Rte. 6, 5 km east of Cavendish •
900-acre century hog farm with
grain, soybeans • Four o/n units,
queen and double beds, two B&S,
1/2 B, one whirlpool • Colour TV
and VCR • Pets permitted
RATES: $35-$45 (2), $5 add'l
person • Open June 15-Sept. 15 •
MC, Visa accepted • Special rates
June 15-30 and Aug. 21-31

North Milton
Country Garden Inn Bed & Breakfast ★★★½
Velda Buell, Winsloe RR 10, C1E 1Z4
(902) 566-4344
Toll free 1-800-308-9259
On Rte. 7, 5.4 km north off Rte. 2 •
Country inn on 10 acres • Two o/n
units, private B&S, one with
Jacuzzi • TV and VCR • No pets,
please • Non-smoking only
FEATURES: Family room • Central
to most attractions, ten minutes to
Cavendish and North Shore beaches
*RATES: $75-$105 • Country
breakfast • Open year-round •
Romance packages available*

North Rustico
Andy's Surfside Inn ★★
A.G. Doyle, Box 5, Charlottetown,
C1A 7K2
(902) 963-2405,
winter (902) 892-7994/0844
On Doyle's Cove in National Park
• Eight o/n units, four B&S •
Centrally located colour TVs
FEATURES: Laundry facilities •
Kitchen facilities • Ocean view •
Antique furnishings • Gas barbecue
• Bicycles • Beach on premises
*RATES: $35-$50 (2), $5 add'l
person, no GST or park entry fee •
Open June 1-Oct. 30 • Off-season
rates in June, Sept. and Oct. •
Weekly $1800 (complete house)*

North Rustico
MacLure Bed & Breakfast ★★½
John & Naomi MacLure, Cavendish
Road, RR 2, Hunter River, C0A 1N0
(902) 963-2239
Rte. 6, 3 km east of Cavendish
intersection • Three o/n units, one
B&S, one S, one with double and
single, one with double, one with
two doubles • Four colour TVs
FEATURES: Deep-sea fishing,
hiking and biking in National Park •
Near Green Gables House, golf
course, Cavendish Beach
*RATES: $35-$45 (2), $5 add'l
person • Breakfast extra • Open
year-round • Off-season rates before
June 30 and after Labour Day*

North Tryon
K.A.T.W.E.N. Tourist Lodge
Cathy & Wendall Muttart, Albany
RR 2, C0B 1A0
(902) 855-2675
Three o/n units, one S • One B&W TV
*RATES: $35 (2) • Breakfast extra •
Open June 1-Sept. 30 • Weekly $210
(2)*

O'Leary
The MacDonald Home ★★★
Adrienne & Stanley MacDonald,
568 Main Street, Box 129, O'Leary,
C0B 1V0
(902) 859-3457/2606
Fax (902) 859-3834
Toll free 1-800-565-3457
Large early 1900s heritage home •
Two o/n units, separate B • Centrally
located TV • Telephone • Cot and
high chair available • No pets, please
FEATURES: Recognized by PEI
Museum and Heritage Foundation •
Antiques • Fireplace • Living room
• Grand piano in parlour •
Whirlpool for guest use
*RATES: $45 (2) • Weekly
$200-$250 (2) • Breakfast • Open
year-round • MC, Visa • Off-season
rates • TIAPEI Member*

Orwell Cove
MacLean's Century Farm Tourist Home ★★
Edison & Lucille MacLean, Vernon Bridge PO, C0A 2E0
(902) 659-2694
Two km off Rte. 1, midway between Charlottetown and Wood Islands • Overlooking Orwell Bay • Three o/n units, one B&S, 1/2 B, double and single beds
FEATURES: This is a 300-acre working family farm
RATES: $30 (2), $6 add'l person • Breakfast extra • Open year-round • Weekly $175 (2), $30 add'l person • TIAPEI Member

Panmure Island
Partridge's Bed & Breakfast ★½
Mrs. Gertrude Partridge, Panmure Island, RR 2, Montague, C0A 1R0
Tel & Fax (902) 838-4687
Six o/n units, three B, two S, three with private B, colour TV, double and single bed, two with double, one with twin singles • three with shared B • Cots, crib available • Children under 6 free • Pets permitted
FEATURES: Kitchen, laundry privileges • Barbecue • Picnic tables • Bicycles, rowboat, canoe free • Near white, sandy beach
RATES:$40-$50 (2), $10 add'l person • Continental breakfast • Open June 1-Sept. 30 • Weekly $240- $300 (2), $60 add'l person • Off-season rates available • TIAPEI Member

Park Corner
Beds of Lavender ★★½
Hank & Clara Williams, Kensington RR 2, Park Corner, C0B 1M0
(902) 886-3114
On Rte. 20 (Blue Heron Drive, 8 km north of New London) • New home with shaker-style furnishings overlooking Lake of Shining Waters • Three o/n units, one S, 1/2 B, two with double beds and one single ($25) • Cot available • No pets • Non-smoking only
FEATURES: Complimentary evening snacks • Light breakfast of juice, home-made muffins, toast, cereal and beverage • Smoke detectors throughout • Winter: 47 Mohican Rd., Cornfield Point, Old Saybrook, CT, USA 06475, (203) 388-2587
RATES: $40 (2), $10 add'l person, no GST • Breakfast • Open mid-June to mid-Oct. • TIAPEI Member

Pinette
Midge's Bed & Breakfast
Eleanore & Gaston Laquerre, Pinette, RR 3, Belle River, C0A 1B0
(902) 659-2333
Three o/n units, one B&S
FEATURES: Beach on premises
RATES: $30 (2), $10 add'l person • Breakfast • Open May 1-Oct. 31 • Weekly $175 (2), $60 add'l person

Rice Point
Straitview Farm
Bed & Breakfast ★★
Louis & Marina Burdett, RR 2,
Cornwall, C0A 1H0
(902) 675-2071
On Rte. 19, 24 km from
Charlottetown • Three o/n units, one
B&S, one with double and single
bed, one with two double beds and
couch, one with queen waterbed,
separate bathroom for guests • Cot
available • Non-smoking only
FEATURES: Explore our nature
trail • Farm pets
*RATES: $25 (1), $30 (2), $5 add'l
person • Open May 1-Nov. 30 •
Weekly $200 (2), $35 add'l person,
breakfast extra • TIAPEI Member*

Richmond
Mom's
Bed 'N' Breakfast ★★½
Mrs. Erma Gaudet MacArthur,
Richmond, C0B 1Y0
(902) 854-2419
Junction Rte.s. 2 and 127, 3 km off

Lady Slipper
Dr. •
Heritage
home 1875 •
Four o/n
units, two
B&S, 1/2 B,
double beds,
one with
private B • No pets, please •
Non-smoking only
FEATURES: Modern comfort, two
verandas • Parlour with piano •
Dining room with antiques • Bicycle
storage • Close to beaches, golf
*RATES: $40 (2), $75 (4), $7 add'l
person • Breakfast • Open June to
Oct. 15 • AE, MC, Visa accepted •
Off-season rates available •
PEIBBA; TIAPEI Member*

Roseneath
Roseneath
Bed 'N' Breakfast
Brenda & Edgar Dewar, Cardigan
RR 6, C0A 1G0
(902) 838-4590
Off Rte. 4, near Pooles Corner •
Quiet 1870s home with antiques
and collectibles overlooking
Brudenell River • Four o/n units,
one B&S, two S • No pets, please •
Non-smoking only
FEATURES: Morning coffee in
room • Evening tea • Enclosed
veranda • Bicycles, fishing rods
available • Nature trails through
property • Seal-watching cruises,
Crowbush Cove, Brudenell golf
courses nearby
*RATES: $50-$60 (2) •
Home-cooked breakfast • Open
June 1-Sept. 30 • Cat on premises*

Rusticoville
Cois Farraige ★★½
B. Montgomery, Hunter River RR 2,
C0A 1N0
(902) 963-3148
Rte. 6, 10 km east of Cavendish •
Restored century home, shore
frontage with view of Rustico Bay
from deck • Three o/n units, two
B&S, one with queen-size bed,
private S and Jacuzzi, two with
double beds • Children over ten,
please • Non-smoking only
FEATURES: Minutes from
golfing, deep-sea fishing, craft
stores and famous lobster and
seafood suppers • Minutes from
beaches • Cois Farraige means
"beside the sea"
*RATES: $45-$55 (2), $10 add'l
person • Full breakfast • Open May
1-Oct. 31 • Weekly $300-$370 (2),
off-season rates available*

St. Catherines
Buena Vista Farm
Judith Gay, Cornwall RR 2, C0A 1H0
(902) 675-3363
Horse farm overlooking scenic river
• Three o/n units, one B&S •
Colour TV in rooms • Pets
permitted • Non-smoking only
FEATURES: Equestrian park, golf
courses, sandy beaches, canoe
rentals, provincial parks, attractions,
historic sites nearby • Fifteen
minutes to Charlottetown, 30
minutes to Green Gables House
*RATES: $35-$45 (2) • Open June
1-Sept. 30*

St. Catherines
Serenity Waters
Bed & Breakfast
Gloria Green, Box 962, Cornwall,
C0A 1H0
(902) 675-3624
Off TransCanada Hwy, on Rte. 9 •
Two o/n units, one B&S, one
Jacuzzi • Colour TV and VCR
*RATES: $30-$65 (1-2) • Open
mid-June to Sept. 1 • Weekly
$180-$395 (1-2)*

Skinners Pond
Keefe's Farm Tourist
Home
Mrs. Freda Keefe, Tignish, RR 2,
C0B 2B0
(902) 882-2686
Two o/n units, 1B&S • Pets permitted
FEATURES: Meals extra
*RATES: $25 (2), $3 add'l person •
Open year-round*

Souris
Church Street Tourist
Home ★★
Jimmy Hughes, 8 Church Street,
Box 381, Souris, C0A 2B0

(902) 687-3065
Toll free 1-800-242-8361
(Apr. 1-Nov. 31)
Corner of Church and Main Streets,
at Ultramar station • Three o/n
units, double beds, shared B&S •
TV in sitting room • Telephone •
Cot available
FEATURES: Dining room 180m •
Ten minutes walk to Magdalen
Islands Ferry • Sandy beaches,
water-skiing and surfboarding
nearby • Migratory bird-hunting in
season
*RATES: $35 (1-2), $5 add'l person
• Open Apr. 1-Oct. 31*

Souris
The Matthew House
Inn ★★★★
Linda Anderson, Box 151, Souris,
C0A 2B0
(902) 687-3461
On Breakwater St., Harbourside,
near Magdalen Islands ferry •
Award-winning Victorian Heritage
Inn • Five o/n units, queen beds,
private B&S or S • TV and VCR in
rooms • Telephone in rooms •
Non-smoking only
FEATURES: Fresh flowers from
cutting gardens • Multilingual •
Licensed dining by reservation •
Period art • Four fireplaces •
Library, parlour • Porches •
Mountain bicycles, spa, exercise
room, harbour boatslip, coastline
cruise • Antique shop • Maps to
secluded beaches, fishing spots,
cycling trails provided
*RATES: $95-$145 (2), $25 add'l
person • Full fireside breakfast •
Open June 1-Oct. 15 • Major credit
cards • Weekly rates available •
TIAPEI Member*

Souris
The Nautical Nook Bed & Breakfast ★★★
Marie Mossey, Box 635, Souris, C0A 2B0
(902) 687-3329
Decorative, clean and spacious home with spectacular view of Souris Harbour • Three o/n units, one B&S, 1/2 B, queen beds • TV available
FEATURES: Enjoy your stay with friendly fishing family • Mussel meals on Saturday with reservation • Minutes to beaches • Ten minutes from Magdalen Islands ferry
RATES: $40 (2), $8 add'l person • Continental breakfast • Open year-round • Off-season by arrangements

Souris
A Place to Stay – The Hannan House
Jay & Betty Hannan, 9 Longworth Street, Box 607, Souris, C0A 2B0
(902) 687-4626
Toll free 1-800-655-STAY
Nine o/n units, queen, double and twin beds, three B&S • TV in lounge • Pets permitted • Non-smoking only
FEATURES: Laundry facilities • Kitchen facilities • Dining hall • Barbeque • Deck • Dormitory available • Mountain bike rentals • Minutes to beaches and Magdalen Islands ferry
RATES: $45-$55 (1-2), $10 add'l person • Open year-round • Off-season rates available • Reservations required after Oct. 15 • TIAPEI Member

South Lake
The Sandpiper Bed & Breakfast ★★★
Murray & Linda Giguère-Fraser, RR 1, South Lake, C0A 1K0
(902) 357-2189
On Rte. 16 • Quiet home with magnificent ocean view, 2 km off Confederation Trail • Three o/n units, one B, one S, two with double bed, one with queen-size bed • One colour TV • Pets permitted, usually on leash • Non-smoking only
FEATURES: Bilingual • Mussel dinner on Saturday with reservation • Barbecue, picnic table • Bird carving, tole painting • Home-made food • Deep-sea & tuna fishing arranged • Minutes to Singing Sand beaches • Fifteen minutes to Magdelene Islands ferry
RATES: $45 (2), $10 add'l person • Breakfast • Open year-round • Weekly $300 (2), $60 add'l person

South Melville
Share Our Home Bed & Breakfast
Renate Ostick, Mill Road, South Melville, Crapaud RR 1, C0A 1J0
(902) 658-2221
Quiet location in the Bonshaw Hills • Two o/n units, shared B&S • Non-smoking only
FEATURES: Beach nearby • Half-hour drive to ferries, Green Gables, Charlottetown
RATES: $35-$40 (1-2), $10 add'l person • Open June 15-Sept. 15 • Cash or travellers' cheques only • Senior citizens' discount • Weekly $210-$240 (1-2), $60 add'l person

South Rustico
Barachois Inn ★★★½
Judy K. & Gary MacDonald, Box
1022, Charlottetown, C1A 7M4
(902) 963-2194
Church Rd., Rte. 243 • Victorian
house (1870), recently restored with
antique furnishings and works of art
• Four o/n units, private B&S or S •
Not suitable for very young
children • No pets, please •
Non-smoking only
FEATURES: View of Rustico Bay
• Suites available • 6 km from
Cavendish National Park and Anne
of Green Gables, 17 km from
Charlottetown
*RATES: $110-$125, $18 add'l
person • Open May 1-Oct. 31 •
Reservations recommended, deposit
required, cancellation policy •
TIAPEI Member*

Springhill
Ford's
Bed & Breakfast ★★½
David Ford, RR 2, Tyne Valley,
C0B 2C0
(902) 831-2487
Toll free 1-800-297-3113
MacArthur Road, 1 km off Hwy 2,
2 km off Lady Slipper Dr.,
Summerside • Newly remodeled
home • Two o/n units, queen beds,
shared B, private entrance, ceiling
fan • Colour TV and VCR in sitting
room • Cot available
FEATURES: Sitting room • Patio •
Back Road Gallery 1 km • Dinner
theatre, Mill River Golf nearby
*RATES: $40 (2), $10 add'l person
• Full breakfast • Open May 1-
Dec. 15 • Visa accepted • Weekly
$240 (2), $70 add'l person*

St. Peters Bay
The Crab 'N' Apple
Bed & Breakfast
Richard Renaud & Seana
Evans-Renaud, Box 9, St. Peters
Bay, C0A 2A0
Tel & Fax (902) 961-3165
Rte. 2, 1 km west from junction
Rte.s. 2 and 313 • Quaint home,
beautiful view of St. Peters Bay •
Three o/n units, one B&S, two with
double bed, one with twin beds •
Cots and crib available • Children
welcome • Pets permitted, usually on
leash • Non-smoking rooms available
FEATURES: Large cedar sun room
• Bilingual • Laundry facilities
nearby • Other meals available with
packages or off-season • Twenty
minute drive to Atlantic salmon
fishing, Links at Crowbush Cove,
Brudenell golf courses
*RATES: $30 (1), $40 (2), $8 add'l
person • Continental breakfast •
Open year-round • MC, Visa
accepted • Winter accommodations
by reservation only • Weekly $260
(2), golf packages available •
Off-season rates before June 26,
after Sept. 5 • PEIBBA Member*

Stanhope
Campbell's Tourist
Home & Housekeeping
Unit ★★
Mary & Malcolm Campbell, Little
York RR 1, Stanhope, C0A 1P0
(902) 672-2421
Two o/n units, one B&S
FEATURES: Apartment also
available
*RATES: $40 (2), $6 add'l person,
taxes included • Light breakfast •
Open year-round • Weekly $250
(2), $40 add'l person • TIAPEI
Member*

Stanley Bridge
Linden Cove Resort ★★½
Buddie & Helen MacEwan, Box
737, Kensington, C0B 1M0
(902) 886-2524
Fax (902) 886-3222
Rte. 238, off Rte. 6 • Waterfront
property on New London Bay • Four
o/n units, one B&S, one S • Two
colour TVs • Partial accessibility •
No pets, please • Non-smoking only
FEATURES: Antique furnishings •
Prize-winning flowers • Picnic
tables • Barbecues • Sports
equipment • Business access to
computer, fax, internet • Beach,
antique shop on premises •
Housekeeping units available •
Cavendish Beach, restaurants,
entertainment nearby
*RATES: $100-$120 (1-4), $8 add'l
person • Open June 15-Sept. 15 •
MC, Visa accepted • TIAPEI Member*

Stanley Bridge
The Smallmans ★★½
Helen Smallman, 329 Poplar
Aveneu, Summerside, C1N 2B7
(902) 886-2846/436-5892
On Rte. 254, 3 km south of Stanley
Bridge • Scenic, tranquil riverside
setting • Three o/n units, one B&S •
TV available • VCR available • Cot
and crib available • No pets, please
• Non-smoking only
FEATURES: Complimentary
evening coffee • Barbecue • Picnic
table • Bird-watching • Beach on
premises • Boating, swimming •
Near Cavendish, lobster suppers,
attractions, Green Gables nearby
*RATES: $35-$45 (2), $10 add'l
person • Breakfast with home-made
jams and muffins • Open early June
to late Sept. • Off-season rates in
June and Sept. • ATO; KATA;
NLTA; PEIBBA Member*

Summerside Area
The Arbor Inn ★★½
Jo Ann & Ian Doughart, 380
MacEwen Road, Summerside,
C1N 4X8
(902) 436-6847
Toll free 1-800-361-6847
Minutes from downtown
Summerside • Attractive setting •
One o/n units • Non-smoking only
FEATURES: Royalty suite
available with queen canopy bed,
Jacuzzi, music • Drive to beaches
*RATES: $95 (2), $10 add'l person
over 12 yrs. • Ensuite light
breakfast • Open year-round • MC
and Visa accepted • Weekly $525
(2), rates for romance packages
available • TIAPEI Member*

Summerside Area
Beladen Farm Tourist Home ★★
Adrian & Isabell Dekker, RR 2,
Sherbrooke, C1N 4J8
(902) 436-6612
Off Rte. 2 on Dekker Rd. • On beef
farm • Two o/n units, one B&S
with double bed and ceiling fans •
TV in living room
FEATURES: Dining room and
lounges nearby • Beach nearby
*RATES: $30 (2) • Continental
breakfast • Open June 1-Sept. 30*

Summerside Area
Birchvale Farm Bed & Breakfast ★★½
Arnold & Barbara Waugh, RR 3,
Wilmot Valley, C1N 4J9
(902) 436-3803/888-7331
Toll free 1-800-463-3803
Three km off Rte. 1A on Rte. 120,
between Rte.s. 1A and 107. Twenty
minutes from ferry and Cavendish •
Active farm in family for six

decades (growing potatoes, barley and beef) • Three o/n units with double, single and queen beds, 2 1/2 B&S • Cable TV • No pets • Non-smoking only
FEATURES: 12th year hosting guests • Trout fishing
RATES: $28-$35 (2), $8 add'l person • Continental breakfast • Open May 1-Oct. 31 • Visa accepted • TIAPEI Member

Summerside Area
Blue Heron Country Bed & Breakfast ★★★
Willard & June Waugh, RR 3, North Bedeque, C1N 4J9
(902) 436-4843
1-800-575-8233
On Rte. 1A, 20 minutes from ferry • Charming family farm grows potatoes and grain • Four o/n units, one private B with queen-size bed, shared B&S and S • Non-smoking only
FEATURES: Relaxing atmosphere • Evening snack • Western riding stable • Supervised instructions at stable
RATES: $40-$50 (2), $10 add'l person • Breakfast • Open year-round • TIAPEI Member

Summerside Area
Country at Heart Bed & Breakfast ★★½
Carl & Vivian Wright, RR 3, North Bedeque, C1N 4J9
(902) 436-9879
Toll free 1-800-463-9879
Off Rte. 1A on Rte. 181 (Taylor Rd.), 2 km east of Summerside, 20 minutes to Borden ferry, 30 minutes to Cavendish • Two-storey home in peaceful farming community • Four o/n units, private B, shared B&S

and 1/2 B, double beds • Non-smoking only
FEATURES: Complimentary evening snack • Picnic table & barbecue • Fans available • 2 km to riding stables
RATES: $35-$50 (2), $8 add'l person • Continental breakfast • Open year-round • Off-season rates Sept. 15-June 15 • TIAPEI Member

Summerside Area
"The Island Way" Farm Bed & Breakfast ★★½
Gordon & Ruth Anne Waugh, RR3, North Bedeque, C1N 4J9
(902) 436-7405
Fax (902) 888-2385
Toll free 1-800-361-3435
Rte. 1A • Family farm, situated in a tranquil setting on Wilmot River • Four o/n units, one B&S, three S • Pets permitted, usually on leash • Non-smoking only
FEATURES: Stately turn-of-the-century farm home full of character and charm of days gone by • Riding stable • Footpath along shore bank • Back roads for cycling • Crafts for sale
RATES: $40-$60 (2), $10 add'l person • Breakfast • Open May 1-Sept. 30 • Romance, riding, family and craft packages available • TIAPEI Member

Summerside Area
MacDonald's
Bed & Breakfast
Ms. Hazel MacDonald, 142 Walker
Avenue, Summerside, C1N 4W8
(902) 436-6878
Off Granville Street, behind
Country Fair Mall and Sears • Two
o/n units, one B&S, one S • TV •
Telephone • Non-smoking only
*RATES: $45-$50 (2) • Continental
breakfast • Open June 1-Sept. 30 •
Weekly $270-$345 (2)*

Summerside Area
Paneau Bed & Breakfast
Muriel & Gerard Gallant, 11 North
Drive, Summerside, C1N 4E7
(902) 436-0543
Minutes from downtown, 25
minutes from Borden ferry •
Century home with large shaded
yard • Five o/n units, two B&S,
three with queen-size beds, one
with double bed, one with twin
singles • TV in living room • Guest
telephone • Cot and crib available •
Pets on leash permitted
FEATURES: Coffee always
available • Evening snacks •
Outdoor games, deck and barbecue
available • Home cooking
*RATES: $30-$35 (2), $10 add'l
person • Full breakfast • Open May
1-Nov. 30 • Weekly $185-$210 (2) •
Off-season rates before July and
after Sept. 30*

Summerside Area
Silver Fox Inn ★★★
Julie Simmons, 61 Granville Street,
Summerside, C1N 2Z3
(902) 436-4033
Toll free 1-800-565-4033
Historic house (1892) designed by
architect W.C. Harris • Six o/n units,
private B or B&S • Not suitable for

children under 10 yrs •
Non-smoking only
FEATURES: Spacious rooms with
fireplaces and fine woodwork, period
furnishings • Close to Summerside's
business and shopping district
*RATES: $65-$80, $10 add'l person •
Continental breakfast • Open
year-round • AE, MC, Visa accepted
• Off-season rates before June 1 and
after Sept. 30 • TIAPEI Member*

Summerside Area
Willowgreen Farm
Bed & Breakfast ★★ ½
Steven & Laura Read, 111 Bishop
Drive, Summerside, C1N 5Z8
(902) 436-4420
Located behind The College of
Piping • Family homestead, tranquil
and relaxed atmosphere. This is a
working farm "in town" • Four o/n
units, one B, one S, quilts • Horses
welcome • Non-smoking only
FEATURES: Country walks
*RATES: $35-$40 (2), $7 add'l
person • Continental breakfast •
Open year-round • Weekly
$210-240 (2)*

Summerside Area
Wilmot Tourist Home
Elmer Gallant, 114 Gaudet
Crescent, Summerside, C1N 5E1
(902) 888-2733
Off Rte. 1A • Three o/n units, two
B&S • Partial accessibility • Pets
permitted
*RATES: $30 (2) • Continental
breakfast • Open year-round*

Tignish
Chaisson Homestead
Anita Chaisson, 156 Chaisson
Road, Tignish, C0B 2B0
(902) 882-2566

One o/n unit, one B&S • Cot
available
FEATURES: Bilingual •
Restaurant 800 m • Ocean beach
800 m
RATES: $35 (2), $6 add'l person •
Breakfast • Open April 15-Oct. 15 •
Off-season rates after Sept. 1

Tignish
Maple Street Inn
Bed & Breakfast ★★½
Jackie & Elmer Arsenault, 216 1/2
Maple Street, Box 96, Tignish, C0B 2B0
(902) 882-3428
Four o/n units, one B&S • Colour
TV • Non-smoking only
RATES: $30-$40 (1-2), $10 add'l
person • Full breakfast • Open June
1-Oct. 31 • Weekly $180-$250 (1-2)
• Full breakfast

Tignish
Tignish Heritage Inn ★★★
Tignish Initiatives, Box 398,
Tignish, C0B 2B0
(902) 882-2491
Fax (902) 882-3144
Behind St. Simon and St. Jude
Church • Restored convent (c.1868)
with spacious grounds in quiet
surroundings • Nine o/n units,
private B&S • Cots available •
Children under 6 yrs free •
Smoking rooms available
FEATURES: Laundry facilities •
Kitchen facilities • Close to North
Cape, parks and beaches • Walk to
museums, restaurants and shopping
• Hostel available
RATES: $60-$75 (1-2), $10 add'l
person • Continental breakfast •
Open year-round • Mid-Sept. –
mid-June by reservation only •
Weekly $360-$450 (1-2)

Tyne Valley
The Doctor's Inn
Bed & Breakfast ★★½
Paul & Jean Offer, Tyne Valley,
C0B 2C0
(902) 831-3057
Rte. 167, 30 km west of
Summerside • Landscaped village
home, c. 1860 • Two o/n units,
shared B • Pets permitted, usually
on leash
FEATURES: Three-acre market
gardens provide fresh vegetables •
Special dining by arrangement •
Recommended in *Where to Eat in*
Canada '92-'95 • Living room with
fireplace • Cross-country skiing in
winter • 4 km from Green Park and
river swimming
RATES: $55 (2), $10 add'l person
• Breakfast • Open year-round •
Visa accepted • Weekly $330 (2),
$60 add'l person

Tyne Valley
Valleyview
Bed & Breakfast
Betty MacIsaac, Box 85, Tyne
Valley, C0B 2C0
(902) 831-3490
Two o/n units, one B&S • Kitchen
privileges • Cable TV in living
room • Pets permitted, usually on
leash • Non-smoking only
FEATURES: Village has all
necessary amenities • Close to
Green Park Provincial Park and golf
course
RATES: $30 (2) • Continental
breakfast • Open June-Aug. •
Weekly $130 (2)

Urbainville
Chez Yvette
Bed & Breakfast ★★★
Yvette Deschenes, Box 63,
Urbainville, C0B 2E0
(902) 854-2966
Rte. 124 off Rte. 2 in the
Évangéline Region • Four o/n units,
one B&S, one S, two with one
double bed, one with queen-size
bed, one with two single beds •
Three colour TVs • Cots available
FEATURES: Bilingual
*RATES: $50 (1-2), $10 add'l
person • Continental breakfast •
Open year-round • Weekly $300
(2), $70 add'l person • Off-season
rates Oct. 1-May 1, $40 (1-2)*

Vernon Bridge
Blair Hall
Guest Home ★★★
Jim Culbert, Vernon Bridge, C0A 2E0
(902) 651-2202
Toll free 1-800-268-7005
On TransCanada Hwy, 15 minutes
east of Charlottetown • Five o/n
units, one B&S, one S, 1/2 B, two
with double beds, one twin beds,
one 3/4 bed, one queen bed, sofa
bed, private balcony
FEATURES: Laundry nearby •
Unique wake-up call, coffee in room
in morning • Private collection of
antiques • Lobster suppers, videos,
and historic village nearby
*RATES: $48-$52 (2), $10 add'l
person • Full breakfast • Open May
1-Dec. 1 • Visa accepted • Weekly
$288-$312 (2), $60 add'l person*

Victoria
Dunrovin Lodge,
Cottages and Farm
Mrs. Kay MacQuarrie Wood, Box
40, Victoria, C0A 2G0

(902) 658-2375
Pioneers in farm vacations (c.1802)
• Two o/n units, one B&S, one B •
Pets permitted, usually on leash
FEATURES: Family-operated •
Babysitting • Horseback riding •
Beach on premises • Museum,
playhouse, provincial park, clam
digging, recreational facility nearby
*RATES: $38-$42 (2), $20 add'l
adult, $6 add'l child • Meals extra •
Open June 22-Sept. 14 • Family
and senior citizens' rates • Weekly
$265-$290 (2), $100-$135 add'l
adult, $40 add'l child • TIAPEI
Member*

Victoria
Lealands Farm Inn
Bryce & Joan Boswell, Crapaud,
C0A 1J0
(902) 658-2173
Historical ocean-front inn located in
scenic fishing village of Victoria •
Four o/n units, one B&S
FEATURES: Picnic tables,
barbecue • Variety of farm animals
• 1/4 mile from beach, quaint shops
and live theatre
*RATES: $45 (2), $5 add'l person •
Continental breakfast • Open June
1-Sept. 30*

Victoria
Orient Hotel ★★★
Darrell Tschirhart & Lee Jolliffe,
Main Street, Victoria-by-the-Sea,
C0A 2G0 • Reservations: Box 162,
Charlottetown, C1A 7K4
(902) 658-2503
Fax: (902) 658-2078
Toll free 1-800-565-ORIENT
Heritage inn, c.1900 • Six o/n units,
private S or B&S • Partially
accessible • Non-smoking only

FEATURES: Tca Shop • Dining by reservation • Views of countryside, shore • Suites available
RATES: $85-$95 (2), $15 add'l person • Full breakfast • Open May 1-Oct. 31 • AE, DC, MC, Visa accepted • Off-season rates before June 15 and after Sept. 15 • Deposit required • HIAC Member

Victoria
Something Different Inn Bed & Breakfast
Kate Lehmann, Box 7, Victoria, C0A 2G0
(902) 658-2347
Quiet, pre-Confederation home • Three o/n units, one B&S, one S • Non-smoking only
FEATURES: Ocean/pastoral views • Five-minute walk to Victoria and beaches • Close to attractions, Cavendish, Borden and Charlottetown
RATES: $36.35-$54.50 (1-2), $20 add'l person • Breakfast • Open year-round • Off-season rates available • Weekly $220-$301 (1-2), $100 add'l person

Victoria
Victoria Village Inn
Pam Stevenson & Jay deNottbeck, Box 1, Victoria-by-the-Sea, C0A 2G0
(902) 658-2483
1800s heritage inn • Six o/n units, one B&S, three S • Non-smoking only
FEATURES: Fine linens and duvets • "The Post and Bean" post office and coffee shop on premises
RATES: $65-$85 (2) • Open year-round • Visa accepted • Off-season rates Sept. 15-June 15

West Point
Red Capes Inn ★★★
Barry and Ada Ellis, RR 1, West Cape, O'Leary, C0B 1V0
(902) 859-3150/2199
On west shore, Rte. 14 (Lady Slipper Dr.), 4 km north of West Point Lighthouse • Modern home finished with pine, cathedral ceiling, stone fireplace, "star war" gallery • Two o/n units, one B&S for guests only, queen size brass beds, ceiling fans, oceanview balcony • Colour TV • Non-smoking only
FEATURES: Swimming • Suite available • Beaches and restaurant nearby • Free videos
RATES: $43 (2), $65-$75 (suite), no GST • Fruit plate, eggs and pastrami, or continental breakfast included • Open mid-May to mid-Oct. • Tel. reservations begin May 6

West Point
Stewart Memorial House Bed & Breakfast ★★½
Audrey MacDonald, West Point, C0B 1V0
(902) 839-2970/1939
On Rte. 14 (Lady Slipper Drive) • New house modelled after Big Philip Stewart original • Four o/n units, three double, one private and three shared B• Colour TV and VCR
FEATURES: Displays of artifacts, geneology, history • Antiques, mats, quilts • Evening coffee, tea, snacks available • One km to Cedar Dunes Provincial Park • Next to Fred's Country Store
RATES: $50-$70 • Full breakfast • Open year-round • Off-season rates Oct. 16-June 15 • Weekly rates available

West Point

West Point Lighthouse ★★★

Carol Livingstone, O'Leary RR 2, C0B 1V0
http://www.maine.com/lights/others.htm
(902) 859-3605
Toll free 1-800-764-6854
Rte. 14 (Lady Slipper Drive) • Canada's only inn in functioning restored lighthouse • Nine o/n units, double and queen, quilts, private B&S • Colour TV and VCR in guest lounge • Partial accessibility • Children under 10 yrs $5 • Non-smoking only
FEATURES: In Fodor's *Great Canadian Inns,* "Cross Country Cooking" TV show, and commemorative postage stamp • Licensed dining room • Evening sweets and coffee • Museum • Patio • Whirlpool • Beach on premises • Nature trails • Clam digging, fishing, biking
RATES: $70-$120 (2), $10 add'l person over 10 yrs, deposit required • Breakfast extra • Open June 1-Sept. 29 • AE, MC, Visa accepted • Off-season rates before June 16 and after Sept. 3 • Weekly $420-$840 (2), packages available • TIAPEI Member

Winsloe North

Cudmore's Chumleigh Tourist Home ★★

James & Marjorie Cudmore, North Winsloe RR 9, C1E 1Z3
(902) 368-1300
On Rte. 233 • Century home with antique furniture • Three o/n units, double beds, one B&S, one S
FEATURES: Kitchen facilities • Five minutes to beach, fifteen minutes to Charlottetown

RATES: $25-$30 (2), $5 add'l person • Open May 20-Sept. 30 • Weekly $150-$160 (2), $10 add'l person

Woodville Mills

Woodlands Country Inn ★★★

Mary Cameron, RR 1, Cardigan, C0A 1G0
(902) 583-2275
Bays and Dunes Drive, ten minutes from Pooles Corner Visitor Centre • Elegant Victorian estate • Four o/n units, one B, one S, double rooms • Pets permitted, usually on leash • Non-smoking only
FEATURES: Period furnishings • Bilingual • Library • Billiards room, table tennis • Fireplace • Movies • Picnics available • Barbecue pit • Bicycles • Private beach, boating, tennis, golf nearby
RATES: $60 (1-2), $10 add'l person • Full breakfast • Open June-Sept. • Visa accepted • Weekly $380 (2), $60 add'l person • PEIBBA Member

Comments and suggestions

Dear Traveller,

If you have comments about a B&B included in this guide, or if you have come across a B&B we missed which should be listed in future editions, please send us details using this handy form.

Name of B&B_____

Address _____

Phone_____

Comments _____

_____

_____

_____

_____

Your name_____

Your address _____

Your phone (daytime)_____

Date _____

Please mail this form to:

The Editor
Atlantic Canada Bed & Breakfasts
Formac Publishing Co Ltd
5502 Atlantic Street
Halifax NS B3H 1G4
Canada

Order form

Like to order another of our guide publications? Just use this handy form:

Please send me the following:

	Price	Qty	Total
Nova Scotia: A Colour Guidebook	$19.95		
New Brunswick: A Colour Guidebook	$19.95		
PEI: A Colour Guidebook	$19.95		
Halifax: A Colour Guidebook	$15.95		
Exploring Nova Scotia	$19.95		

Shipping and handling ($3.50 first book, $1.00 each thereafter) _____

GST (Canadian residents only) _____

TOTAL_____

I enclose a cheque for $_____

OR

Please debit my credit card:
__ Visa __ Mastercard __ American Express

Card number _____ Expiry _____

Signature_____

Name_____

Address _____

Postal code _____

Send your order to:
Formac Distributing,
5502 Atlantic Street
Halifax N.S.   B3H 1G4

Use our toll-free credit card order line for faster service
1- 800-565-1975 (Monday-Friday 9 am - 5 pm Atlantic time)